PENGUIN BOOKS

WELLINGTON AS MILITARY COMMANDER

Michael Glover read history at St John's College, Cambridge. After serving in the British army during the Second World War, he joined the British Council and worked in Britain and abroad before becoming a professional author. He wrote many articles on Napoleonic and Victorian warfare and his books include *The Peninsular War 1807-1814: A Concise Military History*, *Wellington As Military Commander*, *Wellington's Peninsular Victories*, *Wellington's Army in the Peninsular 1808-1814*, *Rorke's Drift: A Victorian Epic*, *Warfare from Waterloo to Mons* and *The Napoleonic Wars: An Illustrated History 1792-1815*.

WELLINGTON
as Military commander

MICHAEL GLOVER

PENGUIN BOOKS

Dedicated, by permission,
to Field-Marshal the Earl Alexander of Tunis, K.G.

PENGUIN BOOKS

Published by the Penguin Group
Penguin Books Ltd, 80 Strand, London WC2R ORL, England
Penguin Putnam Inc., 375 Hudson Street, New York, New York 10014, USA
Penguin Books Australia Ltd, 250 Camberwell Road, Camberwell, Victoria 3124, Australia
Penguin Books Canada Ltd, 10 Alcorn Avenue, Toronto, Ontario, Canada M4V 3B2
Penguin Books India (P) Ltd, 11 Community Centre, Panchsheel Park, New Delhi – 110 017, India
Penguin Books (NZ) Ltd, Cnr Rosedale and Airborne Roads, Albany, Auckland, New Zealand
Penguin Books (South Africa) (Pty) Ltd, 24 Sturdee Avenue, Rosebank 2196, South Africa

Penguin Books Ltd, Registered Offices: 80 Strand, London WC2R ORL, England

www.penguin.com

First published by B. T. Batsford Ltd 1968
Published as a Classic Penguin 2001

3

Copyright © Michael Glover, 1968
All rights reserved

Printed and bound in Great Britain by Cox & Wyman Ltd, Reading, Berkshire

CONTENTS

LIST OF ILLUSTRATIONS

LIST OF MAPS

ACKNOWLEDGMENT

Figs. 6 and 16 are reproduced by gracious permission of Her Majesty The Queen.

The Author and Publishers wish to thank the following for permission to reproduce the illustrations which appear in this book:

The Trustees of the British Museum for Figs. 18a and 18b.

Lieutenant-Colonel Dickson Burnaby for Fig. 21.

National Army Museum, R.M.A. Sandhurst, Camberley, Surrey, for Figs. 5 and 5d.

The National Portrait Gallery for Figs. 5b, 5c, 12a, 12b, 13 and 14a.

His Grace the Duke of Northumberland for Fig. 1.

The Parker Gallery for Fig. 3.

The Royal Artillery Institution, Woolwich, for Fig. 9.

The Royal Engineers' Corps Committee for Fig. 14b.

Scottish National Portrait Gallery for Fig. 11.

United Services Club, Committee of Management, for Figs. 15a and 15b.

Ministry of Public Building and Works for Fig. 4. (Crown Copyright.)

The Trustees of the Victoria and Albert Museum for Figs. 2, 7, 8, and 17.

His Grace the Duke of Wellington, K.G., for Fig. 5a.

PREFACE

As the most successful soldier in English history and the father-figure of early Victorian England, the Duke of Wellington has been the subject of countless biographies and studies. In his lifetime he was, in his own words, 'much exposed to authors'. General Sir John Jones, who served under the Duke as an Engineer, told how he sat opposite the great man in a carriage and watched him reading 'a ponderous quarto recital of the Battle of Waterloo'. As he read, he used a great blunt-ended pencil to mark against paragraph after paragraph the letters 'L' or 'DL'. When Sir John was bold enough to ask what these letters meant, the Duke replied shortly, ' "Lie" and "Damned Lie", to be sure.'

In writing this book, I have been acutely conscious of the ghostly Duke and his great blunt-ended pencil. In describing his active career as a soldier, I have tried to set his campaigns fairly against the background of the state of the British Army during the long French wars around the turn of the nineteenth century. When describing the decisions which Wellington had to take, I have tried to give the reader all the information which Wellington had at that moment and no more. It is absurd, though popular, to judge a man on the basis of a situation which he did not and could not know to exist. To my mind, the mark 'HS' standing for 'hindsight' in the margin would be quite as damning as 'DL'.

Among many people who have helped me with this book I should like first to mention my cousin, Richard Glover, whose book *Peninsula Preparation* has been of the greatest assistance to me. I have also received advice and assistance from General Sir James Marshall-Cornwall. Brigadier J. Stephenson and the library staff of the Royal United Services Institution have again been most helpful and tolerant towards my deplorable habit of keeping too many books for too long. I am also most grateful to my old friend Mrs. Jane Sleeman, who typed the final version of the manuscript and reduced my spelling to some kind of system.

Most of all I must thank my wife who, with my daughter, has given me the encouragement, advice and assistance without which the whole undertaking would have been impossible.

KING GEORGE'S ARMY

There are risks in a British warfare, unknown in any other service.

General Sir Ralph Abercromby

On the morning of the battle of Waterloo, Marshal Soult, as Chief of Staff, thought it his duty to draw the attention of the Emperor to the imprudence of attacking the Duke of Wellington in a position of his own choosing. It was not the first time he had tried to make this point. It was a subject on which he could fairly be said to be an expert. He had made the same mistake at Sorauren and beside the river Nive. Napoleon rejected his advice and snapped: 'You think Wellington is a great general because you have been beaten by him. I tell you that Wellington is a bad general, that the English are bad troops, and that this will be a picnic.' 'I hope so,' said Soult. Thinking it over in St. Helena, Napoleon revised his judgment. Wellington, he admitted, was his equal as a general, with 'the advantage of having more prudence'. When, on 4th July 1821, the news of Napoleon's death reached England the Duke modestly remarked, 'Now I think I may say I am the most successful general alive.'

The British Isles have never been a nursery for great generals. Considering that since Britain has had a regular army there has scarcely been a year in which British troops have not been on active service somewhere in the world, it is remarkable that only two British soldiers, Marlborough and Wellington, can lay claim to being Great Commanders. The reason for this dearth lies in two factors; the low esteem in which the British army is held in peacetime and the inability of the essentially civilian-minded British people to devise a system of directing their armed forces in time of war. Marlborough had the supreme advantage of effectively controlling the civil government from before Blenheim until after Malplaquet. Wellington had no such influence, and to understand his achievement it is necessary to know something of the system within which he had to work.

Eighteenth-century England disliked and distrusted its army. It was, in theory, the last effective weapon left in the King's hand, the only remaining royal threat to the settlement of the Glorious Revolution. Not the least of the causes of the Civil War had been the Parliamentary demand for control of the military forces of the realm. These forces consisted of the militia, a cumbrous and inefficient feudal levy which could only be called into the field to meet an immediate local emergency. Leaving aside the Yeomen of the Guard, King Charles I had no army but this. The Parliamentary demand to control it led directly to the day when one of their own generals cleared the House of Commons with a file of professional soldiers.

At the Restoration, command of the army was restored to the King and there was now a professional army. It was a small force, little more than a bodyguard and a garrison for Tangier, but it was a standing army and the country was never again able to dispense with it. Throughout the eighteenth century Members of Parliament, for the most part those of the Whig persuasion, dilated against the danger to the constitution which a standing army represented, and even more about its cost, but gradually, with the worst possible grace, they learned to live with it.

Although the command of the army remained in the King's hands, Parliament took care that effective control was their own. Discipline was maintained only by the annual passing of the Mutiny Act and the funds needed for the army had annually to be authorised on a number of Parliamentary votes, but far more effective than either of these annual rituals was the utter fragmentation of command and administration which not only made it impossible for Crown or generals to organise a military *coup* but made it all but impossible to carry out a military operation against a national enemy.

Any operation of war required the sanction of a Secretary of State. If operations were to be undertaken in a foreign country, responsibility lay with the Foreign Secretary. In India or the colonies, the Colonial Secretary must give the word. To meet a threat of invasion everything depended on the Home Secretary. On occasions the co-operation of two Secretaries might be needed. Thus, if the Foreign Office initiated an attack on Cadiz, it would be necessary to secure the concurrence of the Colonial authorities as the garrison and port facilities of Gibraltar would certainly be essential to success. Since the largest part of the army at home was stationed in Ireland, little could be done without obtaining the consent of the Lord Lieutenant to the reduction of his garrison.

In 1794, William Pitt made one of his rare constructive contributions to the conduct of the war when he appointed a Secretary of State for War with the task of co-ordinating all military operations. This was an enlightened step, but its value was all but nullified by the appointment he made to the post. Henry Dundas was Pitt's closest adviser and drinking companion, but his grasp of grand strategy was no greater than that of any other middle-aged Scots lawyer. His time, moreover, was already heavily committed since he continued to hold the offices of President

14

of the Board of Control of the East India Company (for which he had to answer in the House of Commons), Treasurer of the Navy, Chancellor of the University of St. Andrews and manager, on the government's behalf, of all Scottish elections. In 1798, the Secretaryship of State for the Colonies was added to his burdens and stayed with his successors after his resignation in 1801.

In any case the new Secretary of State's part in directing operations went little further than selecting the theatre of war, outlining, usually in vague terms, the intention and recommending to the Crown a suitable officer to hold the chief command. He had no connection with the War Office, which was presided over by the Secretary at War, a junior Minister who was responsible for the administration of the army. It was he who prepared the army estimates and answered questions in the House concerning military administration. Although he had no say in deciding where troops should go, it was his responsibility to sign the order authorising their movement.

The office of Secretary at War was a relic of the days when the King commanded the army in person and needed a secretary to despatch his military business. Burke's reforms had transformed him into a political figure of secondary importance charged, by the House of Commons, with seeing that the army spent as little money as possible and ensuring that what it had to spend was spent in as cumbersome and troublesome manner as experienced Treasury civil servants could devise. In the first years of the French Revolutionary war, the post was held by Sir George Yonge, a West Country borough owner* of doubtful reputation whose main occupation was trying to keep in his own hands the profitable patronage of the army which had, in the past, enabled him to dispose of commissions to infants in arms and young ladies. He was sent off as Governor to the Cape of Good Hope before the turn of the century only to be recalled in 1801 after being involved in a dubious contract for supplying the garrison with rotten meat. His successors were stronger on probity but less given to activity until, in 1809, Lord Palmerston was appointed and held the office until 1828.

It was none of the War Office's job to concern itself with what the army did. The Secretary at War was only responsible to see that whatever it did was administered in a proper form. Still less was it concerned with questions of tactics, drill or discipline. These were the concerns of the Commander-in-Chief, with his office at the Horse Guards.

As an economy the office of Commander-in-Chief was usually left vacant in peace-time, his powers of patronage, that is to say, the power to appoint to commissions and commands, being appropriated to the Secretary at War and his military duties going, for the most part, by

* Sir George Yonge and his ancestors 'represented Honiton continuously in Parliament for 101 years up to 1796, through 29 Parliaments (Namier, *Politics at the Accession of George III*, p. 164).

default, but at the outbreak of the French war Pitt recognised that it would be necessary to fill the post once more and appointed General Lord Amherst. In the Seven Years War Amherst had rendered distinguished service in North America, but by 1793 he was 76 years old and in failing health. He had, however, the advantage of having done the job before, from 1778 to 1782. His military staff, at the time of his appointment, consisted of half a dozen officers, at the head of whom stood the Adjutant-General, a comparative youngster of 65 whose first active service had been fighting against Bonnie Prince Charlie. The patronage, when it could be wrested away from Sir George Yonge, was administered by a civilian clerk at a salary of £182 a year.

By 1795 it was clear that Amherst, although 'a worthy and respectable old man', was producing nothing but chaos at the Horse Guards and he was promoted to field-marshal and superseded by the Duke of York. From this time on the Horse Guards became an increasingly efficient organisation. The Duke, whose competence as a field commander was little above average, was an excellent administrator and a clear-headed and conscientious staff officer. His reforms will be touched upon later. At the moment it is sufficient to say that, as far as was in his power, he made the army into an efficient fighting machine and enabled it, in time, to win victories in the hands of a first-class commander.

Unfortunately his power was very limited for, despite his high-sounding title,* his command extended only to the army, and the army, as it was then understood, comprised only the regiments of cavalry and infantry. He had influence over neither the administrative services nor the Artillery and Engineers.

These last were the jealously guarded preserve of the Master-General of the Ordnance who was, in addition, the government's principal military adviser and as such had a seat in the Cabinet.

The office of Master-General dated back to at least 1483. It was one of the great offices of state and had not been held by a commoner since 1682. Between the Glorious Revolution and Waterloo the incumbents had comprised seven dukes, two marquesses, six earls and three viscounts. Most of them were soldiers of distinction, Marlborough and Ligonier among them, but they had one thing apart from their nobility in common; none of them had ever served in either the Artillery or the Engineers. Not that the control of these two corps was the full extent of the Master-General's task. His department had the responsibility of providing all military stores, from muskets to camp kettles, to the army proper, of supplying (and manufacturing) cannon for both the army and the navy, and for the supply of maps.

* On his original appointment the Duke of York was 'Field-Marshal on the Staff'. In 1798 he became 'Commander-in-Chief in Great Britain', in 1799 'Captain-General of the Forces' and in 1801 'Commander-in-Chief of the Forces in Great Britain and Ireland'.

The office of Master-General was not considered a full-time occupation. Lord Cornwallis did not feel it necessary to resign it when he took up his duties as Lord Lieutenant of Ireland in 1798, and Lord Chatham continued in the post while commanding the ill-fated Walcheren expedition in 1809.

The Master-General presided over a Board of Ordnance which consisted of one military member, the Lieutenant-General, who had direct responsibility for the Artillery and Engineers, and four civilians, the Surveyor-General, the Clerk of the Ordnance, the Storekeeper and the Clerk of the Deliveries. Relations between the civil and military members and their subordinates were as bad as possible. In one instance the Clerk of the Cheque to the Board, a civilian, had tried to force his way on to the parade ground at Woolwich during the Commandant's inspection. Having browbeaten a sentry and the garrison sergeant-major, he strode on to the ground and eventually came to fisticuffs with the Commandant himself.[1]

The two Ordnance Corps were organised in a manner calculated to cause confusion and inconvenience. The Royal Artillery consisted of officers and gunners, but after 1794 was dependent on a separate corps for its drivers,* although this anomaly never applied to the Royal Horse Artillery (founded in 1793). Similarly, in the Engineers the officers belonged to a different corps from the other ranks.

Whatever the defect of the Ordnance Office, it must be said to their credit that they possessed, and had possessed since 1741, the only establishment for military education in the United Kingdom, the Royal Military Academy at Woolwich, and that it was only in the Ordnance Corps that officers received any formal training in their duties.

Supplying an army in the field was no concern of the War Office, of the Commander-in-Chief or of the Master-General. The provision of food, forage and transport was the business of the Treasury, which maintained no peace-time organisation to deal with such a task. The theory of army supply was simple. A force disembarking on a foreign shore would be accompanied by Treasury representatives, commissaries, who would contract with local merchants to supply all that the regulations demanded and deliver it to the troops in hired wagons. In a fertile and well-developed theatre of war, such as the Netherlands, this arrangement had been known to work quite well, given a competent commissary. Since most expeditions landed on inhospitable shores, where the local suppliers were suspicious of being paid in bills on

---

* Before this time the artillery were dependent on peasants hired for the duty. This practice did not cease immediately on the formation of the Corps of Artillery Drivers. As late as 1798 a report of an inspection at Woolwich records that the guns were drawn by 'contract drivers on foot, hired for the occasion, dressed in white smocks with blue collars and cuffs, and armed with long carter's whips of the ordinary farm pattern' (Duncan II 32).

London and where the arrangements were in the hands of a commissary of no experience whatsoever, the army frequently went hungry. It was, of course, not easy for the Treasury to find competent representatives. It was a difficult job, and commissaries had an unenviable reputation, not always unjustified, for lining their own pockets. In Wellington's words: 'The prejudice of society against a Commissary almost prevents him from receiving the common respect due to the character of a gentleman.' [2] To some of those recruited this respect was certainly not due, and as Wellington wrote on another occasion: 'I think that a person who has an itch for taking purses is not a fit person to be a Deputy Commissary General.' [3] Commissaries were responsible for supplies to all arms, but those who supplied the Ordnance Corps had a chain of command different from those supplying the infantry and cavalry, the two chains joining only within the Treasury in Whitehall.

In that the pay of the army emanated from the Exchequer, it was a Treasury responsibility, but the task of distributing it to regiments fell to the Paymaster-General (more usually the Joint Paymasters-General), who had a seat in Parliament and answered questions on matters connected with pay, although the estimates on which the pay was based were drawn up by the Secretary at War.

Military matters within Great Britain could only be carried on with the concurrence of the Home Secretary. With him lay the responsibility for all the Reserve forces, the Militia, Yeomanry and Volunteers. He also controlled regular troops enrolled for home service only (Fencibles). Indirectly he was concerned with the movement of troops overseas since, in the days before a police force existed, only the army was available to quell civil disturbance and the views of the Home Office had always been sought lest the garrison of the kingdom should fall below the safety limit. Ireland, of course, was a different matter. Until 1802 Ireland had its own military establishment, complete with a parallel structure of control including a Master-General of the Irish Ordnance at the head of the Regiment of Royal Irish Artillery and Royal Irish Engineers. After the Act of Union, the regular forces of the kingdoms were amalgamated and the Lord Lieutenant had no more concern with military matters than had the Home Secretary, except in so far as the internal state of Ireland was always more explosive than that of England.

Leaving aside the Judge Advocate-General, who was a political appointee with a seat in Parliament, the remaining bodies concerned with the functioning of the army were of less political consequence and owed an allegiance, frequently shadowy, to one or other of the bodies already mentioned. The most confusing, and the least efficient, was the Medical Board. This consisted of the Physician-General, the Surgeon-General and the Inspector-General of Hospitals, and was controlled, as far as it was controlled, jointly by the War Office and the Horse Guards.

The Board appointed doctors and surgeons to regiments and had some supervisory responsibility for the supply of hospital stores and medicines. This supply, however, was the charge of the Purveyor-General and the Apothecary-General respectively. The efficiency of the supply of stores had not been improved by the fact that the office of Purveyor-General had been made hereditary in the previous reign. The Ordnance Corps had, naturally, their own medical arrangements, as they had also for the appointment of chaplains.

Other offices came and, sometimes, went. The Transport Board, staffed by naval officers, saw to movement by sea, the Barrackmaster-General built barracks, a board of general officers supervised the quality of regimental clothing, the Commissioners for Chelsea Hospital made provision for some disabled soldiers, there was a Commissary-General for Musters and, between 1799 and 1807, there was an Inspector-General of Recruiting who was independent of both the War Office and the Horse Guards.

Despite all this elaborate superstructure there was a chronic shortage of troops. The establishment of the army at the outbreak of war in 1793 was about 40,000 rank and file,* exclusive of 15,000 men on the Irish establishment and 4,000 artillerymen. The actual strength was far lower, about 38,000 men for both establishments, from which had to be found the garrisons for the colonies and India. At the outbreak of war the disposable force in the United Kingdom was so small that the only military assistance which could immediately be sent to the allies in the Netherlands was a weak brigade of Foot Guards, less than 2,000 all ranks, without artillery, medical supplies or reserve ammunition. A month later it was found possible to despatch 123 gunners and three battalions of infantry, but these had been so hastily recruited that the Adjutant-General was obliged to write to the commander in the field: 'I am afraid that you will not reap the advantage that you might have expected from the brigade of the Line just sent over to you, as so considerable a part of it is composed of undisciplined and raw recruits; and how they are to be disposed of until they can be taught their business I am at a loss to imagine. I was not consulted upon the subject until it was too late to remedy the evil.' [4]

Great, though unco-ordinated, efforts were made to increase the strength of the army. The militia were embodied; Fencible regiments raised for home defence; every kind of device was employed to raise recruits, ranging from the use of contractors to an abortive attempt to impose conscription on the unemployed, but try as Ministers would,

* Establishments and returns in the army were normally given as 'rank and file', that is, private soldiers and corporals. Officers, sergeants and drummers were returned separately. To reach a true total, one-eighth should be added to the number of rank and file.

they could not keep recruiting for the regular army at a level to enable it to meet its commitments.

There were two principal reasons for this. The first was the government's attempt to defeat France by seizing her West Indian colonies. This was intended to ruin France economically or, alternatively, to provide useful bargaining counters at a peace conference. Plausible as these objects may have been (and the fact that Dundas was known as 'a powerful advocate for the sugar importers'[5] must make them suspect), the effect on the army was deplorable. Although battle casualties were moderate in number, the disease rates were appallingly high. To give one example, when General Grey captured Martinique in 1794, he took to the island a force of 7,000 men. Of these only 2,000 survived. Of the officers, who must have numbered about 400, 27 were killed or mortally wounded in action and 170 died of disease.[6] In all, during the years 1793, 1794, 1795 and 1796, the campaigns in the West Indies cost the army, in death and permanent disablement, 80,000 men, of whom half died.[7] During this period the total of enlistments for the regular army was 112,000, and since many of these, having been raised by crimps, were found to be unusable from physical or mental deficiencies, or were foreign troops who deserted at the first opportunity, it can fairly be said that the campaigns in the West Indies succeeded in nullifying all the efforts made during that time to increase the strength of the army.

Worse than this, they strengthened the existing prejudice against joining the army. At best, no respectable working-class family cared to see a son go for a soldier. To do so was the last resort of the shiftless.* If to the disgrace of enlisting was to be added the near certainty of death in a fever-stricken tropical island, it is small wonder that even the most idle and drunken were reluctant to take the King's Shilling, the more so since they could get better financial terms by enlisting for home service only.†

'Our army is composed of the scum of the earth—the mere scum of the earth. People talk of their enlisting from their fine military feeling —all stuff—no such thing. Some of our men enlist from having got bastard children, some for minor offences, many more for drink.'[8] High-minded historians of a later age have censured Wellington for these words, though they have usually passed over his proud addition, 'it really is wonderful that we should have made them the fine fellows they are.' All the evidence goes to show that the Duke spoke no more

* As late as 1877, when William Robertson, later a field-marshal and C.I.G.S., joined the Seventeenth Lancers as a trooper, his mother, wife of a village tailor and postmaster, wrote to him: 'What cause have you for such a low life? . . . [the army] is a refuge for all idle people. I shall name it to no one for I am ashamed to think of it. I would rather bury you than see you in a red coat.'

† A marriage allowance was paid to men in the militia but not to regulars, even if serving overseas.

than the truth. A sergeant of the Seventh Fusiliers wrote that the 'army was composed of the lowest orders. Many, if not the most of them were ignorant, idle and drunken.' [9] A guardsman admitted that 'Of those who voluntarily enlist, some few are driven by poverty . . . some have disgraced themselves in their situation or employment, many have committed misdemeanours which expose them to the penalties of the law of the land, and most are confirmed drunkards.' [10]

Wellington may have done an injustice to a small minority who joined from admirable patriotic motives, but there can be no doubt that they were few in number. By far the greatest part of the army were induced to join in quite a different way. A recruiting sergeant told Sergeant Donaldson of the different ways he used for persuading men to join, some by preying on their fears of unemployment, some, particularly ploughboys, by telling them 'how many recruits had been made sergeants when they enlisted—how many were now officers. If you saw an officer pass while you were speaking, no matter whether you knew him or not, tell him he was only a recruit a year ago; but now he's so proud he won't speak to you. If this won't do, don't give up the chase —keep to him. . . . You must keep him drinking—don't let him go to the door without one of your party with him until he is passed the doctor and attested.

'Your last resort was to get him drunk, and then slip a shilling in his pocket, get him home to your billet, and next morning swear he enlisted, bring all your party to prove it, get him persuaded to pass the doctor. Should he pass, you must try every means in your power to get him to drink, blow him up with a fine story, get him inveigled to the magistrate in some shape or other, and get him attested; but by no means let him out of your hands.' [11]

It needed this kind of persuasion to enlist men for the army. Leaving aside the perils of the West Indies, there was little except a bounty on attestation and the prospect of liquor and loot to make a man join. The pay of a private of the line was seven shillings a week, from which four shillings a week were stopped before he received it to cover the cost of his rations. A further eighteenpence was deducted for the upkeep of his necessaries, his personal equipment. The remaining one and sixpence was paid over to the soldier less charges for washing his shirts and supplying him with cleaning materials.

In the cavalry of the line the private soldier was fractionally better off since his pay was fourteen shillings a week, although five shillings and threepence of this was deducted for the forage of his horse, leaving him threepence a day better paid than his infantry colleague.

The rations for which so large a proportion of a man's pay was deducted consisted, each day and invariably, of one pound of meat, one and a half pounds of bread (or one pound of biscuit) and a quart of beer (or a pint of wine or a third of a pint of spirits in countries where these were more easily obtainable). There were no cooks and the men took their turn, irrespective of their culinary abilities, at preparing the meat in the two possible guises, stew and soup. Two meals daily were provided, breakfast and a midday meal. If the soldier felt the need for further sustenance he must provide it himself—if he could find the money. In overseas stations, fresh meat was replaced by salt pork, even in New South Wales where fresh meat abounded.

At the outbreak of the war, the majority of the troops in England were quartered in inns. Barracks for 20,000 men did exist, but they were for the most part wrongly sited to enable the troops to perform their primary function of keeping the peace in the manufacturing towns. Pitt set about building barracks up and down the country. He entrusted the work to a new official, the Barrackmaster-General, but omitted, largely because of Opposition hostility to the idea of building barracks, to obtain a Parliamentary vote to cover the expense, financing the operation out of a nebulous subhead called the 'Extraordinaries of the army'. Nor did he ensure that there was any control over the expenditure of the money. In 1804, after the Barrackmaster-General had held office for 12 years, an enquiry was made into the affairs of his office. It was found that more than nine million pounds had been expended but that there were no accounts to show where the money had gone. The Barrackmaster-General, Oliver de Lancey, was dismissed for 'culpable carelessness', but was rewarded with a pension of six pounds a day and the colonelcy of the Seventeenth Light Dragoons. He had succeeded in building a large number of small and inconvenient barracks in which the space allocated to each soldier was less than that provided for convicts. This was made possible by the refusal of the authorities to provide the soldier with a bed of his own, insisting that four of them should share a wooden crib.

Barracks, or rather small military police stations, had existed in Ireland for many years, but the detachments they housed were so small that regiments were scattered to such an extent that it was impossible to train even a company together and military efficiency fell to a very low level, especially in the cavalry where the four regiments on the Irish establishment, which had not left the country for decades, were found to be wholly useless for any operation.

Discipline was savage by modern standards, although it was scarcely more so than the civilian penal code and was almost humane when compared with the navy. Its actual savagery varied from regiment to regiment depending on the character of the commanding officer.

Marriage was almost forbidden to the soldier. Six men in every company of about a hundred were permitted to have wives 'on the strength'. These fortunate men were forced to house their wives and children in the communal barrack-room with no more privacy than could be provided by a blanket hung up as a screen. These wives, in return for their

22

privileged position, were expected to do the washing of all the officers and men. For the unfortunate 94, the army could only lay down that 'Marriage is to be discouraged as much as possible. Officers must explain to the men the many miseries that women are exposed to, and by every sort of persuasion they must prevent their marrying if possible.'[12] Should a regiment be ordered overseas, only the wives 'on the strength' could accompany it and what happened to any woman who had been rash enough to marry outside the quota was explicitly not the army's concern. Marriage allowance was paid only to militiamen who could not be sent abroad.

Adding to all these discomforts and neglects an uncomfortable and barely serviceable uniform, which the public despised, it would have been little less than a miracle if the vast bulk of the army had not been recruited from 'the mere scum of the earth'.

Junior officers were scarcely better off than their men. An ensign in the infantry of the line was paid 4/8d. a day; a cornet in the dragoons 8/-. From this they had to feed and clothe themselves and the cornet had to provide and feed his horses. The pay of all officers was subject to deductions amounting to about one-fifth of the whole for poundage (a commission to the regimental agent), taxes and a fixed contribution towards the upkeep of the hospitals for old soldiers at Chelsea and Kilmainham.* There were further charges for messing and a subscription for the regimental band. There was even a fee payable to the War Office for receiving a commission. This fee was increased with every subsequent promotion.

Worst of all was the cost of uniform. An ensign newly commissioned into the Fifty-second had to lay out £46 for the bare essentials. To his tailor he had to pay £12 12s. for two regimental coatees, £4 4s. for two pairs of blue pantaloons and £1 14s. 6d. for a pair of buff breeches. His hatter's bill was £2 3s. 6d. and the bootmaker charged £5 19s. for two pairs of boots and two of shoes. From the sword cutler he obtained a regimental sabre (£4 4s.), a buff sword belt (14s.), two leather sword knots (7s.), a 'regulation swordknot for reviews' (9s.), four silver bugles

---

* Samuel Briscall, newly joined as a chaplain at a major's rate of pay, found his first issue of pay abated as follows:

31 days' pay @ 16/–				£24 16 0
Less Poundage @ 12d.				
in the £	£1	4	9	
Additional —do—	£1	4	9	
Poundage @ 6d. in the £		12	4½	
Hospital Allowance @ one				
day's pay per annum		1	4	
Property Tax	£2	3	3½	
	£5	6	6	£ 5 6 6
Sum received:				£19 9 6

for 'the corners of the coatees' (15s.), a breastplate for his shoulder belt (£1 7s.) and two pairs of silver epaulettes (£9). The tailor, boot-maker and sword cutler each charged him half a crown for a 'box for packing'. On top of this officers of the Fifty-second were required by their colonel, John Moore, to have a spy glass and compass (£3) and a 'case of mathematical instruments, common size' (£1). Dressing a cavalry officer was much more expensive. It was estimated that a cornet of light dragoons would require £169 10s. for his uniform and £151 19s. 6d. for horses and horse furniture.

One officer in five purchased his commission, the price varying from £400 for an ensigncy in a 'marching regiment of foot' to £6,700 for a lieutenant colonelcy in the Foot Guards.* Only commissions which had existed before the war could be purchased, and all commissions in newly raised units and resulting from the expansion of existing regi-ments were free. Moreover a commission was not heritable property; its value was lost if the owner died and the vacancy caused by his death would be filled by seniority within his regiment.

Purchase was a survival of the days when regiments were raised at the expense of their colonels who subcontracted to their officers for the raising of recruits. The continuance of purchase had few influential supporters, and would long before have been abolished if there had been any chance that Parliament would vote money to buy out the owners of existing purchased commissions. It had one outstanding advantage in that it allowed a purchase officer to retire, providing himself with a 'golden handshake' from the sale of his own property—his commis-sion.† This was important since Parliament also declined to provide retirement pensions and an officer without private means or a purchased commission had to soldier on despite age and infirmities since he could not afford to leave the service. As a result there were far too many elderly officers in the senior regimental ranks.

The only stated qualifications for a commission, purchased or free, were that the applicant should have reached his sixteenth year and be able to produce a recommendation from a major or above that he was 'a gentleman fully qualified to hold an ensigncy/cornetcy'. There was no definition of what constituted a gentleman but it is clear that no narrow definition was used, little more than a reasonable facility in reading and writing.

The Royal Military College, founded in 1802, provided only four in

* Paying more than the regulation price for a commission could lead to an officer being dismissed from the army. It was nevertheless done, although not much in wartime except for captaincies and majorities in much sought after regiments. The market in ensigncies and cornetcies was very slack and it could take as long as seven years to sell a cornetcy in an unfashionable cavalry regiment.

† Purchase was an anachronism in 1800 but it should be remembered that a similar system for doctors, the sale of practices, was not abolished until after the Second World War.

every hundred officers commissioned in the time of the Peninsular war. Half as many again were promoted from the ranks, some of them by way of ensigncies in the Portuguese army. Another $4\frac{1}{2}\%$ of new officers were Volunteers, that is young men who were officer material and served in the ranks, carrying a musket but messing with the officers, until a vacancy as an ensign became available. A much larger proportion (19%) were officers of the militia, the home defence force. Any militia officer could obtain an ensigncy in the line if he could induce twenty of his militiamen to enlist in the regular army. These ensigncies for militia officers were supernumerary but ranked with the established ranks for all purposes including promotion by seniority. Two-thirds of all new commissions went to young men of no military experience who had to learn their drill at the hands of the adjutant when they joined their regiment.

Any healthy and literate young man could obtain a commission without difficulty. Those who purchased their first commissions did so for one of two reasons—to get into the regiment of his choice or to ensure himself a career in the army after the war, as it was clear that those with purchased commissions would have to be retained while most of the rest would be put on half pay, a pittance amounting, after deductions for agent's commission, to £31 15s. 4d. a year for an ensign and only £86 13s. 9d. for a captain.

Once the first commission was obtained promotion went largely by seniority. For every two men who purchased promotion, seven obtained it by seniority and one by the exercise of the Commander-in-Chief's patronage. There had been flagrant abuses in the use of the patronage before the Duke of York became head of the army. He, however, went to the opposite extreme. In theory every promotion not effected by purchase and not resulting from the death of an officer was at the Duke's disposal. This left in his hands four out of every ten promotions, but he used less than half of his opportunities. Where he did use the patronage it was almost always in favour of long-service officers who had fallen behind their contemporaries by the inequalities of promotion in different regiments.* He had a strong belief in the virtues of promotion by seniority but his insistence on justice made it extremely difficult for generals to obtain promotion on merit for their subordinates.

Promotion by seniority could be a slow business. The step from lieutenant to captain averaged about seven years although it could take less than three. It was nevertheless possible for a man from the ranks

---

* As an example of these inequalities the experience of two single battalion regiments may be quoted. Between 1809 and Waterloo the Sixty-eighth Foot suffered 18 officer deaths resulting in 39 promotions and appointments. The Ninety-ninth had only 2 deaths with 5 promotions. The death of a major resulted in four vacancies (captain to major, lieutenant to captain, ensign to lieutenant and the appointment of an ensign).

to rise high in his profession. Jacob Brunt enlisted in 1770 and served in the ranks through the American War of Independence. He became quartermaster * and in 1793 an ensign in the Fifty-fifth. He was gazetted lieutenant-colonel in 1811 in the Eighty-third. John Elley, one of Wellington's most trusted staff officers, was the son of a Holborn eating-house keeper. He enlisted as a trooper in the Blues and was given a cornetcy in the regiment in 1791. By Waterloo he was a regimental lieutenant-colonel and a colonel by brevet. He died a lieutenant-general.

In the infantry and cavalry promotion was something of a gamble. The speed with which an officer rose depended on the number of his seniors who died, were promoted outside the regiment, exchanged into other regiments,† resigned or retired.‡ There was no element of chance in the promotion of officers in the two Ordnance corps. In the Artillery and Engineers, promotion went by unrelieved seniority. There were no purchased commissions and few officers with private means. Consequently there were no retirements and few resignations. Without retirement pensions Ordnance officers could not afford to leave the service. As a result both corps had at their head a collection of senior officers too old to go on active service. Their juniors could only wait patiently until they died in their beds. In 1809 no regimental lieutenant-colonel in the Royal Artillery had less than twenty-six years' service after leaving Woolwich. None of them was less than a year older than Lieutenant-General Sir Arthur Wellesley. Even with brevet promotion (i.e. promotion in the army rather than in the regiment) it was very unusual for an Ordnance officer to become a lieutenant-colonel in less than twenty years. George Fead, who was commissioned in the Artillery in 1757, took 36 years.

Once a man had reached the rank of lieutenant-colonel, whether by purchase, seniority or brevet, his promotion went strictly by seniority. He could count on becoming a general if he lived long enough and avoided being cashiered. The length of time that it took to climb the ladder was determined by the demand for senior officers. Thus, at the outbreak of the war in 1793 a newly made lieutenant-colonel would take only three years to become a colonel, six more to be a major-general and another six to be a lieutenant-general, and this applied equally to young Arthur Wellesley who achieved his lieutenant-colonelcy in the Thirty-third in 1793, fought with distinction in Flanders, India and Denmark, and to Charles Barton of the Guards who became a lieutenant-colonel a month after Wellesley and never served further afield than Windsor. Both became lieutenant-generals in April

* At this time quartermasters did not hold commissions except in the Royal Horse Guards (Blues).

† A man could sell his rank but not his seniority. If a captain sold his captaincy the purchaser went to the bottom of the regimental captains' list and captains junior to the seller moved up one place.

‡ Purchase officers retired; those with free commissions resigned.

1808. Later in the war the time taken to rise from lieutenant-colonel to colonel lengthened to eight years, but the next step to major-general took a much shorter time, about two and a half years. Seniority within the service was immutable; the date a man achieved his lieutenant-colonelcy dictated his seniority for the rest of his life. Whatever his competence he could never be asked to serve under a man whose lieutenant-colonel's commission was dated a day later than his own.* Fortunately brevet promotion to lieutenant-colonel was sufficient to enable an officer to get his foot on the ladder of promotion to general. Had it not been for this it would seldom have been possible for officers of the Ordnance Corps to rise above the rank of full colonel. Hew Ross, one of the most distinguished artillery officers in the Peninsula, did not receive his regimental rank of lieutenant-colonel until 12 years after he had received the brevet.

The system of promoting senior officers entirely by seniority was absurd and inconvenient but it had its compensations. There was no limit to the number of generals who could be created since there was no establishment for them. Promotion to colonel or to any of the ranks of general officer carried, until 1814, no pay. If a man received an appointment as colonel or general 'on the staff', he received the pay for that position as long as he held it. The moment he relinquished it he reverted to the pay of his regimental rank, which was not infrequently that of captain or major. In 1814 Major-General Horace Churchill was subsisting himself as a Captain Commissary in the Corps of Royal Artillery Drivers. Some generals held colonelcies of regiments, a profitable appointment since, apart from the pay, there was a substantial and legitimate profit to be made from the supply of clothing to the men. Other generals held 'governments', the governorship of some colony or fortress. These ranged from full-time colonial posts, such as Gibraltar or Jamaica, to sinecures in England, such as the Governorship of Gravesend and Tilbury or the Captaincy of the Garrison of St. Mawes. There were, notwithstanding these appointments, several hundred generals who drew no pay, except in their regimental rank, and many who had seen no service for many decades.

The advantage of this flexible system of promotion was that it made it possible to promote a junior general by pushing up a step all those in front of him at no cost to the Treasury. Thus, when in 1813, it was thought desirable for diplomatic reasons to promote Major-General Charles Stewart, brother to Lord Castlereagh and formerly Wellington's Adjutant-General, to lieutenant-general after four years in his existing

* There was only one exception, Wellington himself. He went to the Peninsula as a junior lieutenant-general and received the local rank of general in the Peninsula in 1811. He was never a substantive general, as his promotion to field-marshal in 1813 enabled him to leapfrog about 140 senior officers. If he had had to await the normal promotion, he would have become a general in 1819.

rank, the matter was easily arranged. Sixty-two senior major-generals were promoted above him, although fewer than 20 of them had seen active service since the turn of the century, three had not been in action since the American War of Independence and one had last seen an enemy in 1756 when he had been taken prisoner following Byng's failure to relieve Minorca. To relieve pressure on the list of lieutenant-generals 29 were promoted general, of whom seven had been on active service in the past 14 years and one had fought at Minden in 1759. So remorseless was the system that even Oliver de Lancey, whom we have seen removed as Barrackmaster-General for financial irregularities, duly became a general in 1812.

The first 15 years of the war against France brought little prestige to the British Army. Most of the French colonies in the Caribbean were captured and most of the Dutch overseas possessions were taken, for the most part bloodlessly. Every British foray to the continent of Europe ended in humiliation, and a crackbrained venture into Latin America in disgrace. Ministers were still tempted by wild-cat schemes for dispersing the army in pursuit of improbable commercial gains. As late as 1806, Colonel Robert Craufurd received orders to take a force to the west coast of South America, seize Chile and Peru and establish a chain of posts across the continent, a distance of 900 miles of unmapped country, to make communication with another force which, it was hoped, would be holding Buenos Aires. Craufurd was allocated 4,800 men for this enterprise which, fortunately, was cancelled just before it sailed.

There were a few bright portents. Twice, at Alexandria in 1801 and at Maida in 1806, British troops decisively defeated French armies on equal terms. It was noticeable that on each occasion the British were near enough to the sea to be victualled by the Royal Navy and to throw no strain on the Commissariat service. These victories were, in the eyes of Europe, more than balanced by the abortive expedition to Hanover in 1805–06 and the surrender at Buenos Aires in 1807.

Beneath the surface there was a considerable improvement which was to make the army once more a force to be taken into account by the French Empire. Once the Duke of York was established as Commander-in-Chief at the Horse Guards he took in hand the internal management of the army. All military appointments, except commanders-in-chief for expeditions overseas, were kept firmly in military hands. New regulations were put into force, in 1800, whereby no one could receive a captaincy until he had served two years as a subaltern, or a majority without a minimum of six years' service. In future no one could receive a first commission until he had reached his sixteenth year, and a small but not ineffective start was made in military education for officers in the infantry and cavalry, although generations were to pass away before such training became compulsory or even usual. To increase the efficiency of the officers, annual confidential reports were instituted. This was not a popular move. An officer with a most distinguished record of service in the Peninsula wrote of 'that wicked and degrading institution . . . which is smoothly termed *confidential* reports, thus turning the Army . . . into a graduated corps of spies from the ensign up to the general. Great Britain does not reflect that by encouraging these confidential and clandestine reports, she is inflicting a severe censure on the laws and morals of the nation, as not being sufficient to govern by open and legitimate means.' [13]

The Duke of York did what he could to improve the position of the private soldier, though the Treasury and the Parliamentary Opposition limited his efforts in this direction.* Nevertheless he achieved much. Greatcoats became a standard issue and were supplied by the Board of Ordnance rather than, as with the rest of the men's clothing, by the colonels of regiments. Military hospitals were built, with special wards for soldiers' wives. The establishment of chaplains was increased and the chaplains forced actually to attend to the troops. Cheap postal rates for troops on active service were introduced, and a new regulation ensured that the names of soldiers who became casualties on active service should be returned to the Horse Guards instead of the established practice of reporting only how many were killed and wounded. For the benefit of soldiers' children the Duke of York's School was founded in Chelsea as 'an asylum for educating one thousand children, the legal offspring of British soldiers'. All these things were small in themselves, but the cumulative effect was to show, even to the soldiers themselves, that their welfare was a subject near to the heart of the King's favourite son. The more humane attitude which they engendered showed too at a lower level when generals like Sir John Moore and colonels like Kenneth M'Kenzie and Coote Manningham set out to treat their men as if they were human beings, capable of thought and of assuming responsibility.

Training was taken firmly in hand. A number of drill books had been issued during the eighteenth century, but they had been regularly disregarded and every regiment drilled and manoeuvred as its commander or his adjutant thought best. The American War of Independence had made the situation worse since almost all the operations there had been performed by small numbers in broken country. If Britain was to engage the French on the continent of Europe the basic strength of the army must reside in the steadiness and precise manoeuvre of the line. The thin skirmishing order learnt in America would not do against the

* When, to meet the likelihood of actual starvation amongst the troops due to the rise in the cost of food, the ration allowance was increased by Royal Warrant, the Whigs attacked the increase as an attempt to attach the loyalty of the troops more firmly to the Crown rather than to Parliament.

mass formation of the enemy. In *Rules and Regulations for the Movement of His Majesty's Infantry* issued by command in 1792 and written by General David Dundas, the practice of the whole of the army was standardised, or rather it was laid down that it should be standardised. Regiments were so accustomed to following their own ideas that the *Rules and Regulations* were widely ignored until the Duke of York came to the Horse Guards and saw that they were enforced. Henceforth every battalion conformed to Dundas' 18 manoeuvres and it became possible to give orders to a brigade where previously it had been necessary to give as many orders as there were battalions present, since each would have been trained to work only on their own system of commands.

The lessons of the American War were not disregarded, but it was recognised that skirmishing was a specialist duty. Each battalion already had a light company which was trained to act in front of the line. The Duke of York went further and introduced battalions of light infantry and of riflemen whose purpose was to shield the line of battle against anything but mass assault. From the training of these new corps, especially the Forty-third, Fifty-second, Sixtieth (5th Battalion) and Ninety-fifth, emerged a whole new conception of tactics and a revolution in the relationship within regiments between officers and men, since in their kind of warfare soldiers of any rank could no longer be trained as unthinking automata.

The Duke also tried to reform the training of the cavalry, which in 1793 was at an abysmally low level. He made certain reforms, notably in the handling and design of sabres, but his success was not comparable with that which he achieved with the infantry. To the end of the war, the British cavalry was able to perform brilliantly in the set-piece charge under favourable conditions, but never mastered the subtler techniques of pursuit and outpost duty.

Nor was progress confined to the Horse Guards. At the Board of Ordnance there were hopeful signs. The Royal Horse Artillery was founded in 1793 and quickly became the most efficient artillery in the army. The Corps of Artillery Drivers was formed and, even if its conception was anachronistic, it was a great deal better than the haphazard arrangements which had preceded it. When in 1800 it was decided to arm the Ninety-fifth with a rifle, the Board distinguished itself by assembling 40 different types of rifle, conducting competitive tests at Woolwich and choosing an excellent and serviceable piece, designed by Ezekiel Baker, which in capable hands was accurate up to 300 yards compared with the 50 yards of a common musket.

In artillery weapons, the Board showed enterprise. A more effective type of gunpowder was devised, the shrapnel shell was introduced and even rockets were used, though their effect was likely to be more psychological than real owing to their erratic performance.

The provision of maps was undertaken, though this was a slow business. By 1805, when the fear of invasion was finally lifted, the Board had succeeded in producing maps of Sussex, Kent and Essex, although economy dictated that they be published commercially by a private printer. Overseas the map situation was still unsatisfactory, and when Wellesley landed in Portugal in 1808 he was equipped with an excellent map of the environs of Lisbon but had been unable to secure any map of the country around Vimeiro where he actually had to meet the French.

The Ordnance were less successful in two fields, in the preparations for a siege and in the work of the Royal Engineers. It was apparently assumed that sieges would not form part of military operations throughout the war and although a number of siege guns were available at Woolwich they were few and unduly precious. Furthermore the training of men, especially in the ranks, for siege operations had been almost wholly neglected. As to Engineers, they were rare and their training tended to be of a formal kind concerned more with fortification than field engineering. They were, however, notably brave and this in itself was almost a drawback since in any siege operation a high proportion of the small complement of Royal Engineers inevitably became casualties. It is indicative of the lack of confidence which the Duke of York felt in the usefulness of the Engineers that he formed a rival body, the Royal Staff Corps, under the control of the Horse Guards, which rendered notable service in the less formal parts of field engineering.

One other person contributed notably to the regeneration of the army: Lord Castlereagh. He had two terms as Secretary of State for War, seven months from July 1805 and more than two years from July 1807. During this time he was responsible for three great improvements. He succeeded in bringing the army up to an effective strength, he refused to undertake military operations without taking sound military advice, and he established a 'disposable force', 40,000 strong, with troop transports for 10,000 always standing by, so that in future Britain could take advantage of an opportunity to intervene on the continent without having to pause to scrape together men to form an expeditionary force.

Through the efforts of the Duke of York and Castlereagh, the British Army had been restored to a position where it was, for its numbers, a formidable force (provided some way could be improvised to feed it); all that it now needed was a worthwhile and practical objective and a competent field commander. In 1808 both were available.

CHAPTER TWO

ENSIGN TO MAJOR-GENERAL

Dash at the first party that comes into your neighbourhood . . .
and the campaign will be our own.

Wellesley to Stevenson, 17 August 1803

Arthur Wesley,* third surviving son of Garret, Earl of Mornington, was born in Dublin in April 1769. His father, a somewhat ineffective noble-man of musical tastes, died 12 years later without leaving any notable impression on any of his four sons or two daughters. At the time of his death his estate was encumbered with debts. His widow, daughter of an Irish viscount, was a determined lady without a high opinion of Arthur, to whom she was accustomed to refer as her 'awkward son'. It is illustrative of her feelings for him that she could not correctly recall the date of his birth, insisting always that it was 1st May, an error suffi-ciently proved by the registers of St. Peter's, Dublin, where his christen-ing is recorded on 30th April.

Arthur Wesley had an erratic education, attending in succession the diocesan school of Meath, a preparatory school in Chelsea and Eton. In contrast to his elder brother Richard, now Earl of Mornington, he gave no promise of academic brilliance and was noted as an idle, solitary child whose only distinction at Eton was to have defeated Sydney Smith's elder brother in a bout of fisticuffs. At the age of 15, his mother, deciding that she could not afford to keep him at Eton, with-drew him and took him to Brussels, from whence he was sent to a semi-military academy at Angers where he learned French, good manners and very little else. As was often the way with younger sons in penur-ious noble families, his mother decided that the army was the only place for him and his brother, by now a junior lord of the Treasury, used his influence to place him. 'Let me remind you,' wrote Mornington to the Lord Lieutenant of Ireland, 'of a younger brother of mine, whom you were so kind as to take into consideration for a commission in the army. He is here at this moment and perfectly idle. It is a matter of indifference to me what commission he gets so long as he gets it soon.' [1]

On 7th March 1787, a few weeks short of his eighteenth birthday,

---

* The family name had been Colley until it was changed in 1728 to Wesley, when Wellington's grandfather inherited the estates of his cousin Garret Wesley. The second Lord Mornington changed it to Wellesley in 1798.

Arthur Wesley was commissioned as an ensign in the Seventy-third Foot. He never served with the regiment, which was then in India, but on Christmas Day of the same year he bought a lieutenancy in the Seventy-sixth. With this regiment he may have served for a few days before they sailed for India while he, on 23rd January 1788, transferred to the Forty-first. He remained on their regimental books for 18 months before moving on to the Twelfth Light Dragoons. June 1791 saw him purchase a captaincy in the Fifty-eighth, but his regimental service was slight since in November 1787 he had been appointed A.D.C. to the Marquis of Buckingham, Lord Lieutenant of Ireland, a post he held for six years, during which time he became a member of the Irish Parliament for the family borough of Trim. In that capacity one of his few recorded speeches was in favour of giving Roman Catholics the vote.

The outbreak of war with France found him at his post in Viceregal Lodge, Dublin, and a captain in the Eighteenth Light Dragoons. He immediately bought himself, with a loan from his brother, a majority in the Thirty-third and by the time that the regiment landed at Ostend on 25th June 1794, he had commanded it as lieutenant-colonel for nine months. He was 25.

The campaign of 1793–95 in the Netherlands was not one in which many British soldiers distinguished themselves. Wesley was one of the few who did. When on 15th September the British, retiring in some disorder from an abortive assault on Boxtel, found themselves harried by French cavalry, the Thirty-third were deployed in line, on the initiative of their commander, across the path of their pursuers. A single volley decided the French to call off the pursuit. Wesley was rewarded with the command of a brigade and spent most of the rest of the year guarding a stretch of the Waal. It was a dreary task—'the French keep us in a perpetual state of alarm, we turn out once, sometimes twice, every night; the officers and men are harassed to death. . . . I have not had the clothes off my back for a long time and generally spend the greater part of the night upon the bank of the river.'[2] The army's headquarters were grossly inefficient. 'From October to January . . . I only saw one general officer from headquarters, which was old Sir David Dundas. We had letters from England, and I declare that those letters told us more of what was passing at headquarters than we learned from headquarters themselves.'[3] After a long and painful retreat through snow-covered Holland and North Germany, the army re-embarked at Bremen with no more than 6,000 men in 33 battalions. 'I learned,' said Wesley, later in life, 'what one ought not to do, and that is always something.'[4]

Having seen his regiment safely established in Warley Barracks in Essex, Colonel Wesley went on leave to Ireland. He was sickened by the incompetence of the army in the Netherlands: 'I see the manner in which military offices are filled.'[5] He applied to the Lord Lieutenant

33

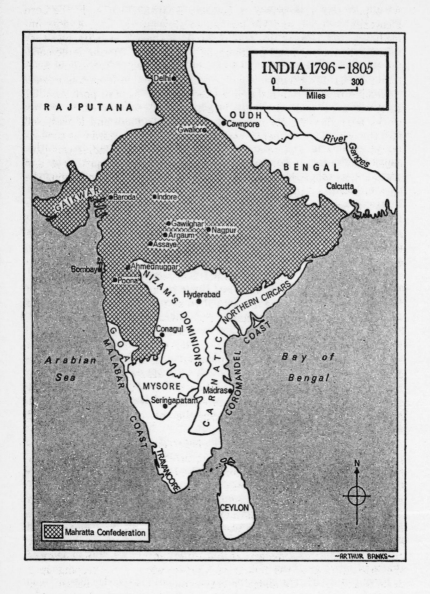

INDIA 1796-1805

0   Miles   300

RAJPUTANA

Delhi

OUDH
Cawnpore

Gwalior

River Ganges

BENGAL

GAIKWAR

Baroda

Indore

Calcutta

Gawilghar
Argaum
Assaye

Nagpur

Bombay

Poona

Ahmednuggar

NIZAM'S DOMINIONS

Hyderabad

NORTHERN CIRCARS

Conagul

GOA

MALABAR COAST

Arabian
Sea

MYSORE

Seringapatam

CARNATIC

Madras

COROMANDEL COAST

Bay of
Bengal

TRAVANCORE

N

CEYLON

Mahratta Confederation

~ARTHUR BANKS~

for a post on the Revenue or Treasury Boards. Fortunately the Lord Lieutenant refused, and Wesley had to stay in the army. Almost immediately the Thirty-third was ordered to the West Indies and they sailed with their colonel in command. Again good fortune intervened, for the West Indies was more likely to bring death from yellow fever than military advancement. The fleet sailed from Southampton on 15th November only to run into a gale which blew it back to port. Another start was made and this time a hurricane was encountered. It was six weeks later that Wesley managed to regain England and it was well into the following year before the whole of the Thirty-third was concentrated once more at Poole. The posting to the West Indies was cancelled and India substituted. The regiment sailed in April 1796 and Wesley, who was sick when they left, followed in a warship, joining the battalion at the Cape. They arrived at Calcutta in February 1797.

To one brought up in the Ascendancy, India was not greatly different from Ireland. The weather was warmer, the natives darker skinned, but at least their religions were tolerated. When he arrived British India was quiet and he could turn his attention to drilling his regiment, writing a long and detailed memorandum for the Governor-General on the best method of capturing Manila, and some large-scale carousing. The memorandum was so impressive that it earned him a command in the expedition which was dispatched to seize Java as a first step, but was recalled on reaching Penang. The carousing he soon abandoned, becoming convinced that there was 'but one receipt for good health in this country and that is to live moderately, to drink little or no wine, to use exercise, to keep the mind employed and, if possible, to keep in good humour with the world'.[6] He was soon afterwards noted as being 'very abstemious with wine: drank four or five glasses with people at dinner, and about a pint of claret afterwards'.[7] At about the same time he gave up playing the violin, perhaps the only taste he had inherited from his father.

If he was disappointed of gaining distinction in Java and the Philippines, a greater opportunity soon occurred. In May 1798 his elder brother, the Earl of Mornington, arrived in Calcutta as Governor-General. He was a man of lavish tastes, particularly in buildings and women, but he had a genuine determination to clean up the corruption that was so outstanding a feature of the East India Company at that time and to see that justice was done equally between Indians and British. He also, very wisely, relied on his brother Arthur for military advice. The peace of India was at that time menaced by an old enemy of the British, Tippoo, the Sultan of Mysore, who, while keeping up a devious and ostensibly amicable correspondence with the British, was simultaneously intriguing with the French in Mauritius (Ile de France) to gain their backing in a renewed attempt to expel the British. Meanwhile the Sultan's army was being trained by French officers. Mornington was anxious to put down this troublemaker immediately, but he was for a time dissuaded by his brother's urging, partly on military, partly on political grounds, that his 'propositions to Tippoo ought to be moderate, at least so much so as to make it probable that he will acquiesce in them'.[8] Indeed, he pressed the Governor so hard to be patient 'that I am afraid I shall be accused of boring Mornington'.[9] Meanwhile he supervised the assembly of an effective army round Madras and recommended that the army of the Nizam of Hyderabad, a weak but friendly ruler subject to much pressure from Tippoo, should be secured for the British cause. This was briskly done. The Nizam's French officers were removed and replaced with British, and 14,000 sepoys added to the troops available for use against Tippoo.

Eventually in March 1799 it became obvious that Tippoo had no intention of reaching any kind of an arrangement with the British, and Mysore was invaded from both Madras and Bombay. The Governor-General had announced his intention of accompanying the Madras contingent, commanded by General Harris, but was sharply discouraged by a letter from his brother telling him that 'your presence in the camp, instead of giving confidence to the general, would in fact deprive him of the command of the army . . . If I were in General Harris's situation and you joined the army, I should quit it.' [10] Colonel Wellesley's own command within the force consisted of a division composed of 'the 33rd, six excellent battalions of the company's sepoys, four rapscallion battalions of the Nizam's which, however, behaved well, and really about 10,000 (which they call 25,000) cavalry of all nations, some good and some bad, and twenty-six pieces of cannon'.[11] A very reasonable command for a colonel of 30.

The campaign against Tippoo was not a very significant one except that during it he suffered one of his very rare reverses. When the army was within three miles of Tippoo's capital, Seringapatam, Wellesley was ordered to take a clump of trees, the Sultanpettah Tope, about half a mile in front of the British lines. On Harris' orders the attempt was made by Wellesley at the head of the Thirty-third. 'On the night of the 5th we made an attack upon the enemy's outposts which, at least on my side, was not quite so successful as could have been wished. The fact was that the night was very dark, that the enemy expected us, and were strongly posted in an almost impenetrable jungle. We lost an officer killed, and others and some men wounded; and at last as I could not find out the post which it was desirable I should occupy, I was obliged to desist from the attack. . . . I got a slight touch on the knee, from which I have felt no inconvenience . . . and I have come to a determination, when in my power, never to suffer an attack to be made by night upon an enemy who is prepared and strongly posted, and whose posts have not been reconnoitered by daylight.' [12] General Harris recalled that Wellesley came to report his failure 'in a good deal of agitation'. The following morning the Thirty-third, led by their colonel, took the Tope without difficulty.

Seringapatam was besieged and fell after a month to an assault led by Major-General Baird. Tippoo's body was found in the captured town. Wellesley was assigned as Governor of Seringapatam, a post he held to the great satisfaction of the inhabitants until the end of 1800. It was a difficult task of civil administration, difficult because it entailed delicate points of British custom. Muslim law and expediency. The daughters of Tippoo 'ought not to be allowed to marry. A Musulman would found a pretension either to a large pension, or even to the government of Mysore, upon his connection with one of Tippoo's daughters.' With the sons it was different. 'There ought to be no restriction whatever upon the Princes to take as many women, either as wives or concubines, as they may think proper. They cannot employ their money in a more harmless way; and the consideration of the future expense of the support of a few more women, after their death, is trifling.' [13]

Between these troublesome problems he engaged in his first campaign as an independent commander, a four-month operation against a powerful brigand, Doondia Wao, who described himself as King of the Two Worlds and commanded an army which at times consisted of about 40,000 men. Doondia carried on his depredations in the north of Mysore and the south of the Mahratta country and his force was so formidable that the Mahrattas, no mean fighting men, refused to face him. It was a difficult and tedious campaign. The country was broken and Wellesley's army had always to drag behind it a slow-moving supply train. Time and again the British aimed blows which fell in the air or on some inconsiderable detachment of Doondia's army which, living by the pillage of the countryside, was infinitely more mobile. The British commander was faced with the same problem that, in later years, his French opponents in the Peninsula were to face with the guerrillas. By determination and by adapting his tactics, Wellesley succeeded in a way that the French were never to do. On 10th September 1800, Doondia, with the hard core of his force, 5,000 strong, was intercepted at Conagul. Wellesley had with him only four regiments of cavalry, two British and two Indian, hardly 2,000 sabres, and Doondia took up a strong position. Rather than risk giving him the chance to slip away as he had done so often before, Wellesley formed his regiments in a single line and charged. The enemy broke and Doondia's body was found amongst the dead. There was some clearing up still to be done but the campaign was over. It only remained for Wellesley to take under his protection his fallen adversary's four-year-old son, whose education he arranged and to whom he paid a small income for the rest of his life.

It was two and a half years before Wellesley took the field again. Before that, in April 1802, he had been promoted major-general in fulfilment of what he had described a year or two before as 'my highest ambition'.[14] In the meantime he had been offered the command of, and had made all the administrative arrangements for, a force destined to co-operate from the Red Sea with Abercromby's successful expedition to Egypt. Shortly before the expedition sailed he was superseded, to his immense chagrin, by a senior officer. Hurt and angry as he was, he agreed to go as second in command, only to be prevented by an attack of the 'Malabar itch—a much worse kind of itch than ours—it would not yield to brimstone. Dr. Scott cured me at last by baths in nitric acid; they were so strong that the towels which dried me on coming out were quite burnt.'[15]

The new war which broke out in 1803 was conducted in the territory of the Mahratta Confederation. The Confederation, a loose association of princelings, covered, in an irregular diamond shape, the whole of central India. To the south it stretched 200 miles beyond Bombay, to east and west it reached the sea, and the northernmost tip was north of Delhi. The main component states were Baroda, Gwalior, Indore, Nagpur and Poona, and these five were, in shifting combinations, constantly at war with each other. In the latter half of 1802, Holkar of Indore had defeated Scindia of Gwalior and the Peshwa (chief minister) of the Confederation and had seized the latter's capital, Poona. The Peshwa thereupon allied himself with the British, who dispatched Wellesley with 19,000 men to recover Poona. This task he achieved bloodlessly in April 1803.

There followed a long period of tortuous negotiation not, as might have been supposed, with Holkar, the aggressor, who had withdrawn to his own dominions, but with the Peshwa's former ally, Scindia, who was showing aggressive tendencies and was coming increasingly under French influence. The talks lasted until August, by which time it was clear that Scindia had no intention of coming to a satisfactory agreement, whereupon the Governor-General gave orders for Scindia's dominions to be invaded from the north by an army under General Lake, whose base was at Cawnpore, and from the south-west by Wellesley from the direction of Poona.

Wellesley's army was divided into three parts. To the north some 4,000 men under Colonel John Murray were to operate in Gaikwar and Baroda, the latter state being in alliance with the British. In the east 9,500 men under Colonel Stevenson operated from the dominions of the Nizam of Hyderabad, and between them Wellesley himself, with 11,000 men, covered Poona.

During the months of wrangling it was exceedingly difficult to put the army into suitable shape for campaigning and even more difficult to keep it supplied, for Holkar's men had stripped the country around Poona and the Governor of Bombay adopted an obstructive attitude to all Wellesley's requests for supplies. Nor was the problem of transport an easy one. 'Our distresses increase upon us for want of cattle', complained Wellesley as the army slowly moved up towards the hostile border. 'I was obliged to leave behind this morning 500 loads of stores, and 100 of provisions. You will be a judge of the mortality of cattle from the following statement. There was a muster on the 15th, and there were 500 good carriage bullocks, in the grain and provision department more than were required for the loads, and a sufficiency in the stores [department]. The consumption between the 15th and the 18th was 250 loads of provisions; and yet on the 18th the deficiency of carriage [bullocks] is found to be 100, making the loss of cattle in the provision department, in three days, 850 bullocks. In the store department it has been, in the same period of time, about 600. The gun cattle kept up well, notwithstanding the bad weather; but it is by force of exertion.' [16]

On 6th August permission was received to start hostilities against Scindia. It was raining hard and continuously at the time and it was not until the 8th that the army was able to move forward. When it did move no time was wasted. On the first day the fortified town of Ahmednuggar was stormed out of hand, although it had a garrison of 2,000, half of them regular troops under French officers. The survivors took refuge in a fort within the town where they were bombarded into submission by 12th August. There was no doubt that Wellesley was putting into practice the advice he gave at this time to Stevenson, commanding the detached column away to his right! 'Dash at the first party that comes into your neighbourhood. . . . If you adopt this plan, and succeed in cutting up, or driving to a distance, one good party, the campaign will be our own. A long defensive war will ruin us, and will answer no purpose whatever. By any other plan than that above proposed, we will lose our supplies, do what we will.' [17]

Using Ahmednuggar as a base, and drawing on the rich districts around it, he plunged deep into the Mahratta country, turning eastward when he heard that Scindia was planning a raid on Hyderabad. His object was to bring Scindia to battle. With this in mind, he declined to join his own army with that of Stevenson since this would not only increase the difficulty of feeding the army but would make it easier for the enemy to elude him.

On 23rd September, soon after midday, he came upon the combined armies of Scindia and the Rajah of Berar encamped at the junction of the rivers Kaitna and Juah, near the village of Assaye, 220 miles east-north-east of Bombay. The Mahratta strength was well above 40,000 men, including 10,000 regular infantry with French officers, more than 20,000 cavalry, a large force of irregular infantry and over 100 pieces of artillery served by efficient French-trained gunners. Their position was 'confoundedly strong and difficult of access'.[18] Between Wellesley and the Mahrattas was the river Kaitna which was broad and fordable only in a few well guarded places.

Having left garrisons in Ahmednuggar and other vital centres, Wellesley had in hand 7,000 men. Of these about 1,800 were British, the Nineteenth Light Dragoons, the Seventy-fourth and Seventy-eighth Foot and 160 artillerymen. There were besides three regiments of native cavalry and five battalions of sepoys. His artillery amounted to 22 guns, most of them of light calibre. Stevenson's column was out of touch. Wellesley decided to attack as soon as his infantry came up. 'I decided upon the immediate attack because I saw clearly that, if I attempted to return to my camp, I should have been followed thither by the whole of the enemy's cavalry, and I might have suffered some loss; instead of attacking I might have been attacked the next morning; and, at all events, I might have found it very difficult to secure my baggage.' [19]

The immediate problem, once the decision was taken, was how to get at the enemy. There were only two possible approaches since a frontal attack was ruled out by the broad river with its defended fords. He could either turn their right, the flank away from the junction of the Kaitna with the Juah, or turn their left. It would not be feasible to make a wide swing round their left, which would entail crossing both rivers in the presence of a numerically superior enemy; but if a crossing could be made in the narrow gap between the Mahratta left and the river junction, it would be possible to draw up the army at right angles to the enemy line with both its flanks resting on rivers and thus secured from cavalry. His native guides assured him that there was no ford in this gap but Wellesley could see that in this stretch there were two villages facing each other across the river. 'I immediately said to myself that men could not have built villages so close to one another on opposite sides of a stream without some habitual means of communication, either by boats or a ford—most probably by the latter. On that conjecture or rather reasoning, in defiance of all my guides and informers, I took the desperate resolution, as it seemed, of marching for the river, and I was right. I found a passage, crossed my army over, had no more to fear from the enemy's cloud of cavalry, and my army, small as it was, was just enough to fill the space between the two streams, so that my flanks were secure.' [20]

'As the infantry approached the river', wrote an officer of the East India Company's Engineers, 'the enemy's guns opened on it, but without much effect. No sooner, however, did the head of the column begin to ascend the opposite bank, than it was met by a shower of shot from a battery advanced near the bank for that purpose, which, continuing without intermission, caused us severe loss. At this time the General's orderly dragoon had the top of his head carried off by a cannon ball, but the body being kept in its seat by the valise, holsters, and other appendages of a cavalry saddle, it was some time before the terrified horse could rid himself of the ghastly burden, in the endeavour to effect which he kicked and plunged, and dashed the poor man's brains in our faces, to our no small danger and annoyance. Being ordered forward to examine the ground in the direction of the enemy . . . I observed, on gaining the top of the high ground between the two rivers, the enemy's infantry in the act of changing their front, and taking up a new position, with their right to the river Kaitna and their left on the village of Assaye. On returning to the General, I found that not supposing the enemy to be capable of such a manoeuvre in the face of an attacking force, he had, in conformity with his original intention of attacking them in flank, already formed the infantry in two lines, while the cavalry . . . was drawn up as a reserve in the rear.' [21]

'I intended at that time to throw my right up to Assaye,' wrote Wellesley. 'When the enemy changed their position, they threw their left to Assaye, in which village they had some infantry, and it was surrounded by cannon. When I saw that . . . I altered my plan; and determined to manoeuvre by my left, knowing that the village of Assaye must fall when the right should be beat. Orders were given accordingly. However, by one of those unlucky accidents which frequently happen, the officer commanding the piquets, which were upon the right, led immediately up to the village of Assaye: the 74th regiment, which was upon the right of the second line, followed them. There was a large break in our line between these corps and those on our left. They were exposed to a most terrible cannonade from Assaye, and were charged by the [enemy] cavalry; consequently, in the piquets and the 74th regiment we sustained the greatest part of our loss.' [22]

Fortunately the left wing did all that could be expected of it. They broke the Mahratta right and swung to their own right to take the Mahratta left in flank. 'I cannot write in too strong terms of the conduct of the troops', Wellesley reported. 'They advanced in the best order, and with the greatest steadiness, under a most destructive fire, against a body of infantry far superior in number, who appeared determined to contend with them to the last, and who were driven from their guns only with the bayonet; and notwithstanding the numbers of the enemy's cavalry, and the repeated demonstrations they made of an intention to charge, they were kept at a distance by our infantry.' [23]

Meanwhile the British and Native cavalry, led by Lieutenant-Colonel Maxwell of the Nineteenth, charged in on the enemy right in support of the Seventy-fourth. The Mahrattas stood their ground bravely, fighting their guns to the last, but the Nineteenth were not to be stopped and came 'pouring through the enemy's left like a torrent that had burst its banks, bearing along the broken and scattered materials which had opposed it'.[24]

The Mahratta centre was able to retire in good order and take up further position, but by this time their spirit was broken. Only the garrison of Assaye continued to put up a strong defence, beating off determined attacks from two sepoy battalions. Their cavalry, which had shown little enterprise during the day, now began to leave the field. The infantry of their centre beat off a further charge from the Nineteenth, in the course of which Colonel Maxwell was killed, and then withdrew. Wellesley was left in possession of the field and 98 captured guns: 1,200 Mahratta dead were counted.

Out of Wellesley's 7,000 men, almost 1,600 were casualties, 644 of the casualties falling on his 1,800 Europeans. It was a heavy price to pay and Wellesley felt it deeply. Having given what orders he could to succour the wounded, he sank down on the ground, sitting with his head between his knees, absolutely silent. Eventually he slept fitfully, suffering from nightmares.

Stevenson's force joined the next day, and having left its doctors to tend to Wellesley's wounded, pushed on in the wake of Scindia's army. It was not until 8th October that Wellesley, having secured the safety of his wounded, was able to take the field again.

Assaye was Wellington's first major victory. With the possible exception of the forcing of the Douro six years later, it was the most risky operation he ever undertook. It was quite unexpected that he should find the whole of Scindia's army at Assaye. All his information led him to believe that only the infantry was present. Nevertheless he determined on immediate attack. His line of attack, across the unknown ford, a ford which all local advice believed not to exist, was a stroke of the greatest boldness. If the ford had been imaginary the army would have to countermarch, which must have led to some disorder in the presence of an overwhelming force of enemy horse. Nor, in view of the strength of the Mahratta cavalry, could their position be reconnoitred except by natives of doubtful reliability. Once the army was across the river, Wellesley learned two lessons which he never afterwards forgot. The first was never to assume that the enemy would stay still while he manoeuvred around them. The second was not to underrate the enemy. He had crossed the Kaitna in the firm belief that the enemy army would not be sufficiently well trained to form briskly to their flank. In fact they did so, in the words of an observer, 'in the most steady manner possible, though not exactly according to Dundas; for each battalion came up into the new alignment in line, the whole body thus executing a kind of echelon movement on a large scale'.[25]

His reactions at the moment when he learned that his attempt to fall on the enemy's flank had failed, were typical of his behaviour on many later occasions when he found that his appreciation of the enemy's intentions had been wrong. 'I never,' wrote one of his staff officers, 'saw a man so cool and collected as he was the whole time.'[26] Imperturbably, he changed his plan and called for his left to advance rather than his right. Equally typical of his later performance was his comment on the man who caused most of the loss in the battle by pressing on against the heavily defended village despite orders not to do so. 'I do not wish to cast any reflection upon the officer who led the piquets. I lament the consequences of his mistake, but I must acknowledge that it was not possible for a man to lead a body into a hotter fire than he did the piquets on that day.' [27] Seven years later, when Robert Craufurd hazarded the Light Division contrary to orders, suffering 300 unnecessary casualties, Wellesley wrote: 'If I am to be hanged for it, I cannot accuse a man who I believe has meant well, and whose error is one of judgment, and not of intention; and indeed I must add that although my errors, and those of others also, are visited heavily upon me, this is not the way in which any, much less a British, army can be commanded.' [28]

As soon as the army was able to move forward again, Wellesley secured possession of most of the Deccan. This produced immediate results. On 10th November Scindia opened peace talks, and one of his principal subordinates brought 3,000 irregular troops to join Wellesley's army. The peace talks were abortive. It was Wellesley's overriding condition that Scindia should withdraw his forces to the eastward, and this despite his promises the Mahratta declined to do. It was therefore necessary to deal with him once more. On 29th November the combined forces of Wellesley and Stevenson came up with Scindia's army at Argaum. The British force, one British and five Native regiments with three British and 12 Native battalions, amounted to about 11,000 men and had beside about 4,000 irregular cavalry of doubtful value and loyalty. Scindia had with him more than 30,000 men, including 10,000 regular infantry. Despite the fact that his army had been marching for nine hours, Wellesley decided to attack.

The battle began badly. The three battalions of Native infantry which formed the advanced guard fell into a panic when the bullock drivers, with the guns which accompanied them, fled through their ranks. Wellesley immediately rallied them, as 12 years later at Waterloo he was to rally the Brunswickers. 'What do you think of nearly three entire battalions, who behaved so admirably in the battle of Assaye being broke and running off, when the cannonade commenced at Argaum, which was not to be compared with that at Assaye? Luckily, I happened to be at no great distance from them, and I was able to rally them and to re-establish the battle. If I had not been there, I am convinced we should have lost the day.' [29]

After this initial set-back everything went well. 'I formed the army into two lines; the infantry in the first, the cavalry in the second, and supporting the right; and the Mysore and Mogul [irregular] cavalry the left. . . . When formed, the whole advanced in the greatest order; the 74th and 79th regiments were attacked by a large body (supposed to be Persians), and all these were destroyed. Scindia's cavalry charged the

1st battalion 6th [Native Infantry] regiment, which was on the left of our line, and were repulsed; and their whole line retired in disorder before our troops, leaving in our hands thirty-eight pieces of cannon and all their ammunition. The British cavalry then pursued them for several miles, destroyed great numbers, took many elephants and camels and much baggage. The Mogul and Mysore cavalry also pursued the fugitives, and did them great mischief.' [30] 'If we had had daylight an hour more, not a man would have escaped. . . . The troops were under arms, and I was in the saddle, from six in the morning until twelve at night.' [31]

The British casualties at Argaum were astonishingly light; only about 360, of whom 160 were Europeans. The enemy losses could not be assessed.

The remnant of the Mahratta infantry took refuge in Gawilghar, 50 miles from the battle field, a fortress perched in sharp mountains, a place of great natural strength. There was no safety for them there. By 8th December Wellesley and Stevenson had surrounded them. There was a delay of a few days while heavy guns were manhandled up the rocky heights, but on the 13th the British batteries opened and two days later the place was stormed. The Rajah of Berar sued for peace and Scindia marched away to counter General Lake's moves against his northern territories.

Apart from a brisk cavalry operation, which he commanded in person, against some banditti who had raided into the dominions of the Nizam of Hyderabad, the storm of Gawilghar was Wellesley's last active service in India. He stayed in the country, dealing for the most part with civil affairs in Poona and Seringapatam, until March 1805, when, having suffered another severe bout of fever and being convinced that there was little chance of achieving further military distinction in the sub-continent, he sailed for England.

He was almost 36, a major-general of three years' standing, with two substantial victories to his credit, and an additional Knight Commander of the Bath. He owed his rise to this eminence, in almost equal proportions, to three factors: his brother's influence, good luck and his own abilities.

A gift * of £6,000 from his brother had put him in line for automatic promotion by enabling him to purchase, at the age of 24, a lieutenant-colonelcy after less than six years' service. Young as this appears by modern standards, it was by no means unusual amongst his contemporaries. Edward Paget, Charles Stewart and Henry Fane were all lieutenant-colonels at 19. From that time Wellesley's promotion went forward by what the Commander-in-Chief described as 'the usual mode of progressive advancement'.[32] Neither influence, nor the fact that he

* This was originally a loan, but when, with the aid of Indian prize money, Wellesley offered to pay it back, his brother refused to accept it.

was one of the few officers to distinguish himself in the campaigns in Flanders, could do anything to change his place on the list of colonels.

Good luck stepped in when he decided to accompany his regiment to India in 1796. As a full colonel there was no question of his being required to go, and when he embarked he can have had no foreknowledge that his brother would be appointed Governor-General and follow him to Calcutta a year later. Before his brother's arrival his obvious abilities had earned him the position of confidential military adviser to Mornington's predecessor, Sir John Shore, who, for the expedition to Manila, had offered him the command of 7,000 men, as many as he was to command at Assaye. This offer he declined, judging it more proper to act as second-in-command to a more senior officer.

Mornington, on his arrival, gave his brother no command, but used him only for the invidious task of acting as unofficial adviser to the Governor of Madras. That Wellesley received a command in the expedition against Seringapatam was another stroke of good luck. An officer due to lead a brigade was killed in a duel and Wellesley was the only replacement available. That the Nizam of Hyderabad asked that his contingent should be added to Wellesley's command may, perhaps, partly have been a compliment to the Governor-General, but it is fair to suppose that knowing Wellesley, the Nizam would have been convinced that the Colonel was a man to be trusted.

It is possible that there was some element of family influence in Wellesley's appointment to command the southern army against the Mahrattas in 1803. Unfriendly critics, both in India and in England, were not slow to draw attention to the fact that the Governor-General's young brother had been given a plum job. That his campaign against Doondia had shown that he was the most capable major-general in south India was overlooked in the glee of circulating a lively piece of malicious gossip. There were few British generals with a victory even of the small scale of Conagul to their credit in 1803, and in the whole history of the world there are few generals who could claim, as Wellesley could, to have put down decisively a guerrilla force operating in strength in difficult country. Assaye and Argaum finally proved that if his appointment was jobbery, it was at least a thoroughly beneficent job. The Mahrattas were no mean opponents, as the unfortunate Colonel Monson found in 1804.

Wellesley took with him when he embarked an address from the inhabitants of Seringapatam expressing their 'gratitude for the tranquillity, security, and happiness we have enjoyed under your auspicious protection; respect for the brilliant exploits you have achieved; and reverence for your benevolence and affability'.[33] In a general order published in Madras on taking leave of his troops, he gave them his military testament, a statement of the guiding principles of his life: 'He earnestly recommends to the officers of the army, never to lose sight of the principles of the military service, to preserve the discipline of the troops, and to encourage, in their respective corps, the spirit of gentlemen and of soldiers, as the most certain road to the achievement of everything which is great in their profession.' [34]

He was very sea-sick on the voyage home, but the journey was broken by a three-week stay on St. Helena. 'The Island,' he told his brother, 'is beautiful, and the climate apparently the most healthy I ever lived in.' [35]

CHAPTER THREE

POLITICAL GENERAL

> You may think about dinner, for there is nothing more for soldiers to do this day.
>
> *Wellesley, 21st August 1808*

Landing in England on 10th September 1805, Wellesley was at any rate financially secure. 'When I came from India I had 42 or 43,000 Pounds which I made as follows. I got 5,000 £ prize money at Seringapatam; 25,000 £ prize money in the Mahratta war; the Court of Directors gave me 4,000 £ for having been commander in Mysore; and the Govt. paid me about 2,000 £ in one sum in arrears of an allowance as Comg. Officer at Seringapatam; & the remainder as interest upon these sums, savings &c during the time I was in India.' [1]

From the military point of view his situation was not so satisfactory. As an unemployed major-general, his only pay was that of a lieutenant-colonel of the Thirty-third. There were more than a hundred major-generals on the army list and there were not commands for half of them. Moreover he belonged to a family which was a target for a prolonged campaign of political smearing. Officers who made their reputation in India have always been viewed with some suspicion in Whitehall. The Horse Guards, he remarked, 'thought very little of anyone who had served in India. An Indian victory was not only no grounds for confidence, but it was actually a cause for suspicion.' [2] There were some compensating factors. The Secretary for War, Lord Castlereagh, an old friend from the Irish House of Commons, recognised his value and sought his advice. Pitt, soon to die, consulted him, and announced that he 'was quite unlike all other military men with whom I have conversed. He never makes a difficulty or hides his ignorance in vague generalities. If I put a question to him he answers it distinctly; if I want an explanation, he gives it clearly; if I desire an opinion, I get from him one supported by reasons that are always sound. He is a very remarkable man.'

Despite his influential friends, it was November before Wellesley was given a command. Even then it was scarcely what he had been accustomed to—three battalions of the line, less than 1,700 rank and file. Nor was the expedition for which they were detailed a propitious one. All through the summer Pitt had been trying to build up a third coalition against Napoleon. Vast Russian and Austrian armies were put in the field, supported by British gold. To act with them a British force was intended to operate in North Europe, reconquering, as a side issue, the King's Hanoverian domains. Men were hastily scraped together. The first great Austrian army surrendered at Ulm on 20th October, the day before Nelson destroyed the Franco-Spanish fleet at Trafalgar. A month later the first British contingent, 11,000 men, for the most part Germans, landed at Cuxhaven. They occupied Bremen but made no contact with the French. At the beginning of December the Russian and Austrian armies were routed at Austerlitz. Before the second division of British troops, amongst whom was Wellesley, had landed in Germany, Austria and France had made peace at Pressburg. The British, reinforced up to 26,000 men, stayed in Germany until mid-February and then sailed home. They had enlisted a few hundred recruits for the King's German Legion, they had offended the King of Prussia, but they had not caused Napoleon a moment's worry.

On his return Wellesley, now Colonel of the Thirty-third, was appointed to command a brigade at Hastings. Had there been at that moment a danger of invasion it would have been a key post, but Trafalgar had stilled that fear for the time being. He filled in his time by getting married and being elected Member of Parliament for Rye. His object in going to Parliament was to defend his brother the Marquis, whose Indian proceedings were under vicious attack. The seat he took was a Whig pocket borough in the gift of Lord Grenville, then Prime Minister. His election cost him £367 17s. His speeches in the House did him credit and helped to restore his brother's good name, but he soon found himself at odds with his Whig patron and changed to the Cornish pocket borough of Mitchell.

In April 1806 Britain declared war on Prussia and at midsummer, while Charles James Fox, as Foreign Secretary, was trying to find a basis for a negotiated peace with France, an eccentric commodore succeeded in capturing Buenos Aires as a private venture. His military force, such as it was, was commanded by William Carr Beresford, later to be one of Wellesley's most trusted lieutenants. Before the news had reached England, Beresford and his whole force had been captured, but the country, and especially the City, went into wild excitement at the thought of opening up the rich South American market. By the end of the year large reinforcements had sailed to the South Atlantic and finding Buenos Aires closed to them, captured Montevideo instead. Meanwhile Napoleon followed England's example and declared war on Prussia. He, however, took some action and destroyed the Prussian army at Jena on 14th October. Next month he dictated the Berlin Decrees from the Prussian capital. His aim now was to destroy England through her commerce. The desire for the South American market was not ill-timed, but it was quite impractical.

The first half of 1807 was a disastrous one for British arms. The Royal Navy made a pointless and humiliating demonstration off Constantinople. A small army landed in Egypt with the vaguest instructions as to what they should do. They were surprised at Rosetta and lost heavily. They hung on until September and then withdrew. In the Argentine things went worst of all. General Whitelocke attempted, at the beginning of July, to retake Buenos Aires. His plan, a simultaneous advance by 13 small unconnected columns into a geometrically laid-out town, must be the most inept in the whole history of war. He was forced to capitulate, court martialled on his return and cashiered.

The Ministry responsible for all this dispersed and ill-directed effort, the Ministry of All the Talents, resigned in March. In its place there ruled a Tory Cabinet under the moribund Duke of Portland. Castlereagh returned to be Secretary of State for War; to Ireland as Chief Secretary went Sir Arthur Wellesley.

The appointment of Castlereagh was important for three reasons. He managed, as none of his predecessors had done, to put recruiting for the army on a sound and expanding footing; he called into being a 'disposable force', an expeditionary army with transports always standing by to take advantage of any favourable opportunity for intervention on the continent; he relied on Wellesley for military advice. Sooner or later it was bound to happen that the 'disposable force', intended to be 40,000 strong, would be sent into action under the Secretary of War's principal, if unofficial, military adviser.

It was natural enough to send a soldier to be the effective executive head of the government in Ireland. The country had been in open rebellion in 1798 and its troubled state was a standing invitation to a French invasion. Wellesley tackled the work with his usual application but with a certain disdain. He dealt with the constant applications for posts in the civil service and the church with punctuality and civility. He firmly declined to allow the claims of the Belleisle Yeomanry to elect their captain, although he was unwilling to appoint to them a person 'who may be disagreeable to them'. Equally firmly he refused to oblige his sister 'respecting the appointment of Mr. Marshall to command a Dublin packet. There is no vacancy in a packet, and I cannot pretend to make an engagement to dispose in any particular manner of a vacancy which may occur. If a vacancy should occur, I think it may be expected that the Duke of Richmond [the Lord Lieutenant] or I have naval friends of merit, but not rich, to whom we may be desirous of giving such a provision.' [3]

Elections he managed as to the manner born:

'My dear Sir,
    Have you any influence over, or could you get at, Captain Anderson at Kilternan? We want him very much to support

49

Falkiner tomorrow. He has ten votes, and they would be most material.

Urge him on the ground of the Protestant interest, and on Talbot's revolutionary speech on the first day of the election, and on Wogan Brown's speech today. Brigade Major Cosby can get at Captain Anderson.

There is no time to be lost, as we must make an effort early tomorrow.' [4]

His own election for Tralee was effected with a minimum of fuss.

However busy he was, he was determined that nothing should stand in the way of his military career. While there was no fighting to be done he was content to serve the country in a civil capacity, but the moment a chance of active service showed itself he was determined to be off. 'I acknowledge that I shall not be satisfied if I allowed any opportunity to pass by without offering myself.' [5] Hearing from Castlereagh that a secret expedition was assembling, Wellesley applied for leave from Ireland and a command in the expedition. He got both.

The secret expedition, which turned out to be directed against Copenhagen, was the most successful British venture since the Peace of Amiens. Trafalgar had largely destroyed the French and Spanish navies, but there were around the coasts of Europe sufficient men-of-war to give Napoleon command of the sea if he could secure and concentrate them. Russia, for some years Britain's ally, had a substantial fleet and so had Denmark. The Russians, who were decisively beaten at Friedland on 14th June, were bound to agree to exclude British trade from their ports. Denmark was under great French pressure to do the same and showed signs of conforming. In March 1807 the Foreign Secretary, Lord Howick (later Lord Grey of the Reform Bill), had written to the Danish Ambassador: 'If Danish neutrality consists in mere assertion and . . . remonstrance against England, and in the most unqualified acquiescences in every extravagant demand of the enemy . . . the King . . . would take such measures as may be necessary to secure his own honour and the country's welfare against injury, which must necessarily arise from a continuance of such conduct.' [6] The impending defection of the Russians forced the Cabinet's hand. They determined to seize the Danish fleet. They hoped to do it without bloodshed. As they wrote to their diplomatic agent who accompanied the expedition: 'If a sword is drawn or a shot fired, it will be a matter of sincere regret to His Majesty.' [7]

The military arrangements went with unprecedented smoothness. On the 18th and 19th of July Admiral Gambier and General Lord Cathcart, the naval and military commanders, were given their orders. On the 29th 18,000 men sailed for Copenhagen. There they were to rendezvous with a further 8,000 who were already in the Baltic trying to co-operate with the King of Sweden, England's only remaining continental ally.

Wellesley was appointed to command the Reserve, the smallest of the three divisions but traditionally the formation used for the most difficult tasks. As William Napier remarked to his mother, 'We are the Reserve; that is the men reserved for the most dangerous service.' [8]

Wellesley's command was not a big one but it was of excellent quality. All four battalions, the Forty-third, Fifty-second, Ninety-second Highlanders and Ninety-fifth Rifles, later distinguished themselves in the Peninsula. But the Horse Guards insisted on sending out with him what Wellesley later described as a 'dry nurse . . . They gave me General [Richard] Stewart as second in command, that is, in reality intended for first in command, though I was the first in name. Well, during the embarkation, the voyage out and the disembarkation, General Stewart did everything. I saw no objection to anything he suggested, and all went à merveille. At last, however, we came up with the enemy. Stewart, as usual, was beginning his suggestions and arrangements, but I stopped him short with "Come, come, it's my turn now". I immediately made my own dispositions, assigned him to command one of the wings, gave him my orders, attacked the enemy and beat them. Stewart, like a man of sense, saw in a moment that I understood my business, and subsided.' [9]

The fleet arrived off Kronborg Castle on 3rd August and exchanged salutes with the fortress. All was civility until the Diplomatic Agent went ashore and made his propositions. The Danish fleet, 13 ships of the line and 14 frigates, should be given into the care of the British until the end of the war. All the dockyard stores should be handed over against payment and any ships building in the yards should be destroyed. The Danes refused. There was much debate and on 16th August the British began to go ashore. It seems that General Stewart's arrangements did not go as smoothly as Wellesley supposed. An officer of the Forty-third wrote: 'Some of our generals have dreadfully thick skulls, for I never saw any fair in Ireland so confused as the landing: had they opposed us, the remains of the army would have been on their way to England.' [10]

There was little fighting. What there was fell to Wellesley's force. A small Danish corps advanced to relieve Copenhagen and but for the disobedience of a Hanoverian officer, the Reserve would have surrounded them and taken them all prisoner. As it was, Wellesley with three and a half battalions 'fell in with them to the amount of about 9,000 at Kioge; fired one volley; the 92nd charged and they ran in all directions'.[11]

The Danes made no further attempt to raise the siege of their capital, nor would they surrender it. With the greatest reluctance, Lord Cathcart authorised the bombardment of Copenhagen. He had never cared for his orders to secure, by force if necessary, the fleet of a friendly neutral and he knew that every officer in his army agreed with him. They had, as a staff officer wrote, 'to steel our hearts against all the feelings of humanity'. The bombardment continued through two days and three nights. The city 'was in flames a quarter of an hour after the bombardment began, and continued so in a slight degree the whole of Thursday. But at night the timber yard took fire, and the conflagration became much more general during the whole of Friday; and the wind which was high during the whole of the time, carrying the flames directly over the town, increased it to such a degree that on Friday night the appearance was rather that of a volcano during a violent eruption than anything I can conceive.' [12]

On the third morning the Danes recognised the inevitable and sent out a flag of truce. Arthur Wellesley was sent to them to negotiate a capitulation. Lord Cathcart was delighted to have a member of the government on the spot to arrange the details of the surrender. Whatever the reactions in England might be to these unsavoury operations, he, Cathcart, had only obeyed his orders and the government could scarcely fail to defend a treaty which had been negotiated by their own Chief Secretary for Ireland.

All went well. The fleet was surrendered and sent away to English ports. The British agreed to evacuate the island of Zealand within six weeks. Then the government, or rather Canning, the Foreign Secretary, had second thoughts. Would it not be well to hold Zealand as the key to the Baltic? Would the Danes agree to this? Failing their agreement, could they not be caught out in some technical infringement of the capitulation which could be used as an excuse for the British to stay in possession? Wellesley was emphatic that they should do no such thing. The island did not command the entrance to the Baltic; it was indefensible; besides, 'I don't know what would be thought of us if after all that has passed, we should break an agreement into which we entered only a week ago'. [13] As for the capitulation itself, 'although I did what I thought was best on that occasion, I shall ever regret that I had any concern in it'. [14] Canning's underhand scheme was dropped and the fleet with the army sailed away on time. Wellesley had preceded it by a month to return to his office in Dublin.

There was an outcry in Parliament. The Whig Opposition worked itself up into a frenzy of self-righteousness over this unprovoked attack on a neutral nation. They conveniently overlooked that it had been a Whig Foreign Secretary who had threatened the Danes with 'all necessary measures' six months before. But even they could not rival the display of affronted virtue given by the Emperor Napoleon. His strictures on English perfidy left no stone unthrown. Four days before the troops had started to disembark against Copenhagen, a joint Franco-Spanish ultimatum had been delivered to the Portuguese Court demanding that Portugal should close her ports to Britain and should declare war against her. While the Danish fleet was being sailed and towed out of Copenhagen harbour, Napoleon announced that 'the House of Braganca has ceased to reign in Europe', and on 30th November General Junot at the head of a French army entered Lisbon while French and Spanish troops occupied all the key fortresses and towns of Portugal. Junot was just in time to see the sails of the Portuguese fleet, fifteen men-of-war, leaving the Tagus for Rio de Janeiro, carrying with it the Portuguese Royal family and escorted by the Royal Navy.

Meanwhile Wellesley was in Dublin dispatching the business of government, writing memoranda on tithes, calling for 'a particular account of the several institutions actually existing in this part of the United Kingdom for the purposes of education. (In order to obtain these returns with the greater uniformity and accuracy, I have the honour to enclose a sufficient number of blank forms according to which his Grace requests the returns be made)', expressing to Mr. Samuel Guinness his concern 'that you should feel yourself aggrieved by any act of the legislature which was proposed by me'. Above all, worrying about the danger of a French invasion, especially before it was known that the Portuguese fleet was in safe hands, when 'a very intelligent priest' in late November informed him that 'the disaffected expect that this country [Ireland] will be invaded from three different ports, Ferrol, Lisbon and Cadiz, and that the expedition from Ferrol will sail first. Letters have recently been received from France via Lisbon. He believes no emissary has come from France; but Pat Traynor, who came about four months ago, remained some time in the Bog of Allen and went to Wicklow. He is probably still in the country. The invasion is expected before Christmas.' [15] In case invasion should come, Wellesley recommended that he, himself, should be given a dormant commission on the staff of the army in Ireland, since 'we are very badly off for want of intelligent general officers'.[16]

In April 1808 the Chief Secretary was promoted to lieutenant-general, one of a batch of 32. He was twenty-ninth on the list, above the Clerk of the Deliveries to the Board of Ordnance, a member of the Board of Claims and a foreign officer, whose service consisted of raising a corps of Chasseurs which had been disbanded. Two of his seniors had seen no foreign service, six were Members of Parliament, and five were the sons of peers. They included Lord Paget and Sir John Hope, who were later to serve under him, Robert Brownrigg, the Quartermaster-General and Sir John Stuart, the victor of Maida.

Before this had happened, in February and March, the French had turned on their former allies, taken over the government of Spain *

* The King and his heir did not resign the throne until the 6th and 10th May, but the French usurpation of the government was effective from 23rd March when Murat occupied Madrid.

and occupied the northern fortresses. The Spaniards were at first stunned by the effrontery of the French seizure and the month of April passed quietly. In May the whole country burst into rebellion against their new masters. Madrid led the way on 2nd May, but there the French were in overpowering strength and it was in the outlying provinces that rebellion took its strongest hold. By 7th June deputies from the Asturias were in London and had seen Castlereagh. The other provinces were not far behind. They asked not for British troops but for money and arms. They were confident that, given these, they could drive out the French by themselves. If British troops were available, the Spaniards urged that they should be sent to Portugal, or at least to some part of Spain other than that from which any particular delegation came.

The British government promised, and supplied, arms and money, but they were in a difficult situation. They had been at war with Spain since 1804,* and their sources of information about that country were small. Their only direct contact with Spaniards was through the Governor of Gibraltar, Sir Hew Dalrymple, who, although technically under siege, maintained unofficial but friendly relations with the Captain-General of Andalusia, Castaños. This state of affairs they endeavoured to remedy by attaching British officers to the various provinces to which they provided supplies, who soon started to send back a flood of information, some of which was of value.

Ministers were anxious to intervene with troops but could not decide where to send them. The numbers sent must in any case be small. Castlereagh's 'disposable force' was already disposed. There were only two small brigades, about 5,000 strong together, in England, both at east coast ports; 10,000 men were cooped up in transports in the harbour of Gothenberg while their commander, Sir John Moore, conducted a fruitless negotiation with the demented King of Sweden for their employment in the Baltic. A further brigade under Major-General Brent Spencer was in transports based on Gibraltar, and 9,000 men were at Cork detailed for another of the government's South American schemes about which Wellesley had been giving somewhat unenthusiastic advice.

Little was known about French strength in Portugal. The best information appeared to be that sent by Admiral Cotton, 'off the Tagus' on 12th June. 'From every account I have been able to procure, there is not more than 4,000 French troops in Lisbon, against whom the populace are highly incensed; so that I feel it a duty to state my opinion that five or six thousand British troops might effect a landing, gain possession of the forts on the banks of the Tagus, and, by co-operating with His Majesty's fleet, give to our possession the whole of the maritime means now collected in the Tagus.'

* Peace between Britain and Spain was proclaimed on 5th July.

If the information on which this proposal was based was accurate, which it was not, the occupation of Lisbon would have been a project valuable in itself and requiring no more resources than were available. Except for the Royal Navy who were anxious to secure the all-weather harbour of Lisbon the country took no interest in Portugal. A crusading fervour swept the country but it was concerned exclusively with Spain. Opposition M.P.s, who had opposed every warlike operation in which the country had been involved since 1793, rallied passionately to the cause of the Spanish patriots. Mr. Sheridan declared that 'there had never existed so happy an opportunity to strike a bold blow for the rescue of the world. Hitherto Buonaparte had run a victorious race, because he had contended against princes without dignity, ministers without wisdom, and countries where the people were indifferent to his success; he had yet to learn what it was to fight against a people who were animated with one spirit against him. Will not the animation of the Spanish mind be excited by the knowledge that their cause is espoused, not by ministers alone, but by the parliament and people of England?' [17] Even Mr. Whitbread, who had been assiduous in advocating negotiations with Napoleon, went on record as believing that 'the Spanish nation was now committed with France: never were people engaged in a more arduous and honourable struggle. It has been falsely and basely stated that I advised the purchase of peace by the abandonment of the Spaniards to their fate. God forbid! A notion so detestable never entered my imagination. Perish the man who could entertain it! Perish this country, rather than its safety should be owing to a compromise so horribly iniquitous.' [18]

As a first step a force was allocated to the Peninsula and Wellesley was designated as its commander. His army was to consist of the 9,000 men at Cork reinforced by two weak battalions from the Irish garrison and some dragoons. Spencer's brigade from Gibraltar was ordered to collect a battalion from the garrison there and join him off the Iberian coast. Another battalion was to come to him from Madeira. When all these elements were assembled Wellesley's force would consist of 17,500 all ranks.

Castlereagh did not issue his orders until 30th June. They were necessarily imprecise. The army was to be employed 'in counteracting the designs of the enemy, and in affording the Spanish and Portuguese nations every possible aid in throwing off the yoke of France.' The method for achieving this desirable end was left vague. 'In the rapid succession in which events must be expected to follow each other, situated as Spain and Portugal now are, much must be left to your decision on the spot. His Majesty is graciously pleased to confide to you the fullest discretion to act according to circumstances, for the benefit of his service; and you may rely on your measures being favourably interpreted, and receiving the most cordial support.' There was no definite instruction to go to either Spain or Portugal. It was clear to the Cabinet that to land troops in Spain would alienate the Spaniards while to land them in Portugal would dissipate the unprecedented all-party support which Ministers were briefly enjoying. The furthest they would go was the broad hint that since the deputies from Galicia and Asturias 'do not desire the employment of any corps of His Majesty's troops in the quarter of Spain from whence they are immediately delegated' it was 'deemed expedient' to direct Wellesley's attention to the possibility of liberating Portugal. As a first step a 'fast sailing frigate' was to precede the convoy to Coruña to 'learn the actual state of things, both in Spain and Portugal'.

These were most unsatisfactory orders to receive. The 'fullest discretion' given to Wellesley meant that it was left to him to take the unpopular decision to go to Portugal. If he won a victory there public opinion would forgive him (and Ministers). If he failed, Ministers could wriggle out of the difficulty.

It was not until 15th July, after Wellesley had sailed, that the Cabinet came to the firm decision that 'the attack upon the Tagus should be considered as the first object to be attended to'. In the meanwhile they had heard that it would be possible to increase greatly the number of troops available. Moore's 10,000 men sailed for home from Gothenberg on 3rd July. They had not recalled that it was necessary for their commander to escape from the arrest under which the King of Sweden had placed him. These and other reinforcements would bring the army's strength in the Peninsula to nearly 40,000. This would necessitate a new commander for the whole force, and while ministers were prepared to leave one of their number 'fullest discretion' at the head of 17,000 men something more definite had to be said to a stranger at the head of 40,000.

Wellesley sailed from Cork on 12th July and landed at Coruña eight days later. The Galician Junta and the people of Coruña 'manifested the greatest satisfaction upon our arrival, received us with the greatest civility and cordiality, illuminated the town at night, and the whole of the inhabitants attended us to our boat when we returned on board the frigate at night'.[19] Reports of the fighting were most encouraging. There was news, for the most part true, of French reverses in Valencia and Catalonia. There was a report that General Dupont's force had been defeated and destroyed in Andalusia. This must have been received by occult means since Dupont was defeated and forced to surrender at Baylen on the day before Wellesley visited Coruña and by human means the news could not possibly have reached Coruña, 400 miles away, within 24 hours. The Spaniards admitted to one setback. 'The great army of Galicia, consisting of 50,000 men, received a check on the 14th of this month from a French corps under Marshal Bessières. The French had not half that number and lost about 7,000 men. . . . The Spaniards lost two pieces of cannon, the French six; the Spaniards retreated about 20 miles from the field of battle towards this province.' It was Wellesley's first experience of the Spanish habit of writing up their own victories and writing down their defeats. Two years later he was to emphasise to one of his divisional commanders: 'I beg you to observe that very little reliance can be placed on the report made to you by any Spanish general at the head of a body of troops. They generally exaggerate on one side or the other, and do not scruple of communicating supposed intelligence, in order to induce those to whom they communicate it to adopt a certain line of action.' [20] In this case, the object of the supposed intelligence was to keep the British troops off Spanish soil. The battle of Medina de Rio Seco had been a resounding defeat for the Spaniards. They had lost 2,200 men, including 1,200 prisoners, and ten guns. The French loss had been scarcely 400. The two Spanish generals concerned, Blake and Cuesta, had quarrelled bitterly on their retreat and divided their armies, Cuesta falling back to Leon and Blake to Astorga. The way to Madrid from France was clear and King Joseph Buonaparte entered the capital on the day that Wellesley was consulting with the Junta.

From Portugal, the news was scarcely more accurate. 'I find that Junot has collected, it is supposed, 12,000 men at Lisbon; and the French still hold Almeida and other points in Portugal with 3,000 more. The three northern provinces of Portugal are in a state of insurrection, and there is a Portuguese army at Oporto, to join which 2,000 Spaniards have marched from Galicia.' [21] The information that northern Portugal was in revolt was true, but the army at Oporto was little more than a rabble of unarmed peasants backed by a few detachments of regulars. The Spanish force really was moving to their support, but such was the condition of relations between Portugal and Spain that the Spanish troops were turned back by the Portuguese frontier guards as an unwanted assistance. Nor was the estimate of the French army in Portugal anything approaching accurate.

One thing Wellesley did deduce, and it became the guiding light of his policy for the years to come. 'It is obvious to me that the French will make no progress in Spain, excepting by the aid of very large armies; and I doubt whether they will find it practical to subsist by the means which the country can afford, or to supply their magazines from France, owing to the badness of the communication.' [22]

Fifteen thousand Frenchmen in Portugal, of whom 12,000 were at Lisbon, was a very different scale of opposition to Admiral Cotton's estimate of 5,000 on which the expedition was based. The chance of a landing close to Lisbon receded sharply, but, with Spencer's force due, the prospect of a successful campaign was still bright provided a safe landing could be made. Spencer, however, was proving elusive. He had been allowed a measure of discretion in his orders to join Wellesley, and since the wind was blowing from the north, letters from Gibraltar and Cadiz were taking a long time to beat up the coast. There was a chance that he might be engaged in some operations in the south from which he could not be extricated.

On the 24th Wellesley arrived in Oporto. There he found a Junta controlled by the Bishop, and a British officer, Colonel Brown, who had been collecting intelligence. Brown estimated the French troops in Portugal at 15,000 of which 10,000 were said to be at Lisbon and Peniche. The remaining 5,000 had been at Almeida and, in early July, had been brought south west, only to be halted south of Coimbra by patriots operating from that city. The Portuguese troops available were exactly estimated at 25,999, but the bulk of these were peasants 'mostly unarmed'. The few regular troops, said Wellesley, were 'composed of detachments of different corps, and cannot in any respect be deemed an efficient force'.[23] It was clear that there could be little useful assistance from the Portuguese army, indeed it could well prove to be a hindrance. It would not do altogether to ignore them but they must be stopped from cluttering up the roads and eating up the supplies on which the British must subsist if they had to move inland away from the fleet. Sir Arthur, therefore, decided that he would make such use as he could of the advanced corps, 6,000 strong, at Coimbra and request the Bishop to collect all the remaining troops at Oporto, well out of the way. He also undertook to send arms for them as soon as possible. The Bishop in his turn promised to supply 150 horses for the cavalry and 500 mules 'of a description which could be applied either to draft or carriage'. These animals were to be available at the mouth of the Mondego.

Wellesley was now almost determined to disembark the force at that river mouth. A volunteer corps, formed from the students at Coimbra University, had seized the small fort at Figueira da Foz which commanded a small harbour. They had been relieved at this post by Royal Marines landed from the fleet. It remained only for Wellesley to sail south to concert the arrangements for landing with Admiral Cotton, who was stationed off the mouth of the Tagus.

By the last day of the month he was back off Mondego Bay and issuing the orders for landing. He was greeted by bad news. 'Spencer has sent me a paper of information stating that the French force in Portugal amounts to 20,000 men; and although he knows I have only 10,000, and that he was not employed on any service in the south [i.e. co-operating with the Spaniards around Cadiz], he has determined to remain on shore at Xeres, near Cadiz.'[24] Not unnaturally he was angry with Spencer, although as it turned out, without justification, for Spencer had only landed his men temporarily at Xeres for their health since they had been for months cooped up in their transports. He also blamed Spencer for the other and more serious piece of bad news.

58

Spencer had sent a copy of his 'paper of information' to England 'where they took the alarm, and ordered out 5,000 men and Moore's corps of 10,000, with several general officers, senior to me, and Sir Hew Dalrymple to command the whole army'.[25] What was more galling was that he heard of his supersession not from Castlereagh direct but in a letter from his brother, William Wellesley Pole, who was Secretary to the Admiralty, and from a roving staff officer sent out by Castlereagh to co-ordinate arrangements. His reply to Whitehall was dignified and dutiful. 'Pole and Burghersh have apprised me of the arrangements for the future command of this army. . . . All I can say upon this subject is that whether I am to command the army or not, or am to quit it, I shall not hurry the operations, or commence one moment sooner than they ought to be commenced, in order that I may acquire the credit of the successes.'[26] In a private letter to his old chief at Dublin Castle, he was more positive. 'I hope I shall have beat Junot before any of them arrive, and then they may do as they please with me.'[27]

Ministers in London had found themselves in a quandary. They had taken the decision to reinforce the army in Portugal almost as soon as Wellesley had sailed from Cork. It is far from clear why the decision was so belated. Probably it was a combination of two factors; the unwonted feeling in Parliament in favour of intervention in the Peninsula, and the knowledge that Moore's force would be returning from Sweden. Moore was three years senior to Wellesley and was known throughout the army as the most competent and experienced general on the list. He was high in the estimation of the Commander-in-Chief and of the King, and was the general most favoured by the Parliamentary Opposition, since, quite apart from his military capabilities, he had been for six years a Whig M.P. It was impossible to remove him from the command of his troops and send them without him to serve under a junior general who was both a Wellesley and a Minister. The fact remained that, although Castlereagh supported him, the remaining Ministers, led by Canning, detested Moore. He had suffered in Naples and Sweden from the views of the Foreign Office and had not hesitated to lay bare their follies in blunt words. The Cabinet did its best to force Moore to resign. They sent him a letter which was a clear invitation to do so. Moore would not oblige them. It was deadlock. The only way out was to appoint a senior general to command both Moore and Wellesley. In theory, the field was wide. There were 70 generals and 91 lieutenant-generals senior to Moore, apart from Field-Marshals the Dukes of York and Kent. The total strength of the army, when the reinforcements had all arrived, would be 37,311. 'There has been,' said Moore, 'no such command since Marlborough for a British officer.' In fact, most of the senior officers were unavailable, decrepit, or discredited. The government pitched on the man who must have seemed the obvious choice, Sir Hew Dalrymple, who for the past two years had been Governor of

Gibraltar. No one in the army was so well informed about events in Spain. For several months past he had been in close touch with the Spanish generals in the south. He was, besides, only 58 and had seen at least one campaign in Flanders, since when he had served satisfactorily in Northern Command and in Guernsey. Lest he should become a casualty and the command revert to Moore, a second-in-command was appointed in Sir Harry Burrard, a 50-year-old Guardsman, an agreeable nonentity whom everyone liked. For good measure, and assuming that he would resign in any case, three further lieutenant-generals senior to Wellesley, John Hope, Lord Paget and Mackenzie Fraser were sent out.

No one had any doubt that the appointment of Dalrymple was a manoeuvre to stop Moore commanding the army, but the way in which it was done made Dalrymple particularly unhappy. Not only was he appointed 'for the present' only but a private letter from Castlereagh accompanying the notification of his appointment recommended Wellesley as an officer 'whom it is desirable, on all accounts, to make the most prominent use the rules of the service will permit'. Dalrymple may not have been very bright, but at least he could see that all was not as it seemed. 'Under all the circumstances of the case, I think it can scarcely be wondered at, that I received these communications with, at least, as much surprise as satisfaction. This ebb and flow of approbation and confidence was not satisfactory; and something seemed to lurk under this most complicated arrangement, which bore, I thought, a most unpromising aspect.' [28]

The troops from England began to sail while Wellesley was off the Mondego. The brigades of Generals Anstruther and Acland left the Downs on 22nd July. Moore's force left Portsmouth on 31st July and a much-needed cavalry regiment followed them ten days later. Wellesley started to land his troops at Figueira da Foz on 1st August. Fortunately the weather was fine and the wind moderate. Even so the surf caused casualties and it was clear that embarkation or disembarkation would be dangerous, if not impossible, when the winter weather set in. It took five days to get his own force of 10,297 on land, and before the operation was complete Spencer appeared with 5,336 more. It was 8th August before Spencer's men were all ashore.

Of the whole force of 15,633, 14,180 were infantry, 15½ battalions, all in good condition, and including one and a half battalions of riflemen, who made up almost one in ten of the infantry strength, a very high proportion for that period. Cavalry were very short, only 372 of the Twentieth Light Dragoons for whom the authorities had found transports for 215 horses. There was more artillery than the available horses could draw and some had to be left on the beach. The guns which actually took the field numbered 18, although for them the draught horses sent out from the Irish commissariat were noted by the senior artillery officer as 'very many of them old, lame, blind and cast-

1 Arthur, Duke of Wellington
From a portrait by George Dawe, 1818

2 British Light Troops: (l. to r.)
Rifleman, 95th Rifles,
Trooper, 23rd Light Dragoons
Private, 43rd Light Infantry
From 'The Military Costume
of Europe', published by
T. Goddard and J. Booth, 1812

3 Royal Artillery: Gunners
From a drawing and etching by J. A. Atkinson, 1807

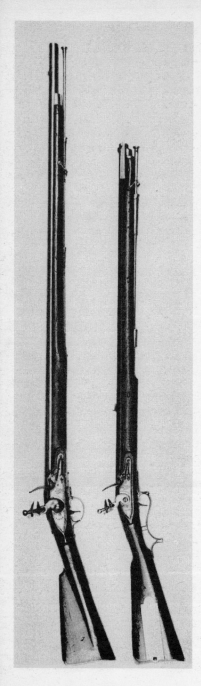

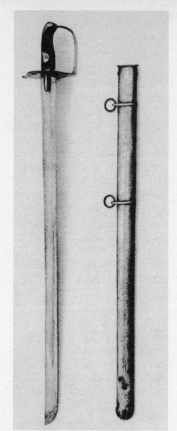

5 Heavy Cavalry Sabre, 35 inches in the blade. Of the type used by Le Marchant's brigade at Salamanca

4 (left) Tower Musket (Light Infantry Pattern)
The barrel is 39 inches long, the calibre 0.75
(right) Baker Rifle.
The barrel is 30 inches long, the calibre 0.615

5a Lieutenant-Colonel the Hon. Arthur
   Wesley, 33rd Regiment
   From a portrait by John Hoppner, c.1795

5b Major-General Sir Arthur Wellesley
   From a portrait by Robert Home, 1804

5c Field-Marshal the Marquis of Wellington
   From a study for a painting by
   Thomas Heaphy, 1813

5d Field-Marshal the Duke of Wellington
   From a portrait by P. E. Stroehling,
   c. 1820

6 Bengal Native Infantry. From a water-colour by 'Green', c. 1790
Reproduced by gracious permission of Her Majesty The Queen

7 Major-General Sir George Murray, Quartermaster-General to the Army in the Peninsula. From a portrait by John Prescott Knight

8 Lieutenant-General Sir Thomas Picton
From a portrait by Sir William Beechey, 1815

off'.[29] Apart from gun carriages and limbers the only means of transport provided from England were four camp-equipment wagons and three forage carts. There were, however, the personnel of two companies of the Irish Wagon Train who were available for driving any local carts which could be acquired. The worst deficiency was in the arrangements for supply. 'I have had the greatest difficulty in organising my commissariat for the march, and that department is very incompetent. . . . The existence of the army depends upon it, and yet the people who manage it are incapable of managing anything outside a counting house.' [30]

He was, notwithstanding, reasonably confident 'that the enemy's force at present in Portugal consists, as far as I am able to form an opinion, of from 16,000 to 18,000 men, of which there are 500 in the fort of Almeida, about the same number in Elvas, about 600 or 800 at Peniche, and 1,600 or 1,800 at Setuval and the remainder for the defence of Lisbon'.[31] Allowing for a garrison in Lisbon itself and for the forts at the mouth of the Tagus, it seemed improbable that Junot could bring more than 12,000 at the most to oppose the British in the field. News, this time confirmed, that Dupont had suffered disaster in Andalusia made it improbable that any reinforcements could reach Junot from Spain.

On 10th August the army set out to the south, keeping as near as possible to the coast so as to be in touch with supplies and reinforcements from the sea. The objective was 'the possession of the harbour and city of Lisbon'.[32] Opposition was to be expected first around Alcobaca where a French advanced guard was believed to be stationed. The Portuguese assistance from Coimbra proved even smaller than was expected. Their general, Bernadino Freire, was so unreasonable in his demands, especially for food, that Wellesley gladly left him behind at Leiria, taking from him only 1,600 infantry and 260 cavalry, a doubling, on paper, of his mounted strength.

Alcobaca, which was reached on the 14th, was found to be clear of the enemy, but the following day contact was made with French outposts around Obidos, where, in the evening, there was a slight skirmish, 'foolishly brought on by the over-eagerness of the Riflemen in the pursuit of an enemy piquet. . . . The troops behaved remarkably well, but not with great prudence.' [33] The local inhabitants estimated that the advanced guard of the French which was in the vicinity was between 3,000 and 4,000 men. Another French corps, 5,000 men, commanded by Loison, was thought to be approaching the British left from the direction of Rio Mayor, about a dozen miles away.

The French advanced guard was met in force near Rolica on the 17th. Neither side intended a battle, Delaborde, the French commander, intended only to delay the British by making them deploy. Wellesley planned to force the French to retire by menacing their flanks. The plans of both sides worked out satisfactorily in the morning, but in the afternoon, when Delaborde had taken up a second position on a ridge of sharp hills a mile south-west of Rolica, battle was joined through the impetuosity of Lieutenant-Colonel Lake of the Twenty-ninth, who launched his battalion in an unauthorised frontal attack, which cost him his life and forced Wellesley to commit several more battalions to support him. Flanking movements compelled the French to retire with the loss of three guns and 600 casualties against 474 to the British, but the whole affair was unnecessary and without significance except to show that, whatever were the deficiencies of Wellesley's army, fighting spirit was not amongst them.

Next morning, news reached the British commander from the sea that the brigades of Acland and Anstruther were off the coast. He consequently moved to his right through Lourinha, arriving early on the 19th at Vimeiro, where he could cover a passable landing beach at the mouth of the Maceira river. His information was that Delaborde's force was holding the strong position of Torres Vedras and that Junot was concentrating the remainder of his field force behind that town. While on the 20th the two brigades were landing, adding the equivalent of seven battalions to his strength, Wellesley gave orders for an advance on the following day. The army was to advance from its right along the coast until the advanced guard reached Mafra, where it would lie across Junot's seaward flank.

That evening the situation changed abruptly. The frigate *Brazen* sailed into Maceira Bay with Sir Harry Burrard aboard. Wellesley immediately went out to the frigate and explained his dispositions and plans. Sir Harry, a cautious man who had not seen the French army since he was taken prisoner on a raid on Ostend in 1798, and had narrowly escaped a similar fate in the Helder expedition in the following year, was alarmed at the initiative which Wellesley intended to take. 'He desired me to suspend all operations and said he would do nothing until he had collected all the force [34] . . . a decision with which I was not pleased any more than I was with the manner in which it was made.' [35] 'I came from the frigate about nine at night, and went to my own quarters with the army, which from the nearness of the enemy I kept on the alert.' [36] 'As I am the "Child of Fortune" and Sir Harry did not chuse to march towards the enemy, the enemy came to us.' [37] 'In the dead of night a fellow came in—a German sergeant or quarter-master—in a great fright—so that his hair seemed actually to stand on end—who told us that the enemy was advancing rapidly, and would soon be on us. I immediately sent round to the generals to order them to get the troops under arms, and soon after the dawn of day we were vigorously attacked. The enemy were first met by the Fiftieth, not a good looking regiment but devilish steady, and brought them to a full stop immediately, and soon drove them back.' [38]

Junot had brought to Vimeiro rather more than 13,000 men, enough he thought to give him equality of numbers with Wellesley, of whose reinforcements he did not know. He had no doubt that the number would suffice; he had left a more than adequate garrison in Lisbon from whence he could have drawn at least three or four thousand more. He suffered, however, from a defect common, and not unnatural, amongst French commanders. He greatly undervalued the British army. He attacked the left centre and extreme left of Wellesley's line in an almost contemptuous series of unconnected attacks, mixing his brigades and divisions in a way certain to cause confusion to his own subordinates. By midday the French were streaming away in disorder, not towards Torres Vedras but eastward towards the Serra da Barragueda and the rugged mass of Monte Junta. For a few fleeting hours there was a chance of seizing Torres Vedras and putting the British army between Junot and Lisbon.

The order to advance was never given. Sir Harry Burrard had arrived on the field during the battle. He had permitted Wellesley to continue in command until the last French attack had been repulsed, but as soon as the danger was over he clamped down with an iron hand of inactivity. There was to be no pursuit. Even Ferguson's brigade, which had 2,000 Frenchmen pinned in a gully, was refused permission to secure them. 'Sir Arthur Wellesley rode to Sir Harry Burrard, and said "Sir Harry now is your time to advance, the enemy are completely beaten, and we shall be in Lisbon in three days. We have a large body of troops which have not been in action, let us move them from the right on Torres Vedras, and I will follow them with the left." Sir Harry Burrard replied that he thought a great deal had been done, very much to the credit of the troops; but that he did not think it advisable to move off the ground in pursuit of the enemy.' [39] Sir Arthur 'turned his horse's head, and with a cold and contemptuous bitterness, said aloud to his aide-de-camp, "You may think about dinner, for there is nothing more for soldiers to do this day".' [40]

'Although', wrote Wellesley the following day, 'we had . . . not less than 17,000 men. . . . Sir Harry did not think these sufficient to defeat 12,000 or 15,000 Frenchmen.' [41] Early next morning Sir Hew Dalrymple arrived on the field and confirmed everything which led to inactivity. In any case it was now too late. The precious opportunity had gone. Junot was back on the direct road to Lisbon and held the Torres Vedras pass. Wellesley had plans, using Moore's corps which was now arriving, to complete the wreck of Junot's army. Sir Hew would not listen. 'I had reason,' said Sir Arthur, 'to believe that I did not possess his confidence; nay more that he was prejudiced against the opinions I should give him.' [42]

That afternoon Dalrymple got an excuse for prolonging his inactivity.

The French general Kellermann arrived to propose a truce, preparatory to an agreement whereby the French should evacuate Portugal. This was agreed. The French army were not to be treated as prisoners of war, but were to be repatriated in British ships with their arms and personal baggage. The Russian squadron in the Tagus were to be treated as if they were in a neutral port. Portuguese subjects who had supported the French during the occupation were to be allowed to go free or to leave the country. At the suggestion of Kellermann, and at the request of Dalrymple, Wellesley signed the armistice on behalf of the British army. 'Sir Hew . . . asked me whether I had any objections to doing so. My answer was that I would sign any paper he wished me to sign. . . . When it was drawn up, I read it over, and . . . gave it to Sir Hew Dalrymple to read, with an observation, that it was an extraordinary paper. He answered that it did not contain anything that had not been settled, and I then signed it.' [43] Sir Hew had realised the advantage of having a Minister of the Crown involved in his dubious piece of negotiation.

Wellesley had his doubts about several of the details, 'although I approve of allowing the French to withdraw from Portugal' now that the chance of destroying their army in the field had been thrown away, not only after the battle of Vimeiro but when the arrival of Moore gave the chance of moving it to Santarem where it would have prevented Junot from attempting the desperate expedient of trying to retire across the Alentejo to Elvas and Spain. Far from hurrying to get Moore ashore, Dalrymple had merely said to him, 'you may land your corps or not as you think proper'.[44] All Wellesley now wanted was to get back to Dublin Castle. He wrote to his brother, 'I wish I was away from this army. Things will not flourish as we are situated. . . . There is no more confidence in me on the part of the Chiefs than if I had been unsuccessful. . . . The General has no plan, or even an idea of a plan, nor do I believe he knows the meaning of the word *Plan*. . . . These people are really more stupid and incapable than any I have yet met with; and if things go on in this disgraceful manner I must quit them.' [45]

Quit them he did at the earliest possible moment but he was not allowed to get away easily. Dalrymple failed to inform the government of the armistice and did not send the definitive convention to them for a week after it had been signed. When the terms of the convention, with which Wellesley had nothing to do, reached England, there was a public outcry. *The Times* wrote: 'The honour of the country has been sacrificed, its fairest hopes blasted, the reputation of its arms stained, the resources of the enemy increased and concentrated, the plunder of our allies sanctioned, the pride of our invincible navy insulted, and the feelings of our gallant seamen injured and corroded beyond expression. A curse, a deep curse, wring the heart and wither the hand that were base enough to devise and execute this cruel injury. . . . Come forth, Sir Arthur Wellesley! You are the man who signed the article in the treaty "that the French army should in no case be considered prisoners of war" to the men who had the very day before conquered them. Human credulity can hardly believe that any thing so monstrously injurious to your country could have entered the heart of the basest of her sons, and still less into yours, which we believe to be proud and imperious enough. . . . Let there be no procrastination in the punishment of the delinquents.' The Whigs were jubilant. Here was a chance to strike at the Wellesley family. Cobbett wrote to Lord Folkestone: 'How the devil will they get over this? Now we have the rascals on the hip. It is evident that he [Wellesley] was the prime cause—the *only* cause—of all the mischief, and that for the motive of thwarting everything *after he was superseded*. Thus do we pay for the arrogance of that damned infernal family.'

The whole nation, from the old King downwards, believed that the fruits of victory had been thrown away. Wellesley's own belief was that he could not defend all the details, 'and two or three unlucky expressions were used, but that the substance and spirit were right. The French had not only the capital, but they had Badajoz, Elvas, Almeida and Santarem—all places that would have required sieges, as also Peniche and the forts of St. Julian and Cascaes, without the possession of which our ships could not enter the Tagus; the season of rough weather was fast approaching, and these places must have been regularly invested; and on the whole the entire evacuation of the forts, the strong places, the capital and the kingdom was all the most sanguine could have desired.' [46]

The public clamour led to a Board of General Officers being appointed to enquire into the convention. Seven elderly generals heard Dalrymple and Burrard rehearse all the arguments for caution. The French army was larger than Wellesley had estimated (indeed it was; there were more than 26,000 French soldiers in Portugal as opposed to a maximum estimate of 18,000; but there were, with Moore's corps, more than 30,000 British in one concentrated body). The communication with the sea might have been broken by a storm on an inhospitable coast. The supply of food might not have been equal to the demands upon it. Everyone wanted to attack Sir Hew, but was careful not to harm the charming Sir Harry. 'Spencer gave evidence that he had seen a reserve strongly posted on the height of Torres Vedras, so I [Wellesley] said to him, "Why, Spencer, I never heard of this reserve before. How is it that you only mention it now?" "Oh," said he, "poor Burrard has so large a family. I had no desire to give pain or trouble to either Burrard or Spencer, and I did not urge any questions on this point.' [47]

Just before Christmas the Board returned a wholly negative report that the evidence was insufficient to say what should have been done, but included a handsome compliment to Wellesley. Dalrymple and Burrard were never re-employed. Wellesley went back to Portugal at the head of the army and stayed with it until it reached Toulouse.

CHAPTER FOUR

THE PENINSULA 1809–11

There are so many entrances into Portugal, the whole country being frontier, that it would be very difficult to prevent the enemy from penetrating; and it is very probable that we should be obliged to confine ourselves to the preservation of that which is most important—the capital.

Wellesley, 25th August 1809

In September 1808 Sir John Moore was given command of an army greater than any entrusted to a British general since Marlborough. In January 1809 the remains of his striking force was evacuated from Coruña by the Royal Navy. It was a repetition of all the British interventions on the Continent since 1793—a brave start, a period of indecision, a hurried evacuation. It was obvious that Moore had won a battle and lost a campaign. What was not clear was that he had created the conditions in which the Peninsular War need not be lost.

Mistrusted by his government, misled by his allies and haunted by his own indecision, Moore had diverted the main thrust of the *Grande Armée* from Lisbon to the barren, irrelevant uplands of Galicia. Had he not spent a month at Salamanca making up his mind, had he not made his reckless advance to Sahagun, his army would have been driven remorselessly back to Lisbon and re-embarked. It is unlikely that there would have been another effective British intervention in the Peninsula.

As it was, Lisbon was saved because the French could not find the troops to seize it. It was defended only by 10,000 British troops and some ineffective Portuguese levies, but until the French could regroup and move a sufficient army against them, Lisbon remained as a port of re-entry, if the British government wished to avail themselves of it.

This the government was reluctant to do. Moore had contended that since the Portuguese had no army, Portugal could not be defended. 'The frontier of Portugal is not defensible against a superior force. It is an open frontier, all equally rugged, but all equally to be penetrated. If the French succeed in Spain, it would be vain to attempt to resist them in Portugal . . . the British must in that event, I conceive, immediately take steps to evacuate the country.' [1] Faced with this opinion, Ministers could be excused for believing that the best thing the British could do would be to quit Portugal immediately. They ignored the condition inserted by Moore: 'If the French succeed in Spain.' The French did not succeed there. They won victory after victory. After Baylen they defeated every Spanish army which they could find in the field but they failed to conquer Spain.

Castlereagh, as usual, consulted Wellesley, who was of the opinion that Portugal could be saved. Certainly the frontiers were indefensible, but what was important was Lisbon, and Lisbon was covered on both sides of the Tagus estuary by compact and powerful defensive positions. As long as the all-weather harbour of Lisbon was secure, a British army could operate profitably in Portugal. It would be an expensive business, but, if the measures he proposed were successful, 'the benefit which will accrue from them will be more than adequate to the expense incurred'.[2] The first step must be to revive the Portuguese army. This need he had foreseen. In August 1808, while his troops were landing at Mondego Bay, he had written: 'My opinion is that Great Britain ought to organise and pay an army in Portugal, consisting of 30,000 Portuguese troops . . . and 20,000 British including 4,000 or 5,000 cavalry. This army . . . would serve as a link between the kingdoms of Galicia and Andalusia; it would give Great Britain the preponderance of the war in the Peninsula; and whatever might be the results of Spanish exertions, Portugal might be saved from the French grasp. . . . If you should adopt this plan you must send every thing from England—arms, ammunition, clothing and accoutrements, flour, oats, &c.'[3]

In March 1809 he adhered to that view. 'I have always been of the opinion that Portugal might be defended whatever might be the outcome of the contest in Spain.' He increased his estimate of the necessary Portuguese strength by adding 40,000 militia to the 30,000 regulars and added that while the Portuguese strength was building, the British contingent ought to be not less than 30,000, 'of which number 4,000 to 5,000 should be cavalry and there should be a large body of artillery', since in those arms the Portuguese were likely to be permanently deficient. Given these conditions, he asserted 'that even if Spain should have been conquered, the French would not [be] able to overrun Portugal with a smaller force than 100,000 men; and that as the contest should continue in Spain this force . . . would be highly useful to the Spaniards and might eventually decide the contest.'[4]

Ministers were not convinced. Many of them, particularly Canning, held that any British troops which could be spared should be sent to Cadiz. It was better, they argued, for a small British army to fight alongside existing Spanish armies than to go to Portugal to fight alone or with a Portuguese army yet to be created, although they had, in February 1809, gone so far as to appoint, at the request of the Portuguese Regency, a British officer, William Carr Beresford, to the command of the Portuguese army.

The question was resolved by the Spanish government. Always reluctant to accept any help but money and arms, they affected to believe that the British had designs to turn Cadiz into a second Gibraltar. In a letter of elaborate politeness and underlying disdain the Spanish Foreign Minister wrote to Canning refusing to accept British troops in Cadiz since the Spaniards had 'just beheld the same troops retreat precipitately from Galicia, leaving Coruña and Ferrol open to our enemies, and instead of directing their march to some other of the many interesting and menaced points, seek shelter in their native country'.[5]

Largely for the wrong reasons the Spaniards had come to the right conclusion. Denied a base at Cadiz, the British were forced to rely on Lisbon. Thereby they reluctantly grasped at their only chance of winning the war. Had the army, no matter who commanded it, landed in Andalusia to act with the armies of Cuesta and his colleagues, it would have been fortunate if it could have been evacuated at half its strength. Its total destruction would have been more than probable.

Having decided to send the disposable force to Portugal, there remained only the choice of a commander. There was little doubt about who should go. In the Cabinet, only Lord Chatham (who hoped for the command himself) disputed the choice of Wellesley. The Horse Guards was in no position to object. The Commander-in-Chief was involved in a Parliamentary storm over the activities of his mistress and had soon to resign. The King agreed to the appointment on the discouraging grounds that Wellesley was 'so young a lieutenant general . . . that he hoped that this consideration would operate with others against any considerable augmentation of that army'.[6]

At the end of March Wellesley was told of his appointment. His letter of service, issued on 2nd April, urged him to 'prepare and equip the British army [in Portugal] for the field' and to 'bring forward the Portuguese army, and render it capable of co-operating with His Majesty's troops. . . . The defence of Portugal you will consider as the first and immediate object of your attention. But as the security of Portugal can only be effectively provided for in connection with the defence of the Peninsula in the larger sense, His Majesty leaves it to your judgement to decide, when your army shall be advanced on the frontier of Portugal, how your efforts can best be combined with the Spanish as well as the Portuguese troops in support of the common cause.'[7] 'It is not His Majesty's intention, in authorising you to co-operate with the Spanish armies in the defence of Portugal and the adjacent Spanish provinces, that you should enter into a campaign in Spain without the express authority of your government.'[8]

He resigned the Chief Secretaryship and made his way to Portsmouth. The news from the Peninsula was grave. 'Affairs are in a critical state in Portugal', he wrote, while waiting for a favourable wind. 'We have accounts from thence of as late a date as 3rd April. Soult had advanced

69

from Galicia . . . on Oporto, which town he took on 29th March. His corps consisted of about 15,000 men. There was another French corps of about 10,000, advancing from Salamanca, and had arrived at San Felices, on the road to Almeida. Marshal Victor, at the head of another, consisting of about 35,000, had lately driven the Spanish army under General Cuesta from the bridge at Almaraz, upon the Tagus; and had since destroyed Cuesta's army in an action fought upon the Guadiana; and had afterwards arrived about the 1st of April at Badajoz.' [9] The British army was being reinforced and would be up to a strength of 23,000 'and whatever Portuguese troops they may have', but the prospect was scarcely bright. Wellesley had a clear appreciation of the enemy's intentions. 'The plan of operation for the French will be to move Victor's corps from Badajoz to Abrantes; then cross the Tagus; and as soon as that corps is ready to move towards Lisbon, to bring on the other two weaker corps from Oporto and Salamanca; and the whole to join in the neighbourhood of Santarem. . . . As soon as the junction and co-operation of the three French corps shall be secure, they will detach from 5,000 to 10,000 men across the Tagus where we have not a man, either British or Portuguese. They will post this corps upon the heights of Almada, which are opposite Lisbon, and in their continuation, command the harbour. As soon as they will have this possession of ground, the admiral will find that he cannot remain there with his ships and the general that he cannot embark his troops; and by this manoeuvre alone the French will obtain possession of Lisbon, most probably before I arrive there.' [10] This was a concise summary of Napoleon's orders at this time, but as yet Wellesley, like Napoleon, was unacquainted with conditions on the Portuguese frontier. With the best of intentions, the French commanders were incapable of such a combination.

It was not until 16th April that the frigate was able to sail. Meanwhile he had two subjects to worry him. Where should he take the army if he found it embarked or embarking, and what should he do if he found that his predecessor had defeated the French. 'In the event of General Craddock's success in any repulse of the enemy, Sir Arthur could not reconcile his feelings to supersede him.' [11] Whatever else he did, Sir Arthur did not fancy himself in the part of Sir Hew Dalrymple.

He arrived in Lisbon on 22nd April. Soult was resting the bulk of his corps at Oporto while he vainly tried to establish some communication with Spain. Lapisse, who commanded the corps at Salamanca, had been so deceived by a handful of Portuguese under the able but unreliable Robert Wilson that he 'turned off to his left, and has marched along the Portuguese frontier to Alcantara, where he crossed the Tagus, and then he went on to Merida on the Guadiana, where he is in communication with the army of Victor'.[12] Victor himself, far from being at Badajoz with 35,000 men, was 60 miles to the east at Medellin with 22,000, waiting to hear that Soult was moving south from Oporto. The news never reached him. Even if Soult could have got his exhausted men forward, no messenger could have reached Victor to tell him of the move. This Wellesley discovered. On 27th April he was told by a French officer that Soult 'was entirely ignorant of the situation of Victor and of all the other French corps in Spain'.[13]

The British force, 23,200 strong,[14] was stationed round Leiria. The nearest French to the north were Soult's cavalry outposts on the river Vouga, 70 miles away. To the east Victor's nearest troops were 150 miles away beyond the great fortresses of Badajoz and Elvas. Victor showed no signs of moving, and the Spanish general Cuesta, who had reconstructed the army broken at Medellin, was lurking around Monasterio in the Sierra Morena ready to march with 23,000 men against the Marshal's rear if he should move against Portugal. Reports from the north of Portugal showed that Soult had diverted much of his strength away from Oporto trying to regain touch with Ney in Galicia and Lapisse whom he still believed to be at Salamanca. The initiative lay with Wellesley if he was strong enough to take it.

Apart from its numbers, Wellesley's army was not a strong force. There were 25 battalions of infantry, of which only three were more than 750 strong. Only five of them had been under his command at Vimeiro and two were battalions made up of detachments left behind by Moore when he marched for Spain. There were no light infantry battalions and only a single, weak battalion of Riflemen, 559 men of 5th Sixtieth.

There were four complete regiments of cavalry and three detached squadrons. Two of the regiments had only just landed and were unfit for immediate service. The British artillery could put in the field 30 guns, but the horses sent out by the Board of Ordnance were 'old, diseased and out of condition'.[15] There was no Horse Artillery and Wellesley's first request for reinforcements was for a troop of that arm.

A number of Portuguese battalions was available, but their appearance was not encouraging, 'the body of men, very bad, the officers worse than anything I have ever seen'.[16] Some Portuguese batteries were, however, horsed and ready for use.

The supply situation was bad. The commissaries were few and inexperienced and there was no money. Before leaving London Wellesley had been assured that he would find £400,000 available—'I have found not quite £100,000 and this sum was in Spanish coins which could not have been circulated in Portugal, excepting at a considerable loss. : . . I have therefore sent the Spanish gold to Cadiz to be exchanged for dollars; and I am now here with the whole army about to proceed to the attack with only £10,000, and with monstrous demands upon us.'[17]

Despite all these drawbacks, Wellesley was determined to attack, and within two days of his arrival he had decided that Soult must be his target.[18] There were known to be about 20,000 French in the north of Portugal, but it was not clear how many of them were available for the defence of Oporto. Silveira, who with a motley collection of Portuguese was facing the French across the Tamega river, estimated that he was opposing 10,000 men and there were reports of a French force at Chaves. Setting aside 4,500 British and 7,000 Portuguese to guard his eastern flank at Abrantes and another British battalion to garrison Lisbon, less than 17,000 British remained for the main enterprise. This was scarcely enough for an operation likely to include the opposed crossing of a formidable river. The only resource was to make up the numbers with Portuguese, whatever they might look like on parade; 7,000 of them were added to the main striking force, 5,000 of them in a body supported by a weak British brigade to act as a flanking column, the remainder in single battalions integrated into British brigades.

Wellesley reached the army's concentration area at Coimbra on 2nd May. A week later he rode out to the north. He forced the Douro under the noses of Soult's army on the 12th and on the 19th the remnants of Soult's army, without its artillery, equipment, military chest and one-fifth of its strength, arrived starving at Orense in Spain.

As soon as it was clear that Soult's retreat could not be intercepted, Wellesley called off the pursuit. His orders forbade an advance into Spain unless it was essential for the security of Portugal, which in this case it was not. 'Of this I am certain,' he wrote on 20th May, 'that Soult will be very little formidable to any body of troops for some little time to come.' [19] Moreover he had given his word to Cuesta to co-operate with him in an operation as soon as Soult was safely out of Portugal.

The co-operation with Cuesta which led to the battle of Talavera was the last manifestation of the underlying belief with which the British had intervened in the Peninsula—that Spanish armies with the support of a British contingent could drive the French from Spain. So strongly was this belief held that in the summer of 1809 the main British military effort, a force of more than 40,000 men, was sent to the mouth of the Scheldt. By the autumn of that year it was clear that if the French were to be expelled from the Peninsula the main weight of the fighting must fall on the British.

Wellesley started on the campaign with high hopes. Napoleon was at war with Austria. While Soult was leading his broken army into Orense, the Emperor was being held to a disadvantageous draw at Aspern and Essling. There would be no reinforcements to spare for Spain. The French armies in Spain, seven corps with a paper strength of 280,000 men, were very large but they were devoted to difficult and diffuse objects. The corps of Mortier, Junot and St. Cyr were in Aragon and Catalonia. Ney, with Soult in support, tried to control Galicia and the eastern Asturias. The problems of suppressing this north-western corner of Spain were so great that they must take many months and Wellesley, when he heard early in May that Mortier's corps was moving out of Aragon up the valley of the Ebro, assumed that he must be marching to Ney's support.* The other two French corps were on the line of the Guadiana facing, in general, south. Sebastiani was around Ciudad Real, south of Madrid, watched by the Spanish army of La Mancha, which greatly outnumbered him. Victor with 23,000 men lay in the area Caceres–Merida–Medellin, observed by the larger numbers of Cuesta's reconstituted army. Victor was the obvious target for Wellesley. His corps was the only one of the seven which threatened Portugal (he raided up to Badajoz and Alcantara in April and May), and Cuesta and Wellesley between them could bring overwhelming numbers against his front and flank. Provided that Venegas could keep Sebastiani's corps occupied, the only reinforcement that Victor could look for was the small central reserve at Madrid. This would make his strength up to 28,000 and against this Wellesley could bring 20,000 British troops with reinforcements on their way, while Cuesta's army numbered over 30,000, 'part of them', Wellesley said, 'good troops'. 'If Victor does not move across the Tagus', he added at the end of May, 'he will be in as bad a scrape as Soult. I hope to receive before long some orders respecting my conduct, supposing I should drive Victor away from the frontiers of Portugal, and should be required by Cuesta or the Junta to pursue him.' [20] Meanwhile the army was ordered to concentrate at Abrantes.

Authority to operate in Spain, providing that Portugal was secure, reached him on 11th June. He was jubilant. He had every hope of reaching Madrid, 'a political object of great importance, in view of the affairs of Europe in general, as well as of those of Spain'.[21] He wrote of the possibility of the French having to retreat over the Ebro. 'The ball is now at my feet, and I hope I shall have strength enough to give it a good kick. I should begin immediately, but I cannot venture to stir without money. The army is two months in arrears; we are head over heels in debt everywhere.' [22]

Money was the key to everything and the government had not sent him any. Despairingly he wrote to the Treasury: 'We have not a shilling or the chance of getting any. The money sent to Cadiz to be exchanged [see p. 71] is not returned, and none can be procured at Lisbon for bills. In short we must have money from England, if we are to continue our operations in this country.' [23] Shortage of money led to other difficulties. Being without pay, the troops took to looting. 'The army behave terribly ill. . . . They plunder in all directions.' [24] There were other shortages too. The forced marches up to and across the Douro and the long road down to Abrantes had destroyed the army's

* Napoleon's intention in moving Mortier to Burgos was unconnected with events in Spain. Its new station was dictated by the possibility that he might be needed in Austria.

boots and the troops could not march again before replacements arrived. The medical services were so short that the army had to march 'without a disposable medical officer, or a blanket to cover a sick man'.[25]

Cuesta proved a difficult ally. Having suffered two major defeats within two years he was resentful of his victorious young colleague, whom he suspected of trying to secure the post of commander-in-chief of all the Spanish armies. He had, in any case, no confidence in the British whose system seemed to him to be 'never to expose their troops, owing to which they never gain decisive victories by land'.[26] By the middle of June Wellesley realised that co-operation would not be easy. 'My correspondence with General Cuesta is a very curious one, and proves him to be as obstinate as any gentleman at the head of an army ought to be.'[27] The Spaniard had put forward three schemes for attacking Victor. Two were dangerous and impractical; the third Wellesley, with some reservations, felt able to accept. Whereupon Cuesta rejected it. In the meantime Victor had retired northwards over the Tagus and Cuesta followed gingerly to the north bank of the Guadiana. It was still possible for Cuesta to hold him on the south while the British attacked his flank from the direction of Plasencia, and although Cuesta suddenly agreed to this plan the British could still not move for lack of money. It was not until 27th June that a convoy of coin* reached Abrantes and Wellesley was able to give the order to march to the Spanish border at Zarza la Mayor, which the advanced guard reached on 2nd July.

By then Victor had moved again, this time to Talavera de la Reina. He did this with no thought of protecting himself against Wellesley's army, of whose presence he was completely unaware, but because he was unable to feed his troops in a more westerly position. Sebastiani, in consequence, had drawn his corps back to Toledo to protect his right flank and when Venegas, dutifully fulfilling his rôle of keeping Sebastiani occupied, advanced towards him, the French general, asserting that he was threatened by 40,000 men, called on Madrid. King Joseph responded by bringing forward the 5,000 men of his reserve and together they chased Venegas back into the mountains south of Ciudad Real, and then retired to Toledo. Thus, when Cuesta and Wellesley eventually came forward, instead of finding Victor isolated around Almaraz, they found him at Talavera with the combined forces of Joseph and Sebastiani, more than 25,000 men, within 50 miles of him at Toledo.

The odds were still reasonable. The allied strength, excluding Venegas, was more than 55,000. The French had less than 50,000 from which they must detach some kind of containing force against Venegas. Cuesta and Wellesley decided to go forward. Already the Spaniards were showing that they could not fulfil the promises they had made to

* This was the money that had been found in Lisbon and sent to Cadiz to be changed into usable coin. Money had still not arrived from England.

supply the British army with food and, more particularly, with transport.

Cuesta became increasingly difficult. On 24th July, after he had wasted a chance of destroying Victor's corps while it was still isolated, Wellesley wrote to London: 'I find Cuesta more and more impractical every day. It is impossible to do business with him and very uncertain that any operation will succeed in which he has any concern. He contrived to lose the whole of yesterday . . owing to the whimsical perversity of his disposition.' [28] Cuesta, thereupon, having refused to attack when the odds were in his favour, insisted on taking forward the Spanish army alone to attack the French combined army of whose position he was uncertain. 'It is evident', wrote Wellesley moderately, 'that Cuesta is too old and has not the talents to conduct in due order the great and confused affairs of a battle.' [29]

On 26th July the Spanish army reappeared in considerable disorder, followed not only by Victor's corps but by the combined forces of Joseph, Victor and Sebastiani, 46,000 men. Venegas, for reasons which have never been satisfactorily explained, had decided to remain stationary in his mountain fastness, checked by the slightest kind of covering force. Fortunately the French pursuit was far from close as Cuesta, apparently out of 'whimsical perverseness', insisted on halting on the eastern side of the Alberche river, fully exposed to a French attack which by good luck never came. Next day he consented to fall back to a position, chosen for him by Wellesley, which was strong enough not to expose to the French the Spanish faults in discipline and training which were now glaringly obvious to the whole British army.

It was not too soon. Next afternoon the French drove in the rearguards of both armies, parts of both of them falling into disorder, and followed this up with a night attack on the key to the British position. By the evening of the 28th, the British, who had borne the whole weight of the French attacks, had lost 5,300 men, more than a quarter of their strength. 'Never,' said Wellesley to his brother, 'was there so murderous a battle.' The Spaniards lost only 1,200 for the French had ignored them on the 28th, assigning no more than 2,500 cavalry to watch the whole of Cuesta's army. The French lost more than both the allied armies together and by the following morning they had retired, leaving a cavalry screen on the east bank of the Alberche. Pursuit was impossible. The British army was scarcely able to tend its wounded and bury its 800 dead. It had been on half rations since the 24th and prospects of further supplies were getting steadily worse. To send the Spanish army forward against even the beaten French force would have been folly. Even Cuesta did not suggest it.

On the day following the battle some of Wellesley's loss in infantry was made good by the arrival of Robert Craufurd with his Light Brigade, three strong and excellent battalions, and four days later there

75

arrived (2nd August) the long-desired troop of Horse Artillery. By that time danger had showed itself from another side.

On 1st August Wellesley wrote to his brother 'On the 30th* I heard of the advance of a French corps towards Plasencia from the neighbourhood of Salamanca. The object of this corps must be to cut off our communications with Portugal. I had long been aware of the possibility that a French corps would endeavour to penetrate through the Puerto de Baños in the mountains which divide Plasencia and Estremadura from Castille; and I had . . . stipulated with General Cuesta to leave in the Puerto de Baños a sufficient detachment to defend it. . . . Unfortunately Cuesta did not send a sufficient detachment, which I did not know until the 29th.' [30] After a long and angry argument with the Spanish general, it was decided that the British should move against this new threat from the north while Cuesta stayed at Talavera to watch Victor. 'I marched on the 3rd', wrote Wellesley, 'leaving the Spanish army to take care of Talavera. My back was hardly turned before old Cuesta quitted his post and followed me under the pretence that he had heard that the army after whom I marched consisted of 30,000 men; and thus he exposed the combined army to be attacked on the one side with 30,000 men and on the other with 25,000. Nearly at the same time I heard that the [French] corps from Plasencia had arrived at Naval Moral between us and the passage of the Tagus at Almaraz. Thus pressed at front and rear, and our only retreat being the bridge at Arzobispo, which if we had delayed the enemy might have destroyed, I determined to retire across the Tagus; and to take up a defensive line upon that river. If I had not determined and acted promptly that retreat would have been cut off.

'In the meantime Cuesta's sudden abandonment of Talavera has lost us a part of our hospital. Everything else and our farther retreat are safe. This is the outline of our disaster.' [31]

By 6th August, thanks to a lightning dash by the Light Brigade over broken country to Almaraz, both the bridges by which the French could cross the Tagus were in safe hands. It had been a very close thing. If Wellesley had delayed his decision to seize the line of the Tagus for 24 hours the French would have been able to take a defensive line between the British and Portugal and the only way to get the British army back to Lisbon would have been by sea from Cadiz. They must inevitably have arrived too late. The reason, apart from the tiresomeness of Cuesta, why Wellesley found himself in this predicament was the unusual one that his knowledge of the enemy's orders was too accurate. As early as 1st July he had had reliable information that the French were evacuating Galicia. A week later he heard that a French general had been captured by guerrillas near Toro carrying despatches

* In his letter of 1st August Wellesley gives the date as 29th. He corrected it to the 30th in his letter of 8th August.

from Soult saying that although he had withdrawn his corps to Zamora 'solely with a view to give repose and to refit . . . Ney remains, and must remain, in Galicia.'.[32] What Wellesley did not know was that Ney had refused to stay in Galicia and had marched his troops into the plains of Leon. His arrival coincided with orders reaching Soult from Paris that he was to take command of the corps of Ney and Mortier besides his own and 'cast the British into the sea'. Soult rightly interpreted these orders liberally and set out to cut the British off from the sea, but the single corps of French, perhaps 20,000 strong, which Wellesley had marched off confidently to attack on 3rd August with 18,000 British troops, was in fact a solid mass of more than 50,000 Frenchmen. Thanks to Wellesley's prompt decision the army was safe and at the end of August fell back south-west to the area Badajoz– Merida where it could be supplied with food from Portugal. Food was unobtainable by the British in Spain. Even where it existed it could not be bought. A commissary reported that around Almendral detachments of Spanish troops threatened to sack any village which supplied bread to their allies.[33] The experiment of co-operating with the Spanish field armies was over. It could not be renewed unless Wellesley had effective command of Spanish troops. 'I regret as much as any man can the necessity of separating from the Spanish armies; but I was at last forced to go, and I believe there was not an officer in the army who did not think I stayed too long. The fault I committed consisted in trusting at all to the Spaniards who I have since found were entirely unworthy of confidence.' [34] If the war in the Peninsula was to be won, a new idea for winning it would have to be devised.

The Tower guns had been fired for the victory at Talavera. The subsequent retreat to the Portuguese frontier came as a heavy blow to public confidence. Talavera had seemed the prelude to a triumphant march to Madrid, perhaps to the Pyrenees. The Opposition in Parliament did not lose the opportunity of accusing Wellesley of being a rash adventurer who had thrust his army into a trap from which it had only escaped by a humiliating scramble to the rear. When a vote of thanks to the victorious commander was moved in the House of Lords Earl Grey denied that there had been a victory and asserted that Wellesley had betrayed 'want of capacity and want of skill'. In the Commons General Tarleton, a hero of the American War, declared that Wellesley's despatches were 'vainglorious, partial and incorrect'. When Wellesley was raised to the peerage as Viscount Wellington, some Members maintained that it was wrong to give a peerage to a man without the means to support his dignities and then opposed the grant of a pension of £2,000 a year to enable him to do so. The Corporation of the City of London joined in with a petition observing the grant of a pension with 'grief and concern' and added that while 'admitting to the utmost extent the valour of Lord

Wellington, we do not recognise in his military conduct any claim to this national remuneration'.

It was a bad summer for Ministers. The Prime Minister, the Duke of Portland, had a stroke in August and, although he continued in office for a few months, he was incapable of controlling his colleagues. The much vaunted Walcheren expedition failed ignominiously through a combination of disease and feeble generalship. The commanding general was a member of the Cabinet and was even being considered as a possible successor to the premiership. Subsequently the two most active members of the government met with pistols on Wimbledon Common and the government collapsed. Its successor, led by Spencer Perceval, had hardly the strength to conduct the business of the House of Commons. Lord Liverpool took over the Secretaryship of State for War and Lord Wellesley moved to the Foreign Office from a short term at the Embassy in Seville during which he had, with more honesty than diplomacy, told the Spanish Foreign Minister that he 'would not trust the protection of a favourite dog to the whole Spanish army'.[35]

Worst of all, the Austrians were defeated at Wagram and forced to make a humiliating peace. With Austria crushed, Prussia humbled and Russia as an ally, there seemed to be no limit to the reinforcements which Napoleon could pour into the Peninsula.

The new government wanted to continue to support Wellington,* but they can scarcely be blamed if they had doubts about the outcome of his operations. Lord Liverpool sought his views. What were the chances of the French achieving the 'complete subjugation' of Spain? Would they be likely to make a serious attack upon Portugal before they had achieved 'a tolerably quiet occupation of every part of Spain north of the Sierra Morena'? What were the prospects of a successful resistance to such an attack should it come? Would it be possible to withdraw the British army safely if such resistance was not 'likely to prove successful'?[36]

Wellington replied confidently. The French could not gain possession of Spain 'if the Spaniards are commonly prudent'. It was more than likely that the French would make the attack on Portugal 'their first objective when their reinforcements will arrive in Spain. I do not think that they will succeed with an army of 70,000 or even of 80,000 men, if they do not make the attack for two or three months, which I believe is now impossible.' The attack, when it came, could be withstood, and even if it could not, 'I am convinced that we could embark after defeat.' [37]

The government were comforted but still uncertain. The argument went on into the following year. Ministers still hankered after transferring the base of operations to Cadiz. As late as February 1810 the Secretary of State was still asserting: 'There can be no doubt that in this country a higher value is set upon Cadiz (connected with the Spanish fleet, arsenals, &c) than upon Lisbon.' [38] The question of evacuation re-

* Wellesley first signed himself 'Wellington' on 16th September 1809.

curred again and again. Should it be from Lisbon or from Peniche? Wellington patiently answered every tremulous enquiry and, bit by bit, built up the government's confidence. It was uphill work. In March Lord Liverpool could still write: 'I should apprise you that a very considerable degree of alarm exists in this country respecting the safety of the British army in Portugal; and as it is always some advantage to know on a question of doubtful policy on which side it may be best to err, I have no difficulty in stating that, under all the circumstances, you would rather be excused for bringing away the army a little too soon than, by remaining in Portugal a little too long, exposing it to those risks from which no military operation can be exempt. I do not mean by this observation that you would be justified in evacuating Portugal before the country was attacked in force by the enemy; but whenever the event shall occur, the chances of a successful defence are considered here by all persons, military as well as civil, so improbable that I could not recommend any attempt at what may be called desperate resistance.' [39]

In the end the decision seems to have been taken by the King himself. George III, having read Wellington's letters, came to 'a very high opinion of Lord Wellington's sense and of the resources of his mind as a soldier; [since] he appears to have weighed the whole of his situation so coolly and maturely, and to have considered every contingency under which he may be placed, not omitting any necessary preparation, His Majesty trusted that his ministers would feel with him the advantage of suffering him to proceed according to his judgement and discretion in the adherence to the principles which he has laid down, unfettered by any instructions which might embarrass him in the execution of his general plan of operations.' [40] This firm assertion of the royal judgment was exactly what Ministers needed to confirm them in leaving the decision to Wellington. From that time forward the continuation of the war in the Peninsula based on Lisbon was never seriously questioned in government circles.

Wellington had placed his confidence in the continuing defensibility of Portugal on the premise that the Spaniards would be 'commonly prudent'. They were no such thing. Hardly had the manoeuvres following Talavera come to an end when they put forward a further plan for a grand offensive on exterior lines, aiming to seize Madrid. Wellington refused to have any part in such a scheme, declaring their plans to be 'rank nonsense'. [41] He repeatedly urged caution on the Junta but his words fell on deaf ears. They were determined to stake everything on a victory. On 19th November the army which had been Cuesta's* was routed and dispersed at Ocaña, south of Madrid. Nine days later the

* Cuesta resigned his command following a stroke in August. He was succeeded by General Eguia who was certainly no more competent than Cuesta. He, in his turn, was superseded by General Areizaga, who seems to have been of about the same standard.

army forming the northern arm of the Spanish pincers was wrecked at Alba de Tormes. For the time being there was no large body of Spanish regular troops to whom the French need pay attention. 'I declare', wrote Wellington, 'that if they had preserved their two armies, or even one of them, the cause was safe. . . . But no! Nothing will answer excepting to fight great battles in plains, in which their defeat is as certain as is the commencement of the battle.' [42]

It was fortunate that King Joseph and Soult threw away all the advantage they had gained by undertaking, in January and February, the occupation of Andalusia. That kingdom was overrun with little difficulty, but by a serious error on the part of the French commanders, joined to a rare flash of intelligence on the part of a Spanish general, the Duke of Alburquerque, the French found Cadiz, which by nature is almost impregnable to an army without command of the sea, sufficiently garrisoned to be able to resist an attack. By the time that the French had brought forward the necessary siege guns and had started to build boats, the garrison was very strong in numbers and was augmented, at the invitation of the Junta, by an Anglo-Portuguese contingent. For the next two years three corps of French troops had always to be stationed in Andalusia to prosecute an abortive siege and hold down the kingdom. It was a drain on French resources which they were increasingly unable to afford.

Meanwhile Wellington was making his preparations to meet the great French attack which he knew must come. The defence of Portugal must be based on 'the preservation of that which is most important—the capital'.[43] 'There are so many entrances into Portugal, the whole country being frontier, that it would be very difficult to prevent the enemy from penetrating.' [44] The only place at which a comparatively small army could be sure of making a stand, with its flanks secure and its position fortified in advance, was on the Lisbon peninsula, where the left could be rested on the Atlantic and the right on the Tagus below the point where it was fordable at any time of year. The orders for the construction of a series of fortified positions across this peninsula, the lines of Torres Vedras, were issued on 20th October 1809, a year (except for nine days) before the French reached them. Knowing that the French would bring overwhelming numbers, Wellington acknowledged that he could not possibly keep them at a distance from the capital. He relied on the devastation of the countryside and the conscription of the entire adult male population of Portugal, both conditions provided for in the ancient laws and customs of the country, to make the position of a French army, faced with an impassable barrier, so intolerable that they must either retreat or starve. It was a decision calling for immense courage. Permitting the French to penetrate deep into Portugal without making any serious attempt to stop them was bound to be unpopular in England. Wellington made it without hesitation. He was amply justified.

It was almost a certainty that the French, when they came, would advance by way of Ciudad Rodrigo and Almeida. There were only two roads from Spain into Portugal which were suitable for a large army. The southern road, dominated at the frontier by Badajoz, was the shortest way to Lisbon and lay across the most favourable country for an army strong in cavalry, but it had two overwhelming disadvantages: it greatly increased the lines of communication with France and it left the invader with the task of forcing the line of the broad Tagus before he could reach Lisbon. There was never any doubt in Wellington's mind which way they would come. As soon as the Spanish armies had been destroyed in the Ocaña campaign, the main bulk of the British troops were moved north from Badajoz to the country west of Ciudad Rodrigo. Only a single British division with some cavalry and Portuguese troops were left to watch the Badajoz road lest the French should stage a diversion from that direction. The main body, four British divisions, two independent Portuguese brigades and four regiments of British cavalry, were deployed in a diamond-shaped formation between Ciudad Rodrigo and the valley of the Mondego with the Light Division, under Robert Craufurd, to the fore in touch with the Spanish garrison of Rodrigo.*

The army was growing slowly. At Talavera the field strength of the army had been 28 battalions (including the Light Brigade) and six regiments of cavalry. By the New Year there were 33 battalions, and three more battalions and a regiment were added before the end of April. Thus at the turn of the year the strength of the army was about 35,000 rank and file (including artillery), although more than a quarter were on the sick list.

There remained the possibility of employing the Portuguese troops. Apart from a single unit, no Portuguese battalions had been involved in the Talavera campaign and the time had been profitably spent in training and disciplining them. Thanks to the efforts of Beresford and his cadre of British officers and N.C.O.s, they had made great strides and by January Wellington was able to report 'that the progress of all these troops in discipline is considerable; that some of the regiments are in very good order; and that I have no doubt but that the whole will prove a useful acquisition to the country'.[45] He was forced to add that 'the cavalry . . . must not be reckoned for much'.[46] They were still, of course, untried troops and Wellington resolved to incorporate them by brigades in British divisions, in the proportion of two British to one Portuguese brigade.† Thus, by midsummer, the main army could count on a strength

---

* The Light Division was formed on 22nd February 1810 from the Light Brigade, hitherto a part of the Third Division, and two battalions of Portuguese Cacadores (light infantry).

† When, in February 1810, this system was first instituted, it applied only to the Third and Fourth Divisions. The First Division never had a Portuguese formation (though it had at times four British brigades), the Second Division had a Portuguese

of 33,000 men, while the detachment under Rowland Hill watching the road from Badajoz numbered about 12,000.

During this period the French were pouring reinforcements into Spain. Before their campaign started in the summer, more than 138,000 men crossed the Pyrenees to bring the total strength of the armies in Spain up to 360,000. Their task was clearly laid down. '*L'Empereur considère qu'il n'y a de dangereux en Espagne que les Anglais; que le reste n'est que de canaille qui ne peut jamais tenir en campagne.*' [47] The French problem lay in deciding how many of these men could be used for invading Portugal to dispose of the English. Nearly 80,000 men were on the rolls of the two corps stationed in Aragon and Catalonia. 74,000 more were in Andalusia. More than as many again were engaged in holding Madrid and the lines of communication through Navarre and Biscay. The gross number of troops detailed for the Portuguese campaign was 130,000, but this figure included not only the very large number of men sick and detached but a corps which was not able to cross the Pyrenees until August and the division needed on the lines of communication from Ciudad Rodrigo as far back as Santander. The striking force which was eventually available was never more than 65,000 men. To command them Napoleon appointed André Massena, Marshal Prince of Essling. In his day there had been few more capable soldiers than Massena in Europe, but by 1810 he was past his best. When he joined his new command at Salamanca in May, one of his most intelligent generals wrote of him: 'He is no longer the Massena of the flashing eyes, mobile face and alert figure I knew in 1799. . . . He is only fifty-two, but looks more than sixty; he is thinner and beginning to stoop; his glance . . . has lost its keenness' [48], while he himself remarked to his assembled commanders: 'Gentlemen, I am here contrary to my own wish; I begin to feel myself too old and weary to go on active service.' [49] Nevertheless he was no contemptible opponent, and Wellington later said of him that he was 'the most dangerous and difficult to deal with' [50] of all his adversaries. Massena's orders were simple. 'He will besiege Ciudad Rodrigo and then Almeida, and will then prepare to march methodically into Portugal, which I do not wish to invade until September, after the hot weather and in particular after the harvest.' [51] The information given him about his enemy was that 'the army of General Wellington is composed of no more than 24,000 British and Germans * and his Portuguese are only 25,000 strong'.

Massena faithfully obeyed his orders. During the spring he did no

---

division of two brigades attached to it (a Portuguese brigade was added to Second Division in June 1811). The Light Division had a Portuguese Cacadores battalion in each of its two brigades. The Fifth, Sixth and Seventh Divisions each acquired a Portuguese brigade on formation.

* Four battalions, one regiment and two batteries consisted of men of the King's German Legion, successors to George III's Hanoverian army.

more than secure his right flank by taking the fortress town of Astorga (22nd April). It was not until 9th July that Ciudad Rodrigo fell after a gallant defence of 24 days. Wellington made no move to save it, although he was under great pressure to do so from the Governor, the Spanish authorities and even from his own officers. 'With an army one fourth inferior in numbers, a part of it being of a doubtful description, and at all events but just made, and not more than one-third the numbers of the enemy's cavalry, it would be an operation of some risk to leave our mountains, and bring on a general action in the plains.' [52] It was no part of Wellington's plan to fight near the frontier and there would have been no more than some slight skirmishing when the French moved forward again had not Craufurd taken it upon himself, contrary to orders, to attempt to dispute the passage of the Coa on 23rd July. He suffered over 300 unnecessary casualties, and the fact that the French suffered even more was the fault of the French commander, Ney, who behaved even more irresponsibly than Craufurd. It had been Wellington's hope that Almeida would put up a stout defence, but in this he was disappointed as an explosion in the main magazine on 26th August robbed the Portuguese garrison of the chances of resisting. By mid-September Massena had his three corps, 65,000 strong, concentrated in the area Guarda–Pinhel and ready to move into the heart of Portugal.

The British army broke contact and fell back before them. Finding that the road which the French had taken ran across the ridge of Busaco, probably the finest defensive position in Europe, Wellington drew up his whole army, including the southern detachment under Hill and the half-formed Fifth Division, and offered battle, opposing 50,000 British and Portuguese to the whole of Massena's army. Foolishly the Frenchman accepted the challenge and was bloodily repulsed (27th September). Wellington continued his retreat. He abandoned Coimbra and, leaving a light rearguard of cavalry to cover the main body, marched steadily south until, by the night of 10th October, the entire army was within the lines of Torres Vedras. When Massena saw the strength of Wellington's position he was astonished. The very existence of this extremely powerful series of fortifications had been an admirably kept secret. Much of the army had assumed that they were retiring on Lisbon to re-embark and even the British Minister in Lisbon, little more than 20 miles away, seems to have been ignorant of them.[53]

Massena and his corps commanders looked at the lines and decided that they were impregnable. French losses had been heavy on the advance, not least when Colonel Nicholas Trant with some Portuguese militia and a handful of dragoons seized Massena's base hospitals at Coimbra and took 5,000 prisoners. The three corps could scarcely put 55,000 men into the field by mid-October. Against this Wellington, who had fallen back on reinforcements, could count on 34,000 British effectives of all ranks and 24,000 Portuguese regulars, to say nothing of two Spanish divisions, 8,000 men, who had sought shelter in the lines. None of these regulars were required to hold the fortifications. This task was performed by 15,000 Portuguese militia and men from the depôts of the regular army. The best that Massena could hope for was that Wellington might emerge from his position, throwing away his advantage, and attack the French in the plains. Wellington had no such intention. 'I think the sure game, and that in which I am likely to lose the fewest men, the most consistent with my instructions and the intentions of the King's government.' [54] It was not that he was happy with this inactivity. It is impossible to read his letters at this time without feeling his longing for taking the offensive, that 'although I have the advantage in numbers, the enemy are in a very good position, which I could not turn with any large force, without laying open my own rear, and the road to the sea. This is the worst of all these strong countries, that they afford equally good positions to both sides.' [55]

Meanwhile the French army was in increasing straits for food. Although the Portuguese, largely through the fault of their Regency, had not laid barren the country to the extent that Wellingon had hoped and ordered, it became increasingly difficult for such a large force to subsist, the more so since their rear was encircled by a flexible and largely invisible ring of Portuguese militia and irregulars drawing support and supplies from the fortresses of Peniche and Abrantes. Every day it became harder for the French to find food; every day they had to go further to forage and the further they went the more of them were murdered by the Portuguese. After almost five weeks in front of the lines, Massena decided that he would destroy his army if he remained there. On the night of the 14th he began a limited retreat to a strong position at Santarem, 20 miles back. Wellington, suspecting that the French objective was Abrantes, followed cautiously and came up to Santarem on the 19th. Thinking that he was opposed by only a rearguard, he issued orders for an attack. Fortunately, the weather made the whole move impossible for it would have been an unduly risky operation. He echeloned his troops between the Rio Mayor, with a strong corps on the south bank of the Tagus, and settled down to wait. It was three and a half months before he was able to advance again.

Massena's retreat brought him within range of new sources of food and forage. It did not, in the long run, make his position any easier. He had still only two courses open to him. To retreat in earnest, either to Spain or to the country north of Coimbra, or to wait for something to turn up. Three eventualities might get him out of his predicament: either Wellington might attack him, which seemed unlikely, or heavy reinforcements might arrive either from Ciudad Rodrigo or from Soult's army in Andalusia. In fact a force of 8,000 men, part of the additional corps that Napoleon had promised him, did arrive at the New Year, but this was scarcely enough to make good his losses from disease, desertion and the activities of the Portuguese around his rear and, indeed, made harder the task of feeding the army.

From the south he heard nothing. The Emperor had omitted to give Soult any orders to assist Massena until it was too late and then gave him instructions which were wholly impractical. Soult compromised by entering Estremadura in January 1811 at the head of 20,000 men and taking Olivenza. This in a very slight measure benefited the army of Portugal since it drew off the 8,000 Spaniards who had been within the lines of Torres Vedras. The Spaniards collected for the defence of Badajoz a not inconsiderable army, but on the 19th February threw it away by sheer carelessness at the battle of the Gevora. Soult was now able to besiege Badajoz, which he lost no time in doing, taking the place on 11th March. By that time his success was irrelevant to Massena's fortunes, and Soult was immediately called back to Andalusia with half his force on hearing that the garrison of Cadiz had sallied against the rear of their besiegers and that the British contingent, under Thomas Graham, had inflicted a sharp defeat on Marshal Victor on Barrosa Hill despite the defection of their Spanish allies.

One other hope kept Massena close to Lisbon—that the British might evacuate the country of their own accord. In this hope he was supported by the Emperor, and not without reason. On 2nd November the Princess Amelia had died. She was George III's favourite daughter and his grief brought back his madness, this time for good. It was widely believed that if the Prince of Wales was made Regent he would dismiss the weak ministry of Spencer Perceval and call in the Whigs, his lifelong friends. 'We are all on the kick and go', asserted Lord Palmerston, the Secretary at War. If the Whigs under Grey took office, there could be no doubt that the army would be withdrawn from Portugal. Ministers delayed as long as they dared, but in February 1811 they were forced to bring in a Regency Bill. The Whigs were jubilant and devoted much thought to the offices they would allocate to one another. The new Prince Regent decided to retain the government and the last of Massena's hopes had gone.

While he waited for starvation to drive Massena away, Wellington had his own worries. 'The present Ministers complain of the expense of the war in the Peninsula, their opponents declare that they would withdraw the army and the conduct of the Spaniards affords a good reason for doing so.' [56] In addition, the Portuguese government was being obstructionist and neglectful of their troops, and even in the British army there was widespread pessimism. General Miles Nightingall, newly arrived in Lisbon to command a brigade, wrote to a colleague in London on 9th February: 'We seem to have got into a situation in which we can do neither one thing nor the other. Advance we cannot and if it was wished to withdraw, I do not think it would be possible.' [57]

Three weeks later, on 2nd March, he reiterated: 'It is quite out of the question for us to advance even if Massena is not reinforced. Massena has not the smallest intention of retreating. I see no prospect of a favourable termination of the campaign.' [58] Three days later the French fell back from Santarem and did not stop until they were in Spain.

Massena took his long-delayed decision to retire just too early to benefit from one of the chances for which he had hoped. Wellington had long determined to attack him and waited only for strong reinforcements promised from England but delayed by bad weather.* The eight battalions and two regiments expected represented such an access of strength that it would be unwise to attack without them, but by the end of February only two battalions had arrived and the infantry were not all in Portugal until 22nd March, the cavalry landing more than a fortnight later.

Massena's intention was not to quit Portugal, although many of his subordinates and all of his troops longed to do so. The Marshal's plan was to put his army on the north bank of the Mondego, with the fertile and unravaged country between Coimbra and Oporto at his back, and hold on there until he was reinforced and able to thrust at Lisbon once more. To do so it was vital to secure a long start over the British and to keep it until the passage of the Mondego had been secured. At first all went well. On the morning following the evacuation of Santarem, a thick mist hung over the Rio Mayor and it was not until a Portuguese made his way across the causeway to the British lines that the outposts knew that the French had decamped. The Light Division set off in pursuit at daybreak, but only one other division and a Portuguese brigade were within supporting distance. Wellington was unprepared for so early a retreat. Two days before he had been of the opinion that it was 'likely that the enemy is about some move, but [we] have been so frequently disappointed that it is impossible to be certain'.[59] Some troops had been brought towards the front, but there were not enough to be able to overwhelm the rearguard. Nevertheless by 7th March touch had been regained and the pressure on Ney's corps covering Massena's rear increased steadily, despite the fact that the advanced guard was in the hands of Sir William Erskine, a thoroughly incompetent officer. On 10th March the French advanced cavalry reached the Mondego opposite Coimbra and found the bridge with two of its arches blown and the ruin guarded by Colonel Trant with a small force of militia and a few guns. Trant was under orders to retire if he was pressed, but the imposing front he presented deterred Montbrun, who commanded the French cavalry. He spent the next two days fruitlessly searching for a ford and found himself opposed at every possible crossing-point. By that time matters were desperate and when on the 12th Ney's rearguard was

* The Fifty-first, as an example, embarked at Spithead on 22nd January. They reached Lisbon on 9th March.

driven out of Redinha, Massena had no choice. He gave orders for a retreat eastwards. It was not a moment too soon. The following day Ney allowed himself to be manoeuvred out of Condeixa and there was a danger that the French army might be cut in two. Massena himself was all but captured by a patrol of German hussars. There were rear-guard actions on 14th and 15th March, but after that the French army abandoned everything that could impede its progress and made off at its best pace for the frontier. Wellington did not attempt to keep up with them. There was no chance of the enemy making an effective stand until they were in touch with supplies of food from Spain and it was useless to fight an action to encourage them to do what they were already determined on doing. Supplies for the allied army had failed and more supplies could only reach them when they could be brought by sea to the mouth of the Mondego. 'Our chief', wrote the acting Adjutant-General, 'had the option of disorganizing his army by a close pursuit without supplies, which while it could last must have been brilliant —or a temporary halt, forgoing the opportunity, not to return, but retaining his army in discipline, supply and efficiency. He chose the latter alternative without a hesitation.' [60] Nevertheless he now knew that the campaign was won. On 20th March, when the French army was still in the triangle Seia–Celorico–Guarda, he gave orders allowing the non-regular troops of South and Central Portugal to stand down, and wrote to the Admiral commanding in the Tagus asking him to send back to England all the troop transports stationed in the Tagus except sufficient to carry 3,000 infantry and 300 cavalry. The evacuation of Portugal no longer needed to be contemplated.

Massena, for the moment, was not prepared to admit utter failure. He attempted a thrust into the country north of the Tagus, but was foiled by his inability to feed his troops or move his guns over the appalling mountain tracks. On 29th March he was manoeuvred out of Guarda, five days later the Second Corps was lucky to escape from an enveloping movement at Sabugal, and by 4th April the only French troops under arms on Portuguese soil were the garrison of Almeida, who were immediately blockaded. The main French army fell back to Salamanca.

Massena had achieved nothing except to devastate the area between Torres Vedras and Leiria and to give the British and Portuguese armies confidence in themselves. He had lost 25,000 men. The whole Army of Portugal had no more than 36 wagons.

Serious as these losses were, Wellington over-estimated them. He reported to London: 'The enemy's loss on this expedition to Portugal is immense; I should think not less than 45,000 including the sick and wounded.' [61] Nevertheless, he did not underrate the chances of the French attempting a counter-attack. The French, he said, 'certainly will not allow this place [Almeida] to fall.' [62] And, much as he would have wished to send the cavalry to the rear in search of forage with which they were 'miserably provided, ... I cannot afford to lose it'.[63] He estimated the French force opposed to him at 40,000,[64] an admirable estimate as the returns for the French army on 15th April gave its strength as 39,546, and his own army at this time could not put many more than 25,000 in the field. There were two reasons for this. As soon as he was certain that Massena was headed for Spain, he had detached Beresford with 19,000 men to Estremadura to attempt to restore the situation at Badajoz, and the supply arrangements for the Portuguese troops which had pursued Massena with him had proved so defective that few of the Portuguese were able to reach the frontier. 'It is really a joke to talk of carrying on the war with these people', he commented bitterly to the British Minister in Lisbon, asking him to urge the Portuguese government to take some steps to feed their troops.[65]

With his army divided by ten days' marching over abominable roads, Wellington decided to use the period that Massena must need to reorganise his army to visit Beresford around Badajoz. He set out on 16th April, spent four days riding hard and five making arrangements for the siege of Badajoz with the inadequate means that were available, starting back on 25th April. On the road north, news reached him that the French were again in strength at Ciudad Rodrigo. By the night of the 28th he was back with the northern army and about to make preparations to resist what was clearly going to be a major French attempt to relieve Almeida.

Had Massena's plans gone aright he would have been only just in time, for it was the French intention to attack on 30th April. Massena, however, was dependent on the support of the Army of the North* for, at the very least, gun teams to move his artillery, having draught horses for only 12 from his own army. Marshal Bessières, who commanded in the north, had promised 10,000 men, and eventually arrived at Rodrigo on the 1st May bringing only 1,700 cavalry, a horse artillery battery and 30 gun teams. Massena, in consequence, could not attack until the 3rd, by which time Wellington was ready for him in a strong position with his right at Fuentes de Oñoro, which suffered only from having a right flank dangerously exposed to an enemy strong in cavalry. In this arm, with Bessières' help, Massena could field 4,500 men against 1,850 on the allied side of whom 300 were Portuguese and far from reliable. Notwithstanding this advantage Massena made his first effort with infantry alone against the strongest part of Wellington's line, the village of Fuentes which he was unable to take. He therefore spent 4th May making a belated reconnaissance and on the day following

* The Army of the North was formed in January 1811 out of the French troops in the triangle Salamanca–Oviedo–Pamplona. Its original strength was about 70,000 men and it was under the command of Marshal Bessières, a cantankerous and uncooperative cavalryman.

attempted a wide-swinging left hook which Wellington met by a hurried re-deployment. By the night of 5th May it was clear that Massena's attempt to relieve Almeida had failed and by the 8th all the French troops had recrossed the Agueda river. It only remained for Wellington to secure the garrison of Almeida, now without hope of relief. In this he was thwarted by the incompetence of his subordinates, especially of Alexander Campbell and Sir William Erskine. Wellington knew well that the garrison was intending to make a dash for freedom. It was equally clear that if they were to escape, their route must lie across the bridge of Barba del Puerco. Erskine was ordered to send thence some cavalry and a regiment of infantry. He actually sent, according to a staff officer, 'a corporal and four men'.[66] Even then the garrison might have been thwarted had it not been for a whole series of mischances and misconduct. 'I have never', wrote Wellington, 'been so much distressed by any military event.'[67]

On this unsatisfactory note the French invasion of Portugal finally came to an end. They never again entered Portuguese territory for more than a raid. For little more than 4,000 battle casualties, the Anglo-Portuguese army over almost a year had made Portugal secure and caused the enemy to lose 30,000 men. It was a defeat such as France had not suffered since the Revolution and was due partly to Napoleon's faulty estimate of the situation but overwhelmingly to Wellington's foresight, patience and determination. Historians have agreed that Massena was ordered to achieve the impossible, but it is hard to believe that he would have found it impossible had his opponent been any other British general than Wellington. As an intelligent British officer wrote in March 1811: 'I do not think Massena deserves to suffer anything in his reputation since he entered Portugal. He seems to have been hurried on by the arrogance of his master into a world of difficulties, and to have made the best of his way out of them. It has been the work of a master.'[68]

CHAPTER FIVE

THE PENINSULA 1811–14

We have certainly altered the nature of the war in Spain; it has
become, to a certain degree, offensive on our part.
Wellington, 27th August 1811

From the fall of Almeida on 11th May until Christmas 1811 there was
a period during which the two sides were in a state of equilibrium. The
allies had a firm grip on Portugal, secured by their possession of Almeida
and Elvas. The French possession of Ciudad Rodrigo and Badajoz ensured that Wellington could make no effective incursion into Spain.
Without assistance the Spaniards in their peripheral fastnesses—Cadiz,
Valencia, Galicia and the mountains of Catalonia and Navarre—could
make no significant threat to the main structure of the French occupation but they could, and did, tie down large French forces.

The Anglo-Portuguese army could put in the field 62,000 of all ranks,
of which 36,000 were British. The main body, the equivalent of seven
infantry divisions and three weak cavalry brigades, was facing Rodrigo.
Around Badajoz the southern corps was 22,000 strong, with the equivalent of four divisions and three weak cavalry brigades.

They were immediately opposed by parts, or the whole, of three
French armies. Behind Rodrigo was the Army of Portugal, to the command of which Marshal Marmont, Duke of Ragusa, had just succeeded
Massena. The army was 44,000 strong but was still recovering from the
retreat from Torres Vedras and was very short of wagons and draught
animals. Behind Marmont lay the Army of the North under Marshal
Bessières. This army had responsibilities stretching back to the Pyrenees
and, at this time, was too small to discharge them. Bessières had brought
only 1,500 cavalry to the Fuentes campaign, but opinion was widespread
in Marmont's army that he could without difficulty have brought 5,000
infantry. It was clear that if Wellington took the offensive towards Salamanca, he must reckon on Marmont being reinforced by at least this
number. On the southern front Beresford, commanding in place of Hill
who was on sick leave, was opposed by the disposable force of the Army
of the South, 25,000 men under Marshal Soult.

There were thus directly opposed 62,000 allies and 70,000 French
(exclusive of the Army of the North). Moreover, while Wellington had
no reinforcements within reach, there were in Spain a further 200,000

Frenchmen 'present under arms' who could in an emergency abandon their normal tasks of holding down the occupied territories and concentrate in overwhelming force to meet a threat from Portugal. The French command structure, with each of the six army commanders responsible only to Paris, made such concerted action unlikely but the possibility could never be left out of Wellington's calculations.

Wellington had no intention of undertaking any major offensive. All he could do was to 'watch for opportunities of undertaking important operations of short duration'.[1] One chance of such a quick and telling blow seemed to present itself immediately after Fuentes de Oñoro. There was a chance that Badajoz could be taken. Beresford had been blockading the town since mid-April and had opened siege works on 8th May. To ensure a temporary numerical superiority over Soult's field force, Wellington sent the 10,000 men of the Third and Seventh Divisions marching south on 14th May, following himself two days later. He reckoned to have 5,000 men more than Soult and hoped he would have the help of up to 10,000 Spaniards under Blake.

Reaching Elvas in three days, he found the situation altered for the worse. Soult had brought forward his troops with great speed. Beresford had stood to meet him at Albuera on 16th May with the support of 13,000 Spaniards. Soult had been repulsed, but the cost to the allies had been appalling: 4,100 British and 500 Portuguese were casualties, a loss equivalent in quantity and greater in quality than the strength of the Seventh Division.

Notwithstanding this reduction in strength Wellington resolved to press on with the attack on Badajoz as soon as the two divisions arrived from the north, which they began to do on 25th May. By this time he knew that Marmont was detaching troops to strengthen Soult and he suspected that the whole Army of Portugal might be brought southward. There must, however, be a short respite before Soult, who had lost more heavily at Albuerta than Beresford, could attack again. The allied troops coming from the Rodrigo front could move in an almost straight line, crossing the Tagus at Vila Velha. The French had to cross far to the east. Thus, while Wellington's men reached the siege in 13 days, Marmont's detachment of roughly equal strength took more than four weeks to join Soult, having had to cross the Tagus as far upstream as Toledo. Wellington had, in fact, about a fortnight in which to seize Badajoz. 'If we don't succeed in a few days we shall not succeed at all, as seventeen or nineteen battalions, and some cavalry, are on their march to join Soult', he wrote at the end of May.[2]

Badly advised by his engineers and with a farcical siege-train of antique Portuguese ordnance, the attempt failed. On 6th June he still believed that there was 'a chance, and in my opinion, not a bad one of obtaining possession of Badajoz',[3] provided it could be done in the next four days, but that night an assault on the walls was repulsed and three days later a second attempt failed. By that time it was known that Marmont was coming south with his whole army. The fleeting chance had gone and was not to recur for nine months. Even though the rest of the army was brought down from the Agueda, marching parallel to Marmont, the French numbers were too great to enable the siege or even a blockade to be continued.

On 18th June Soult and Marmont met in Badajoz. Wellington's army was disposed in a strong position between Elvas and the river Gevora and 'although we have now got upon us the whole disposable force in Spain; and although we are not quite so effective as I should wish, I entertain no apprehension for the result'.[4]

'I have 50,000 men including every Portuguese I can get together and artillery; and about 4,000 cavalry, of which 3,000 are British', wrote Wellington to his brother. 'The French have about 60,000, including 7,000 cavalry, and not including artillery; but they don't like to attack us.'[5] The two armies faced each other for a week but the French commanders had learned better than to attack Wellington, in a position of his own choosing. They thought, moreover, that the Spanish contingent which had been at Albuera was massed with the Anglo-Portuguese, giving the allies equality in numbers. In this they were mistaken. At Wellington's request Blake had led his corps down the western bank of the Guadiana and was slowly getting into a position from which he could threaten Seville, which Soult had left thinly guarded. Simultaneously the Spanish army of Murcia was making demonstrations into Granada.

The confrontation lasted for a week. Then, on 29th June, Soult started detaching divisions to the rear. After a further fortnight had passed while Badajoz was restocked with provisions Marmont and the Army of Portugal marched away to the area Toledo–Talavera in search of food, leaving a single division at Trujillo to act as a link with the Army of the South. All that was left around Badajoz was a corps of 15,000 men under D'Erlon and belonging to Soult's army. Nevertheless Badajoz was safe for the time being. Marmont could join D'Erlon within a week and the allies could not take the town in so short a time. Nor had Wellington any intention of attempting it again. The valley of the Guadinia was notoriously unhealthy in hot weather, as he had discovered after Talavera in 1809. 'The loss of men from the heat of the weather and the unwholesomeness of the climate, if the troops should be obliged to perform any labour during the ensuing six weeks, would exceed what might be expected in a general action.'[6] 'I shall try my hand at something on the north of the Tagus.'[7] On 18th July the main body of the army, seven divisions, started to march north again. Only Rowland Hill, restored to health, with two divisions of infantry and one of cavalry, 13,000 men, was left to observe Badajoz and D'Erlon.

The expedition to the south had been unsuccessful in that it failed to seize Badajoz, but its indirect effects were wholly beneficial. Not only was Andalusia threatened from east and west by Spanish forces, but in the north solid, if temporary, gains were made. From Marmont, Marshal Bessières had accepted, with the worst possible grace, the responsibility for guarding Ciudad Rodrigo. The area under his charge stretched from Rodrigo to the Bidassoa, more than 350 miles as the crow flies. To guard this area he had, apart from garrisons, only four divisions and two brigades of cavalry, scarcely more than 30,000 men. As soon as Marmont was drawn away to the Guadiana, Bessières evacuated the Asturias in order to be able to have some force to support Rodrigo. Soon afterwards the Spanish army of Galicia, finding the force opposed to them weak, succeeded in taking Astorga. Bessières was justifiably despondent. As he wrote to Paris: 'We are occupying too much ground, and wasting our resources; we are grasping at dreams. Cadiz and Badajoz swallow up everything we have: Cadiz because we cannot take it; Badajoz because it needs an army to support it. We should destroy the second and, for the moment, give up hope of gaining the first.' [8] The Marshal had made a very accurate assessment of the situation. When it reached Paris he was recalled and replaced by General Dorsenne, an inferior substitute.

'The next operation which presents itself', Wellington wrote to the Secretary for War in mid-July, 'is the siege of Ciudad Rodrigo, for which I have so far prepared as to have our battering train on the Douro. . . . I am tempted to try this enterprise. But I beg your Lordship to observe that I may be obliged to abandon it.' [9] The siege train had been lying on shipboard in the Tagus since March; Wellington ordered it round to Oporto on 14th May as soon as Almeida had fallen. On 19th July he ordered it to be disembarked and moved by river boat and road to Almeida, an operation which was estimated to take 62 days. Meanwhile the main army was completing its march from Elvas and by 10th August Rodrigo was blockaded by two divisions and the cavalry, with some guerrillas. It was a loose cordon round the town, but it ensured that Rodrigo could not be resupplied without a major operation on the French part, and even if they were prepared to undertake it 'a seasonable diversion will have been afforded to those of the allies who are at present the most pressed'.[10]

Almost immediately bad news began to come in. On 8th August information reached him that there were 20,000 men of the Army of the North around Astorga. This was at least twice the number which could have been expected there. Throughout August news continued to reach him of growing numbers on the road from the French frontier to Valladolid and Salamanca. He had known that new battalions were due to arrive from France, but he had no evidence from which to deduce the vital conclusion, that Napoleon had despatched to Spain three strong divisions of infantry and that, in the first instance, all of them were assigned to the Army of the North. The balance on the Spanish–Portuguese border was, for the moment, swinging to the French side, for while the French were greatly strengthened the allies were reduced by sickness. By mid-September the number of sick in the British army alone was more than 14,000, and the available force on the Rodrigo front was only 46,000 of all ranks. Against this the French armies of Portugal and the North could bring 60,000 without abandoning any vital positions in the interior of Spain.

Sickness was not the only trouble in the allied army. Money was still short and it was difficult to feel much confidence in the English government. Spencer Perceval had proved a surprisingly adequate Prime Minister, but his colleagues were wayward and their majority insecure. Nor, in Portugal, did it seem that their intentions were wholly fixed. Wellington had written earlier in the year: 'I have never been able to obtain any specific instructions, or even a statement of an object. . . . The only instructions which I have . . . are to save the British army; and that is the only object officially stated to me for keeping an army in the Peninsula.' [11] On their side the government had replied only with the cautious declaration that: 'You know our means, both military and financial, are limited; but such as they are, we are determined not to be diverted from the Peninsula to other objects. If we can strike a blow, we will strike it there.' [12]

The blockade of Rodrigo continued throughout August and into September. 'One thing is clear, that if we cannot maintain this blockade, the enemy must bring 50,000 men to oblige us to raise it; and they can undertake nothing else this year, for they must continue to watch this place, and we shall so far save the cause.' [13] The immediate crisis was bound to come in late September for the town was rationed only up to the end of the month and it was inconceivable that the French, with superior numbers, would allow it to be starved into submission. Wellington recognised that it would be dangerous and probably disastrous to fight a general action to the west of Rodrigo where the French superiority in cavalry would be most telling. He made it clear to London that he intended to offer no resistance to the French if they tried to introduce a convoy of provisions into the town with an escort of overwhelming strength. 'I shall have had the satisfaction of obliging the enemy to collect all their troops for the purpose of escorting [the convoy], and thus of contributing to save the army and kingdom of Galicia.' [14]

On 23rd September they came, 58,000 men of the combined armies. The cavalry piquets withdrew before them and the business would have passed without incident if both commanders had not decided to find out the strength of the other. There resulted the four days' fighting between El Bodon and Aldeia da Ponte. The significance of these minor actions was trifling. The most notable result was that Marmont began to form a low estimate of his opponent's skill and determination. It was an estimate that was to cost him his army and his reputation 10 months later.

With Rodrigo supplied and invulnerable, there was nothing that Wellington could do except to revert to his policy of watching for 'opportunities of undertaking important operations of short duration'. 'As long as the enemy remain in their present situation, it is impossible for me to do any thing excepting to keep them in a state of inactivity. Indeed, our army is so sickly, that I can scarcely venture to wish that an opportunity should offer for doing any thing.' [15]

On the French side the Army of the North reoccupied the Asturias and used its disposal formations in hunting guerrillas. The Army of Portugal returned to the valley of the Tagus, between Plasencia and Talavera, in search of food. In Paris the Emperor complained that his armies in Spain had relapsed into a 'defensive attitude' and Wellington was able to report that 'we have certainly altered the nature of the war in Spain, it has become to a certain degree offensive on our part.' [16]

The deadlock was broken by Napoleon himself with two decisions which finally decided the Peninsular War. The first was his resolve to invade Russia. The second was his order to subdue Valencia. The effect of the Russian war was, until after the retreat from Moscow, little felt in Spain. He withdrew only 27,000 men from his armies in the Peninsula. The decision to invade Valencia produced more immediate results.

The task of seizing the last of the great provinces of Spain was entrusted to Marshal Suchet, newly created Duke of Albufera, who commanded the Army of Aragon. Since that army was manifestly too weak to conduct the campaign unaided, the Army of the South was ordered to make demonstrations against the western borders of Valencia while the Armies of the North and Portugal were told to detach troops to Suchet's support. The Army of the North had to send two of its newly arrived divisions to release Suchet's troops on the Ebro, while Marmont was ordered to send 15,000 men to co-operate with the western flank of Suchet's advance. Marmont was assured that 'the English army has 20,000 sick and barely 20,000 able bodied men with the colours, so it is impossible for them to undertake any offensive operations'.[17] Faced with this assurance and with positive orders, Marmont had no option but to despatch two of his divisions and all his light cavalry on a wild-goose chase which took them to Alicante and achieved nothing.

At the time that Marmont made this detachment the British army in Portugal had 34,000 men in the ranks and only 12,000 absent sick.[18] Facing Ciudad Rodrigo there were, including Portuguese, 40,000 men, and their siege train was conveniently situated within the walls of Almeida. Their opponents were so scattered that not more than 30,000 men could be concentrated within three weeks at Salamanca to support Rodrigo.

On Christmas Day, Wellington heard that two divisions of the Army of Portugal were moving eastward. At first it seemed too good to be true. 'I cannot understand these marches and countermarches', he wrote.[19] Soon there was confirmation. Before the New Year further information made the situation clear. The divisions of the Imperial Guard were on the march to the north and the nearest troops of the Army of Portugal had moved from Salamanca to Avila, north-west of Madrid. Orders for the siege of Rodrigo were issued on New Year's Day and although the movement of the siege train was delayed by two days of heavy snow, the place was invested on 8th January. On the night of 19th January the Third and Light Divisions surged over the breaches and the northern doorway between Portugal and Spain was in Wellington's hands, with the loss of only 1,100 officers and men, British and Portuguese. Marmont was at Tordesillas, more than 100 miles away, with 15,000 men and the hope of collecting 40,000 in a fortnight's time.

Wellington had no doubt as to what the next step should be. Having secured the northern doorway, he must obtain the southern, Badajoz. With both these in his hands he could strike out through either, certain that the French could not riposte through the other. On 25th January the heavy battering guns started their wearisome journey southward while the main army stayed in the north to cover the repair of Rodrigo until Marmont, realising that he could achieve nothing, dispersed his army in the valleys of the Douro and the Tagus. It was not until the first week in February that the cavalry and infantry of Wellington's army began to march south.

Marmont clearly appreciated Wellington's purpose, and by stationing three of his seven divisions in the Tagus valley hoped to be able to come to Soult's assistance when Badajoz was attacked. Wellington assumed that he would do so, and when in mid-March Badajoz was invested he sent out two covering forces, one under Graham to ward off Soult coming up from Seville and another around Merida to oppose Marmont moving from the north-east. Soult duly arrived and confronted Graham, although by the time he had gathered an army and crossed the Sierra Morena he was already too late. Marmont never appeared. Napoleon, who was to learn later in the year that armies starved if marched into regions where there was nothing to eat, insisted that the best service which the Army of Portugal could give to Badajoz was to invade northern Portugal. 'Your posture should be offensive, with Salamanca as your base and Almeida as your objective; while the enemy know you are in strength at Salamanca they cannot move south. You must think the English mad if you think they would march against Badajoz while you are at Salamanca and able to reach Lisbon before them.'[20] It was useless for the unfortunate Marshal to explain that: 'If I were to concentrate the army on Salamanca, it could not subsist there a fortnight, [that] if the army moved on Ciudad Rodrigo it could not cross the river Agueda, because that river is unfordable at this season, [and that] the army could not remain three days before Ciudad Rodrigo, for want of provisions.' [21] The Emperor's orders were inflexible. Marmont was to collect his army at Salamanca and 'at least make an incursion into Portugal'.*

Thus, at the end of March, the Army of Portugal approached Ciudad Rodrigo. Marmont summoned the Spanish garrison to surrender and was staunchly defied. There was nothing more he could do to harm it for he had no heavy artillery, the whole of his siege train having been in the town at the time of its capture. Finding Almeida as unshakable as Rodrigo, he could only make a pointless raid as far as Guarda, which he reached on 14th April. The opposition consisted of no more than a small division of Portuguese militia. The day following his occupation of Guarda, Marmont fell back. He had received a despatch giving him the news that Wellington had taken Badajoz ten days earlier. There was no more question of invading Portugal. For the rest of the war Wellington made the moves and the French countered them—when they could.

All this Wellington had foreseen. He realised that Marmont had only one chance of achieving anything and that was that Rodrigo would fall from starvation, the Spaniards having failed properly to provision the fortress. 'Thus,' he wrote angrily, 'by *"mañana"* the Spaniards will lose that place again, unless I should go with the whole army to their assistance.' [22] Had it not been for this worry he might have struck a blow to free Andalusia, knowing that Marmont could not possibly feed his troops in the hilly country inside the Portuguese frontier. 'If Ciudad Rodrigo had been provisioned as I had a right to expect, there was nothing to prevent me from marching to Seville at the head of 40,000 men, the moment the siege of Badajoz was concluded.' [23] In the circumstances he had no option but to return to the Agueda, although, writing in confidence to his brother, he suggested that it might still be possible to go to Andalusia that year. Meanwhile, leaving Hill with his usual corps to watch Estremadura, he marched his army back to the north bank of the Tagus with the main body within reach of Rodrigo.

Having secured Rodrigo and chased Marmont back into Spain, Wellington had a few weeks, while his troops rested, to consider his next move. He had under his hand an army of about 48,000, all ranks, of which 30,000 were British and which, thanks to recent reinforcements, was respectable in cavalry, having ten British regiments amount-

* In a despatch dated 12th March which reached Marmont on the 27th, two days after Wellington had captured the Picurina outwork of Badajoz, and after he had brought the whole of his army around Salamanca to undertake his incursion, he received discretionary orders to move troops to the support of Badajoz.

ing to 3,500 officers and men. Apart from these there was Hill's corps to the south, which was likely to be more than adequate to meet anything that Soult could spare to send against it, supported as it was by the fortresses of Badajoz and Elvas. The total French army in Spain mustered 230,000 effectives, but the majority of these were absorbed in garrison duties and fruitless chases after guerrillas and ragged Spanish regular armies. No single French army could put into the field a force which could match the allies for numbers and any operation he undertook stood an excellent chance of success, provided that the opposing army could be brought to battle under favourable conditions before it could be reinforced by the others. The immediate choice of adversary lay between Soult in Andalusia and Marmont in New Castille. Soult, being burdened by the siege of Cadiz, could bring the fewer men to a battle, but equally could send the fewer to help Marmont. A move into Andalusia would bring Marmont down on his flank and rear. 'It would enable the enemy to bring the largest body of men to act together at one point [which] would be a false move, and this must by all means be avoided.' [24]

'I propose, therefore, as soon as ever the magazines of this army are brought forward, to move forward into Castille, and to endeavour to bring Marmont to a general action.

'I think I can make this movement with safety, excepting always the risk of a general action. I am of opinion also that I shall have the advantage in the action, and that this is the period of all others in which such a measure should be tried.

'In respect of a general action, I believe there is no man in the army who entertains a doubt of its result, and that that sentiment alone would do a great deal to obtain success. But we possess solid physical advantages over the enemy, besides those resulting from recent successes. Our infantry are not in bad order; our cavalry more numerous in relation to the enemy, and the horses in better condition than I have known them since I commanded the army; and the horses of the artillery in the same good condition and complete in numbers, whereas the enemy are I know terribly deficient in that equipment.

'Strong as the enemy are at present, there is no doubt that they are weaker than they have been during the war, or than they are likely to be again, as they will certainly be in some degree reinforced after the harvest, and, very largely so, after Buonaparte's projects in the north [the Russian campaign] shall have been brought to a conclusion. We have a better chance of success now, therefore, than we have ever had; and success obtained now would produce results not to be expected from success over any single French army in the Peninsula on any other occasion.' [25]

The prospect was not all bright. The health of the army was still not all that it might be; on 1st June there were almost 13,000 men on the sick list and a serious shortage of doctors, due to the incompetence of the Medical Board in London. Money, as usual, was a problem. The government was hard pressed to send out a regular supply of coin, and 'if we do not find the means of paying our bills for butchers meat there will be an end to the war at once'.[26] Meanwhile the army went into Spain six months in arrears for pay.

The shortage of cash was particularly serious now that the army was going into Spain. While in Portugal it had been possible to rely to a great extent on depôts which could be supplied from ships sailing to Lisbon and Oporto, whence the stores could be brought forward by river boat at least as far as Abrantes on the Tagus and Lamego on the Douro, so that the overland haul was short. Once into Spain stores must either be carried by pack mules, of which there was a shortage,* or bought from the countryside through which the army was marching. Experience had shown that Spanish farmers were extremely reluctant to accept payment in anything but gold. The situation was particularly bad with the Portuguese troops, whose pay and commissariat arrangements were notoriously sketchy, and the army's muleteers, who were Spanish almost to a man, refused to carry supplies to the Portuguese. 'To oblige Mr. Kennedy [Commissary-General] they would probably once or twice carry provisions to a Portuguese regiment, but they would prefer to quit us and attend to the French to being obliged to perform this duty constantly.'[27] The supply situation was made worse by the absence in England of Commissary-General Kennedy; his replacement was something of a muddler.

Nor was Kennedy the only absentee. Thomas Graham, the second-in-command, was suffering from an eye complaint. Picton, commanding the Third Division, had an open wound from Badajoz. Both had to quit the army soon after it advanced. Craufurd, of the Light Division, had been killed at Rodrigo. George Murray, the Quartermaster-General, had been posted to Ireland and his replacement, a Horse Guards nominee, had not yet arrived. The Adjutant-General was sick in England and his deputy was commanding the Third Division in Picton's place.

At home the situation was far from reassuring. At the end of May news reached Wellington that the Prime Minister, Spencer Perceval, had been shot dead in the lobby of the House of Commons. It was not until early July, by which time the army was more than 100 miles into Spain, that Wellington heard that a new government had been formed. From his point of view it was a reasonably good government. Lord Liverpool, who as Secretary for War had supported him more loyally than he was inclined to believe, became Prime Minister. His old friend

---

* There were some 12,000 mules with the army, but these were required in the forward echelons and could not be spared for bringing supplies from Portugal.

Castlereagh returned as Foreign Secretary and the Secretaryship for War went to Earl Bathurst. All the indications were that it would be a weak government of short duration, but it survived until 1827.

Wellington was not alone in having troubles. The French were in great confusion. Napoleon invaded Russia on 23rd June, and although few in the West believed that he would not be successful, it was clear that the massive movement of the *Grande Armée* eastward would deprive the armies in Spain of reinforcements for the time being. Before starting the campaign the Emperor had entrusted King Joseph with the supreme command of all the armies in Spain, giving him Marshal Jourdan as Chief of Staff. Jourdan was a sound strategist on paper and took a more realistic view of the war in the Peninsula than either Napoleon or the majority of his brother marshals, but his soundness achieved nothing since the subordinate army commanders, with unusual unanimity, declined to obey either Jourdan or King Joseph.

The French knowledge of Wellington's intentions was scanty and inconclusive. As a result the Army of Portugal was scattered between the Asturias and the valley of the Tagus. To keep them in suspense as long as possible, Wellington arranged with British, Sicilian and Spanish forces a number of diversions at peripheral points, of which the largest was a seaborne attack from Sicily on the east coast of Spain, and the most effective a series of raids on the northern ports by Commodore Home Popham with a small naval squadron and two battalions of Royal Marines in close co-operation with the guerrillas of Navarre and Biscay.

On 13th June Wellington, at the head of 50,000 men, of whom 18,000 were Portuguese and 3,500 Spanish, advanced into Spain from Ciudad Rodrigo. The Army of Portugal was widely dispersed, but Wellington was unhappy to find from a captured return that they were stronger by more than 5,000 men than he had anticipated. 'The effective fit for duty are 51,492; of which 48,396 are infantry; 3,204 are cavalry.' [28] 'I am very apprehensive that the advantages of my march into Castille will be confined to regaining the principality of Asturias and to the little advantage which the guerrillas will derive from the evacuation of the different parts of the country by the enemy's posts.' [29]

On 17th June the army reached Salamanca, which the French evacuated, leaving only a garrison of 800 men in three fortified convents commanding the bridge over the Tormes. The reduction of these strongpoints turned out to be a more serious matter than had been anticipated, particularly since Wellington had brought with him no more siege train than four 18-pounders, the guns which had battered Rodrigo and Badajoz having been sent to the assistance of the diversionary force on the east coast, where they were first unused and later shamefully abandoned to the enemy.

Before the Salamanca forts fell on 27th June Marmont had gathered

40,000 men together, being still without one of his divisions which had to be called up from the Asturias. With this incomplete force he threatened Wellington's army, which was drawn up in a strong position covering the siege but, wisely, did not commit himself to an attack. Wellington, equally, declined what seemed to be a good chance of attacking him, thus confirming Marmont's opinion that his opponent was not a commander of the first class.

On the fall of the forts the French army retired behind the Douro and took up a strong position behind the river, with bridgeheads at Toro and Tordesillas. Here, on 7th July, Marmont was joined by his missing division, making his field force up to 50,000, a rough numerical equality with the allies. To offset this he heard to his dismay that Caffarelli, now commanding the Army of the North, had been so alarmed by Home Popham's raids on the coast that he absolutely declined to send to Marmont's support two divisions of infantry which he had promised, despatching in their place only a small force of cavalry. Better news had been sent to him by King Joseph, but all the copies of the King's letter had fallen into Wellington's hands. Joseph had decided that Marmont's situation was so serious that he gave orders for La Mancha and most of Old Castille to be abandoned and was collecting at Madrid all the available troops of the Army of the Centre, about 15,000 men, to march to the aid of the Army of Portugal.

Marmont, however, believed that he was on his own and decided that the only course open to him was to deal with Wellington before the supply of food on the north bank of the Douro failed, as it was soon certain to do, and before the Spanish armies of Galicia and the Asturias started pressing in on his rear. He was strengthened in this determination by the last letter he had received from the King, which had urged just such a move.

By 14th July Wellington knew that Caffarelli had refused to give substantial help and that Joseph was planning to come to Marmont's help with a large force. He knew also that the King had ordered D'Erlon to come north with his corps from the Army of the South. While shrewdly appreciating that D'Erlon would probably not obey this order he could not be certain that Marmont did not know that Joseph was coming to his aid. He was faced, therefore, with the probability that Joseph and Marmont would join forces and, with at least 65,000 men, would greatly outnumber him. In consequence all his actions in the following week were concerned primarily with securing his retreat on Portugal.

On 16th July Marmont attacked across the Douro. Feinting cleverly from Toro and making his real thrust through Tordesillas, he made full use of the advantage offered by the southward bend of the river between these two towns, which gave the French much shorter communication between their flanks. For a short time Wellington was in a critical position, with the whole weight of the French thrust falling on a rear-guard of two divisions and a cavalry brigade. Although he extricated himself with skill, Marmont had undoubtedly out-manoeuvred him and was further reinforced in his belief that he could safely take liberties with him.

Wellington decided to retreat on Salamanca and from 19th to 21st July the two armies moved parallel to each other, frequently within cannon shot, and by the evening of 21st July the allied army was covering Salamanca. Rather than risk the combination of Joseph and Marmont, he was ready to retreat and when, next morning, it was clear that Marmont was attempting to cut him off from Portugal, he duly sent off his baggage to the rear and prepared to follow it. Until the middle of the afternoon it seemed that the campaign, which had opened with such high hopes, would end in a tame retreat to Ciudad Rodrigo. Then Marmont overreached himself.

In his eagerness to turn the allies right, the French commander had over-extended his own army. There was a fleeting chance that the French left could be rolled up and defeated in detail. Wellington recognised it. Remarking to his Spanish liaison officer, *'Marmont est perdu!'* he threw his own right forward and smashed the two leading French divisions. By nightfall the French army, covered by its only intact division, was streaming away to the south in disorder. If the Spaniards had obeyed his orders and held the castle of Alba de Tormes, which commanded the only bridge available for the French retreat, the Army of Portugal would have ceased to exist. As it was General Clausel, who succeeded to the command when Marmont was wounded early in the battle, reported three days later that he had only 20,000 men in the ranks.[*]

Achieved with a loss of only 4,700 men, of whom two-thirds were British, it was the British army's greatest victory since Blenheim. 'You have made the army as popular as the navy has hitherto been', wrote the Prime Minister to the victorious commander,[30] and followed it up with a hopeful authorisation that should 'they who command the French armies in Spain' make any overtures for peace, Wellington could 'conclude any arrangement which may appear desirable for the purpose of accomplishing the great object of entirely clearing the Peninsula of the enemy, and even for other ulterior objects, should they appear to your Lordship practicable'.[31]

Victorious though he was, Wellington was not in a wholly satisfactory situation. As he shepherded the Army of Portugal northwards over the Douro he was aware of King Joseph with his corps of 15,000 men at Segovia and aware too that D'Erlon with his corps of the same strength from Estremadura might at any time obey Joseph's order and join him.

[*] The French casualties were about 15,000 killed, wounded and captured. Some 13,000 more were dispersed and only rejoined their regiments after several days.

Moreover sooner or later Joseph must recall Soult and the remainder of the Army of the South and evacuate Andalusia, as, in fact, he did, on 29th July—although Soult took a long time to obey. Thus, at any time there might be, coming up from the south, a combination of the Armies of the Centre and South which would amount to 65,000 men, even without reinforcements from Suchet's troops in Aragon and Catalonia where Wellington now knew the Anglo-Sicilian force had failed to land. The Army of Portugal was badly damaged but it would not be long before, with reinforcements from the Army of the North, it would be again a menace to be reckoned with. By his success Wellington had brought about the one situation which he could not deal with, the concentration of the bulk of the French armies in Spain.

His best chance was to try to wreck another French army before such a concentration could take place. The obvious target was the Army of the Centre, under King Joseph, against which he could bring double numbers. Therefore, having occupied Valladolid and leaving near it a weak and rather sickly rearguard against the Army of Portugal, he turned south. 'Having discovered that the army under Marshal Marmont continued their retreat upon Burgos, in a state not likely to be able to take the field for some time: and knowing that I could not quit the river Douro [i.e. advance beyond it] in pursuit of them without incurring great inconvenience, and exposing the rear and communications of the army to the operations of the army of the centre under the King, I determined to move upon that army, and to endeavour to bring the King to a general action, or to force him to quit Madrid.' [32]

On 12th August Wellington entered Madrid, to scenes of immense enthusiasm. Joseph scuttled away before him towards Valencia.

While Wellington was thus engaged the remnant of the Army of Portugal showed some signs of life, driving a Spanish garrison out of Valladolid and, with an enterprising raid along the north bank of the Douro, bringing off the beleaguered garrisons of Toro and Zamora. Apart from being angry with the Spaniards for abandoning prisoners and arms in Valladolid, Wellington was not greatly concerned. 'As the allied army would be obliged to attack Toro and Zamora, in case the enemy should not withdraw from these places . . . I do not consider it a misfortune . . . as we shall be saved a long march at an unfavourable season, and an operation which will take time, and in which we must expect to incur some loss.' [33]

His worries were deeper. The army was steadily losing strength despite the arrival of the new battalions of infantry. By mid-August his British troops were reduced to 28,810 in the ranks and there were 18,894 men on the sick list. The news, not unexpected, that war had broken out between Britain and the United States made it unlikely that he would receive much in the way of reinforcements and might seriously reduce his supplies of corn.* Greatest of his concerns was the shortage of general officers. Ill-health and wounds had deprived him of his second-in-command, the commander of his cavalry, the commander of the Portuguese army and the commanders of the Third, Fourth and Fifth Divisions. There was no one to whom he could entrust a corps which might become engaged with a substantial French force. Feeling that Madrid was safe until Soult came up out of Andalusia, by which time Hill could bring up his corps and assume the command around the capital, he decided to leave there his three best but most tired divisions under the competent Major-General Charles Alten, and take the rest of the army north to discourage further the Army of Portugal. 'When I found that the King had decidedly passed the mountains into Valencia, I determined to make use of the time that would elapse before I could go to the south (which I thought it possible I should be obliged to do) in settling our affairs on the Douro, and in establishing a good communication between us and the Spanish Army of Galicia.'

'The probability that Soult would evacuate Andalusia, of which I was aware before I quitted Madrid, or the certainty that he had raised the siege of Cadiz, and abandoned Seville, which I obtained at a subsequent period [7 Sept], was not calculated to induce me to alter this determination. I was certain that whenever Soult should connect himself with Suchet and the King we should be pressed a little on the Tagus, and that it was desirable to remove to a distance all embarrassments, existing on this side, and to strengthen ourselves as much as possible on this side, preparatory to events which might be expected on the Tagus.' [34] Pushing back the Army of Portugal in front of him, Wellington drove the French back from Valladolid and on 17th September reached Burgos. The French evacuated the town but left a garrison in the castle, and on the 19th siege works were begun, although from the start Wellington was 'a little apprehensive that I have not the means to take this castle'.[35] The actual details of the siege are not immediately relevant and will be considered in a later chapter. It is sufficient to say that neither the means, nor the commander's will, were adequate to the task, and the siege dragged on for a month without coming near to success. Meanwhile the French were massing in both the north and the south and his own combinations were going awry.

Wellington calculated that, once the castle of Burgos was in his hands, it could, with the support of two or three Anglo-Portuguese divisions and Spanish forces from Galicia and the Asturias, stand against any force which the Armies of Portugal and the North would be able to bring against it. He rightly anticipated that the main thrust

* Much of the corn imported at Lisbon for the supply of the army came from the United States. In the event the supply was not greatly diminished, except by the depredations of American privateers, as Portugal was not at war with the U.S. and many American merchants were very ready to take advantage of this loophole.

against him would come from the south of the Tagus, from whence 60,000 men could attack him. Hill, who reached Madrid with his corps at the end of September and took over the command from Alten, had with him 31,000 British and Portuguese and 'not less than 12,000 Spaniards, besides innumerable guerrillas'.[36] This force would be sufficient to hold the line of the Tagus, provided the level of the river was high enough—as normally it was in later October—to be unfordable. Apart from this force and the one or two divisions and cavalry which he intended to bring down from Burgos to his support, Wellington reckoned on the assistance of General Ballasteros who, with 15,000 men, had been ordered by the Spanish government to take up a position at Alcaraz from which he could threaten the flank of any French advance against the Tagus. There was by this time an Anglo-Sicilian force at Alicante which ought to have posed some threat to the rear of the combined French armies. In all these hopes Wellington was disappointed. The corps at Alicante did nothing except change its commanders with bewildering rapidity. Ballasteros, hearing that the Cortes had offered to Wellington the supreme command of the Spanish armies, broke into open mutiny and refused to leave Andalusia. Wellington was unable to bring down any support from Burgos, which was still unconquered. The Spanish forces on which he counted in the north proved to be useless and few in number. Worst of all, the rains came late and the Tagus remained fordable at the vital moment. 'If this game had been well played, it would have answered my purpose. Soult and the King could not have remained in Valencia, and they must have crossed the Ebro, where I should have assembled all the allies, and should have worked upon their right flank. Had I any reason to expect that it would be well played? Certainly not. I have never yet known the Spaniards do any thing, much less do any thing well.' [37]

It was not until 19th October that Wellington realised that Soult was advancing on Madrid. Almost at the same time the Army of Portugal, reinforced from the Army of the North, started to drive in on his own outposts. By the 21st he knew that Hill was under pressure and realised that the forces opposed to his own corps were greater than he had estimated. 'I had no reason to believe that the enemy were so strong until I saw them. Fortunately they did not attack me: if they did I must have been destroyed.' [38] Wellingon had 24,000 Anglo-Portuguese and 11,000 Spaniards. His opponents were 53,000. In the south Hill could oppose 31,000 British and Portuguese with 12,000 Spaniards to 60,000 under Soult. The game was up and both parts of the allied armies must retreat.

By 8th November the two corps had joined at Salamanca, and although menaced by a very superior French force on their further retreat to Ciudad Rodrigo their main enemies were the weather, which was abominable, and their own Quartermaster-General, Colonel Willoughby Gordon, who sent all the rations on a road away from the army. The result, added to the usual deterioration in discipline which characterised British retreats in the Peninsula, was that the army lost 5,000,* more than had been killed, wounded and missing at the battle of Salamanca.

On 19th November the army was safely back within the Portuguese frontier. To the Prime Minister Wellington wrote: 'From what I see in the newspapers I am much afraid that the public will be disappointed at the result of the last campaign, notwithstanding that it is in fact the most successful campaign in all its circumstances, and has produced for the cause more important results than any campaign in which a British army has been engaged for the last century. We have taken by siege Ciudad Rodrigo, Badajoz and Salamanca. In the mean time the allies have taken Astorga, Gaudalaxara and Consuegra, besides other places. In the months elapsed since January this army has sent to England little short of 20,000 prisoners and have taken and destroyed, or have themselves the use of the enemy's arsenals in Ciudad Rodrigo, Badajoz, Salamanca, Valladolid, Madrid, Astorga, Seville, the lines before Cadiz, &c; and upon the whole we have taken and destroyed, or we now possess, little short of 3,000 pieces of cannon. The siege of Cadiz has been raised, and all the countries south of the Tagus have been cleared of the enemy.' [39] It was a fair statement of a vast achievement. To the Secretary for War he admitted.: 'I think I have escaped from the worst military situation I was ever in', [40] but to a friend he summed it up: 'In short, I played a game which might succeed (the only one which could succeed) and pushed it to the last: and the parts having failed, as I admit was to be expected, I have at least made a very handsome retreat to the Agueda, with some labour and inconvenience, but without material loss. I believe I have done right.' [41]

The first task that Wellington had to undertake in preparation for the campaign of 1813 was to visit Cadiz to secure what powers he could from his new appointment as generalissimo of the Spanish armies. He did not set out with any high hopes. 'I do not expect much from the exertions of the Spaniards. They cry *viva* and are very fond of us, and hate the French; but they are, in general, the most incapable of useful exertion of all the nations I have known; the most vain, and at the same time the most ignorant, particularly of military affairs, and above all of military affairs in their own country.' [42] It was of the Spanish government and officers that he chiefly complained. He recognised that the Spanish peasant, given rations, pay, equipment and wise leadership could form the basis of a fine army. 'The Spaniards make excellent soldiers. What spoils them is that they have no confidence in their officers—and how should the Spaniards have confidence in such officers as theirs?' [43] The most that could be hoped for was that the com-

* The permanent loss, after stragglers had arrived, was only about 3,000.

manders of Spanish corps could be persuaded to avoid involving their troops in general actions: 'I am afraid that the utmost that we can hope for is to teach them how to avoid being beat.' [44]

He was planning to strike a powerful blow 'as early in the spring as the green forage is on the ground'.[45] 'I propose to get in fortune's way if I should be able to assemble an army sufficiently strong; and we may make a lucky hit in the commencement of the next campaign. But it is obvious that we cannot save the Peninsula by military efforts, unless we can bring the Spaniards forward in some shape or other.' [46] The agreements made in Cadiz seemed to promise that not only would large Spanish armies be available in the field but that nine-tenths of the revenue of every province should be devoted to the maintenance of the army, but in fact most of the Spanish promises were never kept. It cannot have been any surprise to Wellington that he had, in the event, to rely on his own Anglo-Portuguese army.

This army was growing in strength. Although the Horse Guards, in the face of Wellington's protests, had insisted on removing from the Peninsula four regiments and three battalions, all of them weak but seasoned, he received in their place, despite the demands of the American war, four fresh regiments and six battalions. With drafts for his existing units the total strength of the British army in rank and file at the beginning of the year was 58,784, an increase of 9,000 over the figure of 1st January 1812.* Even the money situation had improved due to the government's action in buying gold coin in India and re-minting it into guineas for use in the Peninsula. The supply situation as a whole was improved by the return of Commissary-General Kennedy and the comfort of the troops was increased by the provision of tents and a more convenient type of cooking pot.

Some of the more competent generals returned to the army during the spring, including Thomas Graham, but the most useful return was that of George Murray, the tried and proven Quartermaster-General, who reappeared in March to replace the incompetent and disloyal Gordon, who retired on sick leave with a 'painful disorder' and Wellington's assurance that 'the truth is that your health is, if possible, too robust; and I was frequently apprehensive that you would have had fever in the hot weather'.[47]

The best news of all reached Wellington on his return to headquarters at Freneda, near Rodrigo, on 26th January.† This was nothing less than confirmation of the news, already suspected, that the *Grande Armée* had

---

* The number of men present in the ranks was actually lower at 33,542 compared with 34,386 at 1st January 1812. This was accounted for by a great increase in sick and missing following the November retreat.

† The letter containing this news from the Prime Minister was written on 22nd December and seems to have been a very long time in transit even if it did have to await Wellington's return to H.Q. for a few days.

suffered disaster in Russia. Delayed as was Wellington's knowledge of the Emperor's *débâcle*, he still received it 18 days before the wretched Joseph, who had crept back to Madrid and tried to continue the pretence that he was King of Spain. He was speedily disillusioned. On 14th February he received orders to move out of Madrid and to establish himself at Valladolid. In the weeks that followed he was ordered to send Soult and 20,000 men back to France to assist in rebuilding an army on the eastern front. In future Madrid was to be no more than a town occupied by the French left wing.

To hold the new front which, apart from a flank guard against the Spaniards in the northern mountains, stretched from the Tagus to the Douro, there were available the combined armies of the South, the Centre and Portugal amounting to 100,000 men. Behind them were nearly half that number in the Army of the North. Suchet on the east coast had a further 55,000 men, but these were fully engaged by the operations of three minor Spanish armies and the Anglo-Sicilians at Alicante. Wellington, scraping everything together, British, Portuguese and Spaniards, could put in the field 106,000, of whom 28,000 were Portuguese and 25,000 Spaniards. If the three French armies could concentrate and be reinforced from the Army of the North they would form a mass which, with a quarter of his men Spaniards of doubtful reliability, Wellington could not hope to face in the field. He was, however, full of confidence and had ordered a siege train and supplies to be stationed on board ship at Coruña, 'as it is possible that the events of the next campaign may render it necessary for the army to undertake one or more sieges in the north of Spain'.[48] Burgos was, clearly, one of the places he intended to besiege, indeed the siege train he had requested was 'framed with a view to the siege of Burgos',[49] but there were no other fortresses in that direction on the south of the Ebro or indeed until the neighbourhood of the French frontier.

By the end of March the new disposition of the French armies was clear. 'The King arrived at Valladolid on the 23rd [March], and was still in that city on the 25th. It was expected that the headquarters of the Army of Portugal were to be moved to Palencia. One division of the Army of the South have arrived at Avila; and the first division of the Army of Portugal, hitherto cantoned in that province, have moved towards the Douro. The . . . Army of the South . . . [have] very few troops in La Mancha.'[50] The significant news was of the move of the Army of Portugal. This was the greatest dividend that was paid by the campaign of 1812, for all its disappointing end. The concentration of troops necessary to drive back Wellington from Burgos had required the assembly of every disposable man from the north of Spain. When they returned to their posts they found that the guerrillas of Navarre, Biscay and Cantabria were in control of every acre not garrisoned by the French. It was necessary to reconquer the whole of northern Spain on the left bank of the Ebro. For this the strength of the Army of the North was patently insufficient. Napoleon, not for the first time, underestimated Wellington's strength and ordered the whole of the infantry of the Army of Portugal north to assist in restoring the position. Joseph was left with only 60,000 men on his long front. It was vital that he should be able to take up a strong holding position until he could assemble his reserves. He chose, as Marmont had done, the line of the Douro between Toro and Tordesillas.

Had Wellington followed the same course that he adopted in the previous year it is possible that Joseph might have checked him on the Douro, but he had no intention of doing so. As soon as the first rains fell (28 April) and there was a promise of green forage on the ground, the bulk of the Anglo-Portuguese army moved secretly across the Douro within the Portuguese frontier and assembled around Braganca. South of the river there remained only three divisions, three cavalry brigades, some Spaniards and Wellington himself, whose presence, duly reported by French spies, was the most convincing evidence that it was from here that the blow would fall. There was an infuriating delay while the pontoon train—'our confounded bridge', Wellington called it—was brought forward and at the last moment it was discovered that the Spanish Army of Galicia had no ammunition beyond what was in the men's pouches. It was clear that the Spanish government was as incapable as ever of supplying its troops and indeed 17,000 troops from Andalusia who had been promised made no appearance at all. For the moment Wellington had no patience with them: 'To all these complaints I have one answer, "Either stay and do your best, or go back and I will do my best without you." It will certainly be an eternal disgrace to the Spanish nation if I am to have another campaign in the heart of Spain without the assistance of a single Spanish soldier, excepting guerrillas.'[51]

On 19th May the order was finally given: 'Major General Victor Alten's brigade of Light Cavalry—the Light Division—a body of Sappers and Miners—the brigade of Household Cavalry, and a troop of reserve artillery, will march tomorrow and arrive on the 23rd instant at San Munoz.' It was an undramatic start, but by 26th May the Light Division column, joined on the way by Hill's two divisions from further south, had driven the most forward French division out of Salamanca with hardly a skirmish. The French command received much misinformation from their outposts, including, from Salamanca, the fact that Wellington was sick and travelling behind his army in a carriage. There were rumours of a body of allied troops on the north bank of the Douro, including one that asserted that 2,000 cavalry were in Alcañices (50 miles north-west of Zamora) two days before they arrived. This was ascribed to the Portuguese troops, who were known to have spent the winter north of the river. Two days after Salamanca fell, the only con-

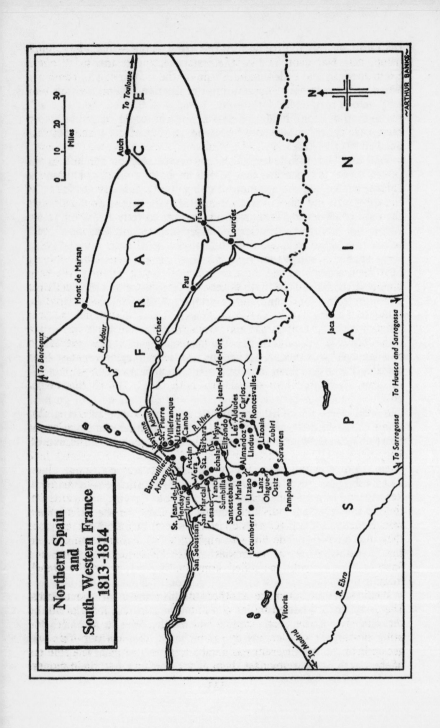

Northern Spain
and
South–Western France
1813–1814

FRANCE

SPAIN

To Toulouse

To Bordeaux

Mont de Marsan

R. Adour

Orthez

Pau

Tarbes

Lourdes

Auch

Jaca

To Huesca and Sarragossa

To Sarragossa

Miles

0   10   20   30

Bayonne
Barrouillet
Arcangues
St. Pierre
Villefranque
Ustaritz
Cambo
R. Nive
St. Jean-Pied-de-Port
Les Aldudes
Val Carlos
Roncesvalles
Lindus
Lizoain
Zubiri
Sorauren
St. Jean-de-Luz
Hendaye
Irun
San Marcial
Vera
Atcain
Sta. Barbara
Echalar
Maya
Elizondo
Almandoz
Lesaca
Yanci
Sumbilla
Santesteban
Dona Maria
Lizaso
Lanz
Olague
Ostiz
Pamplona
Lecumberri
San Sebastian
Vitoria
R. Ebro
To Madrid

~ARTHUR BANKS~

centration of French force was a corps of 20,000 at Medina del Campo, while there was another division and a cavalry brigade, in all about 8,000 men, forward at Toro and Zamora. The rest of the combined armies were marching up from their positions and one division only left Madrid on 27th May.

On 1st June the French discovered the true state of affairs, when their cavalry at Morales, west of Toro, were attacked and severely handled by the Hussar Brigade. Graham, at the head of six divisions, 42,000 men, had crossed the Esla and was rolling up the line of the Douro before it had been manned. On his northern bank were 15,000 Spaniards. By 2nd June King Joseph had realised how serious the situation was and gave orders for a retreat to Burgos, confident that there he could mass 60,000 men in a good position. But Wellington, who by 3rd June had the whole of his army on the north of the Douro, was not to be stopped again by Burgos. The allied army wheeled up to the north and by-passed the town. The initial manoeuvre of overrunning Castille having succeeded, he was going after total victory. 'We keep up our strength, and the army is very healthy, and in better order than I have ever known them.' [52] On 10th June he finally decided that he could go right through to the north of Spain. On that day he sent orders for the battering train and stores lying on board ship at Coruña to be forwarded to Santander, to be landed as soon as the port should be abandoned by the enemy. Nine months before he had expressed the opinion that it would not answer to use Santander as a supply port 'till the army should be firmly established on the Ebro, or probably further on'.[53]

A week later the allied army was across the Ebro without a shot being fired at them. The French had abandoned their position at Burgos, blowing up the castle on finding that they were outflanked. They fell back on the Ebro only to suffer the same fate. On 21st June 58,000 French troops stood for battle at Vitoria against 70,000 allies. By nightfall they were routed, deprived of their baggage and artillery. Retreating over a minor road, the only avenue of escape open to them, they became such an undisciplined mob that the Governor of Pamplona would not open the gates of the town to them for fear of the excesses they might commit. The French kingdom of Spain was at an end. All that remained were the fortresses of San Sebastian, Pamplona and Santoña. By 8th July the allied army had closed up to the French frontier.

Wellington did not make another offensive move for two months. The army was exhausted by its 300-mile advance and, most of all, by the very size of the booty captured at Vitoria. 'We started with the army in the highest order, and up to the day of the battle nothing could get on better. But that event has annihilated all discipline. The soldiers of the army have got amongst them about a million sterling in money.

They were quite incapable of marching.' [54] By 6th July the numbers in the ranks of the British army, which had been 41,547 five days before the battle, had fallen to 34,682, a reduction twice the size of the battle casualties. Wellington calculated the combined loss to the British armies through 'irregularities, straggling, &c for plunder' at over 4,000 men. The supply situation was equally bad. It had been Wellington's intention to change his supply base from Lisbon to Santander, but the navy, due to the demands of the American war and the tendency of naval captains to leave their stations in pursuit of valuable prizes, could not convoy stores around the coast. 'The ships which were ready in the Tagus on the 12th May had not sailed on the 19th June; and our magazines of provisions and military stores, which I expected to find at Santander, have not yet arrived. Of some kinds of ammunition we have none left; and I have been obliged to carry French ammunition of a smaller calibre than ours in reserve. Surely the British navy cannot be so hard run as not to be able to keep up the communication with Lisbon with this army.' [55] The news from elsewhere was not encouraging. On the east coast of Spain, General John Murray who had, on Wellington's orders, undertaken the siege of Tarragona, had lost his head and abandoned his siege train at the approach of imaginary armies. In eastern Europe Napoleon had agreed to an armistice with the Russians and Prussians, while Austria refused to commit herself to either side. If the armistice could be prolonged into a peace treaty, the French could reinforce their army on the Pyrenees to such an extent that they could drive the allies back to Portugal. In any case it was impossible to invade France until San Sebastian and Pamplona, which commanded the roads over the frontier, could be reduced.

Thus the French had a breathing space in which to reorganise their shattered armies. Soult was appointed to the post which he had always coveted, Supreme Commander of the Army in Spain, and the wretched Joseph was sent into exile. Arriving at Bayonne on 11th July, with orders to 'reestablish the Emperor's business in Spain', and to relieve San Sebastian and Pamplona, Soult reorganised the four old armies into three corps, each of three divisions, and a very large reserve division. In all, over and above troops in garrison, he could put in the field more than 70,000 infantry and 7,000 cavalry.

On 25th July he attacked through the Maya and Roncesvalles passes in an attempt to relieve Pamplona. Wellington, whose army was greatly overstretched while covering both sieges, and who was poorly served by his subordinate generals, managed to halt the French onrush at Sorauren on 28th July. By the end of the month Soult was back behind the frontier, having lost 13,000 men.

Soult was not to be deterred. On the last day of August he attacked again nearer the sea in the hope of saving San Sebastian. He employed 41,000 men and the main blow fell on Spanish troops stationed on the hill of San Marcial. There, for the first time since Baylen, the Spaniards won a major battle. Their conduct, reported Wellington, 'was equal to that of any troops I have ever engaged'.[56] San Sebastian fell that morning.

Pamplona held out and Wellington was not prepared to advance. There was no news of the situation in the east where the armistice had been extended. It was clearly unwise to plunge into France until it was certain that the bulk of Napoleon's troops would not be sent to Gascony to oppose him. Meanwhile the Pyrenees was as good a defensive position as any in Europe, but until there was further news from the east, further advance was out of the question. 'We have but one army, and . . . the same men who fought at Vimeiro and Talavera fought the other day at Sorauren; if I am to preserve that army I must proceed with caution.'[57] In fact the war in the east had broken out again at the beginning of August, and Austria had declared war on France on the 11th of the month, but this news did not reach London until 27th August and Wellington did not hear until the second week in September when, pending the fall of Pamplona, he gave orders for a limited offensive on his left flank designed to give him both a bridgehead on the right bank of the Bidassoa and possession of La Rhune, the dominating height in the centre of the French position. Due to the incompetence of the engineer officer charged with bringing forward the pontoon train and the fact that to achieve surprise it was essential to have a convenient low water in the estuary, the attack had to be postponed until 7th October. When it came it was wholly successful. The Fifth Division stormed across the estuary at a point which the French had never conceived to be fordable. The opposition was negligible since a well-thought-out deception plan had directed all Soult's attention to his eastern flank. Further inland the Light Division and Longa's Cantabrians hustled the French out of strong positions around the Pass of Vera. They failed to take La Rhune itself, but the French evacuated it the following day.

Pamplona was finally starved into surrender on 31st October. The communications up to the frontier were at last clear. Soult, recognising that his troops could not be counted upon for an offensive, set them to building fixed defences. They availed him nothing. On 10th November, at the battle of the Nivelle, Wellington's right and centre broke out of the Pyrenees and into the plain between the Nive and the sea, while Soult watched his seaward flank. The last barrier protecting France had fallen and the new French defence line was supported on Bayonne. On the night of the battle Wellington learned that Napoleon had been overwhelmingly defeated at Leipzig.

Soult had his last chance of driving the allies out of France in the second week in December. He had numerical equality, for his opponent had sent back almost all his Spanish troops since their plundering threatened to raise the countryside against the allies.

Determined to break out of the triangle formed by the sea, the Pyrenees and the river Nive, Wellington threw his right wing across the Nive on 9th December. Having short communications through the fortress of Bayonne, Soult was able to attack first on the left bank in the neighbourhood of Biarritz and, having failed there, to swing his main strength back on to the right bank. On 13th December, with six divisions, more than 30,000 men, he attacked Rowland Hill at St. Pierre d'Irube. Hill had only 14,000 men, nine British battalions and 14 Portuguese, and a sharp overnight rise in the Nive had washed away Wellington's bridge so that he could only reinforce Hill by a roundabout route. Hill lost nearly 1,700 men but he stood his ground until reinforcements arrived during the afternoon, when the French were shepherded back into Bayonne. It was Soult's last offensive.

The five days of fighting, known as the battle of the Nive, had cost the French 7,000 men. Shortly afterwards Napoleon demanded from Soult more than twice as many to rebuild the army shattered at Leipzig. Although he received a number of unwilling conscripts to fill up his ranks his field army never again exceeded 42,000 men. Wellington could bring against him 60,000 Anglo-Portuguese, apart from such support as could be obtained from the Spaniards. For two months there was little movement, the weather making the roads impassable, but in mid-February the allies moved their main body eastward, drawing Soult's field force away from Bayonne, which was invested by Wellington's left-hand corps under Sir John Hope. Soult attempted to stand on the Gave de Pau at Orthez (27th February), but, after a shaky start, Wellington out-fought and out-manoeuvred him. By 24th March Soult's entire army was penned up in Toulouse where on Easter Sunday, 10th April, Wellington attacked and defeated him for the last time.

Next day, a British officer rode into Toulouse from Paris. 'He found Wellington pulling on his boots, in his shirt. He had entered Toulouse an hour before. "I have extraordinary news for you."

"Ay, I thought so. I knew we should have peace; I've long expected it."

"No; Napoleon had abdicated."

"How, abdicated? Ay, 'tis time indeed. You don't say so upon my honour. Hurrah!" said Wellington, turning round on his heel and snapping his fingers.' [58]

CHAPTER SIX

THE PENINSULA—OFFENSIVE

Edward, move on with the Third Division—take that hill to your front—and drive everything before you.
Wellington to Pakenham, 22nd July 1812

Many historians, especially in France, have written Wellington down as a defensively-minded general. It is true that Waterloo, his last and most memorable battle, was wholly defensive, but, for the rest, it is hard to read his letters and study his record without concluding that the offensive was always uppermost in his mind. Assaye and Argaum were both gained on the attack, despite enormous odds. In the Peninsula 14 general actions fought under his immediate command were considered worthy to be marked by the award of battle honours either on the colours of regiments or as clasps on the military general service medal. Of these 14 only six (Vimeiro, Talavera, Busaco, Fuentes de Oñoro, Pyrenees and Nive) were defensive. Even of this number Vimeiro was defensive only because Sir Harry Burrard insisted on cancelling Wellesley's orders to advance. Talavera would have been an attacking battle fought on 23rd July had it not been for the 'whimsical perversity' of Cuesta. Fuentes and Pyrenees were fought to cover the blockades of Almeida and Pamplona, and the fighting on the Nive was the French response to a bold offensive move by Wellington. Only Busaco was wholly defensive in character, fought to blood the Portuguese and because Wellington could not resist the temptation to inflict a sharp defeat on the French when they offered him the chance to do so under conditions of the greatest safety. The balance of eight offensive to six defensive actions tilts still further if the crossings of the Douro and the Bidassoa, omitted for some reason from the list of battle honours, are included.

The following pages describe three of the more hazardous of Wellington's offensive operations, the forcing of the Douro in 1809, Salamanca in 1812 and Toulouse in 1814.

The forcing of the Douro, 12th May, 1809

When Wellesley returned to Lisbon in 1809, his thoughts turned immediately to the attack. Victor at Merida and Soult at Oporto both

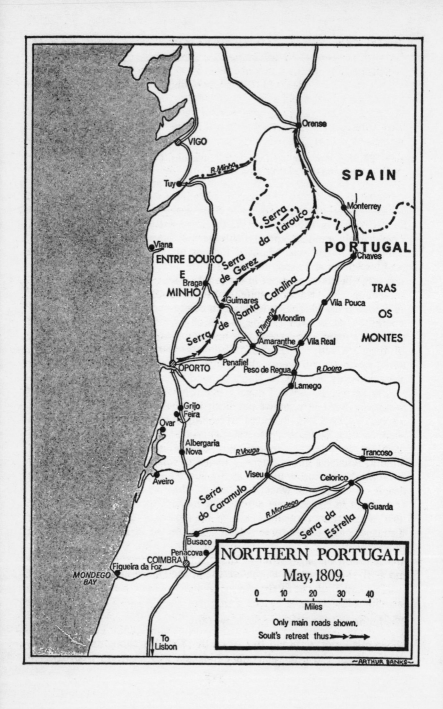

NORTHERN PORTUGAL
May, 1809.

0   10   20   30   40
Miles

Only main roads shown.
Soult's retreat thus ➤➤➤

~ARTHUR BANKS~

presented themselves as targets. There is no doubt that his preference lay with striking at Victor, a move which he hoped would lead to the recapture of Madrid. 'I should prefer an attack upon Victor in concert with Cuesta, if Soult was not in possession of a fertile province of this kingdom and of the favourite town of Oporto, of which it is most desirable to deprive him; and if any operation upon Victor, connected with Cuesta's movements, would not require time to concert it, which may as well be employed in dislodging Soult from the North of Portugal.' [1] Either way he was going to attack, first on one side, then on the other. If Soult could be disposed of while the more ambitious plan was maturing, so much the better.

No time was wasted. Landing at Lisbon on 22nd April and faced with a heavy round of official receptions and desk work, it was only five days before Wellesley issued orders for the concentration of the army at Coimbra. On the sixth day he rode out of Lisbon to join them. Having set aside a small covering force on the eastern frontier, he had in hand 17,500 British and 6,700 Portuguese, the latter of unpromising appearance. In addition, 'General Silveira, with a Portuguese corps, is in Tras os Montes; but I am not acquainted with its strength or composition.' [2] His knowledge of Soult's strength was scanty. He believed the French to number between 15,000 and 20,000 and thought that for the most part they were in and around Oporto with 'some posts on the river Tamega . . . and it is supposed that he wishes to secure for himself the option of retreating through the Tras os Montes, if he should find it necessary.' [3]

His plan was for the main body of the army, seven brigades of infantry, 1,300 cavalry and 24 guns, to move directly upon Soult while Beresford with 6,000 men, including a British brigade, marched northeast to help Silveira block the eastern escape route by taking up a position at Vila Real. All this supposed that Silveira was capable of holding the line of the Tamega which meant, in effect, the bridge at Amarante, since the river was nowhere fordable and all the other bridges had been destroyed.

In fact Silveira lost the vital bridge on the night of 4th May and was driven in disorder behind the Douro at Peso de Regua, north of Lamego. News of this reached Wellesley on 7th May, but he heard at the same time that Soult was preparing to evacuate Oporto and that his retreat would be through Vila Real. He wrote to Beresford: 'Now upon all this question, what shall we do; my opinion is, that we are not sufficiently strong in British troops to make such an attack upon Oporto as will oblige them to evacuate that town, and to post such a corps at Vila Real as will effectively cut them off. . . . I acknowledge that I should not like to see a British brigade supported by 6,000 or 8,000 Portuguese troops, in *any but a very good post*, exposed to be attacked by the French army.' Reluctantly he concluded: 'We must be content therefore with preventing them from crossing the Douro', and urged Beresford to take up a position around Lamego so that the French, when driven out of Oporto, would have to retreat by a mountainous route north of the Douro which would do the maximum harm to their morale and equipment. He gave Beresford wide discretion to act according to circumstances, telling him that the occupation of Vila Real 'would be a most important step if you could venture upon it', but recommending him not to do so 'unless you should know that the post is of such a description that you will be able to hold it for two or three or more days, [as] I must observe that they would have every facility and probably time to attack you at Vila Real before I could arrive in a situation to assist you.'[4]

Wellesley seems to have marched north from Coimbra with no firm idea of how he was to dispossess Soult of Oporto. The city is on the north bank of the Douro; the river is as wide as the Thames at Westminster and the only bridge was constructed of boats which would be drawn in to the city on his approach. He pinned his main hope on destroying Soult's advanced guard, which he estimated at 4,000 men and which was posted between Oporto and the river Vouga 38 miles to the south. To do this he planned a waterborne movement up the west flank to coincide with a frontal drive by the main body of his force. Rowland Hill, with his own brigade and Cameron's, was to move by fishing boats from Aveiro up the lagoon to Ovar so as to be in a position to fall on the flank of the French as they fell back under pressure from the cavalry and the other five bridges.

The plan failed. By sunrise on 10th May Hill had got his first lift of 1,500 men established at Ovar but found that the nearest French force, which was at Feira, was too strong for him and showed no signs of retreating. The main army had been hopelessly delayed by the difficulties of the road and by lack of experience of marching at night. An officer of the leading cavalry regiment described how 'we moved about eleven at night, and immediately on passing the Vouga the road ascends through a narrow pass, admitting only one horse at a time. The men from constant halts and delays fell asleep; and what is but too common, lost the man before them and so the road.'[5] Behind the cavalry the infantry were still further delayed when some artillery wagons broke down in the defile. There was a skirmish, but the French were able to withdraw in good order, offering no opportunity to Hill, whose second lift did not reach him until dark. On the following day there was another skirmish at Grijo, which achieved nothing except to show that some of the Portuguese regulars were not as worthless as many of the British believed. By midnight the French army was complete on the north bank of the Douro, having lost only 250 men.

The problem of crossing the Douro remained and Soult considered it insoluble except by a sea-borne flanking movement. He had already decided to retire to the east, but he intended to take his time about doing so. He sent off his heavy baggage during the night of the 11th, but did not plan to move his main body until the 13th so that his march would not be hindered by his impedimenta at a time when he might have to fight rearguard actions. Having allowed a generous escort to the convoy he had 10,000 men in hand and, apart from sentries on the town quays, was guarding in strength only the stretch of the Douro between Oporto and the sea. All boats had been cleared away from the south bank.

Soon after dawn on 12th May, Colonel Waters, a British officer in the Portuguese service, discovered that a Portuguese barber had brought a rowing boat across to the south bank. With the help of some peasants Waters succeeded in bringing to the south bank four wine barges, each capable of carrying 30 men. The movement was screened from the city by a bend in the river where cliffs overhung the banks on both sides. When this was reported to Wellesley, who still had no plan for seizing Oporto, he recognised that he had a chance that could never recur. Immediately he ordered Hill's brigade to start crossing in the barges and to get possession of a half-built seminary on the north bank, the movement being covered by three batteries of six-pounders on the opposite height. At the same time he ordered John Murray, with two battalions and two squadrons, to march along the south bank to the ford at Barca Avintas, five miles upstream, to delay the French retreat by the eastern road.

The French watch on the upstream bank was disgracefully casual. Three times the unwieldy barges had crossed the river, and more than 600 of the Buffs were safely established in the seminary before the French were able to attack them with three battalions. The attack was swept away by the British guns firing across the river. Three further battalions renewed the attempt, but by this time there were almost two battalions of British firing from excellent cover within the walls, the artillery fire was no less telling and the result was the same. The only French troops available to make a third attempt were the brigade guarding the quays.* In desperation Soult called them up, but as they left their station the citizens of Oporto launched every boat they could find and ferried two brigades on to the town quays. Oporto was lost and Soult could do nothing but order the evacuation of the town. The French, many of them in disorder, set out at their best pace on the road to Penafiel and Vila Real. John Murray, an unenterprising officer, did nothing to obstruct them, although Charles Stewart, the Adjutant-General, led Murray's two squadrons against the rearguard.

Unknown to both Wellesley and Soult there was now a bare chance that the whole of Soult's corps could be destroyed. With Beresford's

* A complete French division was to the west of the town watching for a landing from the sea and could not be brought up in time to be of use.

corps close behind him, Silveira had recrossed the Douro at Peso de Regua on 10th May. Loison, commanding the French division in that direction, had counter-attacked and been beaten off. Unforgivably he had not only retired to Amarante but omitted to tell Soult that he had done so. Beresford sent up Silveira's corps to face him across the Tamega while his own men filed across the Tagus at Peso de Regua, the British brigade being in the rear. The French position was impregnable to Silveira's partly trained Portuguese, but Loison decided to retire and did so in the small hours on 13th May. Moreover he retired north-west, towards Braga at exactly the time when Soult was counting on retiring due east on the abandoned bridge at Amarante. Soult heard the news, the first message he had received from Loison since 7th May, at about the time that Loison's rearguard marched off north-west. His position was desperate. He could not risk forcing the passage of the Tamega with Wellesley at his rear; there was no road to the north by which he could rejoin Loison. To the south was the Douro and to the west Wellesley. Abandoning his artillery, baggage and plunder, he led his army by a mule track to the north and rejoined Loison at Guimaraes on 14th May. Wellesley was still ignorant that the French had lost Amarante and it was not until late on the 13th that he heard that Soult had taken to the mountains behind Penafiel. Up to that time he had contented himself with sending Murray with the cavalry and some light companies up the Penafiel road. Ignorant of the great chance that was open to him, he was giving his troops a much-needed rest while the artillery and supplies were brought across the Douro on improvised ferries. Soult had swept up all the food in Oporto when planning his leisurely retreat and the British were almost without rations.

As soon as he heard the real situation, Wellesley acted with great speed. He ordered Beresford to move on Chaves and set his own army marching northward. So fast did his advanced guard move that they occupied Braga before the French dragoons could reach it, convincing Soult that the northern escape route by Vigo was closed to him.

Beresford heard of the fall of Oporto on 14th May from a captured French commissary. Immediately he ordered Silveira to march on Chaves to deny the French the defiles on the road between Braga and Chaves. His own force, still somewhat in the rear, was directed to move by forced marches on Chaves. Beresford had been given a wide measure of discretion and he used it to the full. Every decision he took was right and agreed fully with the orders he eventually got from Wellesley.* Unfortunately Silveira also used his initiative and used it wrongly. Instead of marching on an interception course by Mondim he had taken

* Communications between Wellesley and Beresford were extremely slow since couriers had to travel by Lamego and the south bank of the Douro. Wellesley's letter written at noon on 12th May announcing the fall of Oporto did not reach Beresford until the morning of 15th May.

the eastern road to Chaves by Vila Pouca. Thereby he lost a day which could never be recovered.

Wellesley had headed Soult off from the Vigo road, but he had no chance of catching up with him. The most he could do was to press the French rearguard. If Soult was to be intercepted it must be by Beresford. It was no fault of his that he failed. The British brigade moved out of Amarante early in the morning of 15th May, and an Assistant Surgeon has described their march. 'The rain fell in torrents, and, for the sake of expedition, our troops were ordered to cross a river breast high. Those who had horses were now employed in the water to catch the men as they were floating and wading about unable from the weight of their packs and previous fatigues to get through without help. After crossing it we marched onward and arrived at about four o'clock in the large town. Here we were halted for one half hour to refresh ourselves and were then ordered to proceed onward a forced march. The night was exceptionally dark in consequence of which the regiments lost each other. The roads were dreadful, [we] were frequently kept standing for ten minutes up to the knees in water. About twelve o'clock midnight we arrived in a small village. The first object is to find cover for the men—officers must do as well as they can. Many found difficulty to find a place to put their heads. . . . On the following morning at three o'clock we marched onwards. In consequence of much rain many of our men were now without shoes and stockings, and also some of the officers. I fortunately, in an old house I broke into, found an old pair of shoes, in consequence of which I threw my boots, now worn out, away. We arrived at a village at about eight o'clock at night and were there halted. On the following morning we pushed on another forced march. The rain continued and this march knocked up our Regiment. Half of it were walking over rocks without a shoe and their feet cut, so as to be unable to proceed.' [6]

They reached Chaves early on the 17th and the next day they were called upon to make another forced march towards Salamonde to fill the gap that had been left by Silveira's eccentric march. It was all in vain. Although they got sight of the French and the 87th secured the carcass of a pig which the French had just killed for themselves, Soult took to the mountains again, and crossed the Sierra de Larouco to Orense. Further pursuit was useless. To follow the French over the mountains would only destroy the army, whose commissariat arrangements were already under more strain than they could bear. Moreover, there was no chance of being able to catch up. 'It is obvious,' wrote Wellesley, 'that if an army throw away all its cannon, equipments, and everything that could strengthen it, and can enable it to act together as a body; and abandons all those who are entitled to its protection, but add to its weight and impede its progress; it must be able to march by roads through which it cannot be followed, with any prospect of being

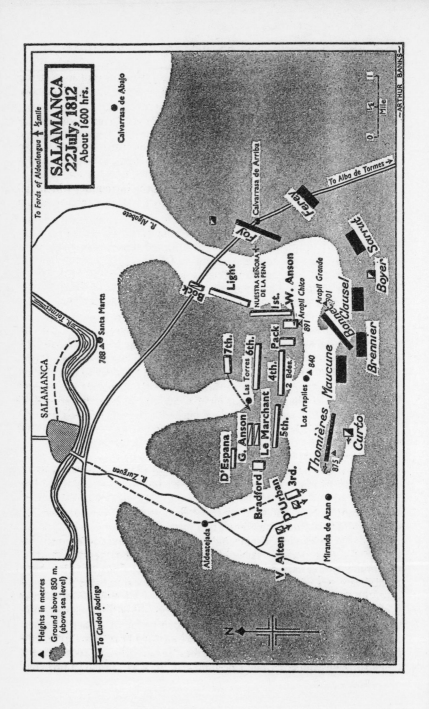

SALAMANCA
22 July, 1812
About 1600 hrs.

To Fords of Aldealengua ½ mile

Calvarrasa de Abajo

R. Argabete

To Alba de Tormes →

Calvarrasa de Arriba

Ferey

Foy

Sarrut

Light

Boyer

Bock

NUESTRA SEÑORA
DE LA PENA

L.W. Anson

1st.

Clausel

Arapil Grande

Bonne

891

Arapil Chico

901

Brennier

788 ▲ Santa Marta

7th.

6th.

Pack

4th.

Las Torres

2 Bdes.

Los Arapiles ● ▲ 840

Maucune

SALAMANCA

Thomières

G. Anson

Le Marchant

5th.

Curto

D'Espana

▲ 875

R. Zurguen

Bradford

D'Urban

3rd.

V. Alten

R. Tormes

To Ciudad Rodrigo

Aldeatejada

Miranda de Azan ●

N

▲ Heights in metres
Ground above 850 m.
(above sea level)

→ To Ciudad Rodrigo

Mile

0   ½   1

~ARTHUR BANKS~

overtaken, by an army which has not made the same sacrifices.' [7]

In any case there was no necessity to follow. Northern Portugal was clear of the enemy, Soult's corps had lost everything except its clothing and personal weapons and arrived in Spain without 4,000 of its men. The allied loss was about a tenth that of the French.

In the forcing of the Douro and the recapture of Oporto, Wellesley was greatly helped by the carelessness and over-confidence of Soult and the unaccountable behaviour of Loison, but this cannot detract from the greatness of his achievement or his genius in profiting from his opponents' errors. Soult's corps was out of the war for two months while it refitted and Wellesley had shown that the intrepidity which had won Assaye was not a characteristic only to be shown against Indian troops.

Salamanca, 22nd July, 1812

Later in 1809 Wellesley undertook the promised offensive operation in co-operation with Cuesta. He set out with high hopes. 'Portugal was safe, our army disposable, and [there was] every prospect that it was sufficiently strong, with the Spanish troops that had kept the French in check, to penetrate to Madrid at least.' [8] The movement which culminated at Talavera was, due to the incompetence of the Spaniards, almost a disaster. From that time, for 30 months, Wellington had to play a defensive rôle, regulating his movements by those of the French. It was a rôle that ill-matched his own inclinations. Watching Massena's army starve in front of Torres Vedras, he remarked longingly to his staff: 'I could lick those fellows any day, but it would cost me 10,000 men, and, as this is the last army England has got, we must take care of it.' [9]

Although on Massena's retreat in the spring of 1811 there were chances, notably at Foz do Arouce and Sabugal, for opportunist attacks which Wellington took and profited by as far as his fumbling subordinates permitted, it was not until the summer of 1812, with Ciudad Rodrigo and Badajoz firmly in his hands, that he was able to contemplate a major offensive movement.

The new move could not be conceived on the scale of the Talavera campaign, as an operation to drive the French back behind the Ebro. It must be a limited stroke aiming to destroy a single French army before it could be supported by any of the others. Wellington set out his intentions clearly in mid-May: 'I propose ... to move forward into Castille, and to endeavour, if possible, to bring Marmont to a general action.' [10]

This being his aim, it is strange that he seems to have neglected his first opportunity for doing so. By the night of 17th June Salamanca was in allied hands except for the three fortified convents which commanded the bridge over the Tormes. One division, the Sixth, was entrusted with the attack on these strong-points while the remainder of the army, 45,000 of all ranks and arms, British, Portuguese and Spanish, took up a strong position on the line of heights covering the north and east of the city. He was certainly right not to press further forward at this stage. His supply system was already sufficiently strained without pushing into the plains, while the only convenient bridge over the Tormes was controlled by the enemy. Three days later, however, he had an opportunity of inflicting a devastating defeat on the Army of Portugal without making an appreciable advance. Marmont advanced to the foot of the allied position with little more than 20,000 men. Wellington made no move. The temerity with which Marmont had advanced led him to believe that the French would encompass their own ruin by attacking him. He even left them in possession of the village of Morisco which a heavy French attack had wrested from a single British battalion after a short, hard struggle. For the moment he was counting on a French attack to give him a cheap and easy victory. 'I had a favourable opportunity of attacking the enemy, of which, however, I did not think it proper to avail myself ... [as] it was probable he had advanced with the intention to attack us, and in the position which we occupied, I considered it advantageous to be attacked: and that the action would be attended by less loss on our side.' [11] To a companion he remarked, 'Damn'd tempting', but he resisted the temptation.

Marmont clung to his exposed position for two days while most of his rear divisions closed up on him, bringing his strength up to more than 35,000 men. Still Wellington refused to be drawn, spending his days watching the French movements, sheltering from the sun under a blanket rigged up by men of the Forty-third. There was some long-range shelling. One evening when he was giving orders to some of his generals, 'several round shot came amongst them, and one close to Lord Wellington, he having a map in his hand. Very little confusion was occasioned—his Lordship moved a few paces, and continued his directions.' [12] Opinion among his officers was divided about what should be done. The French were a tempting target. They were inferior both in infantry and cavalry and, if they were forced to retreat, there was in their rear a vast plain in which a defeated army could be massacred by well-directed cavalry. 'Some people,' wrote a staff officer, 'say it is a pity Ld. Wn. did not attack him on the 20th before his reinforcements arrived, and when he was so near us. But I think Ld. Wn. knows what is right to do. He must to have attacked him given up the advantage of his position, and advanced along a plain a very great distance, without any cover exposed to a very heavy fire. He must have forced two villages, and his loss would be much greater than by waiting for the enemy, and a very great victory to his army would be almost a defeat.

For if this army gets crippled very much it cannot continue the operations.' [13] Right or wrong, Wellington decided not to attack. He may have lost, through overcaution, the chance of a resounding victory. In the event, his passivity led Marmont into an over-confidence which cost him his army a month later. Meanwhile the French Marshal, having vainly tried to turn the allied right across the Tormes, heard on 27th June that the Salamanca forts had fallen and retired the following day. By 1st July the armies faced each other across the Douro.

The position taken up by the Army of Portugal on the north bank of the Douro was an extremely strong one. The main bulk of the army was around Tordesillas with their left at Simancas, protected by the Pisguera river, and their right at Pollos. A detachment of, first one and later two, divisions was held at Toro. Marmont took care by constant movements along this road to leave his opponent in doubt as to the route by which he might attack. He was well sited for such deception since the Toro–Tordesillas road forms with the Douro, a triangle with its apex pointing south, so that, although French divisions could move from one flank to another by a good road 20 miles long, the British on the south bank would have to march almost twice as far by rough country tracks. To add to the strength of the position, the French had bridgeheads at both ends of the line and commanded most of the few fords. By 7th July Bonnet, with the division from the Asturias, had come up and the Army of Portugal reached its potential fighting strength of 49,000.

Wellington's first reaction to this situation was to attack. On 3rd July he sent a reconnaissance across the river at Pollos. 'I made our light infantry (the 60th) pass the Douro this day under the fire of our cannon, and I left them on the right of the river this afternoon, notwithstanding the enemy's fire. We had no body hurt. The enemy, about eight battalions, took post on a height about a mile or more from the river, there being a plain between them and the river I think we could have dislodged them; but it would have answered no purpose. The enemy are too near for us to keep the post, unless we should pass over the whole army; which it would not be desirable to do, unless we shall have found at least one more passage for infantry. I have heard of another at Castro Nuño, which I have sent officers to look at.' [14] He was not over-sanguine, even at this stage. While he was perfectly ready to put the campaign to the test of a general action if the conditions were anything like equal, it was obviously rash to attempt to attack an army which he reckoned as more powerful than his own across a wide river. To a staff officer who was returning to England, he said: 'I think you have seen the end of it. . . . I shan't fight him without an advantage, nor he me, I believe.' [15] Meanwhile bad news was coming to him in a steady stream. Graham and Picton, two of his best subordinates, had to return to England for their health. Intercepted messages told him that King Joseph had ordered troops from the Armies of the North, South and Aragon to Marmont's support. He had no news of the effectiveness of Home Popham's diversions on the north coast and his latest information of the proposed diversion against Suchet from Sicily was that Bentinck had decided to send his troops to Italy instead. The Army of Galicia, on which he had counted to disrupt Marmont's right, fumbled around Astorga and made no contribution to the deadlock on the Douro. The final blow was an intercepted message that King Joseph was marching to support Marmont with '19,000 men of whom 5,000 cavalry, but this account is much exaggerated, or many of the troops must be Spanish Juramentados.' [16]

On the north bank of the river, Marmont was in almost as much distress as Wellington on the south. He was convinced that the Army of the North would do nothing to help him and he was ignorant of Joseph's determination to support him. His own army was grumbling openly about his timidity and his last orders from Madrid had urged him to seek a battle. After a fortnight's stand on the Douro he made an elaborate and successful feint at Toro and attacked in strength at Tordesillas. Wellington, extricating himself from a very difficult position, fell steadily back and for some days the two armies moved southwest on parallel lines towards Salamanca, the French always having a slight advantage owing to their better marching power.

It was now the turn of the British to be despondent and to feel that their commander was acting timidly. By the night of 21st July the allied army was astride the river Tormes covering Salamanca on its eastern side, while the French advanced guard were across the same river at Huerta and in a position to continue their manoeuvre of turning the allied right as they had done for days past. The surgeon of the Fortieth wrote that evening: 'without fighting they have compelled us to retrograde all the way from the Douro to this place, and it even now is very doubtful whether we shall be able to maintain ourselves at Salamanca, as in the event of their continuing to move by their left, we must of necessity move parallel with them and uncover it. Events may yet turn out well, but at present I fear we have gained but little popularity by our irruption into the North of Spain.' [17]

Wellington's view was not dissimilar. 'The enemy's object hitherto has been to cut off my communication with Salamanca and Ciudad Rodrigo, the want of which he knows well would distress us very materially. The wheat harvest has not yet been reaped in Castille, and even if we had money, we could not procure any thing from the country, unless we should follow the example of the enemy, and lay waste whole districts, in order to procure a scanty subsistence of unripe wheat for the troops.

'It would answer no purpose to attempt to retaliate upon the enemy, even if it were practicable. The French armies have never any secure communication beyond the ground which they occupy; and provided the enemy opposed to them is not too strong for them, they are indifferent in respect to the quarter from which their operations are directed, or on which side they carry them on.

'I have therefore determined to cross the Tormes, if the enemy should; to cover Salamanca as long as I can; and above all, not to give up our communication with Ciudad Rodrigo; and not to fight an action, unless under very advantageous circumstances, or it should become absolutely necessary.' [18]

Here was one of the disadvantages under which Wellington always laboured in the Peninsula. The French army had no inhibitions about living off the country, indeed they were trained to do so. Such a course was impossible for the British, firstly because they were operating in a friendly country which could not be pillaged without sacrificing the very real advantages, especially in the supply of information, which Spanish support implied; secondly because the training and discipline of the British army was based on the assumption that regular rations would be supplied. If the plunder of the Spanish peasantry was authorised the army would become a disorderly mob, as they had shown signs of doing when rations were short on the retreat to Coruña and in the weeks following Talavera. Thus at any time it was open to the French to threaten the supply lines of the allies, while the allies could make no effective counter since there were no French supply lines to attack.

Dawn on 22nd July found the allies with their main body on the south bank of the Tormes, their leading division, the Fourth, holding the Lesser Arapile, a rocky knoll about 400 feet above river level and three miles south of the fords of Santa Maria. On the north bank there remained only the Third Division and a Portuguese cavalry brigade. The total strength was 51,000 men of all ranks, of which 30,000 were British (including Germans), 18,000 Portuguese, and the remainder Spaniards. There were 10 British and 2 Portuguese regiments of cavalry, 46 British, 37 Portuguese and 5 Spanish battalions, 48 British and 6 Portuguese guns.

A few miles to their front the French army, 25 squadrons and 73 battalions with 78 guns, in all 48,500 men, were pushing southward trying to turn the allied right as they had tried to do every day since they had crossed the Douro on 16th July. Wellington, basing himself on a captured return, over-estimated the French strength by about 3,000 men and knew as Marmont did not, that King Joseph was marching to Marmont's support with '10,000 to 12,000 men, with a large proportion of cavalry'.[19] He learned on the morning of the 22nd that 1,700 cavalry with 20 guns from the Army of the North had reached Pollos on 20th July and would join Marmont on either that day or the day following. It was, therefore, Wellington's last chance to attack with what seemed to be roughly equal numbers. He was still determined not to fight unless the circumstances gave reason to suppose that the French would be heavily defeated, but throughout the early part of the day he was in an aggressive mood which had been absent in the previous week.

The first fighting of the day took place when French skirmishers, protecting the march of their columns to the south, pushed in against the outposts of the Seventh Division which was covering the main road from Salamanca to the south-west, and was the only large body of allied troops in sight of the French, the remainder being hidden from view by a low ridge which ran from the river to the Lesser Arapile. It was not a very dangerous move, but Wellington reacted strongly, sending two battalions against them, and throughout the morning there was bickering around the chapel of Nuestra Señora de la Peña, the Light Division later relieving the Seventh in this sector. Not long afterwards it was realised that the Lesser Arapile was dominated by another knoll, the Greater Arapile, about 1,000 yards to the south. The importance of this had been underestimated by the commanders on the spot, Beresford and Cole, who had misjudged the distance in the dawn light. As soon as Wellington saw the situation he ordered a Portuguese battalion to seize the knoll. In this they were frustrated, as a French battalion reached the summit first. For a time Wellington determined to capture the height and ordered the First Division to form in the plain to the north of it, but caution prevailed and the division countermarched to the ridge. Opinion in the army attributed the change of plan to Marshal Beresford, but as one cavalry officer commented: 'Lord W. is so little influenced, or, indeed, allows any person to say a word, that his attending to the marshal was considered singular. From all I could collect and observe the peer was a little nervous.' [20]

It was now past midday and Wellington had brought the bulk of his troops to a position facing south along a ridge at right angles to his original position, which was held only by the First and Light Divisions, flanked on the north by a brigade of heavy cavalry. The Lesser Arapile was still held by a British brigade of Fourth Division and the remainder of that Division, with the Fifth, Sixth and Seventh Divisions, two Portuguese brigades, the Spanish troops and the bulk of the cavalry faced south. The Third Division, formerly the rearguard on the north bank of the Tormes, was marching through Salamanca to take its place on the right of the new east–west line. The baggage of the army, escorted by a regiment of Portuguese dragoons, had already set out on the road to Rodrigo. There was not a man in the allied army who did not believe that they would set out that evening for the Portuguese frontier.

No one held this belief more strongly than Marshal Marmont. The impression he had gained of Wellington in the last month, added to that which he retained from El Bodon the previous summer, was, as we have seen, that his opponent was a timid commander and one with whom he could take liberties. His information about the allied position and strength was slight. He could see the Light Division with their flanking cavalry opposite Nuestra Señora and William Anson's infantry brigade on the Lesser Arapile. To the west of them the light companies of the Guards held the village of Los Arapiles in the dip in front of the east–west ridge with about a division in support. All the other allied divisions were in dead ground and the clouds of dust raised by the baggage and the Third Division convinced him that apart from a rear-guard of two or three divisions the allied army was in retreat for Rodrigo. His aim was 'an advantageous rearguard action, in which, using my full force late in the day, with only a part of the British army left in front of me, I should probably score a point'.[21] On these false premises he decided to press his leading divisions westward along a ridge parallel with that occupied by the allies and to turn the right flank of what he took to be their rearguard. Three divisions were committed to this thrust, while three more remained on and behind the Greater Arapile and two stood on the original north–south alignment. At the best of times it would have been a dangerous move; as it was carried out it was disastrous. As the French divisions advanced along the ridge they became separated and there was much straggling within each division.

Wellington's staff was having a belated meal in a farm house on the ridge above Los Arapiles. 'While they were eating, [Wellington] rode into the enclosure; he refused to alight, and advised them to make haste; he seemed anxious and on the look-out. At last they persuaded him to take a bit of bread and the leg from a roast fowl, which he was eating without a knife from his fingers, when suddenly', said his Spanish liaison officer, 'they saw him throw the leg of the fowl far away over his shoulder, and gallop out of the yard calling on them to follow him. I knew that something *very serious* was about to happen when *an article so precious as the leg of a roast fowl* was thus thrown away.'[22] Wellington had seen that the French divisions were no longer within supporting distance of each other and that the chance for which he had waited so patiently had come. Marmont had made a mistake.

In the stretch between the Greater Arapile and the village of Miranda de Azan, a distance of less than three miles, were 14,000 French infantry and 1,700 cavalry, out of formation and with their horsemen riding on the safe, southerly side of the ridge. Throwing the Third Division with some light cavalry at their head and more than four divisions and two cavalry brigades at their flank, Wellington was able to bring 32,000 infantry and 2,000 cavalry against them. Wallace's brigade, leading the Third Division, was the first to engage. They struck at the head of Thomières' division which had led the French advance. Edward Pakenham, Wellington's brother-in-law, commanding the division in Picton's absence, led them on horseback up the end of the ridge, ordering them to change from column to line without halting and holding them back until they were within a few yards of the enemy and had sustained one heavy and regular volley without firing a shot in return. Then, 'seeing the proper moment had arrived, [he] called out to Wallace "to let them loose". The three regiments ran onward and [Thomières' division] which but a few minutes before was so formidable, loosened and fell in pieces before 1,500 of invincible British soldiers fighting in a line of only two deep.

'Wallace, seeing the terrible confusion that prevailed in the enemy's column, pressed on with the brigade, calling to his soldiers "to push home to the muzzle". A vast number were killed in this charge of bayonets, but the men, wearied by their exertions, the intolerable heat of the weather, and famishing from thirst, were nearly run to a standstill.' [23] Thomières' division was destroyed as a fighting force. Its commander and almost half its strength were casualties; it lost an eagle and the six guns of the divisional battery. The survivors fled eastward along the ridge to the cover of the supporting divisions, only to be caught up in an even heavier attack.

Against the divisions of Maucune and Brennier, which occupied the space between Thomières' division and that of Bonnet on the Greater Arapile, Wellington deployed four Anglo-Portuguese divisions. The first line consisted of the Fifth Division with the Fourth (less one brigade) on its left while the Sixth and Seventh formed the second line. A Portuguese brigade covered each flank of the main attack and Carlos de España's Spaniards were in support. Also on the right flank was Le Marchant's heavy cavalry brigade. As soon as Pakenham's division was launched against Thomières, Wellington rode to James Leith, commanding the Fifth Division. He gave him detailed instructions on the formation in which his troops should be drawn up: 'in two [two deep] lines, the first of which was composed of the Royal, 9th and 38th regiments, with part of the 4th regiment, from General Pringle's brigade, necessarily brought forward for the purpose of equalising the lines, of which the second was formed by the remainder of General Pringle's brigade, and the whole of General Spry's Portuguese infantry.

'Lord Wellington on this, as on all occasions, gave his orders in a clear concise and spirited manner; there was no appearance of contemplating a doubtful result; all he directed was as to time and formation, and his instructions concluded with commands that the enemy should be overthrown and driven from the field. He then proceeded towards the 4th division.' [24]

There was some delay while Bradford's Portuguese brigade came up to its place on the right of Leith and then the whole line went forward. 'Occasionally every soldier was visible, the sun shining bright upon their arms, while at intervals all were enveloped in a dense cloud of dust, from whence at times, issued the animating cheer of British infantry.' [25] On the left there was more delay as the Fourth Division (Lowry Cole) had to file through the village of Arapiles and re-form line on the south side.

In consequence, the Fifth Division was the first in action. The slope up which they were advancing was crowned by French artillery and the divisions' light companies had to clear away a swarm of *tirailleurs*. The main body of Maucune's division was beyond the crest and only became visible to the advancing British as they topped the rise. The French were 'drawn up in contiguous squares, the front rank kneeling, and prepared to fire when the drum beat for its commencement. All was still and quiet in these squares—not a musket was discharged until the whole opened. Nearly at the same moment General Leith ordered the line to fire and charge. . . . In an instant every individual present was enveloped in smoke and obscurity. No struggle for ascendancy took place; the French squares were penetrated, broken and discomfited; the victorious division pressed forward, not against troops opposed, but a mass of disorganised men, flying in all directions.' [26]

As Maucune's division broke, adding to the fugitives already streaming in from Thomières' division on their left, Stapleton Cotton sent in Le Marchant's heavy cavalry brigade. He had Wellington's order to 'charge in at all hazards' and he chose his moment to a nicety. Twelve hundred 'big men on big horses',[27] with heavy sabres, 35 inches in the blade, galloped in from over the right shoulder of Leith's men, the Third Division opening their ranks to let them through. The mass of broken infantry was the answer to a cavalryman's prayers. The Dragoons knew exactly what to do. Their commander was the author of the *Rules and Regulations for the Sword Exercise*. 'A person on horseback is elevated so much above those acting on foot, that it is necessary for him to bend the elbow, in order to take a sweep to give his cut with effect: and this may be securely done, as the sword arm is not exposed in the contest [with infantry]. . . . It should be remembered that little force is requisite to produce effect from the application of the edge, if conducted with skill. . . . No cut can be made with effect or security where the weapon does not free itself at once from the object to which it is applied; otherwise it must turn in the hand, and give a contusion rather than a cut; for which reason those wounds are most severe, which are made nearest to the point.' [28]

The Dragoons made three attacks, losing their commander and more than 100 men, but, by the time they had galloped themselves to a standstill the whole French left was broken. Clausel, who succeeded to command of the French when Marmont was wounded, made a gallant attempt to counter-attack with troops from his centre when the excusable failure of Pack's Portuguese to storm the Greater Arapile exposed the left of the Fourth Division, but the quick-wittedness of

Beresford and the irresistible forward march of the Sixth Division from the second line swept the French away.

'There was no mistake,' wrote Wellington, 'everything went on as it ought; and there never was an army beaten in so short a time. If we had another hour of daylight, not a man would have passed the Tormes.' [29] As it was, he led forward the Light and First Divisions from his left wing to cut the French off from the ford of Huerta. The pursuit continued until half past twelve at night [30] but found nothing. The drive on Huerta had been ordered on the assumption that the bridge at Alba de Tormes and the castle which commanded it were safely in the hands of the Spaniards but, as usual, the Spaniards were not where they were supposed to be. 'They would all have been taken if Carlos de España had left the garrison at Alba de Tormes as I wished and desired; or having taken it away, as I believe, before he was aware of my wishes, he would have informed me it was not there. If he had I should have marched in the night upon Alba, where I should have caught them all.' [31]

Next morning the pursuit was pressed in the right direction and the advanced guard of cavalry coming up with the French rearguard at Garcia Hernandez scored one of the most remarkable triumphs of the war. The French troops consisted of Foy's division, the only infantry which had escaped devastating loss on the previous day, and a brigade of *chasseurs*. The allied advanced guard consisted only of five cavalry regiments, but they had Wellington's orders to press on. Four squadrons of Light Dragoons drove away the *chasseurs* 'which fled, leaving the infantry to their fate',[32] and Bock led the two regiments of Heavy Dragoons of the King's German Legion against Foy's infantry drawn up in squares. For the only time in the Peninsula steady infantry, properly in formation, were ridden down by cavalry. Three battalions were broken. The French suffered 1,100 casualties against 127 to the Germans.

Salamanca decided the Peninsular War. There were many battles and some dangerous days still to come, but by his sudden, unpremeditated attack Wellington established a moral ascendancy over the French which he never subsequently lost, even when, having entered Madrid as a conquering hero and laid siege to Burgos, he had, apparently ignominiously, to retreat to the Portuguese frontier in November of the same year. Foy, the most competent and, in the Peninsula, the most experienced of the French divisional commanders, confided to his diary that it raised Wellington to the level of Marlborough. Marlborough had been a sinister figure in French military history, a man whom even Napoleon admitted to have been one of the great commanders of all time. Wellington, himself, remarked in his modest way: 'I do not believe that there are many soldiers who were in that action who are likely to face us again till they shall be very largely reinforced indeed.' [33]

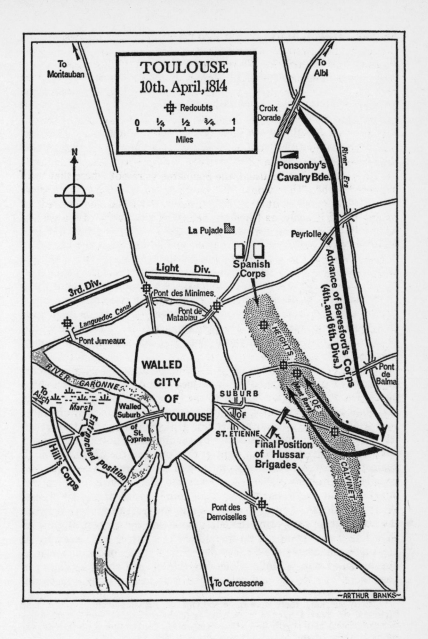

TOULOUSE
10th. April, 1814

⊞ Redoubts

0   ¼   ½   ¾   1

Miles

N

To Montauban

To Albi

Croix Dorade

Ponsonby's Cavalry Bde.

River Ers

La Pujade

Peyriolle

Light   Div.

Spanish Corps

3rd. Div.

Pont des Minimes

Advance of Beresford's Corps (4th. and 6th. Divs.)

Languedoc Canal

Pont de Matablau

Pont Jumeaux

HEIGHTS

Pont de Balma

RIVER GARONNE

WALLED CITY OF TOULOUSE

SUBURB

To Auch

Marsh

Walled Suburb of St. Cyprien

OF

Entrenched position

ST. ETIENNE

Mont Rave

OF

Hill's Corps

Final Position of Hussar Brigades

CALVINET

Pont des Demoiselles

To Carcassone

~ARTHUR BANKS~

By mid-November 1813 the allied army was established in France, although penned in the triangle formed by the Pyrenees, the river Nive and the Bay of Biscay. The French army had, under Soult's leadership, regained something of its old dash and skill only to be repulsed by the British at Sorauren and the Spaniards at Sán Marcial. Since then they had suffered defeats on the lines of the Bidassoa and the Nivelle and had relinquished the line of the Pyrenees, the finest natural defensive barrier in Europe.

From that time forward Wellington treated Soult and his men with something approaching contempt. The weather, which made the roads impassable, was almost as formidable an adversary as the Duke of Dalmatia. As soon as it cleared sufficiently, Wellington did not hesitate to divide his army by passing Hill's corps across the river Nive (9th December), although he knew that he was giving Soult the chance to attack either part in greatly superior strength. In the previous year he had written to a timorous general that 'His Majesty and the public have a right to expect of us that we should place a reasonable confidence in the gallantry and discipline of the troops under our command and I have the satisfaction of reflecting that, having tried them frequently, they have never failed me.' [34] The performance of Hill's two divisions at St. Pierre on 13th December was a more than adequate confirmation of his belief.

At Orthez (27th February 1814), Wellington attacked with such confidence that, early in the battle, it seemed that he might suffer a sharp check. His numbers were inferior to the French, 33,000 against 37,000, and Soult held a very strong position except that his left was vulnerable to a wide flanking movement. Sending Hill's corps to turn the French left, Wellington opened the battle by sending the Fourth and Seventh Divisions against the French right at St. Boes and the Third and Sixth against the centre. Both attacks failed and the Fourth Division suffered heavily. The only available reserve was the Light Division, which was much under strength, having two of its four* British battalions absent. Wellington does not seem to have been in the least dismayed. Between the French troops opposing the left column and the nearest support on their left, a re-entrant ran up the hill. To reach it, it was necessary to cross a marsh. Seeing the commander of the Fifty-second riding near to him he called out, ' "Hollo, Colborne, ride on and see if artillery can pass there." I rode on, and galloped back as fast as I could and said,

---

* Strictly speaking, there were three and two half British battalions in the Light Divisions, viz. 1/43rd, 1/52nd, 1/95th Rifles (eight companies) and 2/95th Rifles (six companies) and 3/95th Rifles (five companies). On the day of Orthez 1/43rd and 1/95th were absent collecting new clothing.

"Yes, anything can pass!" "Well, then, make haste, take your regiment on and deploy into the plain. I leave it to your disposition." ' [35] The Fifty-second marched in column down the forward slope, deployed into line on the level ground, and advanced. 'They did it beautifully', recalled their colonel. 'The French were keeping up a heavy fire, but fortunately all the balls passed over our heads. . . . Though the men were over their knees in the marsh they trotted up in the finest order.' [36] Simultaneously the Third Division renewed their attack to the right of the Fifty-second and Hill's turning movement began to take effect on the extreme right. Soult's army broke and fled in disorder.

The final act took place on Easter Sunday, 10th April 1814. Soult had led his entire field army, 42,000 men, into the defensive works surrounding Toulouse. Against this Wellington could bring 45,000 infantry, of which 15,000 were Spaniards, and rather less than 5,000 cavalry. 'The town of Toulouse', wrote the Quartermaster-General, 'and its environs present a position of very great military strength, in which the assailant has numerous important obstacles to overcome. This is especially the case when it is approached, as it was by the allied army in 1814, from the south west for, the town being situated on the eastern side of the Garonne, that broad and rapid river is to be passed before it can be attacked. But as the Garonne forms at Toulouse a re-entrant angle with respect to an enemy on the left bank, the suburb of St. Cyprien, which is opposite to the town in that re-entering angle, forms a *tête-de-pont* most advantageously situated for covering the stone bridge and renders Toulouse quite unassailable in that direction. Neither could an attempt to force the passage of the river against a strong and vigilant enemy be made with any prospect of success.' [37] It was clear, therefore, that any attack on Toulouse must be made from the east bank. Here the problem was scarcely less difficult, for the Languedoc Canal (Canal du Midi) covered the north and west faces of the town, being quite unfordable and having only six bridges, all of them defended by substantial works. Moreover, an approach from the south, the only face not covered by a water obstacle, was not available to Wellington since he had omitted to bring forward sufficient pontoons to bridge both the Garonne and the river Ariege, which joins it about eight miles south of the town. Given that the St. Cyprien bridgehead was unassailable, Wellington had no option but to put his striking force across the Garonne below Toulouse (i.e. to the north) and attack from the north and east. On this side, to the east of the Languedoc Canal, there is a long height known as the Mont Rave or Heights of Calvinet. If this hill could be secured, Toulouse would be at the mercy of the allied artillery and would quickly become untenable. Recognising this, Soult had crowned the Mont Rave with redoubts and fortified buildings and had detailed four of his seven divisions to its defence. Two more covered the northern approaches and one only occupied St. Cyprien on the western bank of the Garonne.

A further water obstacle, the river Ers, confined any attempt to attack Mont Rave from the east. This river, unfordable and with few and narrow bridges, ran north and south, parallel to the heights. 'The country beyond the Ers had', wrote Wellington, 'been reconnoitred, and it was found impossible to manoeuvre on it, for the purpose of repairing or forming new bridges, with a view to the passage of that river. It was necessary to march between Mont Calvinet and the river Ers, the distance not being greater from the works upon the summit anywhere than 2,000 yards, diminishing to 1,000 yards, and in some places to 500 yards. The distance to be marched was not less than 2 miles under the fire of the enemy's position.' [38]

The implementation of this hazardous march across the enemy's front was entrusted to Marshal Beresford with the Fourth and Sixth Anglo-Portuguese Divisions, the Hussar* Brigade being attached to cover their southern flank. A further Hussar Brigade (18th British and 1st German) under Major von Gruben, was ordered to move down the east bank of the Ers, clear away any French piquets, cross the canal where it could and operate on the southern flank of the Hussar brigade. Beresford was given discretion to choose the moment for turning the column to the right and assail the heights. Their object was 'the right of the enemy's position'. Timed to coincide with Beresford's attack, 10,000 Spaniards under General Manuel Freyre were to assail the northern end of the height. Freyre's instructions are an interesting example of the difficulties of giving orders at a time when detailed maps were not available. 'On arriving at Croix Dorade, General Freyre will form his troops into two columns. The right column, keeping to the right of the Albi road, will advance to an alley of cypress trees, which there is between that road and La Pujade. The left Spanish column will enter the Albi road near the church of Croix Dorade, and it will thence move forward of a height which there is to the left of that road, nearly in line with the alley of cypress trees already mentioned.' [39] On the right of the Spaniards the Light and Third Divisions were to threaten the bridges over the Languedoc Canal on the north side of Toulouse. 'The operations of these two divisions are meant, however, more as diversions than as real attacks, it not being expected that they will be able to force any of the passes of the canal.' [40] Hill's corps (2nd Anglo-Portuguese, Le Cor's Portuguese and Morillo's Spanish divisions) was to demonstrate against the St. Cyprien bridgehead.

It was an extremely daring plan, but the only one that could have succeeded. The Anglo-Portuguese army was divided into three separate portions each of two divisions. Hill's corps was separated from the Third and Light by the Garonne. They, in their turn, were separated

* Seventh, Tenth, Fifteenth Hussars under Lord Edward Somerset.

from Beresford's corps by a large body of Spaniards of doubtful reliability and, increasingly, by distance. In reserve, behind the Spaniards Wellington could spare only a brigade of heavy cavalry and some Portuguese nine-pounders. Worst of all, Wellington, for the first time in all his attacks, had to leave command of the main stroke in the hands of another. It was clear that his own place must be near the Spaniards and that the whole conduct of the flank march must be left to Beresford.

The cavalry opened the battle by clearing away Soult's piquets, especially good work being done by the German hussars, who swept down the east bank of the Ers, driving two French regiments before them with such speed that although the French managed to blow the bridge at Balma, directly to the east of Toulouse, they were forestalled at the bridge at Revel, nearly three miles farther south. At about the same time Hill and Picton opened their diversionary attacks, Hill's corps actually mastering the outer defences of St. Cyprien, although wisely abstaining from attacking the forbidding main line. Meanwhile Beresford's corps, the Hussars leading, followed by the Fourth and Sixth Divisions 'in three parallel columns of lines by brigades, in the common order of march, sections of three in front',[41] with their light companies deployed to cover their exposed flank, started to march south. They did not suffer as much on this two-mile march as might have been expected as most of the French shot passed over their heads and fell either in or over the river.

Hardly had they reached their station opposite the south end of Mont Rave than General Freyre launched his Spaniards at the northern end of the hill. 'Although a full half a mile from the enemy', wrote an officer in the Light Division on their right, 'they started in double quick time. "This", we said, "won't last long." They, however, drove the French from some entrenchments on the side of the hill, and continued to ascend until they reached a high-road, which, being cut out of the side of the hill, afforded them shelter from the fire of the enemy. Here they came to a halt; and not all the endeavours of their officers, many of whom set a gallant example, could make them move a step further; the French, perceiving this, after a little time sent down a strong body of *voltigeurs* who, firing right among the Spaniards, sent them headlong down the hill. Our division immediately formed line, and the Spaniards, passing through the intervals, rallied in our rear. They were much mortified at their defeat, and bore rather sulkily the taunts of our Portuguese, who were not sorry to have a wipe at their neighbours.'[42] Following this repulse, and on his own initiative, Picton turned the Third Division's diversion into a serious attack on the canal defences and suffered 300 unnecessary casualties. Wellington was thus left with no reserve to cover a repulse except the Light Division and the heavy cavalry, while Soult was able to bring his reserve division to reinforce the two already opposed to Beresford on the southern end of the hill.

Beresford's column found it more difficult than they had expected to turn to their right and deploy, having between their line of advance and the foot of the hill 'a wet ditch and a marshy meadow. . . . We ran along the bank until we came to a place where we could leap the ditch and formed on the swampy ground beyond it,' said a sergeant of the Black Watch. 'We had scarcely formed when a strong column of the enemy, with drums beating a march, descended the hill in our front, and thinking from the nature of the ground that we should neither be able to advance or retreat, rushed down confident of success. For us to retire would have been scarcely practicable; the bank from which we had leaped down was too high in several places to leap back from such uncertain footing, for we were sinking to the ankles, and sometimes deeper at every step; to advance was the only alternative, and it was taken.

'The light companies of the division were by this time in our front, and without any hesitation dashed forward; we followed fast, and the opposing column reascended the hill, and left us the undisputed masters of the valley.' [43]

The French who had given way were from Taupin's division and seem to have lost heart when their commander was killed and when they received amongst their close-packed ranks a few rockets, a weapon which few of them can have seen before. The two divisions then forced their way to the crest of the hill without too much difficulty although threatened by cavalry on their left. It was when they reached the crest that their troubles began. 'Here we were exposed to a destructive fire of round shot, shell grape, and musketry, while we had not as yet got one gun up, owing to the numerous obstructions that lay in the way. . . . The light companies advanced, and maintained a very unequal skirmish with the enemy, who lay securely posted behind their breastworks and batteries, and in the redoubts, from all of which they took the most deadly aim.' [44] One redoubt was captured by an impetuous charge of the Sixty-first who presented so fearsome an appearance that the garrison took to its heels at their approach, but Beresford wisely declined to advance further until his gunners, with infinite labour, had got their pieces up the hill.

During the pause which ensued the Spaniards essayed a second attack, although this time they avoided the direct assault up the north end of the heights, 'and got between them and the canal, where they suffered from a cross fire. As might have been expected, they came tumbling back.[45] Lord Wellington said to Pakenham,* "There I am, with nothing between me and the enemy!" Pakenham said, "Well, I suppose you'll order up the Light Division now," and he replied, "I'll be hanged if I do!" ' [46]

Eventually Beresford's artillery was in position and he ordered a

* Sir Edward Pakenham, Adjutant-General and Wellington's brother-in-law.

further advance northward, covering his left flank with two brigades of cavalry and the Portuguese brigade of Fourth Division. It was a trying and dangerous advance against a heavy fire of musketry and cannon. 'The field had been lately roughly ploughed or under fallow, and when a man fell he tripped the one behind, thus the ranks were opening as we approached the point whence all this hostile vengeance proceeded; but the rush forward had received an impulse from desperation. . . . In a minute every obstacle was surmounted; the enemy fled as we leaped over the trenches and mounds like a pack of noisy hounds in pursuit, frightening them more with our wild hurrahs than actually hurting them by ball or bayonet.' [47] This determined advance by the Sixth Division succeeded in storming the two redoubts in the centre of Mont Calvinet, but almost immediately the French recaptured both of them, counter-attacking in great strength before the Forty-second and Seventy-ninth could consolidate their position. The Highlanders tried to regain possession, but were repulsed, and it was not until the other British brigade of Sixth Division was thrown in that the centre of the ridge was consolidated.

It was now four o'clock and another pause to reorganise was imperative. The Sixth Division was almost worn out. The Forty-second had lost 26 officers and 386 men and had its colours carried by sergeants, all the subalterns being casualties. The Seventy-ninth had scarcely 250 men on their feet. The Sixty-first was commanded by the adjutant. It was essential to bring the Fourth Division through the Sixth to carry out the final assault, the attack on the French redoubt at the northern end of the ridge which the Spaniards had once more failed to storm.

The last attack never took place. At about five o'clock Soult admitted defeat by withdrawing his troops from the northern redoubt, a retreat they were, perforce, allowed to carry on without interference. By nightfall the whole of Mont Rave was in allied hands and Toulouse would be at their mercy as soon as heavy guns could be got on to the summit. The victory had cost the allies more than 4,000 casualties, twice the cost to the French. But, despite all the efforts of French historians to prove, from the repulse of the Spaniards, that the day was a defeat for Wellington, Toulouse was a great victory. Wellington's intention had been to gain Mont Calvinet. By evening he was firmly established upon it. By dawn on the second day following, Soult had evacuated Toulouse, marching to the south for Carcassonne. He knew it would be disastrous to attempt to retain the town with the allies in a position to dominate it. That evening news was received that the war was over.

Toulouse was the messiest of Wellington's attacking battles. In no other were so many mistakes made. Wellington was set a particularly difficult problem by the topography of the place. The solution he devised was the only one that could have succeeded and it worked. It entailed, however, leaving far too much to the initiative of others, and although Beresford carried out his difficult task to perfection, the antics of Picton and the unreliability of the Spaniards brought the whole battle nearer to a defeat than Wellington had been since the Native Infantry broke at Argaum. It may be said that he would have been wiser and safer to use the Third and Light Divisions to storm the end of the hill, leaving the Spaniards to carry out the diversion on the north face of the town, but it was on those two divisions, the best in his army, that he counted as a reserve in case of a repulse. It would never have answered to have British troops retreating on to Spaniards. He had done much to bring on the morale of the Spaniards and had forced them to win a defensive victory at San Marcial in the previous year, but to expect them to cover a British repulse would have been asking too much, not only of the Spaniards but of the British and Portuguese. As it was he took a chance, in response to repeated requests from the Spanish generals, by allowing them to try to gain an offensive victory. The gamble failed—but Wellington was never averse to taking a chance.

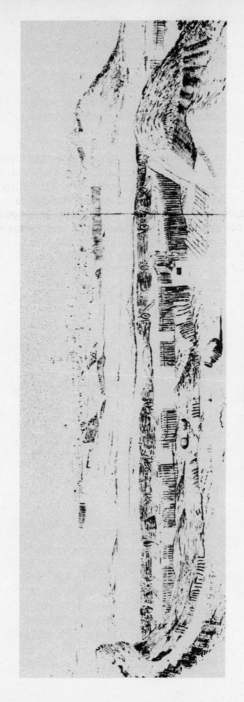

9 The breaches at Badajoz from the Battery in the Gorge of the Picurina Fort
From a drawing by Major John May, April 1812

10 (overleaf) The Battle of the Pyrenees-Sorauren 28th July 1813
From the painting by I. M. Wright (etched by H. Moses,
aquatinted by F. C. Lewis), 1814

11 Lieutenant-General Sir Hew Dalrymple Bt.
From a painting by J. Jackson (Engraved by C. Turner), 1829

12a Lieutenant-General Sir
Edward Paget
From a portrait by
Robert Home, c. 1828

12b Lieutenant-General Sir
Rowland Hill (1st Lord
Hill)
From a water-colour by
George Richmond c.1834

13 Lieutenant-General Henry Paget, Earl of Uxbridge (later Marquis of Angelsea)
From a portrait by Sir William Beechey, c. 1817

14a Marshal Sir William Carr
Beresford
From a study for a painting
by Thomas Heaphy, 1813

14b Lieutenant-Colonel
Sir Richard Fletcher, Bt.,
Royal Engineers
From a portrait attributed
to J. Barwell, c. 1813

15a Lieutenant-General Sir Thomas
Graham, Lord Lyndedoch
From a portrait by Sir Thomas
Lawrence c. 1816

15b Lieutenant-General Sir Stapleton
Cotton, Lord Combermere
From a portrait by Sir William Ross

CHAPTER SEVEN

THE PENINSULA—DEFENSIVE

> I could lick those fellows any day, but it would cost me 10,000 men, and as this is the last army England has, we must take care of it.
>
> *Wellington at Torres Vedras, 1810*

Historians have tended to assume that Wellington's genius for defence lay in his ability to choose a defensive position—one with secure flanks and in which the main line of battle could be concealed in dead ground until the enemy were within range of the devastating volleys which were the pride and most effective counter-blow of the British infantry. To this they add his insistence on covering his position with a heavy screen of skirmishers* which held off the French *tirailleurs* and harassed their columns of attack until they came within range of the main line.

All this is true, but it is only a part of the story. So effective was his choice of ground in the early days of the Peninsular War that, after Vimeiro, Talavera † and Busaco, the French commanders declined to attempt to break through a British line in a position of Wellington's choosing. By the spring of 1811 Wellington could write: 'really these attacks in column against our line are very contemptible',[1] and at the same time his French opponents came to the same conclusion. From then onwards they either declined to attack Wellington at all (*cf.* the Elvas position in June 1811) or attempted to move against his flank (*cf.* Fuentes de Oñoro). The only exceptions were Soult's frontal attacks at Sorauren, when he was desperate for time, and at St. Pierre, when both the British flanks were secured on rivers. Soult seems to have learned his lesson and, on the morning of Waterloo, he cautioned the Emperor against a frontal attack, only to receive an insulting reply.

The real tests of Wellington's defensive abilities are the occasions

* The number of men trained for skirmishing amounted to about one-fifth of the strength of each division. As an example, the Fifth Division in May 1811 had a total strength of 5,158 all ranks. Of these there were 1,070 trained skirmishers, made up of a battalion of Cacadores (484), two companies of Brunswick Oels (69 and 68), six British light companies (*c.* 320) and four Portuguese light companies (*c.* 130).

† At Talavera the shape of the ground made it impossible to find a reverse slope position for the Guards and K.G.L. brigades, who were in consequence much exposed to artillery fire before the French attack.

when his opponents did not give him the opportunity to pick a position
and settle his army into it. It is intended, therefore, to examine two such
occasions, Fuentes de Oñoro and the Pyrenees.

Fuentes de Oñoro, 3rd–5th May, 1811

The morale of the Anglo-Portuguese army was high in the spring of
1811. They had liberated Portugal in the face of a numerically superior
army which had suffered, by battle, disease and desertion, 25,000
casualties. In their last two engagements, at Foz do Arouce and Sabugal,
they had defeated the French almost with ignominy. By the end of April
the ration situation, which a month earlier had been badly strained,
was restored. The army looked forward to a short period of rest, confident that they could thrash the French any time they attacked.

Wellington's immediate task was the blockade of Almeida, which he
believed, wrongly, to be 'ill supplied with provisions'.[2] To this object
he allocated the Sixth Division and Pack's Portuguese brigade. As a
covering force the cavalry and the Light Division watched the line of
the Agueda with the Fifth Division in support. The remainder of the
army, three divisions and an independent brigade, was billeted to the
south around Fuentes de Oñoro. The total strength available was not
very great, less than 40,000 men, since 20,000 more were detached
under Beresford in Estremadura in an attempt to recapture Badajoz.
The chief weakness was in cavalry. There were only four British regiments, of which only one had more than 400 sabres, and two Portuguese units so weak that their combined strength was only 300. With
four British and four Portuguese batteries, 48 guns could be put in the
field.

Massena had taken the Army of Portugal back to Salamanca. With
42,000 infantry and 3,000 cavalry, it was strong in numbers but very
weak in wagons and draught animals, while its morale left much to be
desired. In mid-April, therefore, Wellington was not in any apprehension that they would come back at him. Writing that 'I do not think the
enemy have the means or inclination to interrupt [the blockade]',[3] he
set out to visit Beresford near Badajoz, intending to be away from the
main army for not more than three weeks.[4] Meanwhile, the command
in the north was left with Sir Brent Spencer, a choice dictated by Sir
Brent's seniority rather than his merits, and one which caused some
consternation in the army. He was, wrote a brigade commander, 'as
good a fellow as possible to meet at a country club, but as to succeeding
Wellington it is damnation to him'.[5]

Wellington set out for the south on 15th April and reached Elvas on
the 20th. Hardly had he gone when there was a flurry of activity on the
line of the Agueda while the French garrison of Ciudad Rodrigo was
revictualled and made some reconnaissances. There was skirmishing on

16th and 22nd April and Wellington curtailed his stay in the south to one of four days. He reached his headquarters again on the 28th. By that time the French were obviously on the move. On the following day Massena, who had some reinforcements from Marshal Bessières and the Army of the North, had concentrated at Rodrigo a force of 48,000 men, consisting of four corps of infantry amounting to 42,000 infantry, 4,500 cavalry and 38 guns. On the 30th April Wellington gave out his preliminary order to oppose an attempt to relieve Almeida. The blockade was to be maintained by Pack's brigade of Portuguese strengthened with a single British battalion. The remainder of the army, 34,000 infantry, 1,500 cavalry and 48 guns were to take up a line between two rivulets, the Dos Casas and the Turones, which flow north and south about two miles apart. Both streams run in gorges, which, north of the main road from Rodrigo to Almeida, are impassable to formed bodies of troops. South of that road the banks, especially of the more easterly, the Dos Casas, are still steep and there is between them a splendid defensive position where the watershed between them forms the Spanish-Portuguese frontier. The rise in the floor of the Dos Casas valley reduces the value of this position towards the south. Near Alameda, in the north, the climb from the stream to the crest about a mile to the west is some 400 feet. At Fuentes de Oñoro, eight miles to the south, the rise is only 140 feet, but the ground is still formidable. South of Fuentes there is a gap of five miles to Nave de Haver, beyond which there is the broken ground of the foothills of the Sierra de Gata. The five-mile gap was for the most part passable for formed bodies of troops although it was partially broken by woods and marshes.

Knowing that Massena's army was in no state to embark on another full-scale invasion of Portugal, it was clear to Wellington that the concentration of troops at Ciudad Rodrigo must be intended only for a limited operation and there was no doubt that the operation intended was to raise the blockade of Almeida. His intention was equally precise. On 1st May he reported to London: 'I do not intend to allow them to relieve this place, unless I should be convinced that they have such a superiority of force as to render the result of a contest for this point doubtful. The enemy may be stronger than they were when they were obliged to evacuate Portugal, and they may be reinforced by detachments of troops, particularly the Guards, under the command of Marshal Bessières; but I still feel confident that they have it not in their power to defeat the allied army in a general action; and I hope to prevent them relieving this place, unless they should bring the contest to that issue in a situation unfavourable to us.' [6]

Wellington was equally certain where the blow would fall. In mid-April he had written: 'It is probable that they will move their whole army, or the greatest part of it, upon Ciudad Rodrigo from whence they would turn the heads of the ravines of the . . . Dos Casas and

143

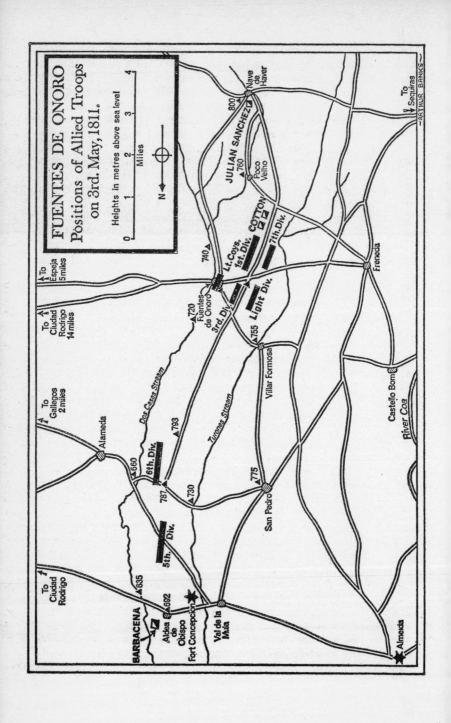

Turon[es].' [7] His warning orders issued on 30th April arranged for the army to occupy the 13-mile line between Fort Concepcion and Nave de Haver, although 'the body of the army will be drawn towards the left'.[8]

Having left a force to continue the blockade of Almeida, there were 37,500 men, including six infantry divisions, available to hold the line. Two points had especially to be guarded. On the northern end of the line the two roads from Rodrigo to Almeida, the road by which if the French were to succeed they must bring their supply wagons, must be blocked. The rest of the army must be prepared to defend the heads of the ravines of the Dos Casas and Turones rivers. Wellington, therefore, allocated two divisions, the Fifth and Sixth, to guard the northern end of the line, with Barbacena's 300 Portuguese horse as a flank guard, and directed that the remaining four divisions with the British cavalry should take post around the heads of the ravines. Between the two wings of the army there was a gap of four miles, but it was a reasonable assumption that the French, with their memories of Busaco, would not attempt to attack across the steep rocky ravine of the Dos Casas. No troops were allocated to hold the gap between Fuentes and Nave de Haver, but in the latter village the mounted Guerrilla of Don Julian Sanchez was stationed in observation.

The French army began to move out of Ciudad Rodrigo on the morning of 2nd May. One column marched in the direction of the allied left wing, the other towards Fuentes de Oñoro. The allied covering force, consisting of the British cavalry and the Light Division under Sir Stapleton Cotton, which had orders not to dispute the country in front of the Dos Casas, fell back before them 'without firing a shot' [9] and by nightfall occupied the villages of Gallegos and Espeja. Next morning the French advance continued until the line of the Dos Casas was reached, and Cotton's force took their place among the rest of the allied army, already in their positions.

Wellington had divided the four divisions available to him into two bodies. The two strongest divisions, the First (7,565 all ranks) and the Third (5,480), together with Ashworth's Portuguese brigade (2,539) were formed into a corps under Sir Brent Spencer* and to them was assigned the task of defending Fuentes de Oñoro and the ridge behind it. The two remaining divisions, the Seventh (4,590) and the Light (3,815), were held in reserve under Wellington's own direction ready to be moved 'to the direction which the enemy appears to give to the principal part of his force'.

The village of Fuentes is built on the slopes of two parallel spurs which run out from the main ridge towards the Dos Casas. The northern

* Nightingall MS letter of 9th May 1811: 'as Sir Brent Spencer commanded the two divisions in line (1st and 3rd), the 1st was placed under my immediate command'. Major-General Nightingall was the senior brigade commander in the First Division.

spur is crowned with the village church and the southern by a Calvary. Both are about 500 yards back from the stream and about 60 feet higher. The village is built of granite, is full of winding streets and is intersected in every direction by walls of the same material.[10] While the main body of Spencer's corps was held at the crest of the ridge, nearly a mile behind the church, the village itself was occupied by a strong body of picked troops, the light companies of Spencer's corps (less the Guards)* under Lieutenant-Colonel Williams of the Sixtieth supported by a weak battalion, the Eighty-third, from the Third Division. In all, the garrison was about 2,500 strong. In the flatter country to the south of the village, Sir Stapleton Cotton deployed his four British cavalry regiments as a flank guard.

Massena's army was still in the two columns in which it had left Rodrigo. In the north were the corps of Reynier and Junot, 16,000 men, and to the south were those of Loison and D'Erlon with the reserve cavalry of the Army of Portugal, together with the two cavalry brigades which Bessières had brought from the Army of the North, making up a mass of more than 30,000 of which 3,500 were cavalry. Thus at both ends of the front the French had a clear numerical advantage: 16,000 to 11,000 at the north and 30,000 to 15,000 opposite Fuentes. With a most cursory reconnaissance, reminiscent of his negligence at Busaco, Massena ordered a demonstration on his right and an immediate assault by Loison's corps on the village of Fuentes.

The feint in the north looked, at one time, sufficiently threatening for the Light Division to be detached in that direction, although its services were not required. The assault on the village was more serious. The attack was entrusted to Ferey's division, whose leading brigade charged across the stream and established itself in the lower houses. Colonel Williams counter-attacked and drove them back to the water, but before the allies could be reformed Ferey threw in the rest of his division and drove the defenders back to the upper outskirts around the church. The disorganisation of the light companies was increased by the use in the attack of a battalion of the French *Légion Hanovérienne* which, being dressed in red coats, 'was at first taken for a British regiment, and they had time to form up and give us a volley before the mistake was discovered'.[11] This setback was partially compensated when the French artillery, making the same mistake, opened fire on their Hanoverian allies, but, with Colonel Williams seriously wounded, the position was critical. Wellington, therefore, 'being aware of the advantage which [the French] would derive from the possession [of the village] in their subsequent operations . . . reinforced the village successively with the 71st regiment, the 79th, and the 24th. . . . The

* None of the authorities mention the presence in the village of the light companies of Ashworth's Portuguese brigade. They certainly suffered casualties on 3rd May so I assume they were present.

71st charged the enemy and drove them from a part of the village of which they had obtained a momentary possession. The contest continued until night, when our troops remained in possession of the whole.' [12]

Massena, having put 14 battalions into the fight, found that he had gained no more than the few scattered buildings on the eastern side of the stream, at a cost of 650 casualties. He therefore devoted the next day to making a reconnaissance and to regrouping his troops. He decided to turn the allied right through the gap between Fuentes de Oñoro and Nave de Haver and then to assault northwards along the ridge which formed the allied position. With this end in view he concentrated the two infantry divisions of D'Erlon's corps behind Ferey's division, opposite Fuentes, making a mass of 14,000 infantry ready to renew the assault on the village, and moved three infantry divisions, 17,000 men, with 3,500 cavalry to the southward. Only the 11,000 men of Reynier's corps remained opposite the allied left.

Although these troop movements took place under cover of darkness, Wellington guessed from Massena's quiescence on 4th May that some new development was planned for the following day. Having seen patrols opposite the gap south of Fuentes, he concluded that his first appreciation had been right and that Massena would attempt to turn the heads of the ravines. 'I . . . imagined that the enemy would endeavour to obtain possession of Fuentes de Oñoro, and of the ground occupied by the troops behind that village, by crossing the Dos Casas at Poco Velho [about two miles south of Fuentes]; and in the evening I moved the 7th division, under Major-General Houston, to the right, in order, if possible, to protect that passage.' [13]

This was one of the most questionable moves which Wellington ever made. His intention being to cover the blockade of Almeida there was little point in extending his right. His eventual fighting line, if pressed, must be the southern face of the Fuentes position, which was almost as strong as the eastern. It therefore seems extraordinary that he should have risked a weak and inexperienced division* in open country in face of an overwhelming cavalry force. The reason usually given for this detachment is Wellington's concern for his rear in case of having to retire. The great weakness of the Fuentes position is that, upwards of five miles behind it, the substantial river Coa runs in a rocky gorge. In

* The Seventh Division had been formed in March and had only two brigades. The British brigade contained only two native British battalions (51st and 85th), both newly arrived from England. The brigade was completed by the Chasseurs Britanniques, a battalion of French émigrés much given to desertion, and eight companies of the Brunswick Oels light infantry, of which Wellington remarked: 'I am not very fastidious about troops; I have them of all sorts, sizes and nations; but Germans in the Peninsula pass for Englishmen; and it is really not creditable to be a soldier of the same nation as these people' (SD vii 38). The other brigade was Doyle's Portuguese.

May the fords are few and dangerous and there were only three bridges within reach of Fuentes. That in the north was uncomfortably close to Almeida, although it was not actually commanded by the guns of the fortress. The most southerly bridge, at Sequiras, west of Nave de Haver, might be lost if the French broke through the Fuentes–Nave gap. This would leave only the bridge at Castello Bom, which would certainly be inadequate for the whole army if they had to retire in a hurry. Wellington himself, in his despatch on the battle, said that he 'occupied Poco Velho and that neighbourhood in the hopes that I should be able to maintain the communication with Sabugal [south of Sequiras] as well as provide for the blockade'.[14] This seems to be an inadequate explanation, as he knew well that the French were in no condition to make a deep penetration into Portugal and he was besides 'confident that they have it not in their power to defeat the allied army in a general action' (see p. 143). Napier suggests that the move was made as a result of Spencer's 'earnest suggestions',[15] but it seems unlikely that Wellington would have been swayed by a general whom he believed to be 'exceedingly puzzle headed'.[16]

The truth seems to be either that Wellington greatly underestimated the strength of the French flanking swing or that he feared a cavalry raid across the Turones aimed at disrupting his communications. Whatever the reasons, he later regretted it. In 1813, talking at the headquarters dinner table, he said that he 'committed a fault by extending his right too much to Poco Velho; and that, if the French had taken advantage of it, there might have been bad consequences, but that they permitted him to recover himself and change his front before their face'.[17]

Whatever the reason, Houston moved the Seventh Division during the night a clear two miles to the south of Fuentes and took up a position with two battalions, one British and one Portuguese, in the village of Poco Velho and his remaining troops in support on high ground to the west of them. As soon as it was light, the size of the French flanking force became apparent. Three divisions of infantry were moving on Poco Velho while on their left, already on the west bank of the Dos Casas, was a mass of cavalry which swept the guerrillas out of Nave de Haver without a shot being fired.

Quick to realise his mistake, Wellington dispatched all his British cavalry and the Light Division to rescue Houston and his men. Poco Velho was lost immediately, the Eighty-fifth and 6th Cacadores being swept out by 6,000 French infantry, but their retreat was in good order and the French infantry was prevented from pursuing them by the Riflemen and Cacadores of the Light Division, who established themselves in a small wood to the north of the village and held back Marchand's division with a steady accurate fire. South-west of them, the remainder of the Seventh Division was drawn up on the high ground.

148

The Fifty-first were in a dip on the forward slope, with the Chasseurs Britanniques on the crest behind firing over their heads. In front of them 'an officer of Huzzars soon showed himself on the brow, he viewed us with much attention then coolly turned round in his saddle and waved his sword. In an instant the brow was covered with cavalry. This was the critical moment . . . and their trumpeter was sounding the charge, when Colonel Mainwaring gave the words "Ready, Present, Fire". For a moment the smoke hindered us from seeing the effect of our fire, but we soon saw plenty of horses and men stretched not many yards from us. The C.B. Regt now opened a fire, as did the Portuguese over our heads. It was a dangerous but necessary expedient, as our fire was not sufficient to stop the cavalry, so we were obliged to lay down and load. The confusion amongst the enemy was great, and as soon as the fire could be stopped a squadron of the 1st Royal and of the 14th Light Dragoons gallantly dashed in amongst the enemy and performed wonders, but they were soon obliged to fall back—for the enemy outnumbered them twenty to one.' [18]

Under cover of the Light Division, and of repeated gallant charges by the small force of British cavalry, the Seventh Division retired by regiments in succession. Eventually they took up a position astride the Turones to the west of Fuentes, with one brigade on the east bank and another thrown somewhat forward on the west. As soon as they were safely on their way, Craufurd ordered the riflemen out of the wood and formed the Light Division into battalion squares. Then, changing to 'column at quarter distance ready to form square at any moment if charged by cavalry',[19] they marched the two miles back to the main position. 'A body of cavalry hovered about us, but from our formidable appearance and the steady manner with which the movement was conducted, the enemy did not charge us.' [20] The retreat of the Light Division was regarded by those watching from above Fuentes as a most dangerous and impressive manoeuvre. To the men who took part it was a routine operation and George Simmons of the Rifles wrote sadly to his parents his regret that the division had not been 'hotly engaged'.[21] The real heroes were the four regiments of cavalry, the Royal Dragoons, the Fourteenth and Sixteenth Light Dragoons and the First Hussars, King's German Legion, together with the Horse Artillery troops of Ross and Bull who, outnumbered three to one, always managed to hold the French back. The fact that the French did not fight with their usual skill, possibly because, as at least three witnesses assert, 'their cavalry were all drunk and fought like madmen',[22] and that there was dissension between the cavalry commanders of the Armies of Portugal and the North, can do nothing to detract from their gallantry and enterprise. It was the finest achievement of British light cavalry throughout the war.

By the time that the Light Division were back to the main position, Wellington had changed his front. Certain that no French force could fight its way across the Dos Casas and up the ridge north of Fuentes, the First and Third Divisions had been wheeled to face south. Their left was now in touch with the defenders of the village; their right stretched to the Seventh Division astride the Turones. When, rather belatedly, the infantry of Massena's left closed up to this position they made no attempt to attack it. 'Their success', wrote Wellington's Adjutant-General, 'amounted to nothing more than the occupation of some ground; they had in no respect broken our ranks, and they were as far from turning them as ever.' [23] Nor were the French any more successful in their second attempt to storm the village of Fuentes. On this occasion the garrison consisted of three battalions, the Seventy-first and Seventy-ninth in the village and the Twenty-fourth in support. Against these the French used first Ferey's division, then 18 grenadier companies of D'Erlon's corps, and finally the rest of D'Erlon's two divisions. With such a constant supply of fresh troops to contend with, the defenders, although sparingly fed with light companies and Cacadores from the main position, were eventually forced back in bitter street fighting. 'The town presented a shocking sight: our Highlanders lay dead in heaps, while the other regiments, while less remarkable in dress, were scarcely so in the number of their slain. The French grenadiers, with their immense caps and gaudy plumes, lay in piles of ten and twenty together.' [24] Finally the French fought their way to the church at the top of the village and the Highlanders 'were fighting with the French Grenadiers across the tombstones and graves'.[25]

Behind the churchyard, Mackinnon's brigade had been drawn up in reserve when the Assistant Adjutant-General, Edward Pakenham, rode up to the Colonel of the Eighty-eighth. ' "Do you see that, Wallace?" said Pakenham. "I do," replied the Colonel, "and I would rather drive the French out of the town than cover a retreat across the Coa." "Perhaps," said Sir Edward, "his lordship don't think it tenable." Wallace answering said, "I shall take it with my regiment and keep it too." "Will you?" was the reply, "I'll go and tell Lord Wellington so." In a moment or two Pakenham returned at a gallop, and, waving his hat, called out, "He says you may go—come along, Wallace." ' [26]

Charging down the hill 'with fixed bayonets in column of sections, left in front, in double quick time, their firelocks at the trail', the Seventy-fourth and Eighty-eighth swept the French away and threw them across the stream at the foot of the hill. D'Erlon used his few intact battalions to shield the survivors. The storm of Fuentes had failed and it was not renewed. Meanwhile, on the new south-facing alignment of Spencer's corps there was little more than skirmishing, although the light companies of the Guards were severely cut up when they were incautiously extended in the presence of cavalry. At nightfall the fighting stopped, the French having lost 2,260, the allies 1,550.

Next day Massena gave the order to feed his troops out of the stores which had been collected to revictual Almeida. He no longer believed in the possibility of achieving his object, although it was not until 10th May that he withdrew his troops on Rodrigo and acknowledged defeat. The allies were reinforced in their belief that they could beat the French any day and the only man who had any doubts about the affair was Wellington himself. Writing to his brother seven weeks later he said: 'Lord Liverpool was quite right not to move [a vote of] thanks [in Parliament] for the battle at Fuentes, it was the most difficult one I was ever concerned in. If Boney had been there, we should have been beaten.' [27] He was, however, gratified by the humanity of his troops. 'The village of Fuentes de Oñoro having been the field of battle the other day, and not having been much improved by this circumstance, they immediately and voluntarily subscribed to raise a sum of money, to be given to the inhabitants as a compensation for the damage which their properties have sustained in the contest.' [28]

The Pyrenees, 25th July–2nd August 1813

Apart from the untidy and almost disastrous skirmishing at El Bodon, Wellington was not called upon to fight a defensive action for more than two years after Fuentes de Oñoro. Twice, in June and November 1812, he offered battle outside Salamanca, but on each occasion the French declined to oblige him. By July 1813 the situation was vastly different from that which he had faced on the Portuguese frontier in the summer of 1811. The French kingdom of Spain had collapsed, King Joseph had been exiled to his country estate and the allied armies had closed up to the Franco-Spanish frontier. In the previous month Wellington had inflicted, at Vitoria, a crushing defeat on the combined French armies, taking all their artillery and baggage. Wellington was now a field-marshal, and his troops were confirmed in their belief that no Frenchman could withstand them. The Portuguese had served their apprenticeship and could be relied upon to stand beside their British allies. On 21st July Wellington 'talking of the Portuguese, said that it was extraordinary just now to observe their conduct; that no troops could behave better; that they never had now a notion of turning; and that nothing could equal their forwardness now, and willing, ready tempers'.[29]

The Field-Marshal was not so pleased with his British troops. They had fought magnificently at Vitoria, but their indiscipline after the battle had gone far to prevent an effectual pursuit. 'It is', he wrote to the Horse Guards on 18th July, 'an unrivalled army for fighting, if the soldiers can only be kept in their ranks. The inferior officers . . . never attend to an order . . . and therefore never obey it when obedience becomes troublesome, or difficult, or important.' [30] The casualties at Vitoria had amounted to little more than 5,000 British, Portuguese and

Spanish, but 'by the states of [8th July] we had 12,500 less under arms than we had on the day before the battle. They are not in the hospitals, nor are they killed, nor have they fallen into the hands of the enemy as prisoners. . . . I believe they are concealed in the villages in the mountains.' [31]

Nor were the troops the only source of concern. News had come in from the east coast of Spain that Sir John Murray had fled incontinently from before Tarragona in the face of a chimera of his own imagining, abandoning his siege train to the incredulous garrison of the place, and leaving Suchet and the French Armies of Valencia and Catalonia free to move against Wellington's right and rear by the valley of the Ebro. The supply situation, now principally the concern of the Royal Navy, was very insecure. 'I am certain,' wrote Wellington, 'that it will not be denied, that since Great Britain became a naval power, a British army has never been left in such a situation, and that at a moment when it is most important to us to preserve, and to the enemy to interrupt, the communication by the coast. If they only take the ship with our shoes, we must halt for six weeks. . . . The enemy have reinforced *by sea* the only two posts they have on the north coast of Spain.' [32]

For the time being the whole posture of the allies had to be defensive. As long as the French held San Sebastian and Pamplona, each commanding one of the two main routes from Spain to France, it would be folly to undertake the invasion of France even if news of the military situation in east Europe gave some assurance that the Emperor would not be able to reinforce the Pyrenean front from Germany. Before going further it was essential that the two fortresses should be reduced. Meantime they were 40 miles apart as the crow flies and the effort to cover them both gravely strained the strength of the army. 'The truth is,' wrote Wellington, 'that having two objects in hand, viz. the siege of San Sebastian and the blockade of Pamplona, we are not so strong at any point as we ought to be.' [33]

The topography did not make the task easy. Although the whole country was hilly and broken there was an overriding pattern of mountain features. The main Pyrenean chain bifurcates north-east of Pamplona, slightly to the west of the Pass of Roncesvalles. The main range continues westward as the Sierra de Aralar, which links the Pyrenees to the mountains of Cantabria. To the north-west of Roncesvalles there run a complex of mountainous spurs which culminate, south of St. Jean de Luz, in the massif of La Rhune. Thus the force which blockaded and covered Pamplona was cut off from the main army by the Sierra de Aralar, which was crossed by few roads, of which only one, the Pass of Velate, had any serious pretension to being passable.

It was inevitable that the French would make a major effort to relieve one or other of the beleaguered towns. Information from behind the enemy lines was less plentiful than it had been when the French had been operating in Spain, first because the two armies were separated by a mountain barrier and more because the guerrillas were no longer able to intercept despatches now that the French were stationed on their own soil. By the middle of the month there were indications that the enemy was weakening his seaward flank and concentrating around St. Jean Pied de Port, but this last did not have to mean more than that the force under Clausel which had been driven back into France through the pass of Jaca after Vitoria had regained touch with the main body. It was not until 18th July that the first news came, through peasants, that Marshal Soult had arrived to take command of a united Army of Spain.*

There were three roads by which Soult could advance. The main road from Bayonne to Vitoria crossed the lower Bidassoa near Irun and was the most direct route to San Sebastian. The river bridge at Behobie had been burnt when the French retreated over it and the river was not fordable, so that to use this approach would require a pontoon train. Sixteen miles to the south-east was a good road over the Col de Maya which led straight to Pamplona. To reach San Sebastian by this route the French would have to advance south and south-west down the Baztan valley for 12 miles beyond the pass until it reached Elizondo and then swing north, a clumsy and unlikely manoeuvre. Finally, to the east of the bifurcation of the Pyrenees, there was the Pass of Roncesvalles beyond which the road ran, fairly directly but through a succession of good defensive positions, some 26 miles to Pamplona. There were, in addition, a number of minor passes through which supporting attacks might be put. To guard this front and to prosecute the two sieges, Wellington had available rather more than 100,000 effectives of all ranks and arms, of whom about a third, 36,000, were Spaniards.

Wellington disposed his infantry strength into what amounted to four corps, with two divisions held in army reserve. On the left, the seaward flank, Sir Thomas Graham commanded. His responsibility comprised the siege of San Sebastian and the covering force guarding the Bidassoa where it formed the Franco-Spanish frontier. For this he was allocated the First and Fifth Divisions, a brigade of Portuguese and the 15,000 Spaniards of the Asturian and Galician armies. On their right and coming directly under Wellington, whose headquarters were at Lesaca, were the Light Division guarding the Pass of Vera and the Seventh which held the Pass of Echelar. Sir Rowland Hill held the Maya Pass and Baztan Valley with his usual corps (less one brigade). Two British brigades under William Stewart held the Maya itself and three Portuguese brigades watched the small passes which run eastward out of the Baztan into the French valley of Baigorry, the most southerly of these brigades, at Les Aldudes, being the only formation established

---

* Soult joined the army on 12th July with orders to combine the remains of the Armies of the North, South, Centre and Portugal into a single force, which could put into the field rather more than 70,000 men over and above garrisons and depots.

on French soil. The right-hand corps comprised 11,000 men under Sir Lowry Cole and guarded the Pass of Roncesvalles. The troops allocated to Sir Lowry were his own Fourth Division, Byng's brigade of Second Division and Morillo's 4,000 Spaniards. Far out to the east Saragossa and Jaca were watched by the former guerrillas of Mina and Duran, now regular troops, lest Suchet should attempt to intervene from Catalonia.

It was less than a week before Soult attacked that Wellington was able to provide any reserve to his extended line. On 17th July the 17,500 men of the Spanish 'Army of Reserve of Andalusia' arrived to take over the blockade of Pamplona, thus releasing the Third and Sixth Divisions, which went into reserve, the Third at Olague and the Sixth at San Estevan, one either side of the Pass of Velate. The cavalry was useless in this broken country and, apart from two bridges kept forward for communication work, was billeted back at Vitoria.

Wellington's appreciation of Soult's probable moves was conditioned by the state of the two fortresses he was besieging. Pamplona, he knew, was provisioned for some weeks to come and was unlikely to fall. San Sebastian, on the other hand, was being steadily battered by siege guns. An apparently practical breach was blown on 23rd July and it was intended to storm on the following day. It seemed that San Sebastian was in imminent danger and that it must, therefore, be the object of Soult's first attack. Wellingon was reinforced in this belief by the news that the French were assembling bridging material at Urugne, between St. Jean de Luz and the Bidassoa. The day before the attack began he was still wedded to this belief. 'I have undoubted intelligence that Soult has moved the greater part of his force towards St. Jean Pied de Port, leaving at Urugne the boats which are two complete bridges. It would appear, therefore, that he entertains serious designs to draw our attention from the side of Irun, and then attempt to pass the river.' [34] While he realised he might be wrong in this appreciation he did not feel greatly concerned since the positions both at Maya and at Roncesvalles were naturally strong and, if resolutely defended, should be able to impose enough delay on the enemy for a sufficient force to be collected in front of Pamplona to deny it to the enemy.

The assault on San Sebastian had to be postponed until the 25th, and when it was launched it failed. Wellington, who had left all the arrangements to Graham, was at his headquarters at Lesaca. He heard the news about eleven o'clock in the morning and at once ordered his horse and rode off to see Graham about a renewal of the assault. Hardly had he gone beyond reach of recall than heavy firing was heard from the allied right. No news arrived until the middle of the afternoon, when a message arrived from the Seventh Division at Echelar relaying a report that the French had attacked the Second Division at Maya and had been repulsed. The sound of firing could, however, still be heard. The Quartermaster-General, George Murray, in charge of headquarters during Wellington's absence, sent to the commanders of the Seventh and Light Divisions to tell them that 'It will be a proper precaution that your division should be prepared to make a movement this evening should it be necessary.' [35] He also ordered a troop of Horse Artillery to move immediately from Vera to San Estevan.

When Wellington returned after dark to Lesaca there was still no news from Maya. At nine o'clock a message reached him saying that Cole had been attacked in force at Roncesvalles but that up to midday the line had been held. 'It is impossible', he wrote at 10 p.m., 'to judge of Soult's plan yet, particularly till I know the result of his operations today. I understand that the enemy were driven off from the Puerto de Maya. One can hardly believe that, with 30,000 men, he proposes to force himself through the passes of the mountains. The remainder of his force, one would think, must come into operation on some other point, either tomorrow or the day after.' [36] Still convinced that Soult would attempt to relieve San Sebastian, Wellington moved no troops, but gave orders to embark the siege train. It was not until the small hours of the 26th that an A.D.C. from Hill arrived with the news that he had ordered the evacuation of the Maya and was concentrating his corps to cover Elizondo, six miles behind the pass.

Wellington's disbelief in Soult's intention to 'force himself through the passes of the mountains' with 30,000 men was ill-founded. Soult had every intention of forcing the passes, but the strength he was bringing forward was not 30,000 but 60,000, apart from 15,000 which he left on the lower Bidassoa to watch Graham. At Maya, D'Erlon with a corps of 20,000 infantry was attacking Stewart, while at Roncesvalles, two corps, 32,000 infantry, with two divisions of cavalry in reserve, were attacking in two columns astride the Val Carlos. The aim of both attacks was Pamplona. The troops were rationed for four days and there was in this mountainous country little chance of their being able to supplement their supplies from the countryside. In any case Soult knew that if he could not relieve Pamplona or achieve a decisive victory over a substantial portion of the allied army within four days the task he had set himself was impossible. After that time Wellington would have concentrated enough troops to drive him back to the frontier.

On 25th July luck was on Soult's side. Not only was Wellington unaware of his intentions and movements but he was poorly served by his subordinate commanders at both Maya and Roncesvalles. At both places the troops fought with a bravery which even they seldom equalled and, helped by their strong positions, brought the French to a standstill, but at nightfall both allied forces retreated. The general most at fault was William Stewart at Maya. Although the finest and most enlightened battalion commander in the army he was quite unsuitable to command a division. 'With the utmost zeal and good intention and abilities, he cannot obey an order', Wellington had written to the Horse Guards, adding that 'it is necessary that he should be under the particular charge of somebody'.[37] His governor at this time was Hill, but Hill, who commanded a wide front, could not always be with him. On the morning of the 25th, Stewart, although he knew that at least 12,000 French were within a mile of his front and, in Wellington's words 'having been prepared to receive the attack, decided that the enemy would not attack him; and he sent half the troops a league to the rear, and ordered the whole to cook, and went himself to Elizondo.* In the meantime the French formed in the wood under the height, on which he had no body. I give the troops great credit for getting out of the scrape as well as they did. With common precaution, General Stewart had enough men to defend the pass.'[38] As it was, the two brigades only escaped a disaster by the timely intervention of a brigade of Seventh Division which came to their aid by a mountain path.

Cole at Roncesvalles had rather more reason for abandoning his position. Having successfully defended it throughout the day, he was harassed by hearing musketry in his right rear and haunted by the fear that he might be surrounded. Nevertheless he had Wellington's specific order to defend the passes 'as effectually as you can without committing the troops against a force so superior that the advantage of the ground would not compensate it',[39] and on the previous day a further letter had been sent to him urging him to maintain the passes 'to the utmost'. Cole's chief fault lay in failing to keep Wellington informed of his intentions; he 'never informed me exactly how far he found it necessary to give way, or let me know by what a superior force he was pressed, and that he intended giving way'.[40]

When, early on the morning of the 26th, Wellington rode from Lesaca to the Second Division at Elizondo, he was not greatly perturbed by the French attacks. 'I suspected that all Soult's plan was merely by manoeuvres to get me out of the hills, and to relieve one or both of the besieged places, as things should turn up and succeed for him; and I expected him shortly to turn around short towards San Sebastian.'[41] With this in mind he did no more than order the Sixth Division at San Estevan to touch in to the left of Hill's corps at Elizondo. With Hill's corps, strengthened by the Sixth Division, blocking the Baztan valley, and the Seventh and Light ready at Echelar and Vera to oppose a possible westward move through the mountains on to Graham's flank, the situation in the centre was well in hand. The only cause for concern was the total lack of news from the right, from whence nothing had

* Taking his entire staff with him. When the attack started Surgeon Walter Henry of the Sixty-sixth was the only commissioned officer at Headquarters (Henry i 166). Command at the pass devolved on the senior brigade commander, Major-General Pringle, who had been with his brigade less than 24 hours. In his previous command one of his staff officers had described Pringle as 'a man who is liked by all the world in private life, and respected by no one in public' (Gomm 287, 21st September 1812).

come dated later than noon the previous day when the position was still intact. As a precaution, the cavalry was ordered up to the Pamplona area and the blockading Spaniards around that town were told to detach troops to support Cole and his immediate reserve, Picton's Third Division. To find out more of the situation, Wellington set out towards Pamplona during the afternoon.

Late in the afternoon of 26th July Wellington reached Almandoz, five miles short of the crest of the Col de Velate. There was still no news from Cole and D'Erlon's troops were not pressing Hill at Elizondo. This last fact decided him to take as few risks as possible on the right flank. He ordered the Sixth Division to march over the Col de Velate at daybreak on the 27th. Simultaneously the Seventh Division was to 'extend to the right . . . to secure the left and rear of Sir Rowland Hill's position'.[42] Scarcely had these orders been despatched when news at last arrived from Cole. A glance at the head of the paper must have shown Wellington that his orders to the Sixth Division had been amply justified. The letter was headed Linzoain, ten miles in rear of the position which Cole was meant to be holding. The tone was despondent. 'It appears by that letter that Sir Lowry Cole looks forward to the likelihood of having to continue to retire upon Pamplona.'[43] The only grounds for encouragement were that Picton and the Third Division should by this time have joined Cole, making the allied strength available in that sector up to 19,000, and that the valley down which they were retiring offered many good defensive positions. Immediately the Quartermaster-General wrote to Picton: 'As you will become the senior General Officer present with the troops between the enemy and Pamplona, when the divisions are united, Lord Wellington has directed me to represent to you how necessary it is that the advance of the enemy in that direction should be checked. Lord Wellington is of opinion, considering the nature of the country, and the very respectable force of good troops which will be at your disposal, that even should the enemy have penetrated beyond Linzoain when you receive this, that he will undoubtedly be stopped between that place and Zubiri.'

Picton was the toughest fighting general in the army, but the command of what amounted to a corps was too much for him. He had brought forward the head of his division to Zubiri and rode forward alone to see how Cole was faring. To the tired men of the Fourth Division who were quite unable to divine why they should continue to retreat in face of an enemy whom they had trounced the previous day, his arrival gave great hope. He rode up in his usual bellicose state 'in a blue military frock-coat and a round hat, riding in the opposite direction to that we were going and I heard him say, "Right about, right about. It is damned odd if 10,000 British cannot show their faces to 30,000 French." '[44] His confidence did not last long. 'When I joined Sir Lowry Cole he had taken up a position about two miles in front of

Zubiri, where he was attacked about half-past three by a very superior force. The enemy were not able to make any impression on the post, though he drove in our sharpshooters, and extended himself much to our right and left, particularly to our right, which was easily turnable. The affair ended with the day, and the country offering no post between this place and Pamplona where it would be safe to hazard anything like an effectual stand against such superior force, I agreed with Lieutenant General Sir L. Cole in opinion that it was advisable to retire. . . . We shall take up a position at as short a distance as practicable from Pamplona. If I had known your Lordship's intentions sooner, I . . . would have endeavoured to give effect to your Lordship's wishes.' [45] So great did Picton's desire to retreat become that he chose for the Third and Fourth Divisions a position so close to Pamplona that the guns of the fortress could fire into their rear. He only brought forward his left to the Sorauren position on the urgent representation of Cole, whose judgment had returned as his responsibilities had grown less.

This continued retreat of his right was, of course, unknown to Wellington on the evening of 26th July, but since Cole's belated report had estimated the French strength opposed to him as 'no less than 35,000 men, and probably more',[46] it was clear at last that Soult was making his main move against Pamplona. He therefore gave orders for the centre of the army to hold the line of the Sierra de Aralar, with Hill's corps blocking the Col de Velate and the Seventh Division the minor passes above Doña Maria on Hill's left. The Light Division was to leave the right-hand end of the line on the Bidassoa to Longa's Spaniards and move to Zubieta with a view to covering the direct road from Pamplona to San Sebastian by way of Irurzun and Tolosa.

At this time Wellington believed that Picton, with the Third and Fourth Divisions and their attendant troops, backed by the Sixth Division and detachments of Spaniards from the blockade of Pamplona, a mass of at least 25,000 troops including seven British infantry brigades, could, at worst, fight delaying actions which would hold the main French threat until he could bring forward enough troops to defeat them. Nevertheless, he did not neglect the possibility of a French breakthrough to Pamplona. Early on the 27th word was sent to Hill that 'if things should not go well towards Pamplona, we may, in that case, have to wheel the army back upon its left, placing the troops now about Pamplona near Irurzun. The centre of the Army between that and Tolosa; the left, under Sir Thomas Graham, remaining nearly where it is.' [47]

While this letter was being written, Wellington was riding over the Col de Velate. Arriving at Ostiz, he was greeted by the news that Picton had fallen back to the Sorauren position less than five miles ahead. This was serious as it meant that the French would shortly command the southern end of the direct road by which reinforcements could join

Picton's corps over the Col de Velate, the road by which the Sixth Division, which Wellington had overtaken, would arrive. Leaving George Murray, his Q.M.G., to divert the reinforcements to a more westerly road through Lizaso, Wellington galloped on, accompanied only by Lord Fitzroy Somerset (the future Lord Raglan), reaching Sorauren village, in the valley below Picton's extreme left, when the French cavalry was no more than a mile away. Despite the well-meant warnings of the peasantry, he dashed off a brief note to Murray, ordering Hill's corps and the Seventh Division to fall back to join him and to urge on the march of the Sixth. With this, Lord Fitzroy galloped back up the Ostiz road just in time to evade the French cavalry scouts. Wellington, himself, turned his horse to the steep slope of Sorauren hill to join Picton and Cole. 'I saw [the French] just near one end of the village as I went out of the other end. . . . It was rather alarming certainly, and a close run thing.' [48]

It was eleven o'clock on 27th July. Soult's men were using the third of their four days' rations. If Pamplona was to be relieved Soult must do it within 24 hours. Like Wellington he had been poorly served by one of his subordinates. Count D'Erlon, commanding his right-hand column, had taken a severe fright on 25th July. The following day he had spent in half-hearted patrol activity and when he finally pushed forward on the 27th his advance was so cautious that he failed even to sight Hill's rearguard.* Whatever D'Erlon was about, Soult received no messages from him and could only hope that, sometime on the 27th or 28th, he would appear from the Col de Velate and take the Sorauren position in flank. With his left column the situation was somewhat better. Clausel's corps of three divisions came up to the ridge facing Cole's position during the morning, but Reille's three divisions had been ordered to advance by tracks and, finding them impassable, had had to fall back to the main road in rear of Clausel. Clausel was anxious to put in an immediate attack and even launched a regiment against an outcrop at the southern end of Cole's position held by two Spanish battalions which stood their ground well and beat off the attack. Soult observed the ground carefully and decided to wait until the following day.

He had good reason for caution. The position Cole had chosen for the allied left was, though lower in height, as formidable as Busaco and was, moreover, only two miles long, with a river on either flank. It was a sharp-fronted ridge which faced another on which Clausel had drawn up his men. Sir John Fortescue describes it graphically when he likens it to 'a leg of mutton with one thick slice cut out'. [49] Somewhat east of the centre a narrow spur connects the two ridges. On this ridge Cole had drawn up 10,000 men consisting of his own Fourth Division (two

---

* D'Erlon claimed to have captured guns and baggage in his advance. Such small captures as he made were due entirely to small parties getting lost and taking the wrong track in the confusing country.

British and one Portuguese brigades), Byng's British brigade from Second Division, Campbell's independent Portuguese brigade and two Spanish regiments of foot. About 3,000 yards to his right rear, drawn up behind a stream, were Picton's 5,000 men of the Third Division, with their left on the river Arga which marked Cole's right. Parallel with them, on the right bank of the Arga on a line of heights, was a large body of Spaniards drawn from the force investing Pamplona.

It was a formidable position and Soult, with only one corps up, was right to hesitate before assaulting it. His doubts were confirmed by the wave of cheering which greeted the arrival of Wellington. 'I cannot,' wrote a British regimental officer, 'adequately express the sense of confidence and assurance that was revived by his presence in the midst of a single division of his army; cheers upon cheers were vehemently raised upon the whole line.' [50] His appearance on the highest part of the British position, wearing his 'grey frock coat, buttoned close up to the chin, with his little cocked hat covered with oilskin, without a feather',[51] was seen by every man in the corps of Cole and Clausel. Most important of all, he was seen by Soult. 'I saw him', said Wellington years later, 'spying at us—then write and send off a letter—I knew what he would be writing and gave my orders accordingly.' Soult was dictating his orders for an attack next morning. One of Wellington's officers wrote that 'we would rather see his long nose in a fight than a reinforcement of ten thousand men';[52] on 27th July Wellington's appearance was literally equivalent to a reinforcement which had not yet been able to arrive.

On the following morning Soult flung five of his divisions at the Sorauren ridge. By that time the Sixth Division was in force on Cole's left. The French attacked repeatedly with great gallantry; it was, wrote Wellington, 'fair bludgeon work. . . . I never saw such fighting as we have had here.' [53] At the end of the day the French had not gained a yard of ground and they had lost more than 3,000 men. The allies had lost almost as many, about 2,600, but they had broken the French offensive. Moreover the allies were receiving regular rations and the French were on the last day's supply of their issue.

The following day was quiet, 'not a shot was fired';[54] neither rations nor reinforcements reached the French, although touch was regained with D'Erlon whose leading divisions reached Lanz and Ostiz. On the British side not only rations but the Seventh Division supplemented Wellington's strength. On the 30th July came the reckoning. Soult, determined not to retreat tamely on Roncesvalles, started to move his whole army, now led by D'Erlon, on Irurzun and the westerly road from Pamplona to San Sebastian. D'Erlon's corps, in greatly superior numbers, succeeded after a day-long battle in pushing back Hill's forward troops across a valley in good order. It was a modest success but the corps of Clausel and Reille had a very different day. To follow D'Erlon they had to move across Wellington's front. This they started to do during the night of 29th–30th July. Dawn found them in some disarray, and still in large numbers, on the ridge facing Sorauren. Wellington advanced with four divisions and two brigades. By nightfall the two French corps could not muster more than 14,000 men out of the 35,000 in their ranks of the previous day. The most easterly French division was forced to retreat due north to Roncesvalles, driving 4,000 stragglers before it. The French army regained their own frontier on 2nd August, and after the thousands of stragglers had rejoined their units, the loss to the army was found to be 13,000 men. The allied loss was 7,000, of which about a third fell at Maya and Roncesvalles.

The operations of 25th–28th July 1813 must rank as the finest example of Wellington's defensive fighting. Covering a long front with bad lateral communication, the initiative was inevitably with his opponent. Wellington had formed a wrong appreciation of Soult's intention and was shamefully served by his subordinate generals, who neither held their positions as they should have done nor sent him information of their actions or intentions. In the outcome he inflicted on the French a defeat more costly in casualties than any they suffered in the Peninsula with the exception of Salamanca. Even while he was working from wholly misleading premises, his anticipation of possibilities always gave him sufficient troops moving towards likely points of danger to avert catastrophe. At Maya, Roncesvalles and Sorauren the infantry fought magnificently. 'I never saw the troops behave so well.' [55] 'The gallant 4th division, which had so frequently been distinguished in this army, surpassed their former good conduct. Every regiment charged with the bayonet, the 40th, 7th, 20th and 23rd, four different times.' [56] Nevertheless the real triumph was personal to Wellington who, under the most difficult circumstances, got sufficient troops to the right place at the right time.

CHAPTER EIGHT

THE PENINSULA—SIEGES

The truth is, that, equipped as we are, the British army are not capable of carrying on a regular siege.

Wellington to Torrens, 7th April 1812

'Everyone knows', asserted Sir Charles Oman, 'that the record of the Peninsular army in the matter of sieges is not the most brilliant page in its annals.' [1] That little of the blame for this state of affairs rests with Wellington can be deduced from the statement of a distinguished Peninsular engineer officer who roundly declared that 'in 1811 the siege establishment of the empire was as imperfect and as uninstructed as in 1793'.[2]

In time of peace Ministers had worked on the economical view that, if war did come, the British army would not be called upon to undertake sieges. Suitable heavy guns did exist in Woolwich Arsenal, but there were neither men to operate them nor transport to move them. Previous to the Peninsular campaigns, siege guns had been manned by men borrowed from the field artillery and, since their employment had been wholly in coastal Flanders, their transport had been the responsibility of the Royal Navy.

There was a small but skilled corps of Royal Engineers, serious-minded, rather pompous officers. An irreverent infantry officer referred, not without justification, to 'all the inherent pomp and acquired gravity of a Royal Engineer'.[3] In April 1809 there were 179 of them, including 9 colonels and 12 lieutenant-colonels, all of whom, since promotion was strictly by seniority, were elderly. From this array they were able, by the end of the year, to send to Portugal 17 officers commanded by the 41-year-old Major Richard Fletcher,* who remained Wellington's Chief Engineer until his death in 1813.

The chance of an engineer surviving for long was small. Of the 21 engineers present at the first siege of Badajoz in May 1811, only 11 survived the war and only five of them were unwounded. In any single siege 50 per cent engineer casualties were not uncommon. Eleven out of 24 were killed or wounded at Badajoz (1812) and 11 out of 18 at San

---

* Fletcher had been a captain, Royal Engineers, since 1801 and had the brevet rank in the army of major since 1807. He became a lieutenant-colonel, R.E., in June 1809, there being no regimental rank of major in the Engineers.

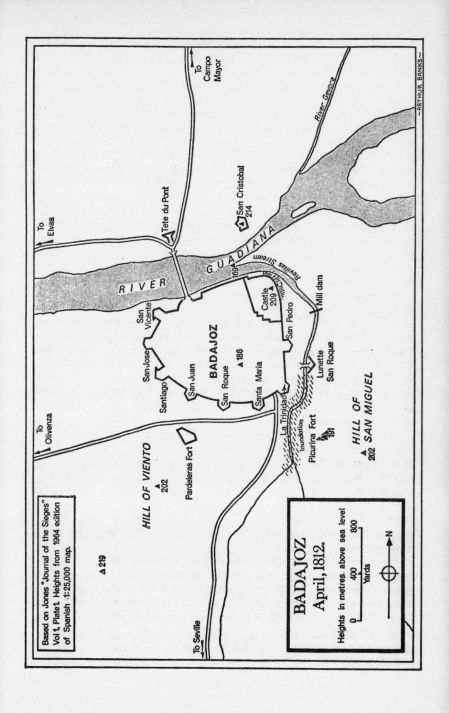

Based on Jones "Journal of the Sieges" Vol.1, Plate1. Heights from 1964 edition of Spanish 1:25,000 map.

To Elvas

To Campo Mayor

River Gevora

Tete du Pont

San Cristobal 214

RIVER GUADIANA

Revillas Stream

San Vicente

Castle 209

Cliff Hill 169

Mill dam

San Pedro

BADAJOZ

San-Jose

186

San Juan

San Roque

Santiago

Santa Maria

Lunette San Roque

To Olivenza

La Trinidad

Inundation

Picurina Fort 191

HILL OF VIENTO 202

Pardeleras Fort

HILL OF SAN MIGUEL 202

219

To Seville

~ARTHUR BANKS~

BADAJOZ April, 1812.

Heights in metres. above sea level

N

0   400   800

Yards

Sebastian. Wellington wrote in May 1812: 'We have had such an expenditure of Engineers that I can hardly wish for any body lest the same
fate befall him that has befallen so many.' [4]

There were no 'other ranks' in the engineers. There did, however,
exist the corps of Royal Military Artificers which, in 1809, consisted of
12 companies of which eight were stationed in the United Kingdom,
two in Gibraltar and one each in the West Indies and Nova Scotia. This
was a very static body of men. A contemporary observed that 'from the
close of the American war, all the companies of the Royal Military
Artificers were kept permanently fixed in their respective stations, both
at home and abroad, where they remained for life, in what may for
military men, be styled a state of vegetation; so that there were, at that
period, a vast number of men who had actually grown grey in the
corps, who had never entered a transport, nor made a single day's
march from the headquarters of their company. Everywhere they inter-
mixed with civilians; they married in a proportion unknown in other
corps; so much so that the number of women and children belonging
to one company was often equal to that of a battalion of the line.' [5]

It was clear that little movement could be expected from such a
body, skilled though they were in the domestic arts of carpentry and
smithery, and the most that a field commander could expect to find
under him was a small detachment, probably drawn from several companies, under the command of a sergeant. When Wellington returned to
the Peninsula in 1809 he found the artificers represented by two sergeants and 27 other ranks. These were augmented, two years later, by
two more sergeants and 57 men 'who had never seen a sap, battery or
trench constructed'. [6]

Badajoz, March–April 1812

Wellington opened his first European siege at the end of May 1811. It
was a makeshift affair based on the hope that Badajoz could be taken
in a fortnight, after which time it was known that an overwhelming
French force would be available to relieve the place. The means available were slender. There were 21 engineers and 25 military artificers,
supplemented by untrained officers and men from the infantry. For a
siege train he relied on guns which could be spared from the armament
of the great Portuguese fortress of Elvas. 'They were,' wrote Major
Dickson who collected them together, 'brass Portuguese guns of the
time of John 4th and his son Alfonso, bearing the dates 1646, 1652,
1653, etc; also some Spanish guns of Philip 3rd and 4th, dates 1620,
1636, etc.' [7] An engineer noted that, 'In general there was room between the shot and the bore to put a man's finger in . . . so that the
practice was necessarily vague and uncertain.' [8]

Following Fletcher's advice, fire was opened, as it had been in Beresford's short attempt earlier in the month, against the castle and the fort of San Cristobal, the two strongest parts of the defences. Assaults were made on 6th and 9th June, but both failed and by that time the armies of Marmont and Soult were closing in and the siege had to be abandoned. Wellington was believed to have muttered to himself that 'if he undertakes another siege, he will be his own engineer'.[9] He was not greatly upset; he had realised from the start that his chances were small and undertook the siege only because the prize was such an important one.

Six months later Ciudad Rodrigo was taken. It was not a first-class fortress. The garrison was small, the breach made by the French in 1810 had been imperfectly repaired and the town was commanded by a hill, the Grand Teson, within range of the walls. A redoubt on the Teson was brilliantly stormed by a detachment of the Light Division under John Colborne on the night of 8th January and on the following days batteries were established on the height. This time the guns were not the Portuguese antiques employed at Badajoz but a full siege train, 34 24-pounders and four 18-pounders, shipped out from England.* By the afternoon of 19th January two practicable breaches had been battered and the assault was delivered that night. The storm cost the allies 560 men, of whom 125 died, including Generals Craufurd and Mackinnon. A high proportion of the casualties were caused by a mine which was exploded after one breach had been won and the fall of the town certain. An artillery officer who joined the stormers because 'I thought I might as well see the whole of the fun', wrote: 'As soon as the French suspected we were coming they threw a quantity of light balls which enabled them to see completely the whole of our troops. Our troops then pushed on and the whole business was finished in less than a quarter of an hour.' [10]

The event was hailed as a great victory partly because of the significance of Rodrigo as one of the two gateways to Spain but more because it was the first successful siege of a European fortress by the British army without naval support since the days of Marlborough.† The problem set to the engineers was not a difficult one. It did not need a trained man to realise that there was only one way of taking Rodrigo. In fact, they did little more than copy the methods the French had used two years before. 'Our engineers', wrote Wellington, 'though brave and

* This siege train had been lying on shipboard in Lisbon harbour at least since March 1811. Wellington had wisely not considered it safe to employ it at the speculative siege of Badajoz in May–June that year. It was very slow moving; even given good weather it would take a fortnight to move it to Badajoz from Alcacar do Sal (east of Setubal), the nearest seaport. This would be a great risk to take in face of a superior enemy.

† This omits the siege of Valenciennes in 1793 in which British troops were engaged and which was commanded by the Duke of York. The majority of the troops involved were Austrians, as was the artillery.

well educated, have never turned their mind to the mode of conducting a regular siege, as it is useless to think of that which, in our service, it is impossible to perform.' [11]

Badajoz, to which Wellington immediately turned his attention, was a very different proposition. It is naturally strong, particularly against an enemy coming from the north. Along that face of the town flows the river Guadiana, between 300 and 500 yards wide. When the river ran high there was no ford between Badajoz and the sea. Upstream the next bridge was at Merida, 30 miles away. Badajoz had been fortified for centuries and, although the neglect of eighteenth-century Spanish governments had allowed it to fall into some disrepair, it remained very formidable. In 1757 orders had been given for the defences to be greatly strengthened, but the work had never been completed. The eight bastions had been rebuilt, each 30 feet high, but the curtain wall was only 23 to 26 feet and some of the masonry was of poor quality. The French, who had been in possession of the town for a year, had greatly strengthened the details of the defences.

At the north-eastern corner of the town, protected to some extent on the east by the mouth of the Revillas stream, the castle stands on a sharp hill, rising more than 100 feet above the Guadiana. Parts of the north-eastern slope are precipitous and nowhere are they easy to climb. Facing it on the north bank of the river are the heights of San Cristobal, rather higher than the castle hill. From San Cristobal much of the interior of the castle is clearly visible. A heavy battery on these heights could make the castle untenable, and to guard against this danger they had been crowned by a fort. 'Its figure is nearly that of a square of 300 feet; the scarp, which is all built of stone, is twenty feet in height, and mostly well covered by a revetted counterscarp.' [12] Communication from the town to San Cristobal is by a stone bridge, 25 arches long, covered, since it is half a mile downstream from the redoubt, by a *tête-de-pont* of no great strength.

To the south and east of the town are low heights which might have been tempting starting places for a besieger. Each of them had been surmounted by a fort of moderate strength, the Pardaleras to the south and the Picurina to the south-east. There was a further minor outwork, the lunette of San Roque, on the eastern side protecting the easiest place over the Revillas stream. The French garrison had 4,700 effectives, there was an adequate provision of guns, ammunition and stores and, in General Phillipon, a governor of proven determination and great skill.

Having set aside 35,000 men in covering forces to guard against the interference of Marmont and Soult, Wellington had available for the work of the siege four Anglo-Portuguese Divisions (Third, Fourth, Fifth and Light) and some additional Portuguese. The siege train consisted of 16 24-pounder guns, 16 howitzers of the same calibre and 20 18-

pounders of Russian manufacture found in the Lisbon arsenal. There were 862 artillerymen, all drawn from field batteries and two-thirds of them Portuguese. Of the 22,367 round shot for the 24-pounders, one-third were designed for either 22- or 23-pounders.[13] Engineers were, as always, in short supply and the operations were started with only 20 (there had been seven casualties at Rodrigo) and 115 artificers.

The French attack in 1811 had started by way of the Pardaleras outwork. The two British attempts in the same year had concentrated on San Cristobal and, to a lesser extent, the castle. Despite the advice of his engineers, who would have preferred a further attack on the castle,[14] Wellington decided to attack the Picurina fort on the south-east, since it was known that 'the counterguard in front of the right angle of the bastion of La Trinidad [which with the bastion of Santa Maria forms the south-eastern angle of the walls] had been left in an unfinished state.' [15] Siege work started against the Picurina on 17th March and, despite delays due to bad weather, the fort was stormed eight days later with the loss of 320 men. Up to this time, six of the 20 engineers had become casualties.

By the evening of 5th April, two breaches, one in the Trinidad bastion and one in the curtain wall between that and Santa Maria, were judged practicable and orders for an assault that night were issued. They were, however, cancelled three hours before the assault went in and the following day a third breach was blown in the right-hand angle of the Trinidad bastion. The orders for the assault were reissued, start time being put at half-past seven. This, most regrettably, had to be postponed until ten o'clock as the necessary arrangements could not be made in time. The French made excellent use of the two and a half hours given to them and, under cover of darkness, covered the breaches with obstacles.

The assault on the three breaches was entrusted to the Light Division on the left and the Fourth Division on the right. Both divisions were to be led by storming parties of 500 men 'attended by twelve ladders'. At the same time the Third Division was to attempt to carry the castle by escalade. To do this they were to pass to the north of the San Roque lunette and cross the Revillas stream on a broken bridge and a mill dam. As a diversion, a Portuguese brigade was to attack the *tête-de-pont* on the north bank of the Guadiana. On the day before the assault took place a further attack was ordered. The Fifth Division was instructed to attempt to escalade the bastion of San Vicente at the north-west corner of the town where the main town wall joins the lower wall along the river front.

Promptly at ten o'clock the Third, Fourth and Light Divisions moved against the fortifications. 'The night was dark, and without moon, and the movements of the columns concealed for a time; but they were soon unmasked by the pale but powerful glare of fire-balls, and in an instant a flood of fire poured over the breaches, sweeping everything before it like the lava down the side of a mountain.' [16] 'The parapet of the whole front poured forth fire. The glare of light occasioned by explosions of gunpowder and other combustibles, by fire-balls, the firing of cannon, incessant peals of musketry, the bursting of shells and hand-grenades, gave to the breaches and to the whole front, an awfully grand appearance.' [17] 'Our columns moved on under a most dreadful fire of grape that mowed down our men like grass. We tore down the palisading and got upon the glacis. My captain was shot in the mouth. Eight or ten officers [of the Ninety-fifth Rifles], and men innumerable, fell to rise no more. Ladders were resting upon the counterscarp from within the ditch. Down these we hurried, and as fast as we got down rushed forward to the breaches, where a most frightful scene of carnage was going on. Fifty times they were stormed, and as often without effect, the French cannon sweeping the ditches with a most destructive fire. The ditch, from the place where we entered to near the top of the breaches, was covered with dead and dying soldiers. If a man fell wounded, ten to one that he ever rose again, for the volleys of musketry and grapeshot that were incessantly poured amongst us made our situation too horrid for description. I had seen some fighting, but nothing like this. We remained passively here to be slaughtered, as we could do the besieged little injury from the ditch.' [18] So great were the difficulties of passing the ditch and so heavy was the fire that it was never possible to form on the far side a sufficiently strong storming party to carry the breach. The small parties that with measureless gallantry struggled up to the crest were either shot down or stopped by the obstacles which Governor Phillipon and his engineers had devised. Looking at these the next day an officer who had tried to surmount them found 'a breast work of sandbags upon [the breach], constructed for the enemy to fire over a strong *chevaux de frise*. Placed in front and across the breaches here and there were large beams studded with long spikes irregularly thrown about to impede our advance. Behind these breast-works the ground was cut and intersected with deep trenches. In the bottom of these trenches were fixed swords and bayonets fixed upon pieces of wood to wound those who fell upon them. The ramparts were lined with live shells and barrels of powder, cart wheels and lumps of wood and iron ready to be thrown into the ditch.' [19] After two hours of this carnage, when they had lost more than 1,800 men, the Fourth and Light Divisions fell back. They had failed to storm the breaches but they had drawn away so many of the garrison to repel them that they had ensured the fall of the town. At the castle the Third Division met with great difficulties. Having clambered up a rocky slope on which it was hardly possible to walk upright, four of their five ladders were broken as they were reared against the wall. They lost more than 500 men but they carried the castle. This, in itself, would have caused the fall of Badajoz on the following morning, but before they could exert a decisive influence on the struggle they would have had to fight a second battle to break out into the town. As it was, the final blow was struck by Leith's Fifth Division at the bastion of San Vicente. So many of the garrison had been called away to oppose the Fourth and Light Divisions that Walker's brigade had, at first, more trouble with the fortifications than with the French: 'The rampart at this point was surrounded by a regular ditch, into which there was no descent but with the assistance of the ladders which we carried, and the rampart itself, nearly 30 ft. high, with revetment. Our 24 ft. ladders, therefore, of which we were supplied with about twenty, had nearly played us a trick; but the parapet above the cordon was climbable on such an occasion to such as were not interfered with from 'above. It was some time before we could establish our footing upon the rampart, but through General Walker's exertions it was at length effected, and we had thrown, or rather lifted, four regiments into the town before midnight.' [20] General Walker's brigade did not have such an uninterrupted progress throughout. Following their orders, the brigade started to make 'a circuit of the interior of the works, to come in rear of the enemy's troops defending the breaches'. As the leading troops moved into the town a panic, absurd in less highly strung circumstances, was started. 'The flame of a portfire struck a terror into the minds of men that artillery, musketry, walls, and the bayonets of French infantry had failed to daunt. Part of General Walker's brigade, mistaking this appearance for the forerunner to the explosion of a mine, broke and were bayoneted back. Fortunately General Leith had advanced part of the right brigade of his division in support of that already in the town. The second battalion of the 38th regiment had ascended, and were formed on the ramparts. When the circumstances above detailed occurred, that corps, being prepared, received the pursuing enemy with a volley and a bayonet charge that speedily terminated all contest. . . . Having succeeded in penetrating and dispersing all his opponents, General Leith sent an officer to report to Lord Wellington that the 5th division was in the town. His bugles sounded the advance in all directions, distracting the enemy's attention, and inducing him to believe that he was to be assailed from all quarters. . . . The 4th and light divisions, which had previously been withdrawn, again advanced, and marched into the town by the breaches.' [21]

Badajoz was won. The cost in casualties for the whole siege was 4,670; for the storm alone 3,713. 'The capture of Badajoz', wrote Wellington to the Secretary for War, 'affords as strong an instance of the gallantry of our troops as has ever been displayed. But I greatly hope that I shall never again be the instrument of putting them to such a test as they were put last night. . . . These great losses could be avoided, and, in my opinion, time gained in every siege, if we had properly

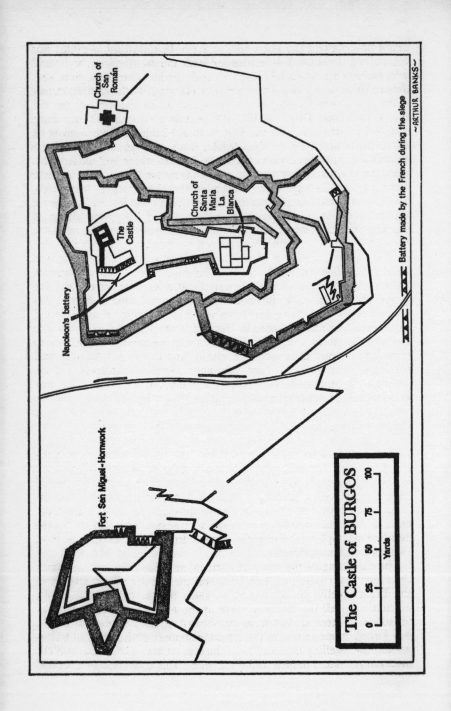

Church of San Román

Church of Santa Maria La Blanca

The Castle

Napoleon's battery

Fort San Miguel-Hornwork

Battery made by the French during the siege

~ARTHUR BANKS~

The Castle of BURGOS

0   25   50   75   100

Yards

trained people to carry them on. . . . When I ordered the assault I was certain that I should lose our best officers and men. It is a cruel situation for any person to be placed in, and I earnestly request your lordship to have a corps of sappers and miners formed without loss of time.'

The capture of Badajoz was a great feat. From that time the initiative passed finally into Wellington's hands. Portugal was safe from everything but the merest raid. Salamanca, Vitoria and every battle up to Toulouse became possible. With such a list of casualties there was bound to be controversy about the details. Wellington had made up his mind to be 'his own engineer' and had chosen to attack from the Picurina fort. The engineers would have had him attack by way of the castle. Anyone who has seen the approach to the castle may be excused for doubting the practicability of that route had the castle been fully manned and supported by the reserves which would have been available had the French strength not been drawn away by the repeated devotion of the Fourth and Light Divisions. On the other hand Wellington's chosen assault on the wall near the Trinidad bastion failed, although the fact that he devoted more men to the attacks on the castle and San Vicente showed that he expected it to fail but reckoned that, heavy as the loss at the breaches might be, it was itself a diversion which would make the other attacks succeed. 'Such an arrangement', wrote a senior engineer officer who was present, 'shows no very great confidence to have been placed in the main operation; and to the correct judgment formed on that head by Lord Wellington, with his firmness and resource, in seconding the assault by such unusual arrangements the army is indebted for its success against Badajoz.' [22]

Burgos, September–October 1812

It was the opinion of Sir John Fortescue that 'beyond all question the abortive siege of Burgos was the most unsatisfactory operation on Wellington's part during the whole of the Peninsular War'.[23] Few would dissent from this opinion, but although it must be admitted that the immediate operations of the siege were costly and ineffective, the long-term effects were wholly beneficial and contributed as much to the eventual triumph of driving the French from Spain as did most of Wellington's major victories.

The shattering of the Army of Portugal at Salamanca led directly to the French evacuation of Andalusia and the other provinces south of the Tagus. Wellington's attempt to seize Burgos led to the French evacuation of all the territory north of the Ebro, except for a handful of isolated fortresses. When, in October 1812, the Army of the North was forced to put 12,000 into the field in support of the Army of Portugal to drive Wellington away from Burgos, control of Navarre and the Biscayan provinces passed to the guerrillas. This could not be tolerated for more than a short time since the main French supply route for the whole of Spain, excepting Catalonia, Valencia and parts of Aragon, lay through the lost district. When the allies were safely shepherded back to Portugal, the Army of the North was quite incapable of reconquering their area of responsibility. To assist them in their task Napoleon had to order the six infantry divisions of the Army of Portugal to march north and operate against the guerrillas. Because of this diversion of strength Wellington was able to set out on the early summer campaign with a comfortable numerical superiority. The fiasco at Burgos led directly to the victory at Vitoria.

The consequence of the victory at Salamanca set Wellington a wholly new problem and one which he continued to be uncertain how to answer. The magnitude of his victory had exposed him to the very dangers which he knew his army could not surmount. The rout of the Army of Portugal meant that the other French armies must concentrate against him and such a concentration would be irresistible. His only hope lay in catching and destroying other single French armies before they could join the concentration. For the moment the Army of Portugal was a negligible factor. To chase it to the Ebro would only exhaust his already tired troops and present a longer and more thinly held flank to a threat from the south. Thus, he moved on Madrid partly in the slight hope that he might be able to trap and destroy the small Army of the Centre, but principally from the need to establish a powerful front against the Army of the South. He knew that Soult must evacuate Andalusia and join King Joseph. Not only was it elementary military sense that he should do so, but he had seen copies of several orders from Joseph to Soult instructing him to move as soon as possible. The fact that Soult did not make contact with Joseph until 2nd October, weeks after he should have done so, was fortuitous. It is never safe for a commander to work on the assumption that his opponent's subordinates will disobey him.

Wellington entered Madrid on 12th August. The Army of the Centre had decamped and there was no sign of Soult. On the other hand the Army of Portugal was showing renewed evidence of activity. On 14th August Clausel reoccupied Valladolid and sent Foy on a raid along the north bank of the Douro. Since the only allied force in this direction, apart from the almost useless Spanish Army of Galicia, was the Sixth Division, which had lost more than a quarter of its strength at Salamanca, reinforced by five newly-arrived battalions and a cavalry brigade, it was clear that more troops would have to march north to drive Clausel back and hold him in check. Wellington, therefore, left in and around Madrid his tiredest and, as it happened, best divisions, the Third, Fourth and Light, and returned to the Douro with the remainder. He saw this move not as a major operation but as a short expedition, after which he and one or two divisions would return to Madrid to act against Soult.

Wishing to establish a block which would prevent the Armies of Portugal and the North debouching into the valley of the Douro, it was natural that he should seek to establish himself at Burgos. The town stands at the south-western end of the defile through which runs the only main road from France to the centre of Spain. South of Burgos the road divides, one branch going to Madrid and thence to Andalusia, while another runs to Valladolid, Salamanca and the Portuguese frontier. With Burgos held against them it would be impossible for support to come to King Joseph and Soult except by way of the lower valley of the Ebro, an intolerable detour. Capturing Burgos would be putting a cork in the bottleneck of the French supply lines.

The advance against Clausel was not very hardly contested on either side. In Wellington's words: 'We passed the Douro on the 6th [September], and drove the French from Valladolid: on the 7th we pushed them on, but not very rigorously, till the 16th, on which day we were joined by about 12,000 men of the army of Galicia.* We then drove the enemy before us to Burgos; on the 17th they retired through the town that night and have since continued their march to Rubena.' [24] They left a garrison of 2,000 men in the castle of Burgos.

It was immediately apparent that the taking of the castle was going to be a more difficult task than previous information had suggested. The Commander, Royal Artillery, wrote: 'We have had a view of the castle which appears a more tough job than might have been supposed. It stands on a knoll above the town and is separated from the remaining part of the height by a deep valley and there is a hornwork unfinished on the height which appears the only approach.' [25] Wellington admitted that he had under-estimated and continued to under-estimate the strength of the place. 'It was not unlike a hill fort in India, and I had got into a good many of them.' [26] The fact was that the castle was not in itself a very powerful obstacle but its natural situation made it extremely formidable, as may be gathered from the description of it given by one of the engineers present. 'The defences were found to occupy a conical hill, and to be of a triple nature nearly all round. The lower or outer line consisted of the old escarp wall of the town or castle, modernised with a shot-proof parapet, and flanks ingeniously procured by means of palisades, or tambours, as the salient or re-entering points.

'The second line was of a nature and profile of a field retrenchment, and well palisaded.

'The third, or upper line, was nearly of a similar construction to the second; and on the most elevated point of the cone, the primitive keep

* 'Ragged rascals' was Wellington's description of them in another letter (WD ix 423 to Bathurst, 12 Sep 12).

had been formed into an interior retrenchment, with a modern heavy casemated battery, named after Napoleon.

'The situation of this fortified post was very commanding, excepting on the side of the hill of St. Michael, the summit of which, at less than 300 yards distance, is nearly on the same level with the upper works of the castle, but separated from them by a deep ravine. This height was occupied by a hornwork of large dimensions; the front scarp of which, hard and slippery, 25 feet in height, stood at an angle of about 60°, and was covered by a counter-scarp 10 feet in depth. The whole interior of the hornwork was under the fire of the battery Napoleon, and its branches were well flanked from the works of the castle.' [27]

The means to reduce the fortress were small, even by the standards of British sieges. There were five Engineer officers and five Military Artificers. Of artillery there were five 24-pounder howitzers, which were useless for anything more than keeping the garrison's heads down, and three 18-pounder guns with 1,306 rounds of round shot. It is scarcely surprising that as early as 20th September Wellington was 'a little apprehensive that I have not the means to take this castle',[28] and that two days later he wrote: 'I hope I may take this place; but I doubt it.'

The fact remained that he had to try. If he could not block the French at Burgos there was no other blocking position further west. With the certainty that, sooner or later, Soult would press in on his southern flank, the Armies of the North and Portugal must be held at Burgos or the allied army might as well retreat immediately on Ciudad Rodrigo. The hornwork was stormed on the night of 19th September.

This was the right start to the operation, but it was done clumsily and at the cost of 421 casualties. Most of these were from the 1st Battalion Black Watch who had only just returned to the Peninsula having been absent since Coruña. They attacked with more gallantry than skill and lost 204 men. 'Our loss', reported Wellington, 'was much greater than it ought to have been; which was to be attributed very much to the inexperience of the 42nd regiment. If I had here some of the troops who had stormed so often, I should not have lost a fourth of the number.' [30]

While batteries were erected for the pitiful siege train, an escalade was attempted on the outer wall on the night of 23rd September. It was repulsed with the loss of 158 men. Six days later a sap was driven to the wall and a mine exploded. It burst in the wrong place and the storming party which started out to take advantage of its effect was repulsed without difficulty. The casualties were slight, only 29, but the cumulative effect of these repulses was having a deplorable effect on the troops.

Meanwhile the artillery was making a poor showing. The first pieces to open on the works were the 24-pounder howitzers. Their fire was so ineffective that they were quickly taken out of action as the amount of powder they used far outweighed any effect they achieved. It was hard to find a position from which the three 18-pounders could fire without being overwhelmed, but on 1st October, when they were eventually established in the third battery which had been dug for them, it was hoped they would have great effect. On that morning the French opened on the new battery with overwhelming fire and before the embrasures had been broken through. Two of the three guns were temporarily disabled, one losing a trunnion, the other being split in the muzzle and having its carriage destroyed. It was not until 4th October that something like a concentration was opened on the place where the mine had exploded on 29th September. Another mine was fired that evening and, with some determined storming by 2nd Battalion Twenty-fourth Foot, a substantial portion of the outer wall was captured and held with the loss of 190 men. From there sapping commenced towards the second wall, although it was much interrupted by two well-conducted sorties by the garrison on the nights of 5th and 8th October.

Wellington was becoming increasingly despondent. 'I do not know what to say of this damned place', he wrote on 5th October. 'Our final success is still doubtful. Luckily, the French give me more time than I have a right to expect.' [31] News was coming in from his front that the Army of Portugal was becoming active again, but fortunately there was still no threat from south of Madrid. He was very anxious to go himself to Madrid but it was impossible. There was no one to whom he could entrust the command of the four divisions around Burgos, the senior officer being Henry Clinton of the Sixth Division who, though a gallant divisional commander, was patently inadequate to be in charge of a corps. It was not until late on 11th October that Edward Paget came up to take over the First Division and act as second-in-command to Wellington. Since he had been away from the Peninsula since 1809, when he had done four days' active service before losing an arm, it was impossible to hand over to him without several days of consultations.

Meanwhile the rains set in and made life miserable for the troops, already much downcast by the lack of progress and the heavy casualties. The rain would have been an acceptable discomfort if it had not fallen only in the north of Spain. 'I hope', wrote Wellington to Hill at Madrid, 'the rain which annoys us so much reaches you likewise, and I should think you will have the Tagus in such a state as to feel no apprehension in regard to the enemy's operation, be their numbers what they may.' [32] Even this consolation was denied to him. No rain fell in the upper reaches of the Tagus and the river south of Madrid remained fordable and no obstacle to Soult. While a third mine was preparing to breach the second line of defences, the experiment was tried of attempting to set fire to the enemy's main store house, in the church of San Blanca, using red-hot shot. This again failed. The building refused to

175

catch 'and a deserter tells me that the only injury we did was to kill a *pharmacien* and derange a commissary from his quarters'.[33]

The final assault was mounted on 18th October. It failed once more, almost certainly because the storming parties employed were too small. There were 170 casualties. Already it had been necessary to draw away troops from the siege to resist the pressure being put on the covering force by the Army of Portugal. This, by itself, did not cause Wellington overmuch concern, but on 21st October news reached him that Soult, unhindered by either Ballasteros or the Tagus, was moving in earnest against Madrid with 60,000 men. The game was up and orders were given for a retreat to join Hill.

The siege of Burgos cost the allies more than 2,000 casualties and, in its immediate effects, achieved nothing. Worse than that, it went some way to undermine the confidence of the army in Wellington. A staff officer wrote home that 'from the moment the siege was seriously undertaken it has always appeared to me that there was more of fondness than firmness, or even obstinacy, in the conduct of an enterprise which all the world saw (and it is absurd that he himself did not see) was entered upon with means inadequate and carried on, certainly many days after the success of it was more than doubtful'.[34] A captain in the Guards asked: 'What possible motives could have determined Lord Wellington to persevere so tenaciously, in a siege when his means were totally inadequate, and to incur daily such a certain loss, with so very faint a prospect of success? Certain it is, however, that no operation since the commencement of his command has so little contributed to raise his character, which, was it not established on so firm a base, would have suffered severely.' [35] There were others even more outspoken.

Wellington knew that he was taking a gamble—the kind of gamble he had taken in June 1811 when he tried to seize Badajoz in a fortnight. He failed, as he had always known that he might, but he was convinced that he had taken the only course open to him. If the defile of Burgos could not be secured, he would have no effective guard for his rear while he was engaged with King Joseph and Soult south of Madrid. If this guard could not be maintained he would be beset from front and rear by 100,000 men. If he won, and if, as did not happen, he received the co-operation of Ballasteros and could secure the line of the Tagus, he would have been able to hold all the ground won at Salamanca. The alternative was a retreat to Rodrigo, which would have demoralised his troops and undermined the stability of the government in London, which was already sufficiently unstable.

Two charges can, perhaps, be brought against Wellington: that he did not ensure that adequate equipment was available for the siege and that he did not press his attacks with sufficient strength. Many critics have truly remarked that there was in Madrid a whole arsenal of heavy artillery which he could have drawn upon and that Sir Home Popham, at Santander, had offered to supply him with 24-pounders from his battleships. While these guns undoubtedly existed, the draught animals to move them did not. It took 10 pairs of oxen to move a 24-pounder over mountain roads and this was a very slow process. It would have taken at least a fortnight to move guns from Madrid to Burgos and the oxen to draw them would have to have been sent from the main army at Burgos, taking almost as long again. To get them from Santander would have taken a somewhat shorter time, although the roads were much worse, but from the oxen leaving Burgos to the time when they returned with the guns three weeks must have elapsed and, in the early days of the siege, it seemed that this time would not be available.

There is more justice in the claim, put forward at the time by the senior engineer present, that the final assault would have succeeded, had larger storming parties been used. Wellington was reluctant to lose more men than he could avoid and there is no doubt that the memories of the holocaust at Badajoz preyed on his mind. To the engineer he said: 'Why expose more men than can ascend the ladders, or enter the work at one time?' [36] To the Secretary of State he wrote: 'It is not easy to take a strong place, well garrisoned, when one has not a sufficient quantity of cannon; when one is obliged to save ammunition on account of the distance of our magazines; and when one is desirous of saving the lives of soldiers. Then, nothing in the way of assault can be done excepting by a British soldier; and we cannot afford to lose them.' [37] Moreover, it can be said that, with the exception of the Guards and some of the German Legion, Wellington was poorly served by his infantry, particularly by the Portuguese. All the evidence goes to show that there was none of the enthusiasm for storming which was so remarkable at the attacks on Rodrigo and Badajoz. There was even less enthusiasm for digging, especially as 'they had to work on rock, barely concealed by the surface of clay, and so hard, that it required extraordinary labour to make the slightest impression on it'.[38] The French sharpshooters were numerous, well concealed and accurate, and the balance of artillery superiority at all times lay with the French. Moreover, the troops had been constantly in movement since the campaign of Ciudad Rodrigo started at the New Year. They were tired and months in arrears with their pay.

Wellington, as was his custom, took the blame for the failure. He felt that had he taken the Third, Fourth and Light Divisions, instead of the First, Fifth, Sixth and Seventh, he might have pulled off his gamble,[39] but in the long run he was prepared to admit: 'It was all my own fault.' [40]

CHAPTER NINE

WATERLOO

I don't think it would have done if I had not been there.
Wellington to Creevey, 19th June 1815

The news that Bonaparte had left Elba and was making for France galvanised the Congress of Vienna into an activity and unanimity which was quite untypical of its previous proceedings. Wellington, who was the British representative at the Congress, wrote: 'Here were are all zeal, and, I think, anxious to take the field. I moderate these sentiments, as much as possible, and get them on paper.' [1] Before long it was agreed, on paper, that Austria, Britain, Russia and Prussia should each put in the field on the frontiers of France 150,000 men. Since Britain would not be able to secure such a number she would make up her share with subsidies in gold for the remainder. Meanwhile, there was to be no war with France, the territory of His Most Christian Majesty (now bustling away to Ghent), but Napoleon Bonaparte was declared to have deprived himself of the protection of the law, having shown that there could be no peace with him.

This, as far as it went, was all very well, but to gather this vast army together would take time, at least as long as it took the Russian contingent to march across Germany. In the meantime Napoleon reestablished himself in France, where he had to hand a very substantial army and a large reserve of discharged veterans who were only too eager to rally to him.

Wellington reached Brussels to take up the command of the Anglo-Hanoverian army on 4th April. He joined in the social life of the city with a light-heartedness and outward confidence which left Creevey with 'the impression of his having made a very sorry figure, in giving no indication of superior talents'. [2] Beneath the surface it was different, and when Creevey mentioned the Duke's lightheartedness to the British Ambassador he was bluntly told: 'Then he is damned different with you from what he is with me.' [3]

There was every reason for Wellington to be concerned at the difficulties confronting him. He was convinced that Napoleon's best course would be an immediate attack on Brussels, driving the allies before him. This would give him an easy victory to rally France behind him, further humiliate Louis XVIII and bring down the carefully contrived kingdom of the Netherlands, almost the only piece of political arrangement his opponents had been able to agree upon since they had deposed him a year earlier. 'It seems to me that we must be prepared to oppose a *coup-de-main* which might be attempted at any moment' was his opinion on the day after his arrival in Brussels.[4]

Should such a *coup-de-main* be attempted there were not the means in Belgium to resist it. At the time of his arrival the British troops stationed in the Netherlands amounted to 800 cavalry and 11,000 infantry.* There were in addition 3,000 cavalry and 3,000 infantry of the King's German Legion. Owing to the demands of the recently concluded American War, the native British battalions were almost all of the poorest quality and short of numbers. Such men as they had in the ranks were largely boys and sub-standard adults. Even the Horse Guards could not say more of them than that they were 'weak corps and inefficient battalions as had been originally sent to Holland upon a sudden emergency and in the absence of better troops'.[5] Of 17 line battalions, totalling 8,500 men, only eight were over their half strength of 500 men. Three battalions of Guards were somewhat stronger, the weakest having 765, but they too had been made up to strength with boys. Only three battalions and detachments of two others had been in the Peninsular army, and these again had been much diluted with drafts to take the place of time-expired men. The battalions and regiments of the Legion had more experience, but although all the five German cavalry regiments were more than 500 strong only two of the six battalions had that number in the ranks. The most reinforcement that could be looked for, apart from some drafts, was a brigade of heavy cavalry and some infantry battalions which might, or might not, arrive back from America, the earliest being expected about the middle of May. Some more infantry might be spared from Ireland if the state of the country made this possible or if the government could sort out the legal problems involved in calling out the militia at a time when the country was not technically at war.

In support of this small force was the Hanoverian army, 1,000 cavalry and 12,000 infantry, some newly raised regulars, the remainder militia. Apart from a few who had served in Napoleon's Germanic levies, all these men were newly raised and scarcely trained. The whole contingent was deficient in officers. Weak and inefficient as the Hanoverians were, they were unquestionably under Wellington's command. The Netherlands army was, at the beginning of April, very small, amounting to 7,250 men.[6] It was being rapidly expanded, but was completely officered

---

* These figures are for rank and file only and are probably correct. The various returns printed in SD x pp. 1, 49, 716, 717–19, 724, 724–5, are hopelessly confused and contradictory. Some of them include troops which it was hoped would arrive there shortly. Some seem to give totals for all ranks or include veteran battalions. One at least includes two regiments in two different places.

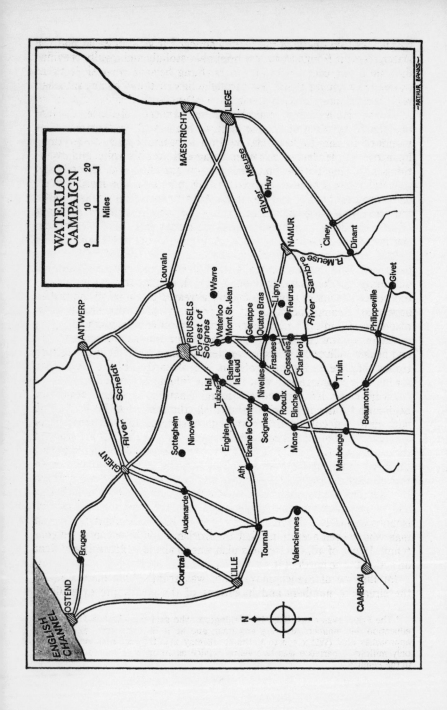

by men who had been in the French service.[7] It was probable that the Dutch element in this raw army might act stolidly and loyally provided they were not called upon to do anything beyond what their slight training had taught them, but the reliability of the Belgians, who had been forced most unwillingly into the Dutch-controlled Kingdom of the Netherlands, must remain doubtful. Another obstacle was the attitude of the King of the Netherlands who, 'with professions in his mouth of a desire to do everything I can suggest, objects to everything I propose. . . . He has given me no command over his army, and everything is for negotiation, first with his son and then with himself; and although he is, I believe, a well-meaning man, he is the most difficult person to deal with I have ever met. He is surrounded by persons who have been in the French service. . . . I would not trust one of them out of my sight.'[8] In despair at the need for more reliable troops, Wellington asked for 12,000 or 15,000 Portuguese troops to be shipped to Belgium. They at least could be used as if they were British and if Beresford were to accompany them, there would be the additional advantage that he, as a Marshal of Portugal, would outrank the 24-year-old Prince of Orange who, having been created a general in the British service as a compliment during the peace, must now inevitably command a corps unless a responsible senior officer could be found.*

The only items in plentiful supply were untrained junior staff officers and general officers. 'We have,' wrote the Duke, 'scarcely more English troops than we have general officers.'[9] It is hard to blame Wellington for his sweeping assertion that it was an 'infamous army'.[10]

Away to his left, around Liège and Namur, a Prussian army was beginning to assemble. Like the British, the ranks had been filled up with drafts of untrained boys and they suffered from a shortage of muskets. In their ranks was a contingent of 14,000 Saxons who, in early May, mutinied and had to be sent away. The temporary commander was Count Gneisenau, a competent but hidebound staff officer, who viewed the Duke with wholly unmerited suspicion on the grounds that his service in India had 'so accustomed himself to duplicity that he had at last become such a master of the art as even to outwit the Nabobs themselves'.[11] His liaison officer at British headquarters was a man who viewed everything that the British did with unconcealed contempt. Worst of all, Gneisenau's plan was to abandon Brussels and fight an action to the north of it.

Intelligence of French movements was scanty. 'Information about the situation, numbers and intentions of the enemy are exceedingly

* The Prince was much liked by Wellington, who said that 'he has a very good education, his manners are very engaging, and he is liked by every person who approaches him' (WD x 390 to Bathurst, 18 May 13). The fact remained that his only military experience was two years' service as an extra A.D.C. to Wellington in the Peninsula.

vague',[12] complained the Duke on his first arrival. It was not easy to improve it. 'In the situation in which we are placed at present, neither at peace nor at war, unable on that account to patrole up to the enemy and ascertain his position by view, or to act offensively upon any part of his line, it is difficult, if not impossible, to combine an operation, because there are no data on which to found any combination.' [13] Much information did come through, some of it from travelling Englishmen, most from French refugees. Most of it was inaccurate, much was contradictory. 'There is,' the Duke complained, 'a good deal of *charlatanism* in what is called procuring intelligence.' [14] Most of the information pointed to Napoleon's position being precarious. This was so widely believed that in early May the Secretary of State was able to assert to Wellington that: 'All the private accounts from Paris concur in representing Bonaparte's power being on the decline, and that he must be overthrown.' [15]

In the two months after Wellington's arrival in Brussels the situation slowly improved. The King of the Netherlands created the Duke a field-marshal and gave him the command of his troops.* Prince Blücher, a fine, tough, attacking soldier for all his 71 years, took over command of the Prussians. With him the Duke quickly built up a close and friendly working arrangement based, apparently, on a total disparity of temperament except that both men were fiercely honest. A new and agreeable liaison officer came from Blücher to Brussels, and to Blücher's headquarters Wellington sent Colonel Hardinge, one of his favourite young officers. The strength of the Prussian army rose to 100,000 infantry. Similarly, the strength of the Anglo-Netherlands army, with its German contingents, Hanoverians, Brunswickers and Nassauers, reached 80,000, of whom 14,000 were cavalry. There were now 22 battalions from the Peninsular army, 'my old Spanish infantry' as Wellington called them. This figure was, however, misleading as many of the men in the ranks were by no means veterans. For example, the Fifty-second, the strongest regiment at Waterloo with 1,079 in the ranks, contained drafts of 36 sergeants and 558 men who had joined it since its return from the South of France. The command and staff structure had also improved immeasurably. Most of the officers in the Quartermaster-General and Adjutant-General's departments were now experienced men who had learned their jobs under Wellington, and of the generals almost all had served in the Peninsula, either commanding formations or units. There were three serious disappointments. Alexander Dickson did not arrive back from America in time to take the chief command of the artillery; George Murray, although appointed, was delayed too long by contrary winds to take over the Quartermaster-

---

* This seems in the first place to have referred only to the infantry. Uxbridge complained that it was not until the morning of the battle of Waterloo that the Netherlands cavalry came under Wellington's command.

Generalship, and the Horse Guards, in direct opposition to Wellington's wishes, insisted on sending Lord Uxbridge to command the cavalry instead of Stapleton Cotton (now Lord Combermere).

The army was no longer 'infamous' but it was still weak. Wellington had asked for '40,000 good British infantry' [16] and 150 field guns and he had got only 20,310 British and 3,285 K.G.L. infantry with 90 British and 18 German field guns. In the long run it was the British and K.G.L. infantry which counted. A fortnight before the battle, Wellington, walking in the park in Brussels with Creevey, saw 'a private soldier of one of our infantry regiments . . . gaping about at the statues and images:—"There" he said, pointing at the soldier, "it all depends upon that article whether we do the business or not. Give me enough of it and I am sure." ' [17]

By the beginning of June it was known that the French army was starting to concentrate on the Belgian frontier. The enemy strength was assessed with reasonable accuracy at around 110,000 infantry and cavalry, but there was no detailed information of Napoleon's intentions. There could be no doubt that the Emperor's aim was to seize Brussels and that to do this he must inflict a decisive defeat on either the Prussian or the Anglo-Netherlands army. The numerical strength of the three armies (Blücher, 99,645 infantry, 13,648 cavalry, 304 guns. Wellington, 56,637 infantry, 14,480 cavalry, 174 guns. Napoleon, 87,650 infantry, 22,236 cavalry and 366 guns*) was such that the French, with a very high proportion of veterans in their ranks, would be more than a match for either of the allied armies if engaged singly but would have only a modest chance of victory against the two of them in combination. Napoleon must therefore defeat one of his opponents before he reached Brussels. To take the city by mere manoeuvring would leave him in an awkward salient with a fully concentrated army at either flank, a dangerous situation which he would be unlikely to risk. It was reasonable to assume that the French would know that the allied army was much extended in its cantonments and that Napoleon, working from previous experience, would expect the British to be sensitive about their lines of communication which ran parallel to the front on the line Brussels–Ghent–Ostend. He might also believe that co-operation between the allies would be defective.

With these considerations in mind, it was probable that the main French thrust would fall in the 75-mile gap between Courtrai and Namur, between the watery coastal plain and the woods and foothills of the Ardennes. There might, of course, be diversionary thrusts outside these limits, possibly as far west as the sea. Within the gap three approaches were open to the French. They could thrust at the allied

* These figures exclude the necessary garrisons of fortresses. Wellington's army had more than 12,000 men in garrison.

right, on either side of the Scheldt, aiming at Ghent; they could strike at the allied left centre, moving on Brussels through Charleroi; they could strike at Brussels through the allied centre by the roads passing through Mons or Ath.

The approach to Ghent would be the longest of the three for reaching Brussels but, being the nearest thing to an open flank in the allied position, offered the best chance of catching one of their armies isolated. Wellington's army could be concentrated on the Scheldt without difficulty, but the furthest Prussian corps was quartered beyond Liège and could scarcely march to Wellington's support in less than four days, even if the attention of Prussian headquarters could not be diverted by demonstrations south of the Sambre. Within four days Napoleon should have had time to deal with Wellington's motley force. The Prussians could then be dealt with at leisure.*

The Charleroi–Brussels axis seemed the most difficult road on which to attack. It was the only part of the front covered by a natural obstacle, the river Sambre, and although the riverline could not be held indefinitely, it should have been possible to impose at least 24 hours' delay there.† Such a delay would greatly simplify the task of concentrating the allied armies, and since it was near the centre of their cantonments, it was the area in which concentration could be achieved most quickly.

The Mons–Brussels line (probably with a second thrust through Ath) gave the greatest chance of success. The road to Brussels was shorter than that through Charleroi. There was no natural obstacle and the artificial obstacle of the fortress of Mons could be by-passed without difficulty. Behind Mons the Anglo-Netherlands army would be concentrated and ripe for destruction before the Prussians, pinned down by demonstrations, could join them.

Wellington recognised that any of these three approaches might be used and quartered his troops accordingly. His own belief, in early June, was that the attack would be through Mons, a belief in which he was strengthened by a report received from an agent in the first week of June which said that it was Napoleon's intention to 'make a false attack on the Prussians, and a real one on the English army'.[18]

The positions of the allied armies were dictated partly by tactical considerations and partly by the necessity of feeding the troops.‡ Four of the British divisions (three of them including a brigade of Hanoverians) were stationed respectively around Audenarde, Ath, Enghien and

---

* Napoleon did not know, and almost certainly did not suspect, that Wellington had promised Blücher to drop his communications with the sea if the need arose.

† It is not known whether the Sambre was fordable. Probably it was not. Certainly no Frenchman seems to have forded it when the attack came.

‡ Belgium is a rich and fertile country, but the harvest was not gathered until after Waterloo and substantial forces had been in the country for many months past.

Soignies and the three Netherlands divisions were at Sotteghem, Roeulx and Nivelles. The Reserve, including a strong British division and the Brunswick contingent, was in Brussels, a newly arrived brigade of Peninsular veterans at Ghent was moving up to Brussels and 7,000 more good Peninsular infantry, returning from America, were expected towards the end of June. The main body of the British and Hanoverian cavalry was in the villages around Ninove. The Netherlands cavalry watched the line of the frontier and there was an intelligence centre at Mons in the charge of Major-General Dörnberg, a Brunswicker in the British service.

Wellington's responsibility for the front stopped a little to the east of Binche. Beyond that was the Prussian 1st Corps, with its head-quarters at Charleroi and its outposts on the south bank of the Sambre on a line from Thuin to Dinant where they were in touch with their 3rd Corps. The 3rd Corps had its main strength in the area Huy–Ciney and to the north of them, across the Meuse, was 2nd Corps with head-quarters at Namur. The 4th Prussian Corps lay around Liège.

By 14th June the information reaching both Blücher and Wellington made it plain that the bulk of the French army was concentrated around Maubeuge. The Prussians began to draw in their more easterly troops. The warning order for this move was passed to Wellington but the executive order, issued at 11.30 p.m., was not. By night there was an indication that parts of the French force had moved somewhat east-wards to Beaumont, but it was still probable that the thrust, when it came, would be by Mons, although an advance by Binche and Nivelles could not be ruled out.

Wellington spent the morning of 15th June at his desk writing, amongst some other routine business, a long memorandum to the Czar making recommendations about the deployment of the Russian armies which were at last beginning to arrive on the Rhine. During the afternoon the Prince of Orange, who commanded the more easterly of Wellington's two corps, rode into Brussels. He had visited the outposts beyond Mons early in the morning and had found all quiet. Shortly before three, when he was due to dine with the Duke, a message reached him that the Prussians had been in action at Thuin and that there was musketry to be heard from the direction of Charleroi. About four o'clock, while the Duke and the Prince were still at dinner, there arrived General Baron Müffling, Blücher's liaison officer, with a note despatched from Charleroi at 9 a.m. saying no more than that the Prussian outposts south of the Sambre were being driven in. Soon after this a further message came in from the Prince of Orange's headquarters reporting that the Prussians had moved eastward from Binche. All was quiet in front of Mons and Maubeuge was now believed to be occupied only by National Guards. At 6 p.m. a message arrived from Prussian head-quarters repeating the information contained in the message from

Charleroi and asking Wellington to concentrate his army, in accordance with previous plans, at Nivelles.

This the Duke was not prepared to do. His only information was that the French had attacked the Prussians on the south bank of the Sambre in the early morning. The Prussian corps commander at Charleroi, General Zieten, had orders to pass all information direct to Brussels. Up to that morning he had been punctilious in doing so. It was fair to assume that he would continue to do so, especially if some important news, such as a major attack on his front, came to hand. There was, in the early evening, no credible reason for believing that the fighting that morning was anything but a feint against the Prussians which could be held on the line of the Sambre and that the real attack would fall further west. All that could safely be done was to order the divisions to concentrate on their respective headquarters, a process which must in any case take some hours. The most westerly division, the Fourth at and beyond Audenarde, was ordered to march eastward while the brigade at Ghent was put in march for Brussels. All were to be 'ready to move at the shortest notice'.

Later in the evening further, though still indefinite, news came in, gained probably from fugitives from the Prussian right flank. From this it appeared that the attack on Charleroi might really be serious. Thereupon at 10 p.m. 'After Orders' were issued calling for the Reserve to move as soon as possible 'by the road to Namur, to the point where the road to Nivelles separates'.* The remainder of the British divisions was to start moving to a concentration area around Nivelles, although clearly some of them would not be able to reach it on the following day.

These orders issued, the Duke, accompanied by Baron Müffling,† went, soon after midnight, to the Duchess of Richmond's ball. Every precaution which could be taken had been taken, the troops were on the move and all now depended on their marching power. His presence at the ball could serve a useful purpose in calming the English civilians, who were showing a tendency to panic. The ballroom made a convenient and agreeable command post. Both corps commanders,‡ the commander of the allied cavalry, three divisional commanders from outside Brussels, eight brigade commanders and the Commander, Royal Artillery, were due to be present,[19] as were most of the allied liaison officers and such senior staff as were not engaged in getting out the orders for the move.

It was after 1 a.m., while supper was being served, that the next news arrived. An A.D.C. from the Prince of Orange's headquarters galloped

* This point was to become famous three days later as the field of Waterloo.
† Müffling does not appear to have been invited to the ball.
‡ According to his biographer, General Lord Hill, commanding 2nd Corps, did not in fact attend.

in with information that the French had penetrated 12 miles north of Charleroi and had been held up by a brigade of Nassauers at Quatre Bras. Wellington had been particularly well served during the day by three of his subordinate commanders. Prince Bernard of Saxe-Weimar, commanding the Nassau brigade which was stationed at Quatre Bras and Frasnes, decided, when his advanced battalion was driven in, that he would stand and fight at Quatre Bras, although he was without orders to do so. His divisional commander, Baron de Perponcher, resolved to support him with his other brigade, and the Prince of Orange's Quartermaster-General, Major-General Constant de Rebecque, hearing of their decision, ignored Wellington's first orders, which would have concentrated Perponcher's division at Nivelles, confirmed Perponcher's decision to support Prince Bernard and ordered other Netherlands troops to start moving to their support. Between the three of them they saved the campaign and the Duke was warm in his thanks to them.

Wellington left the ball to go to bed soon after 2 a.m., announcing his intention to ride out to Quatre Bras at 5 a.m. He had had an unsatisfactory day. He had started with a false appreciation of the enemy's intentions. His allies had given him just enough information to allow him to believe that his appreciation was right and had then stopped sending him news of any kind. When he went back to his house in the Rue Royale after leaving the ball, he still had no information from the Prussians dated later than 9 a.m., although they had been fighting within three hours' ride of Brussels. As it was, the situation could be saved. About the time that Wellington got into bed Picton's Fifth Division and the Brunswick contingent marched out of Brussels by the Namur gate on their way to Waterloo. The Third Division under Charles von Alten, 'by far the best of the Hanoverians',[20] would be assembled at Nivelles, eight miles from Quatre Bras, early the next day. Provided that the French did not make too bold a thrust early in the morning, there was every hope that the situation could be stabilised.

At half past four the Duke was woken on the arrival from Mons of General Dörnberg. From him, at last, he began to get a clear picture of the situation. The French army was across the Sambre, held Gosselies and had its advanced posts at Frasnes and on the outskirts of Fleurus. The Prussian army which had opposed the difficult river crossing with no more than skirmishers, and without troubling to destroy the bridges, was concentrating behind Fleurus with the apparent intention of fighting a decisive battle. Most of this Wellington had already divined from the scraps of information which had come his way. He ordered Dörnberg to ride after Picton with instructions to continue his march beyond Waterloo to Quatre Bras. Orders were sent to the rest of the army to make Quatre Bras their concentration point. About 7 a.m. the Duke was able to mount his horse and set off to the south.

Soon after 9 o'clock Wellington arrived in Quatre Bras and found the crossroads held by 6,000 Nassau and Netherlands troops with eight guns. There was no sign of the French, and since he had no cavalry he could not patrol forward to establish their position. He also learned the whereabouts of Blücher, who was about six miles away. Since, when he had surveyed and approved the positions of Perponcher's division, there was still no sign of the enemy, he rode over to see his ally and, while watching the French columns advance against the Prussian position at Ligny, explained the situation of the Anglo-Netherlands army to Blücher. Having promised to come to his assistance when his divisions came up provided that the position at Quatre Bras was not attacked, he rode back to the crossroads.

Ney, who commanded the French left, had seen nothing in Napoleon's orders to him which required him to hurry his advance that morning. He therefore allowed time for his rear divisions, which were spread over many miles of road, to close up. It was not until after one o'clock that his leading infantry came in touch with Perponcher's outposts. Even then, finding Quatre Bras apparently confidently held, he waited until two divisions of Reille's corps were in hand before launching an attack. Wellington had won the battle of Quatre Bras during the previous five years in the Peninsula. Too often had French commanders, including Ney and Reille, assaulted seemingly lightly held positions only to find concealed brigades of redcoats behind them. Reille remarked to Ney, 'Ce pourrait bien être une bataille d'Espagne, où les Anglais se montreront seulement quand il sera temps. Il est prudent d'attendre pour attaquer que toutes nos troupes soient massées ici.' [21] Ney listened to him and delayed the attack.

As a result it was not until after two that Ney attacked with two divisions, more than 6,000 infantry, supported by 2,000 cavalry. Immediately the French assault developed the defenders were in trouble, but by that time Wellington was back from his meeting with Blücher and the head of Picton's division was arriving. By a narrow margin the attack was held. In the breathing space that followed, the Brunswickers and some Netherlands cavalry came up. Again the French attacked, with greater numbers. Again the situation was desperate and was saved by the arrival of more British battalions, the Third Division. By this time the road to the rear was choked with stragglers from the Brunswickers, whose Duke had been killed at the head of his cavalry, and with Netherlanders. A third French onslaught was foiled by the arrival of the Guards from the First Division after a 15-hour march. At nightfall the position was secure. The allies had lost 4,800 men and the French rather less, but by that time Wellington's army was sufficiently concentrated and there could be no further danger to it from a mere wing of the French army.

South-east of Quatre Bras heavy cannon fire could be heard from the Prussian position at Ligny, rising in a crescendo about three o'clock, when the first French attack went in, and continuing until nightfall. The news from Ligny was scant. Two Prussian officers were sent to give news to Wellington during the afternoon. One of them was wounded on the way and never arrived; the second merely announced that the fight was hard, that the Prussian 4th Corps from Liège would not arrive in time to assist, and that it was probable that the army would be able to retain their position until nightfall. In consequence, it was not until the following morning, when the Duke sent a patrol across to Ligny and found the French in possession, that he realised that his left was in the air. A casual encounter between one of his A.D.C.s and a Prussian corps commander established that the whole Prussian army had retired on Wavre. While waiting for the report of his patrol, Wellington had been chatting with a young captain of the Guards 'for an hour or more, during which time he repeatedly said he was surprised to have heard nothing of Blücher. At length a staff officer arrived, his horse covered with foam, and whispered to the Duke who, without the least change of countenance, gave him some orders and dismissed him. He then turned round to me and said, "Old Blücher has had a damned good licking and gone back to Wavre, eighteen miles. As he has gone back we must go too. I suppose in England they will say we have been licked. I can't help it, as they are gone we must go too." ' [22] By evening the allied army was concentrated on its chosen fighting position at Mount St. Jean, with the village of Waterloo and the forest of Soignes at its back and Wavre less than seven miles to the east.

There was one part of the army which did not join in the concentration. Nearly 18,000 men, mostly Netherlanders but including a British and an Hanoverian brigade, with 20 guns, were stationed 10 miles out on the right flank at Hal and Tubize. In the event these troops were never engaged and would have been of the utmost value at Waterloo on the 18th, but when he stationed them out on the right Wellington was in no position to assume that Napoleon would make a frontal attack on the Mont St. Jean position. During the night of 17th–18th June Wellington knew that the Prussian army was substantially intact and had all its four corps concentrated around Wavre. It was reasonable to suppose that Napoleon, with his strong force of cavalry, would also be aware of this fact. That Napoleon was the victim of an obsession that Blücher's army was retreating in disorder on Liège was unknowable and would certainly be a most insecure assumption on which to plan. Wellington knew that the Prussians would protect his left and that he had an open right flank. Napoleon was acclaimed as the greatest commander of the age, and it was unreasonable to suppose that he would court the battle, in inferior numbers to the joint allied armies, as must result from an attack on Wellington's left. It would also be rash to assume that the Emperor would fall into the error made by Junot at Vimeiro, by Victor at Talavera, by Massena at Busaco, by Soult at Sorauren, and make a frontal attack.*

The possibility of a retreat had also to be considered. Wellington was too much of a realist not to realise that a French breakthrough was possible if the Prussians did not arrive promptly to his support. In quality his army was vastly inferior to the French. His total strength was some 63,000 infantry and cavalry with 154 guns. In his view he had only 35,000 on whom he could rely,[23] and even this figure included the untrained but solid Hanoverians and the raw British battalions, one of which had behaved badly at Quatre Bras. At the same battle the Peninsular battalions in Picton's division had been badly mauled.†

The strength which Napoleon might be able to bring against him was unknowable. Allowing for losses at Quatre Bras and Ligny, the French strength in infantry and cavalry could be supposed to amount to more than 100,000 men, but there was no way of telling how many of these had been detached to watch Blücher. The Prussians believed, and probably informed Wellington, that they had only 15,000 in front of them. If this was so Napoleon could attack at Waterloo with at least 85,000 men, which would make a long defence impossible and retreat inevitable.‡ All that was certain was that the French would attack in superior strength made up of veteran troops and that their artillery would be superior not only in numbers but in weight of metal.

The direction in which Wellington might have to retreat would depend on the line of the French attack. If his right was forced, and both the topography and his dispositions made this unlikely, the army must fall back on Brussels and Wavre. If the centre or left was broken the retreat must be westward on Tubize and Hal, in which case the detachment stationed there would be invaluable as a rallying point.

Wellington's dispositions in front of Waterloo were dictated by the fact that Blücher had promised to come to his help with two corps, and there was every reason to suppose that these would come into action soon after noon. This meant that the left was secure and the centre reasonably so. It was therefore essential to keep the main strength of the army on the right so that even if Blücher failed to arrive and an overwhelming attack broke the allied centre, there would still be an effective 'army-in-being' to operate against the French left. As long as both Wellington and Blücher had their armies substantially intact

* Early on the 18th both Soult and Reille advised Napoleon against a frontal attack. Reille said: 'Bien postée comme Wellington sait le faire, et attaquée en front, je regarde l'infanterie anglaise comme inexpugnable en raison de sa tenacité calme et de la supériorité de son tir.' Napoleon insisted in believing that the battle would be 'L'affaire d'un déjeuner' (Houssaye 311).

† The Forty-second and Ninety-second both lost over 280 men out of strengths of 577 and 621 respectively.

‡ In fact Napoleon had detached 33,000 men under Grouchy to shepherd Blücher away and attacked at Waterloo with 67,000 men and 266 guns.

there was still everything to play for. Wellington could afford to suffer a defeat such as Blücher had suffered at Ligny. Napoleon could not afford another such victory.

The Mont St. Jean position is a long low ridge at right angles to the Charleroi–Brussels road. To the right of the road the ridge swings forward and ends in a re-entrant which covers the right flank. On the left it shades away into woods and from the front of the ridge falls away more steeply. The effective front of the ridge between the re-entrant and the woods is rather less than three miles, a longer front than could be held by the reliable troops available. It was therefore necessary for Wellington to choose the points to which priority must be given. These were two, the centre where the Brussels road crossed the ridge and, most important, the right wing. It was here that he expected to be attacked but, if he were wrong and the French should break his centre, his right wing must remain powerful enough to act as an anvil to the Prussian hammer.

Thus the right wing was defended in great depth. Out in front the grounds and buildings of Hougoumont were defended by Nassau and Hanoverian troops to whom were added, on the evening of the 17th, the four light companies of the Guards. On the ridge behind were the four battalions of Guards, with their right flank covered by a British brigade which included two Peninsular battalions. A British light cavalry brigade was in support. Further to the rear was the Anglo-Hanoverian Second Division, the strongest and freshest division available, which included five battalions from the Peninsular army. Behind them again the Brunswick contingent held the village of Merbraine and Chassé's Netherlands division was in Brain la Leud at the head of the re-entrant. Thus some 22,000 men, including the two brigades of Guards and seven Peninsular battalions, were stationed on the extreme right.

The point where the Brussels road crosses the ridge was also entrusted to reliable infantry. On the right of the road, where some cover is given by the farm of La Haye Sainte, there was a brigade of the German Legion, including three Peninsular battalions, one of them in the farm itself. To the left, behind a fleeting screen provided by a Belgian brigade, were the eight magnificent but battered Peninsular battalions of Picton's division. In support were the two heavy brigades of British cavalry, and at eleven o'clock on the morning of the battle there arrived three more fresh battalions of Peninsular troops returned under Major-General Lambert from the American war.

The extreme left was sparingly held by two British light cavalry brigades with two Hanoverian brigades of infantry linking them to the centre, while the farms in front, on the floor of the valley, were garrisoned with Nassauers.

The right centre, between the Legion battalions above La Haye Sainte and the Guards, was filled with the troops which remained, a raw British brigade much shaken at Quarte Bras, an Hanoverian brigade and another of Nassauers. In rear were two British cavalry brigades and the Netherlands and Hanoverian cavalry, the latter more for show than for use. The right centre was, however, better supported by artillery than the left. Most of the British artillery was held on the right and three batteries originally detailed to the centre and left were later moved to the right of the main road. The only British artillery which remained on the left of the road were the Rocket Troop and, on the extreme flank, a troop of Horse Artillery.

In the battle of the 18th June Wellington was fortunate in that the French, and in particular Napoleon, made almost every mistake that was open to them. Reille's corps used itself up in fruitless attacks, at a severe disadvantage, against Hougoumont. D'Erlon's corps did not make its first attack until about 1 p.m. and then attacked in divisional columns, a formation which long French experience had shown to be ineffective against British infantry and which deprived them of all their advantage in numbers. Ney, with the Emperor's active assistance, threw away the magnificent body of French heavy cavalry by ordering them to charge unbroken squares. At about 6 p.m. the battle was Napoleon's for the taking. La Haye Sainte had fallen, the allied centre and right centre scarcely amounted to a chain of skirmishers. Desperately Ney sent to Napoleon begging to be reinforced. He was contemptuously refused. When, more than an hour later, the Emperor made up his mind to commit the Imperial Guard it was too late. Wellington had brought up his last reserves and the line was complete. The fact that the Guard also attacked in column only made their overthrow more certain. An hour earlier they could have won the battle in almost any formation.

To offset his good fortune, the tardiness of the Prussians came near to causing a British defeat. Wellington had only fought on the understanding that two Prussian corps would support him. There was every reason to suppose that at least the first of these would be in action by 1 p.m. Their vanguard was within sight of the battlefield by mid-morning but it was not until about four o'clock that they managed to draw off any substantial body of infantry * from the force opposing Wellington. It was nearly seven before they became a major menace to Napoleon's right. The long-drawn-out agony of the British and Hanoverian infantry on the ridge was due entirely to the fact that, partly due to sodden roads, partly to bad staff work, the Prussians were six hours late on the field.

In the end the victory was complete. The French army broke and never rallied. Although the allied artillery, the British cavalry and the Prussians all played their part, the greatest share of the credit belongs

* Six thousand infantry of Lobau's corps.

to the British infantry, whose losses were crippling. At the end of the day, Wellington wrote of them: 'I never saw the British infantry behave so well.' [24] It was the highest compliment he could pay them.

Above all it was Wellington's victory. He was more than justified when he said the following day, 'I don't think it would have done if I had not been there.' [25] During the battle he appeared wherever the danger was greatest, heartening the troops and re-arranging the details of their dispositions. Three times he personally led up the wavering Brunswick battalions and the third time they stayed in line and did their duty. A rifleman of the Ninety-fifth recalled how during the French cavalry charges 'while we were in square the second time, the Duke of Wellington and his staff came up to us in all the fire, and saw we had lost our commanding officers; he, himself, gave the word of command; the words he said to our regiment were thus—"95th, unfix your swords, left face and extend yourselves once more, we shall soon have them over the hill"—and then he rode away on our right, and how he escaped being shot God only knows, for all that time the shot was flying like hailstones.' [26] It was incidents like this, repeated time after time, which kept the troops in their ranks. 'Old Nosey' had never been defeated and so long as he was with them everything must come right in the end.

More than that was his handling of the whole campaign. He saw the essential factor that, so long as his army and Blücher's were kept substantially intact, Napoleon could not win. It was unimportant that both at the outbreak of fighting and before Waterloo he misappreciated the enemy's intentions. He was the greatest improviser in the history of war. No eventuality found him unprepared. As he said of his battles against the French marshals, 'They planned their campaigns just as you might make a splendid set of harness. It looks very well, and answers very well, until it gets broken; and then you are done for. Now I make my campaigns of ropes. If anything went wrong, I tied a knot; and went on.' [27] It was this attitude which won Waterloo.

CHAPTER TEN

THE GENERALS

> I have nothing to do with the choice of General Officers sent out here or with their numbers . . . and when they do come, I must employ them as I am ordered.
>
> *Wellington to Vandeleur, 26th April 1813*

During the Peninsular War and, to a lesser extent, in the Waterloo campaign, Wellington suffered from many shortages—coin, transport, an efficient commissariat, doctors, forage and many others—but nothing circumscribed his operations so much as the dearth of competent general officers. 'I am obliged to be everywhere', he wrote in 1811, 'and if absent from any operation, something goes wrong. It is to be hoped that the general and other officers of the army will at last acquire that experience which will teach them that success can only be attained by attention to the most minute details; and by tracing every point of every operation from its origin to its conclusion, and ascertaining that the whole is understood by those who are to execute it.' [1] The hope was not realised.

The system whereby generals in the British army were created (see pp. 26–8) militated against the supply of capable commanders but, with more than 600 officers of the rank of major-general or above on the Army List, it might have been supposed that enough able men could be found to supply an army of nine divisions. Such, however, was not the case and the Horse Guards were constantly at their wits' end to meet Wellington's not very exacting needs. Sometimes, as in the case of Slade, they sent out a known incompetent (see pp. 214–15). On other occasions they posted a general with the most half-hearted recommendations. About General Lumley, who turned out successfully, they could find nothing better to say than that they had 'never thought him a clever man'. [2] When Wellington, on hearing of the arrival of Sir William Erskine, gently remonstrated that he had 'generally understood [him] to be a madman' [3] the Military Secretary glibly replied that 'no doubt he is sometimes a little mad, but in his lucid intervals he is an uncommonly clever fellow; and I trust he will have no fit during the campaign, though he looked a little wild as he embarked'. [4]

Few of the generals who were sent to the Peninsula were men of Wellington's own choosing. He had a hand in the selection of Beresford and probably in that of Hill. Picton and Crauford he asked for and got, possibly because both were embarrassments to the government in England, Picton having been involved in a judicial scandal in the West Indies and Craufurd being the Opposition's most effective spokesman on military matters in the House of Commons. The only other senior officers sent out at Wellington's request were Graham, Houston, Leith and Nightingall.[5] The first three were sound men, although Graham and Houston were in poor health and Leith was wound-prone. Nightingall, who had served under Wellesley at Vimeiro, turned out badly. He was defeatist and hypochondriac and spent most of his six months with the army scheming for an appointment in India. For the rest, Wellington had to take whoever was sent him, only begging the Secretary of State 'not to send me any violent party men ... or we shall be in a bad way indeed'.[6]

The supply of generals fluctuated. At times there was a desperate shortage. In mid-June 1810 Wellington complained that, 'I have now three brigades in this army without officers even of the rank of colonel to command them.'[7] In 1812 the Light Division was commanded for three months by a lieutenant-colonel before a successor could be found for Robert Craufurd. Later in the war there was a glut, which led Wellington to complain that 'we have more general officers than I know how to dispose of'.[8] 'I hope', he wrote, 'I shall have no more new generals; they really do us but little good and they take the place of officers who would be of use.'[9]

It was difficult to dispose of incompetent generals once they had arrived. Always scrupulously fair to people whom he considered were doing their best however inadequate, Wellington set his face against demanding the dismissal of well-intentioned fools.* He tried to insist that some suitable situation should be found for them in the United Kingdom. Of Slade he wrote: 'I conceive that so fit a person as he could not be selected to command a depot of heavy cavalry.'[10] This reluctance to dispose outright of incompetents eventually angered the Duke of York, but Wellington realised that a recall would mean not only professional but, possibly, financial ruin. A general's pay would cease on the day on which his appointment 'on the staff' ended. There was no system of pensions and since such a man could scarcely return to regimental service, his future might depend on the meagre half-pay of a lieutenant-colonel or major. Undoubtedly some generals had private means, but some did not, and Wellington could hardly dismiss only those who could afford to be dismissed. There were some who were useless through no fault of their own, such as General Löw, one of the Germans, 'a very respectable man, but who is by no means fit

---

* This indulgence did not apply to men whom he considered to be rogues. Lightburne, 'whose many little improprieties render him a discreditable person with the army' (WD vi 485) was confidentially denounced and recalled.

for service in this country'.[11] It was worth keeping some very doubtful officers because their inevitable successors would be even worse. 'I do not see,' said Wellington when he received discretionary orders to send home Erskine, Slade and Long, 'that the service would derive much advantage from sending to England any one of the three general officers, in order that Sir Granby Calcraft may command a brigade.' [12]

Fortunately, many generals were only too anxious to slip off to England for longer or shorter periods. Skerrett, the *bête noire* of the Light Division, took sick leave 'as his father was dead and he was heir to an immense property'.[13] Another applied for leave wishing, as Wellington said, 'to unite himself to a lady of easy virtue'.[14] Ill health was the most frequent excuse. Nightingall had not been with the army three weeks before 'the dread of a return of my Rheumatic complaint' put him in mind that 'a few years might be passed in Bengal with great advantage to myself, and Mrs. N. having her brother and a sister married in that country makes the inducement stronger'.[15] Within six months he had gone. Dr. McGrigor tells of a day, during the siege of Burgos, when he was waiting in Wellington's office, 'when two officers came to request leave to go home to England. An Engineer captain first made his request: he had received letters informing him that his wife was dangerously ill, and that the whole of his family was sick. His lordship quickly replied, "No, no, sir, I cannot spare you at this moment." The captain, with a mournful face, fell back. Then a general officer, of noble family, advanced saying, "My lord, I have lately been suffering much from rheumatism———." Without allowing him time to complete his sentence, Lord Wellington rapidly said, "and you want to go to England to be cured. By all means. Go there immediately." The general, surprised at his lordship's tone, looked abashed, but to prevent him saying more, his lordship turned and began to address me.' [16] This incident has often been quoted as an example of Wellington's harshness to junior officers and indulgence to aristocratic seniors, but at that moment he was attempting to besiege Burgos with only five engineer officers and could genuinely not afford to spare one of them, while no excuse could be neglected to dispose of the services of officers of the calibre of Major-General John Hope,* the general concerned.

It was less satisfactory that officers in whom Wellington could place confidence were not only as prone to be wounded or sick as the incompetents, but were just as likely to demand leave for insufficient reasons. When Massena retreated from Santarem in 1811, Wellington was in greater need than usual of the commander of his cavalry and the commander of the Light Division, yet neither were available. Despite Wellington's urgings, Cotton had returned to England to attend to

* Major-General John Hope, great-grandson of the 1st Earl of Hopetoun, must be distinguished from his kinsman, Lieutenant-General Sir John Hope, later 4th Earl of Hopetoun, who did not join Wellington's army until the following year.

his duties as an M.P., while Craufurd had been overcome by the desire to visit his wife.

Difficulties over seniority were another problem. It needed the greatest tact to persuade a general to serve in a position which was not demonstrably senior to a man below him on the Army List. General John Murray left the army rather than run the risk of having to take orders from Beresford who, although nine places below him on the list of generals, might have had to assert seniority as a Marshal of Portugal. General Tilson went so far as to ask 'to be allowed to return to England, if it is intended to employ his services again in co-operation with the Portuguese troops'.[17] *

'The perpetual changes which we are making, owing to the infirmities, or the wounds, or the disinclination of the General Officers to serve in this country, are by no means favourable to the discipline and success of the army; and do not augment the ease of my situation' was Wellington's comment.[18] At times the situation was desperate. Writing in July 1811 he complained: 'as usual, all the officers of the army want to go home, some for their health, others on account of business, and others, I believe, for their pleasure. General Spencer is going, because General Graham has come from Cadiz; General Nightingall is gone; General William Stewart, General Lumley, General Howorth, and Colonel Mackinnon, likewise, on account of their health. General De Grey has asked to go, because he has put his shoulder out; and I have had this morning an application from General Houston for leave to go, as his spleen is out of order. To this list add General Dunlop, General Hay, General Cole and General Alexander Campbell, who have applied to go to settle their affairs. General Leith is still absent.'[19] Thus at one time the army was without, or was likely to lose, five out of eight commanders of divisions, six infantry and one cavalry brigade commanders and the Commander, Royal Artillery.

In all, 85 men of British origin (including Wellington himself) served in Wellington's army in the Peninsular and Waterloo campaigns in the rank of major-general or above, either in command of formations † or in senior staff appointments.‡ Leaving aside Sir Thomas Graham, who

---

* This put him outside the scope of Wellington's protection of incapable generals. 'I only hope', Wellington wrote to London, 'that General Tilson will not be placed on the staff of the army any where else.' (WD iv 428, to Castlereagh 16 June 09). Tilson retracted his 'erroneous military opinion' and was allowed to remain in command of a brigade.

† It was normal at this time for brigades to be commanded by major-generals.

‡ This figure excludes the Hanoverians (Charles and Victor Alten, Bock, Löw and Hinüber), two Brunswickers (Bernewitz and Dörnberg), besides the Prince of Orange, who in the Waterloo campaign held the British rank of general. The Duke of Brunswick, who was killed at Quatre Bras, was a British lieutenant-general but was serving at the head of his own troops. It also excludes two major-generals, Howorth and Borthwick, from the Royal Artillery, Major-General Sir Marmaduke Peacock, who was commandant of Lisbon, and one or two generals who arrived in

joined the army as a lieutenant-colonel at the age of 46, the most striking thing they had in common was their youth. Charles Colville had been commissioned at the age of 11, William Stewart, Le Marchant and Lord Aylmer had been only 12. On average they had started their military life at the age of 17, although Daniel Hoghton had not become an ensign until the advanced age of 24. Their average age on becoming lieutenant-colonels was rather less than 28, although three of them, Henry Fane, Edward Paget and Charles Stewart, had reached that rank at 19. John Hamilton was 40 before becoming a lieutenant-colonel, which was the average age for becoming a major-general, a rank Edward Paget had achieved at 30. By contrast their two Peninsular colleagues in the Royal Artillery, Major-Generals Howorth and Borthwick, had had to serve 22 and 24 years respectively to reach the rank of lieutenant-colonel by brevet and three years longer for regimental rank.

Three of these generals were peers in their own right, the 9th Earl of Dalhousie, the 2nd Earl of Uxbridge and the 5th Baron Aylmer. Fourteen more were the legitimate sons of peers and two, Beresford and Nightingall, were the illegitimate sons of marquesses. The fathers of seven were baronets, three were judges and one was a dean of the Church of Ireland. John Lambert's father was a captain in the Royal Navy and John Byng's uncle had been the unfortunate admiral. The rest were mostly the sons of minor country gentry, although one, Tilson, was the son of a banker.

For the most part their education had been at the hands of tutors, but ten had been to Eton,* eight to Westminster, three to Harrow and one to Charterhouse. Seven had attended universities, three at Oxford, two at Edinburgh, one at Aberdeen and one at Trinity College, Dublin. If their formal education was sketchy, their military education was even more so. Only three had attended the Royal Military College, where another had been an instructor, eight had attended military academies on the Continent, and Stapleton Cotton had attended a similar institution in Bayswater.

Their practical military experience was more thorough. Three of them had fought in the American War of Independence, and 31 in Flanders in 1793–5; 29 had seen service in the West Indies, 16 in India and 26 in Egypt. Five had been in the small force which defeated the French at Maida and 16 on the Walcheren expedition. Three had seen active service with the Royal Navy, one having been present at the Glorious

---

the Peninsula and left hurriedly (e.g. Sir James Erskine who landed in May 1809 and was home by September). Only generals in the British service are included (e.g. Samuel Whittingham, who was a major-general in the Spanish army, is omitted).

* General Constant de Rebecque, the Prince of Orange's chief of staff at Waterloo and the man who saved Quatre Bras by his initiative, was also an Etonian.

First of June, one at the battle of Cape St. Vincent and William Stewart had, at the special request of Lord Nelson, embarked his newly formed riflemen on board H.M.S. *Elephant* for the battle of Copenhagen. In civilian life 17 of them, when they served under Wellington, were or had recently been Members of Parliament * and, apart from Wellington, one had been a Minister.

Casualties amongst the generals were high. Nine were killed in action under Wellington's command, and three more were killed in other theatres before Waterloo. Two died in the Peninsula from disease, and two fell to their deaths from balconies in Lisbon. Two were made prisoners by the French and 30 were wounded. A reckless bravery was one of the hall-marks of British generals, good and bad. Beresford, at Albuera, unhorsed a Polish lancer with his bare hands; when, at St. Pierre, there was an explosion at William Stewart's feet, he merely remarked: 'A shell, sir, very animating', and went on with his conversation. Skerrett was said by his brigade major 'always to be found off his horse, standing in the most exposed spot under the enemy's fire, as stupidly composed for himself as inactive for the welfare of his command'.[20] The only generals of whose gallantry the army seem ever to have had any doubt were Slade, Long and Hay. Slade came from the Coruña campaign with a reputation for shirking fire (see p. 215) which seems not to have been borne out under Wellington's command, whatever his other abilities. Long drew attention to himself by taking an unnecessarily wide sweep round the guns of Campo Mayor in the Albuera campaign. He claimed this was to avoid a 'deep ravine', but to everyone else the obstacle seemed to be something less spectacular. The talk aroused by this incident would probably have died down had not he repeated the mistake a year later when, in March 1812, Hill had directed him to skirt round a wood to cut off a French detachment. Long again went very wide and Hill sent an officer to him with an order to keep closer to the wood. Long's reply was that 'he wished to keep clear of the skirts of the wood', whereupon the officer sent to him 'remarked that the wood must have skirts more extensive than a dragoon's cloak to keep them at such a distance'.[21]

Andrew Hay was unpopular throughout the army. Captain Swabey, R.H.A., knew him to be inhospitable, a man 'who, notwithstanding that I was an old acquaintance, permitted me to sleep, wet as I was, in my clothes, without offering me a blanket'.[22] His fellow brigade commander in Fifth Division, Frederick Robinson, son of a loyalist American colonel, took a more serious view of him. He wrote to his wife that 'Hay . . . is a fool, and I verily believe, with many others on my side, an arrant coward. That he is a paltry plundering old wretch is estab-

---

* This high figure of parliamentarians was less unusual than it seems. In 1809 four generals, 17 lieutenant-generals, 16 major-generals, 12 colonels and 16 lieutenant-colonels were in the House of Commons.

lished beyond doubt. That he is no officer is as clear, and that he wants spirit is firmly believed.' [23]

Bravery was not enough. As Wellington wrote: 'The desire to be forward in engaging the enemy is not uncommon in the British army; but that quality which I wish to see officers possess, who are at the head of troops, is a cool discriminating judgment in action, which will enable them to decide with promptitude how far they can, and ought to go, with propriety; and to convey their orders, and act with such vigor and decision, that the soldiers will look up to them with confidence, in the moment of action, and obey them with alacrity.' [24] It was this that was chiefly lacking among Wellington's generals. Almost all of them were capable battalion commanders and most of them could be trusted at the head of a brigade. It was when they were required to command a division that their failings began to show. 'It requires some discretion and sense to manage such a concern.' [25] This most of the major-generals did not have. 'When I lately informed the establishment for the telegraphs, I trusted to the General Officers commanding divisions to select officers to superintend the telegraphs given in charge to their several divisions; and Major General Hay, being in command [temporarily] of the 5th division, was trusted to select the officer for that division. He has selected one who is quite incapable of managing that or any other concern; and who, if I be not misinformed, is known to Major General Hay to be so stupid as not to be trusted in any way. We have not been able to pass one message from the right to the left of the army on account of the stupidity of this officer.' [26]

A few were so inadequate that news of them filtered through to the Horse Guards. Of Tilson,* of whom Wellington reported that he 'spends the greatest part of his time in England, and is not very energetic when he is here',[27] the Military Secretary wrote: 'I have heard from several quarters that the habitual want of energy in his character, and his indifference to his profession, have rendered him a burden to the army',[28] and he was recalled just before his promotion to lieutenant-general. For the most part, however, the dead-beats remained and a junior cavalry officer was not far from the mark when he wrote home that 'apart from General Hill there is scarcely a general officer in this army of any talent and very few of any activity, except Sir S. Cotton and I suppose no commander ever had so few clever men on his staff almost all of them being coxcomical and old women'.[29]

There was a handful of competent divisional commanders in the army, but they were men who were temperamentally unsuited to command larger formations. The best were Craufurd, Picton, Pakenham and Cole. Robert Craufurd, until his death at Ciudad Rodrigo, was undoubtedly Wellington's favourite. He had many faults, notably a tend-

---

* Tilson had by this time changed his name to Chowne.

ency to indulge in unnecessary and costly actions. His division, the Light, was the best administered in the army, but he took a most cavalier view of orders coming from above. At the time of El Bodon he had established an unauthorised divisional hospital and, when the time came for a hurried retreat, he had to use all the divisional transport to evacuate his sick. 'We have', wrote an officer serving under him, 'in consequence been very ill supplied during our march—frequently without bread when the rest of the army had plenty. Report says that Lord Wellington has strongly expressed his displeasure at this circumstance, but I really believe that he has got off much easier than his lordship would have allowed any other officer in the army to escape.' [30] When Craufurd published the standing orders for the Light Division a subaltern described them as 'the most *tyrannical* and *oppressive* that were ever compiled by a British officer,' [31] and one of his brigade commanders applied to have his brigade removed from Craufurd's command. But these Standing Orders made the Division the most efficient in the army. 'Seven minutes sufficed to get it under arms during the night; a quarter of an hour, day or night, to gather them in order of battle at the alarm posts, with the baggage loaded and assembled at a convenient distance in the rear; and this not upon a concerted signal, but all times certain, and for many months consecutively.' [32] Wellington said of Craufurd's handiwork: 'The Light, 3rd and 4th Divisions were the *élite* of my army, but the Light had this peculiar perfection. No matter what was the arduous service they were employed on, when I rode up the next day, I still found a *division*. They never lost one half the men the other divisions did.' [33] It is a measure of Wellington's confidence in Craufurd that he put him in charge of the Light Division and kept him there at a time when nine senior officers were only commanding brigades in Portugal.

Picton, who detested 'that damned fighting fellow' Craufurd, shared some of his faults. Having successfullly seized the castle of Badajoz in what was meant to be a diversionary attack and having launched the Third Division at Vitoria into a successful attack by intercepting the orders intended for his senior, Lord Dalhousie, he seems to have decided that he was a great tactician. At the Gave d'Oleron (24th February 1814), and at Toulouse, he launched unnecessary and unauthorised attacks, both with heavy casualties suffered for no purpose. When called upon, during the Pyrenees, to decide the actions of a large corps, his nerve failed him altogether (see pp. 157–8), but at the head of the Third Division he was an indomitable figure. 'I found him', said Wellington, 'a rough foul-mouthed devil as ever lived, but he always behaved extremely well; no man could do better the different services I assigned to him.' [34]

Pakenham, very much against his will, spent most of his time in the

Adjutant-General's office, first as deputy to Charles Stewart and latterly in charge on his own account. His reputation has suffered from the circumstances of his death commanding an unwise attack, forced on him by the Royal Navy, against New Orleans. He made his reputation as a fighting general at the head of the Third Division at Salamanca. Wellington, who was his brother-in-law, wrote: 'He made the manoeuvre which led to our success with a celerity and accuracy of which I doubt many are capable. . . . He may not be a genius but [he is] one of the best we have.' [35]

Lowry Cole was the best example of a man who, in command of a division, had reached the limit of his capabilities. With a hot, short-lived Irish temper and a bravery which was remarkable even amongst his colleagues, he was popular with his men in a way in which Craufurd and Picton could never hope to be. His hospitality was renowned throughout the army. 'Cole', said Wellington, 'gives the best dinners.' 'To do this,' remarked one of his guests, 'he now has travelling with him about ten or twelve goats for milk, a cow, and about thirty-six sheep at least, with a shepherd, who always march, feed on the roadside, on the mountains, &c, and encamp with him. When you think of this, that wine and everything is to be carried about, from salt and pepper and tea cups, to saucepans, boilers, dishes, chairs and tables, on mules, you may guess the trouble and expense of a good establishment here.' [36] As long as Cole could confine himself to the command of the Fourth Division and had no difficult decisions to take, all was well. Once given a larger command his normal decision and self-possession left him, as witness his performance at Roncesvalles (see p. 156). After his division had been repulsed from St. Boes at the battle of Orthez, he was in a great state. As the Fifty-second advanced 'we met Sir Lowry Cole coming back with his division and anxiously looking out for support. He was very much excited and said, "Well, Colborne, what's to be done? Here we all are coming back as fast as we can." ' [37] Colonel Colborne confessed to being 'rather provoked, and said, "Have patience and we shall see what's to be done." ' [38]

These four were the best of the divisional commanders. There were others, such as Leith and Hamilton, who were trustworthy but less inspired. The remainder needed constant watching. 'British officers', remarked Wellington, 'require an authority of no mean description, exercised with considerable strictness, to keep them in order and within due bounds.' [39] There was throughout the army a feeling that obedience to orders was optional. 'It is difficult to have an order obeyed by the officers', said Wellington on another occasion, 'if it affects their own convenience.' [40] The most flagrant example occurred during the retreat from Burgos. In the rain-sodden final stages Wellington ordered the First, Sixth and Seventh Divisions to move by a certain road. The three commanders, William Stewart, Henry Clinton and Lord Dalhousie,* decided that the road was too long and too wet and chose another. This brought them to a bridge which was blocked so that they could not cross. Here, eventually, Wellington found them, waiting. What, Wellington was asked, did he say to them? 'Oh, by God, it was too serious to say anything.' [41] † 'What a situation is mine!' he complained to London later. 'It is impossible to prevent incapable men from being sent to the army.' [42]

If it was difficult to find competent divisional commanders, it was all but impossible to find men of the calibre to command a corps of several divisions and all arms. This was the greatest weakness in all the army's operations in the Peninsula. There was no one Wellington could trust with a detached corps. Normally this would have been the task of the second-in-command of the army. It was unfortunate that till late in the war it was difficult to have much confidence in the officers appointed to this post. Edward Paget was the first to hold it and might have satisfied Wellington had he been less unfortunate. When he first arrived with the army in 1809 he was seriously wounded, losing an arm, within four days. He rejoined in 1812 and was captured within five weeks. His successor in 1809 was John Sherbrooke, 'a very good officer', said Wellington, 'but the most passionate man I think I ever knew'.[43] It was impossible to trust any major undertaking to Sherbrooke, and when he went home sick in June 1810 the post passed to Brent Spencer. He, again, was not a man fitted for a major command. Wellington said of him, after the war: 'Spencer was exceedingly puzzle-headed but very formal; he one day came to me, and very slowly said, "Sir, I have the honour reporting that the enemy has evacuated Castello Bono." It was not Castello Bono, but Carpio, as we could all see, and his aide-de-camp whispered him the right word, upon which Spencer began again as slowly and solemnly as before, "Sir I have—the—honour—to—report", and ending once more with Castello Bono, and though he made three several attempts, he could never get rid of Castello Bono. He always would talk of the Thames for the Tagus.' [44]

Spencer left the army in pique when Graham, his senior, was posted north from Cadiz. Thomas Graham, then in his sixty-fourth year, arrived with a ready-made reputation as the victor of Barossa. This was a brilliant small-scale victory at the head of 4,500 men which owed everything to Graham's skill and the bravery of his troops. He was a man of immense personal charm who inspired great devotion in the officers and men who served under him. As a corps commander he

* These are the three names given by Lord Fitzroy Somerset, who, as Wellington's Military Secretary, was in a good position to know, but there is strong evidence to suggest that it was Oswald rather than Clinton.

† According to another account he remarked: 'You see, gentlemen, I know my own business best.'

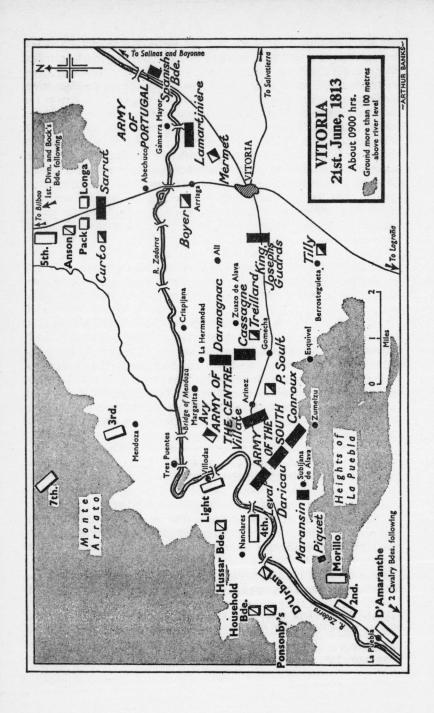

VITORIA
21st June, 1813
About 0900 hrs.
Ground more than 100 metres
above river level

was not particularly successful and his increasing blindness did not help, although he continued to be an intrepid rider, so much so that a young artillery officer who accompanied him on a reconnaissance wrote: 'whether the general is mad or blind I have not decided; it required one of those imperfections to carry him in cold blood over the rocks and precipices. I should have soon have thought of riding from Dover to Calais.'[45]

He spent much of 1812–13 in England on sick leave and got his first chance at the head of a large force at Vitoria. He had under his command about 30,000 men, the First British and Fifth Anglo-Portuguese Divisions with two independent Portuguese brigades, a small but active Spanish division and two cavalry brigades. His opponents were two divisions of the Army of Portugal, about 11,000 men, supported by some 2,000 Spanish renegades and about a battalion's worth of detachments from other French formations, so that his superiority was comfortably more than two to one. His task was to turn the enemy's right while other columns drove in their centre and turned their left. His orders gave him a wide discretion. He was to regulate his movements by the advance of the army but 'not to forgo the advantage of being able to turn the right of the enemy's position, and the town of Vitoria, by moving to the left'.[46] A later instruction urged him to 'turn his whole attention to cutting off the retreat of the enemy by the great road which goes from Vitoria by Tolosa and Irun to France'.[47]

Through no fault of his, Graham's corps was rather late in starting their attack, but by mid-afternoon the great road to France had been cut by Longa's Spanish Division. The Fifth Division was still disputing the main bridge across the Zadorra, but Longa's bridgehead was secure and the Army of Portugal was tied down holding off the Fifth Division. The way would seem to have been open for Graham to use the First Division to 'turn the right of the enemy and the town of Vitoria'. About four o'clock, when the other three columns of the army were ready for their final assault, Graham received another order urging him to 'move forward and press the enemy. He will judge from the force of the enemy, and the obstinacy, or otherwise, of his resistance, whether it will be most expedient to move wide of Vitoria, or to move direct upon that place. . . . Sir T. Graham's movements should be directed in whatever manner will enable the army to reap the most effectual advantages from its success.'[48]

There could be no doubt what the movement should be. With the great road held by Longa and the French divisions opposing the main body of the allied army steadily in retreat, Graham had only to cut the easterly road out of Vitoria to Salvatierra and Pamplona for 50,000 Frenchmen to be cut off from France. If he had done so Vitoria would have been one of the most overwhelming victories of all time. An enterprising commander would have done it on his own initiative long before he received the final order. Of the 4,800 men in the First Division, the Guards brigade had suffered no casualties, the brigade of the German Legion only 54. Two brigades of cavalry, including the German dragoons who had triumphed at Garcia Hernandez, were ready under his hands. Graham preferred to go on slogging it out with the Fifth Division and to follow up his opponent when, eventually, pressure from their flank forced them to withdraw. The French escaped, with little more than their personal weapons, but at least capable of being re-formed and of fighting for another nine months.* Later that year Graham, having led his corps successfully across the Bidassoa, was forced by his health to return to England. A captain in the Guards wrote home: 'We all regret General Graham as a gentleman, but perhaps as *commandant en second* we have not lost much by the exchange.' [49]

Graham's successor was Sir John Hope, four years older than Wellington and his senior in the Army List before Wellington's promotion to field-marshal. He had little chance to show his capabilities at the head of a corps between his arrival and the end of the war. It was because of an error of his judgment that the first day's fighting of the battle of the Nive was so desperate. His reserve, the First Division, was stationed more than five miles to the rear of the main fighting position of the corps and it was a long time, during which they were badly needed, before they could be brought up. It was largely Hope's efforts which retrieved the situation so that he can be held to have made up for his mistake although at a heavy cost in lives and prisoners.† He displayed, on this occasion, the insensate bravery which was so common amongst his colleagues. 'We shall lose him,' said Wellington, 'if he continues to expose himself in fire as he did; indeed his escape was then wonderful. His hat and coat were shot through in many places, besides the wound in his leg. He places himself among the sharpshooters, without, as they do, sheltering himself from the enemy's fire. This will not answer; and I hope that his friends will give him a hint on the subject . . . but it is a delicate subject.' [50] Inevitably, he was eventually wounded and captured in the sortie from Bayonne on 14th April 1814.

Apart from the designated seconds-in-command, three men had the seniority to be considered as possible corps commanders, Cotton, Hill and Beresford. Stapleton Cotton was very capable at the head of a division or more of cavalry but could not, except perhaps in his own estimation, be seriously considered as a commander of all arms. He

* It is only fair to Graham to record that, according to his Deputy Assistant Quartermaster-General, Wellington remarked after Vitoria: 'By God! Graham hit it admirably.'

† The allied army lost 507 prisoners on that day, the highest total for any of Wellington's battles.

did command a corps consisting of the Fourth and Light Divisions and two brigades of cavalry for a short but critical time on the retreat from the Douro in July 1812. He acquitted himself with credit, but it was Wellington's view that Cotton 'is not exactly the person I should select to command an army'.[51]

Rowland Hill commanded an independent corps for longer than any other general. At the head of a divisional group he was excellent, as he showed at the affairs of Arroyomolinos and Almaraz. It is more difficult to assess his capabilities as a corps commander. Although he commanded the Second and Portuguese Divisions with a considerable force of cavalry in Estremadura almost continuously from the end of 1809 until the summer of 1812, the only occasion when the corps came seriously in contact with the enemy was during Hill's absence in England suffering from fever. It can be held that he was unenterprising in the early summer of 1812, when he was confronted with D'Erlon and a substantially smaller force, but it is fair to add that his best chance of attacking D'Erlon came at a time when he was under Wellington's orders not to attack and that after he received permission to go over to the offensive the opportunities were less tempting.

In the campaign of Vitoria he performed well but with no special distinction, while in the Pyrenees he was, through ill-luck or ill-judgment, absent at the critical moment when D'Erlon attacked William Stewart at the Maya. His greatest day was, without doubt, 13th December 1813 when with 14,000 British and Portuguese he held the heights of St. Pierre against six French divisions.

If he was not particularly enterprising he was at least wholly reliable, which is more than can be said for most of his colleagues. Wellington once remarked: 'The best of Hill is that I always know where to find him',[52] and such dependability was worth a host of wayward brilliance. In the summer of 1810 Wellington wrote to him: 'I am convinced that whatever you decide upon will be right.'[53] There were few officers whom the Commander of the Forces could trust in that way.

What is beyond doubt is that no one could find an unkind word to say about him. His charm, kindness and hospitality made him the most popular man in the army, a fact which Wellington gracefully acknowledged. No man, whatever his rank, called at his headquarters without being kindly received and provided with food, shelter and a drink. A sergeant of the Ninety-fourth recalled after the war how, when he delivered a message to 'Daddy Hill', the general saw that he was given a meal, arranged for him to be found quarters and when he had to leave 'ordered his servants to fill my haversack with provision; and when I was going away, he said, "Remember now what I have told you —don't go farther than the village; and here is something for you to get yourself a refreshment when you arrive there." '[54]

William Carr Beresford's work in rebuilding the Portuguese army and making it into an efficient fighting force entitles him to be considered as Wellington's most effective lieutenant. Against his reputation as a corps commander lies the battle of Albuera and a torrent of denigration from William Napier. His reputation in the army was not high even before the battle. Edward Pakenham considered him in April 1811 as 'a clever fellow but no general; his anxiety is too great',[55] while after the battle even the chaplain at headquarters, a charitably minded cleric, could only write grudgingly: 'Beresford appears to have behaved as well as his slender talents promised.'[56] In fact the army and history seem to have been less than just to Beresford at Albuera.

Wellington, writing six weeks after the battle, summed up the feeling of the army when he said: 'They were never determined to fight it; they did not occupy the ground as they ought; they were ready to run away at every moment from the time it commenced till the French retired.'[57]

It is notable that throughout Wellington refers to 'they' rather than to Beresford, for the worst of Beresford's troubles was the presence of the Spaniard, Joachim Blake, Captain-General of the Coronilla, and a Regent of Spain, who, although he had agreed to serve under Beresford's orders, thwarted and disobeyed him at every turn. Beresford, rightly, was far from determined to fight the battle. In his view the siege of Badajoz had not progressed far enough to be worth covering in a general action which was bound to be expensive since his numerical superiority consisted in a rabble of dubious Spaniards and four brigades of untried Portuguese.* Blake refused to consider retiring, he 'would not listen to crossing the Guadiana, and stated that, whether the position was good or bad, you [Wellington] had pointed it out'.[58] Beresford, therefore, was faced with the alternative of abandoning his bellicose ally to certain destruction or standing beside him and fighting it out. The first would have been the wisest course but it was politically unthinkable.

It is hard to find fault with Beresford's dispositions. The two most common criticisms are that he should not have trusted his exposed right to the Spaniards and that he did not defend enough ground on his right. To the first, it can only be answered that the Spaniards were moving in from the right of the position and only arrived in the small hours of the morning, having taken 19 hours to cover seven miles, and were then in such confusion that they could not be sorted out until daylight. If they had been stationed on the left of the army they would not have reached their position until the battle was over. Napier constantly harps on Beresford's failure to take more ground to his right, maintaining that the 'key to the position' was the gentle rise in the ground about 500 yards on the right of the Spaniards' flank at Las Baterias. This argument is quite untenable. The ridge of Albuera is a

* Only one of the Portuguese battalions at Albuera had ever fired a shot in anger.

gently rolling affair with a succession of crests a few feet different in height. If the crest beyond Las Baterias had been occupied the whole battle would have been fought in exactly the same way, but 500 yards south, and with the allied line slightly more tenuous as it would have to be more extended. There is no safe height on which to rest the right flank.*

Beresford misappreciated the line by which Soult would attack,† but, as soon as he realised that his right was threatened, his orders to meet the situation could not have been bettered. He was frustrated by Blake, who first refused to comply with his orders and later complied only partially and tardily. To make matters worse William Stewart then threw away three battalions of the Second Division by inexcusable carelessness in attacking with them in line, in echelon of battalions, while a vastly superior cavalry hovered on their rear and flank. Had Blake and Stewart obeyed their orders and shown even moderate competence, Albuera would have been a standard defensive battle in which Soult would have been repulsed with slight loss to the allies.

The feeling that Beresford was determined on withdrawal was current throughout the army. The evidence for it is slight. The withdrawal of the German Legion battalions from Albuera village may have looked like the beginning of a retreat, but in fact it was Beresford's intention to use them for the task which, in the event, was performed by Cole and the Fourth Division under the urgings of Henry Hardinge, Beresford's very competent Deputy Quartermaster-General. It is possible to feel that Hardinge's plan was better than Beresford's, but the result would have been the same in either case. The only concrete piece of evidence for Beresford's intention to retreat lies in a verbal message given to Alexander Dickson by one of Beresford's Portuguese aides telling him to be prepared to withdraw his guns. It is unlikely that this order originated from Beresford, and Dickson himself was 'from the first induced to attribute Souza's message to a mistake, as neither in my conversation with Lord Beresford was there any allusion to it, nor did anything occur to indicate to me that he was aware of my having received such an order'.[59]

Whatever the army thought of Beresford, he never forfeited Wellington's confidence. This had been given him from the outset. At the end of 1809 it had been Beresford to whom Wellington had wished to entrust the detached corps in Estremadura and it was only after Beresford had declined it on the grounds that 'the then state of the Portuguese army required my personal and entire attention to organise it

* From his description of the battlefield of Albuera, it seems unlikely that Napier had ever seen the ground.

† It is interesting that Beresford at Albuera expected a frontal attack while Wellington at Waterloo, a very similar battlefield, expected an attack on his right flank. Beresford was attacked on the right and Wellington frontally.

and put it into any state of discipline',[60] that the command was given to Hill. It was on Beresford's advice that Wellington cancelled the premature attack by the First Division on the morning of Salamanca and it was his initiative that ordered a Portuguese brigade on to the flank of Clausel's dangerous counter-attack later that day. It was to Beresford that Wellington entrusted the risky and essential flank march at Toulouse and he carried out his task to perfection. He may not have been a general of the first class, but he was, without doubt, the best of Wellington's subordinates both in battle and out of it. 'They tell me', said Wellington, 'that when I am not present, he wants decision; and he certainly embarrassed me a little with his doubts when he commanded in Estremadura; but I am quite certain that he is the only person capable of conducting a large concern.'[61]

CHAPTER ELEVEN

CAVALRY AND ARTILLERY

CAVALRY

Our cavalry is the most delicate instrument in our whole machine.
Wellington to E. Cooke, 16th March 1813

The Peninsula is not good cavalry country. Of the regions in which Wellington's army fought there are only two tracts of country in which it was possible to manoeuvre large bodies of horsemen—the plains between Ciudad Rodrigo and Burgos and those of Estremadura between Badajoz and the Sierra Morena. Inside Portugal a large force of cavalry was more of an encumbrance than an asset. Both the climate and the supply situation made it difficult to keep horses in good condition and losses outside action were always heavy. In August 1809 Captain Ross of the Horse Artillery commented that Fane's brigade 'which landed at Lisbon between four and five months ago, 1,300 strong in horse, is now reduced to 800, and of that number not above 20 horses have been taken or killed by the enemy'.[1] Wellington, writing two years later, observed that 'the Peninsula is the grave of horses; I have lost no less than twelve for my own riding since I have been here'.[2]* He was, therefore, not anxious to be over-reinforced with horsemen. At the beginning of 1810, hearing that the Thirteenth Light Dragoons were on their way to join him, he remarked that this would 'give us more cavalry than we could feed with convenience or than, according to present appearances, we shall require',[3] and at the end of that year he wrote to London: 'I do not recommend that any additional regiments should be sent out.'[4]

As long as the fighting was confined to Portugal this was wise, but once the war moved to the frontiers and the plains beyond he found himself acutely short of mounted troops. In May 1811, when both the corps of his army were engaged in separate general actions in good cavalry country, he was only able to oppose 1,854 (including 312 Portuguese) horsemen to the 4,662 of Massena and Bessières at Fuentes de Oñoro, and 3,889, of whom only 1,164 were British, against Soult's 4,012 at Albuera. The Portuguese cavalry, unlike their infantry, were, he reported, 'worse than useless',[5] while of the Spaniards he said, 'I have never heard any body pretend that in any one instance they have

* Three of these horses were lost in a stable fire in January 1810 (WD v 460).

behaved as soldiers ought to in presence of the enemy. They make no scruple of running off, and after an action are to be found in every village and shady bottom within fifty miles of the field of action.' [6] 'We must not', he came to the conclusion, 'reckon on more than the British.' [7]

By the summer of 1811 Wellington's mind was beginning to turn to operations in Spain and for this a strong augmentation of cavalry was essential. In August 1811 he was writing to London that, 'I am of opinion that we cannot have too much British cavalry'.[8] The government responded well and at Salamanca he was able to field 3,335 British horsemen, apart from nearly 500 Portuguese, against Marmont's 3,379, while still leaving Hill's corps in Estremadura with two British brigades. In 1813 the position was even better: 7,424 British cavalry set out on the Vitoria campaign and King Joseph could only bring 7,000 to the battle. On neither side did the cavalry achieve much at Vitoria as the very success of Wellington's approach march from Portugal to Vitoria took them out of the area in which cavalry could play a decisive rôle.

The cavalry coming out to the Peninsula was found, almost without exception, to require complete retraining, and many of the officers had little notion of their duties. Lieutenant-Colonel Barton of the 2nd Life Guards, who landed at Lisbon with his regiment, was perhaps an extreme example, but there were deplorably many who resembled him. He left the Regimental Veterinary Surgeon and Paymaster in England and was reported to Wellington as being 'not only wholly uninformed of the most common duties of regimental service, but to be wanting in those exertions which your Lordship has a right to expect from every officer serving under you'.[9]

The main functions of cavalry are reconnaissance, the maintenance of the outposts, shock action in battle (the charge) and the pursuit of a broken enemy. The British showed themselves more or less deficient in the first three of these; they had little opportunity to show their ability in the fourth. A few cavalry officers, of whom Captain the Hon. Edward Somers Cocks was the most notable, excelled at reconnaissance. The majority had neither the talent nor the application to succeed in it.

All ranks were untrained in the maintenance of the outposts. 'In England . . . to attempt to give men or officers any idea of outpost duties was considered absurd', wrote a subaltern in the 16th Light Dragoons, 'and when they came abroad, they had all this to learn. The fact was that there was no one to teach them. Sir Stapleton Cotton tried, at Woodbridge in Suffolk, with the 14th and 16th Light Dragoons, and got the enemy's vedettes and his own looking the same way.' [10] By good fortune there was with the army, from 1809, one regiment, the 1st Hussars of the King's German Legion under Frederick von

Arentschildt, who were fully capable of doing this duty and the better English regiments of light cavalry learned from them. Nevertheless the infantry continued to feel more comfortable with the Germans out in front of them. 'If we saw a British dragoon at any time approaching in full speed, it excited no great curiosity among us, but whenever we saw one of the first hussars coming on at a gallop it was high time to gird on our swords and bundle up',[11] was the considered opinion of one Rifle officer. Regiments new out from England had a distressing tendency to lose vedettes in the night and there was a crop of such incidents in the summer of 1811, which tended, as Wellington pointed out, 'to show the difference between old and new troops. The old regiments of cavalry, throughout all their services, and all their losses put together, have not lost so many men as the 2nd Hussars [K.G.L.], the 11th and 13th dragoons, the former in a few days, and the latter in a few months. However, we must make the new as good as the old.'[12]

Shock action was the manoeuvre on which the cavalry most prided itself, but here again its training was insufficient to reap the benefits of the splendidly executed charges. 'In England', wrote the Sixteenth Dragoon previously quoted, 'I never saw nor heard of cavalry taught to charge, disperse and form, which if I taught a regiment one thing it should be that.'[13] The consequences of this lack became obvious at Vimeiro, at Talavera and at Campo Mayor. On each occasion the cavalry executed their charge with great gallantry and precision but could not be stopped, suffering useless casualties in consequence. The worst example occurred in June 1812 near Maguilla when General Slade, having broken two French regiments with an equal force, pursued for several miles, until he was taken in flank by fresh French reserves and driven back beyond his starting-point with more than 160 unnecessary losses, including 118 prisoners. 'I have never', wrote Wellington, 'been more annoyed than by Slade's affair. It is entirely occasioned by the trick our officers of cavalry have acquired of galloping at every thing, and their galloping back as fast as they gallop on the enemy. They never consider their situation, never think of manoeuvring before an enemy—so little that one would think they cannot manoeuvre, except on Wimbledon Common.'[14] Although the cavalry won some handsome cavalry-to-cavalry actions on a small scale, notably under Lumley at Usagre in May 1811, and behaved magnificently covering the retreats at Fuentes de Oñoro and El Bodon, they had little influence on the winning of Wellington's major victories, Salamanca being the only exception and even here they showed evidence of their besetting fault. Le Marchant's brigade charged magnificently, breaking through two bodies of French infantry. Unfortunately they did not stop there. Seeing another brigade of French formed and ready to receive them, Le Marchant led his disordered squadrons against them in a

213

fruitless charge which cost him his own life and that of many of his troopers.

Colonel Augustus Frazer who, since he commanded Wellington's Horse Artillery, was in a position to know, wrote, two days after Waterloo, that 'the Duke's forte is in pursuit of a beaten enemy'.[15] Sir Charles Oman, on the other hand, criticises Wellington for his failure to pursue effectively after Vitoria and Orthez.[16] In neither case does the criticism seem fair. The retreat of the French from Vitoria was through country over which cavalry could not effectively act. General Long wrote on the following day that 'the country was so intersected with impassable ravines and ditches that our advance was broken and impeded at every step',[17] and Captain Bragge of the Third Dragoons a day later said that 'the ground was so intersected with woods and enclosures that the cavalry could not act against their infantry'.[18] It is indicative of the difficulties of getting cavalry forward along the rough track to Salvatierra and Pamplona which the French took that when, on 24th June, effective harassing of the French rear became possible, there were two Rifle battalions keeping up with Victor Alten's cavalry and Ross' Horse Artillery in the advanced guard. The situation after Orthez was not dissimilar. Somerset's cavalry brigade was well forward when the French gave way and almost demolished two French battalions, but the ground which a French author described as 'un terrain de steeple chase',[19] forbade large-scale cavalry movements and the French were able to escape behind the Luy de Béarn.

No one could complain about the pursuit after Salamanca. Although it was impossible for the cavalry to pursue through woods in the darkness of the night which followed the battle, Wellington's cavalry was in pursuit early the following morning. Catching up with the French rearguard at Garcia Hernandez, they achieved the greatest cavalry feat of the war. While Anson's light cavalry drove off their French opposite numbers, von Bock, with the two regiments of heavy dragoons of the German Legion, attacked the French infantry, broke two squares and inflicted 1,100 casualties.

Apart from their weaknesses in horsemanship and training, the chief defect of the British cavalry was their command at brigade level. As soon as Wellington became a field-marshal and at last began to be able to return generals to England, he immediately disposed of four* of his seven cavalry brigadiers. Another, William Erskine, would have joined them had he not averted recall by throwing himself out of a window in Lisbon. Of these the worst was probably Jack Slade. Slade was sent out to Wellington in 1809 as an officer of proved incapacity. He had commanded one of the cavalry brigades under Lord Paget in the Coruña campaign. Lord Paget was in no doubt as to his abilities. Having given him an order, his Lordship called out to one of his

* Victor Alten, George Anson, R. B. Long and J. Slade.

aides-de-camp, whom he ordered to 'ride after the damned stupid fellow and take care he committed no blunder'.[20] Not only was his intelligence suspect, it was widely said in the army that he was a coward. It was observed that on one occasion when ordered to charge at the head of the Tenth Hussars, he kept halting to adjust his stirrup leathers, and on another when one of Paget's plans was 'rendered abortive by . . . the dilatory proceedings of [Slade] who . . . made a long speech to the troops, which he concluded with the energetic peroration of "Blood and Slaughter—March".' [21] Even the mild Sir John Moore had remonstrated with him for riding to the rear with a message which would more properly have been carried by an A.D.C. It was unfortunate that, when Cotton returned to England in the early months of 1811, the immediate charge of the cavalry fell, by seniority, into Slade's hands. Hercules Pakenham wrote that he 'let no possible opportunity of inaction pass him—pretending not to comprehend orders, which the events passing before him would have made comprehensible to a trumpeter—complaining that his hands were tied, and letting the opportunity slip—a curse to the cause, and a disgrace to the service'.[22] He was not even competent at his desk work and drew down upon himself a stinging rebuke from the Adjutant-General that: 'The Commander of the Forces has directed me to express his extreme surprise and his regret that after repeated orders have been issued to the army, any brigade should omit to send in their returns, agreeable to the frequent directions they have received on this head, especially a brigade under a general officer so long in the country as yourself, and certainly so well acquainted with the rules of the service.' [23]

Stupidity was not the only drawback of the cavalry brigadiers. Blindness was another. Sir William Erskine, 'on whose sanity, I am sorry to say, much reliance cannot be placed',[24] was, said Wellington, 'very blind, which is against him at the head of cavalry',[25] while the German, von Bock, was so near-sighted that when he was ordered to make his famous charge at Garcia Hernandez he had to ask a colonel of artillery to 'be good enough to show us the enemy'.[26] Nor were matters improved by the well-meaning efforts of Charles Stewart, Adjutant-General until 1812, who was always fancying himself as a cavalry commander and taking off a few squadrons to conduct a private war. In his anxiety to secure a cavalry command he enlisted the support of the Duke of York. Wellington would have none of it. Telling Stewart that 'although it might be more agreeable to you to take a gallop with the hussars, I think you had better return to your office,' [27] he said firmly to the Horse Guards that 'he labours under two bodily defects, the want of sight and of hearing, which must ever prevent him from forming an immediate judgment of what is going on in the field. . . . I acknowledge that I would hesitate in putting General Stewart at the head of a large body of cavalry to be directed by him.' [28]

Wellington was at least fortunate in his senior cavalry commander in the Peninsula. After General Payne had returned to England with gout in 1810, the command passed to Stapleton Cotton who, apart from two short absences, commanded it for the rest of the war. Although something of a dandy in his dress, he was a solid and reliable cavalryman who had Wellington's complete confidence. 'I do not know where we should find an officer that would command our cavalry half so well as he does', commented Wellington after Salamanca [29] where Cotton had achieved his greatest success in ordering Le Marchant's charge at the critical moment. He also greatly distinguished himself while commanding the cavalry covering the retreat of the northern part of the army from Burgos later that year when, according to an intelligent civilian observer, 'throughout this trying occasion Cotton behaved with great coolness, judgment and gallantry. I was close to him the whole time, and did not observe him for an instant disturbed or confused.' [30] There was no doubt that he was the cavalry commander whom Wellington would wish to have serve under him. 'He commands our cavalry very well; I am certain much better than many who might be sent out to us and might be supposed to be much cleverer than he is.'

The person supposed to be much cleverer than Cotton was Lord Paget, whom Wellington did not want on both personal and professional grounds. When the army was reformed for the Waterloo campaign, Wellington specifically asked for Cotton (by then Lord Combermere) to command his cavalry. At the insistence of the Prince Regent and the Duke of York, Paget (by then Earl of Uxbridge) was sent in his place. The short campaign showed how fortunate it was that he had never commanded the cavalry in the Peninsula.* He had acquired, deservedly, a reputation as a commander of a small division (five regiments) in the Coruña campaign. He had subsequently undertaken the command of the cavalry in the abortive Walcheren expedition, but he had no experience or abilities to enable him to deal with the large body of cavalry (14,482 men including 5,911 British and 2,560 K.G.L.) of which he found himself in charge.

His first action in independent command was scarcely encouraging. On the morning after Quatre Bras, Wellington, as soon as the infantry was well on its way to the rear, left Uxbridge in charge of the cavalry and Horse Artillery rearguard remarking: 'There is the last of the infantry gone and I don't care now.' [31] As the rearguard fell back there was a danger that the stronger French cavalry would get round their flank. At one time Uxbridge came up to Captain Mercer of the Horse

* Lord Paget was offered the cavalry command in the Peninsula in the summer of 1811, as soon as Wellington was made a general in Spain and Portugal, and was thus senior in local rank to Paget. Lord Liverpool informed Wellington that 'Lord Paget declines service altogether in the present circumstances' (SD vii 196, Liverpool to W. 8 Aug 11).

Artillery calling out: ' "Here follow me with two of your guns", and immediately himself led the way into one of the narrow lanes between the gardens. What he intended doing, God knows, but I obeyed. The lane was very little broader than our carriages—there was not room for a horse to have passed them. His lordship and I were in front, the guns and mounted detachments following. What he meant to do I was at a loss to conceive; we could hardly come into action in a lane; to enter on the open was certain destruction. Thus we had arrived at about fifty yards from its termination when a body of chasseurs or hussars appeared there as if waiting for us. The whole transaction appears to me so wild and confused that at times I can hardly believe it to be more than a confused dream—the general-in-chief of the cavalry exposing himself amongst the skirmishers of his rearguard, and literally doing the duty of a cornet! "By God! we are all prisoners" (or some such words), exclaimed Lord Uxbridge, dashing his horse at one of the garden banks, which he cleared, and away he went, leaving us to get out of the scrape the best way we could.' [32]

Not long afterwards Lord Uxbridge decided that another attempt must be made to check the French advanced guard which had occupied the town of Genappe. The head of the French column 'consisted of a troop of lancers, all very young men, mounted on very small horses. For about fifteen minutes they remained in the jaws of the town, their flanks being protected by the houses; and the street not being straight, and those in the rear not knowing that those in the front were halted, they soon became so jammed that they could not go about.' [33] With the lancers jammed, knee to knee, between the houses and unable to retire it was, of course, impossible for a charge against them to succeed. The lancers could not break even if they wished to. If the task was to be attempted at all, it was essential that heavy cavalry should be used. The Household Cavalry brigade was at hand, but Lord Uxbridge would not employ them, preferring to use a light cavalry regiment, the Seventh Hussars, of which he was colonel. 'We might', wrote one of their officers 'as well have charged a house.' [34] 'Of course,' wrote another, 'our charge could make no impression, but we continued cutting at them, and we did not give ground, nor did they move. Their Commanding Officer was cut down, and so was ours, and this state of affairs lasted for some minutes, when they brought down some light artillery, which struck the rear of the right squadron and knocked over some men and horses, impeding the road in our rear. We then received orders to go about from Lord [Uxbridge] who was up with us, but not on the road during all this time.' [35]

These were minor faults due, no doubt, to over-excitement. It was on the day of the battle of Waterloo itself that Uxbridge committed his greatest mistake, the mistake that was to deprive Wellington for the rest of the day of all but a handful of his only reliable heavy cavalry. Uxbridge chose his time to perfection for launching the House-hold and Union brigades against D'Erlon's corps. Nothing could have been better timed, but having launched them he lost all control over them and as a consequence the troops pursued too far. The evidence of Uxbridge's fault is best expressed in his own words: 'I committed a great mistake in having myself led the attack. The *carrière* once begun, the leader is no better than any other man; whereas, if I had placed myself at the head of the 2nd line, there is no saying what great advan-tages might not have accrued from it. I am the less pardonable in having deviated from a principle I had laid down for myself, that I had already suffered from a similar error in an affair . . . where my reserve, instead of steadily forwarding as I had ordered, chose to join in the attack, and at the end of it I had no formed body to take advantage with.' [36] The almost total loss of the heavy brigades at this early stage in the battle could well have been fatal to Wellington's chance of success. Fortunately his skill and the incredible staunchness of his British infantry were more than able to make good the defects of his cavalry commander.

The Duke of York had written to Wellington in 1811 warning him of 'the extreme difficulty of finding a sufficient number of general officers of talent and experience to command cavalry in the field'.[37] The warning was borne out in practice. A few cavalry brigadiers of real merit like Le Marchant and Fane were found and employed. A few more such as Ponsonby and Vandeleur were sent out and performed adequately. For the most part, however, the cavalry was poorly led and ill trained. It was a constant source of worry to Wellington. In 1813 he wrote: 'Our cavalry is the most delicate instrument in our whole machine. Well managed it can perform wonders, and will always be of use, but it is easily put out of order in the field. None of our officers are accustomed to the manoeuvres of large bodies of cavalry; and if any accident were to happen to a large body, such as a brigade of our cavalry, while we should be forward in the plains, we are gone.' [38] In the same year he summed up their achievement. 'Our cavalry never gained a battle yet. When the infantry have beaten the French, then the cavalry, if they can act, make the whole complete, and do wonders; but they never yet beat the French themselves.' [39]

ARTILLERY

The artillery was most judiciously placed by Lieut. Colonel Dickson, and was well served; the army is particularly indebted to that corps.   *Wellington 22nd June, 1813*

The good service performed by the artillery in Wellington's army and the good use Wellington made of his guns have been obscured over the years by the bitterness of artillerymen against the Duke in the years after Waterloo. This is unfortunate since the relations between Wellington and his gunners were, on the whole, reasonably happy and in the letters of Dickson, Frazer and Ross, the three best gunner officers who served under Wellington, it is hard to find traces of the acrimony which appears in the work of later writers. To be sure, artillerymen complained that Wellington made insufficient mention of their doings in his despatches, but this was equally the complaint of many infantry regiments (notably of the Fifty-second after Waterloo). The fact was that Wellington did not write his despatches as a list of recommendations. They were formal documents and a senior officer would be mentioned in them not because he had done well but because he had been present. Anything more than a formal mention of an individual or a regiment was rare in the extreme. There is, in the Dickson papers, a violent outburst from Captain Cairnes R.A. against Wellington's 'abominable intemperance [i.e. sharp temper] and disregard of all consideration of all feeling',[40] but since Wellington had recently, and with regret, taken away Cairnes' carefully-tended gun horses to draw the pontoon train, an outburst of temper was only to be expected. The real animus of the Royal Regiment against Wellington started with the unfortunate arrest of Norman Ramsay in 1813 and burst into flame with the publication in 1872 of a letter written by Wellington to the Master-General of the Ordnance after Waterloo. Both these occurrences will be considered below.

The Royal Artillery represented the only large body of professionally trained officers in the Peninsular army. This, joined to the peculiar situation of the Ordnance Corps, with their loyalties and hopes of advancement centred on the Master-General rather than through Wellington and the Horse Guards, gave them a feeling of apartness which was sensed and sometimes resented by the rest of the army. To many infantry officers their gunner colleagues seemed occasionally to be pedantic and slow thinking. As the army struggled through the mountains of Tras os Montes to reach the start line for the advance north of the Douro in 1813, a staff officer complained: 'These people are as nervous about their guns as the people they fire at are about their shot. ... Their officers require more driving than their horses.'[41]

The sense of apartness was something which the artillery officers, a tight knit group who had been friends and colleagues for years, were anxious to preserve. It had not been many years before the Peninsular War that the bulk of the artillery had been split up into penny packets and used in pairs as 'battalion guns' under the immediate command of infantry colonels, and it was an artillery tenet that control of their guns should never again pass into the hands of infantry officers. Wellington organised his army on a divisional basis; 'one of our divisions', he wrote, 'is in itself a complete army, composed of British and foreign troops, artillery, departments, &c' and it was vital that for such an organisation the troops and batteries* of artillery should be thoroughly integrated into the divisions with which they served. For the most part this worked well in practice and a real comradeship grew up between the gunners and the infantry of their divisions. Such an arrangement, however, clearly detracted from the influence of the Commander, Royal Artillery, and caused concern to the senior officers of the Regiment at Woolwich.

One of the best illustrations of the kind of feeling which was engendered can be found in Major Duncan's *History of the Royal Artillery*. Speaking of the battle of Busaco, he says: 'In the battle . . . Lord Wellington displayed an ignorance of Artillery tactics, from the results of which he was happily saved by the intelligence and gallantry of the representatives of that arm. . . . Instead of massing his Artillery in reserve until the attack should develop itself, the guns were placed, as a rule, in the easiest parts of the position, where it was supposed the French *would* attack.' [42] This was the classic artillery doctrine; the guns kept in rear until they were required and then brought forward with overwhelming effect. At Busaco such a deployment would have been abused. The position is nine miles long and the only lateral communication was a narrow, newly-made track. The fastest that field artillery could move was four miles an hour and the French attacked under cover of a thick mist so that the points of attack were veiled until they were a few hundred yards from the crest of the position. In such circumstances it would have been impossible to bring guns kept in a central reserve into action before the battle had been settled. It only remains to add that Wellington's actual dispositions were such that at each of the two points chosen by the French for attack there were 12 guns, that at another point where a French column happened to arrive, having been lost in the mist, a battery arrived to resist it in a very few moments, and that the point reached by the final French column to attack the (British) right was inaccessible to guns in any case.

Efficient as they were, the artillery in the Peninsula suffered from two malaises. The first was their Corps of Drivers, which was never efficient and which one Horse Artillery officer described as a 'nest of infamy'.[43] Equally serious was a bitterness against the Board of Ordnance and the system of promotion by seniority. 'My despondence', wrote Captain Hew Ross, R.H.A., 'chiefly arises from the unmanly and miserable feelings of our own corps. There has ever been a prejudice in

* Units of foot (i.e. field) artillery were at this time known as companies or brigades (which to make confusion worse were divided into divisions). It seems simpler to refer to a group of six guns by the modern name of battery. A contemporary battery was a field or permanent work of fortification into which guns were put.

16 Light Dragoons escorting artillery. From a water-colour by J. A. Atkinson or T. Ellis, c. 1800
Reproduced by gracious permission of Her Majesty The Queen

17 The Battle of Waterloo, 18th June 1815. From a painting by Sir William Allan, 1843
    Napoleon watching the attack of the Imperial Guard in the final phase of the
    battle. Wellington's reaction on seeing the picture for the first time was 'good
    —very good: not too much smoke!'

18a The action at Campo Mayor, 25th March 1811
From a drawing by William Heath (engraved by J. Hill), 1815

18b Battle of Vitoria, 21st June 1813; bringing in the prisoners
From a drawing by William Heath (etched by I. Clark, aquatinted by
M. Dubourg), 1815

19 India—Waterloo—House of Lords. From a lithograph by L. P. Lassouquère

20 The Battle of Vitoria, 21st June 1813
   From a painting by I. M. Wright (etched by H. Moses, aquatinted by
   F. C. Lewis), 1814

21 Lieutenant-Colonel Alexander Dickson, in the uniform of the Portuguese Artillery
   From a painting by J. Hartrey, c 1819

the heads of our regiment against inferior officers obtaining brevet. Our senior officers, having grown grey themselves in the subaltern ranks, cannot endure the thought of their followers being more fortunate. After seventeen years in the service, I find myself seventy steps from a majority.' [44]

The Artillery and Engineers were until 1813 particularly badly placed since a rule of the Board of Ordnance forbade the grant of brevet rank to second captains (i.e. seconds-in-command of batteries) even if they had been for some years in actual command of their batteries. Eventually 14 second captains of the Peninsular army petitioned the Prince Regent through Wellington for redress of this grievance. Wellington gave his full support. When he read the petition he turned to the Commander of the Royal Artillery and remarked: 'Every word of this is perfectly just and true. I have already recommended some of these officers but I suppose some damned Ordnance trick has prevented their promotion: leave the papers with me and assure the Second Captains that I will do all I can for them.' [45] The petition was granted.

Promotion by seniority alone had a deplorable effect on the quality of the senior artillery officers sent out for the chief command of Wellington's artillery. The first incumbent, Brigadier-General Howorth, was a bumbler. 'I think I shall be lucky if he does not get me into a scrape yet',[46] wrote Wellington after Howorth had complained that he was insufficiently mentioned in the Talavera despatch. His successor, Framingham, lasted only four months and was followed by Major-General Borthwick. 'Report says', wrote Captain Ross, 'that Lord Wellington told him that he wanted an active officer to fill so important a situation as Chief of Artillery, and recommended him to go home.' [47] After Borthwick came Colonel Robe who, although no genius, could manage the work until, unfortunately, he was wounded on the retreat from Burgos. Rather than have another elderly incompetent sent out from Woolwich, Wellington decided to appoint as C.R.A. the next senior artillery officer in the Peninsula, Colonel Fisher, who was highly thought of in the regiment. 'As ... I have reason to be satisfied with the intelligence and zeal of Colonel Fisher, I am not desirous that that officer should be superseded. His health is not good, but I hope he will last out.' [48]

Fisher held the post for six months, after which his uncertain manner in answering Wellington's questions proved too much for the temper of the Commander of the Forces. 'His Lordship in a rage said "Sir, you know nothing", so when Fisher got home he wrote a letter asking for leave which Lord W. answered in his own hand—a letter which gratified Fisher.' [49] This time Wellington was determined to have the man of his own choice. Briskly telling the senior artillery officer in the Peninsula to stay in Lisbon, he gave the command to Alexander Dickson, a mere captain in the regiment but a lieutenant-colonel in the Portuguese service. Dickson, by far the most competent artillery commander in the regiment, stayed in charge, to Wellington's great satisfaction, until the end of the war. He would have been Wellington's choice as Commander of the Royal Artillery for the Waterloo campaign but he arrived back from the American war too late to be available. Instead the command was given to Colonel Sir George Wood. There had been some talk of Wood coming out to succeed Borthwick in the Peninsula. It may have been to avoid his coming that Wellington appointed Fisher and Dickson. Certainly the rumour of his posting caused consternation in the Peninsular artillery. 'Depend upon it', wrote a captain. 'Sir George Wood is too fat.' [50] He is remembered as the man who let the Prussians secure all the captured French guns after Waterloo.

Dickson commanded the loyalty of all the officers who served under him, not least because he always wore a shabby Portuguese uniform to avoid giving offence to those officers serving under him who were his seniors in the British service. Nevertheless the dismissal of Fisher rankled among the gunners and it was particularly unfortunate that scarcely a month later Wellington put Captain Norman Ramsay under arrest. Ramsay, one of the most efficient and popular officers of the Horse Artillery and the hero of a dramatic incident at Fuentes de Oñoro, had commanded a troop with distinction at Vitoria. On the following day he was given verbal orders by Wellington to stay where he was until he received further orders from Wellington himself. Ramsay misunderstood the last part of the order and, next morning, moved his troop on the orders of a staff officer. Thus, when Wellington came to find him, he was gone and he was ordered into arrest for disobeying an order. Many representations were made on his behalf, including one from Sir Thomas Graham, but it was many days before Wellington agreed to release him and even then felt that he could not recommend him for the brevet promotion which he would otherwise have got for his conduct at Vitoria. This incident infuriated the junior officers of the artillery against Wellington and continued to rankle as an injustice. This was a tragedy since it was well known that Wellington 'had a strong liking' [51] for Ramsay. This liking, if anything, made Wellington all the more severe in his dealings with him. All through the war there were frequent examples of orders and regulations being flouted by officers of all ranks and Wellington had frequently to order their arrest and trial. He felt it most important that Ramsay should not appear to escape lightly when he was known to be a favourite. He was, in fact, fortunate that he escaped a court-martial and it was only his good reputation and the growing conviction that he had made a genuine mistake in the interpretation of Wellington's order that saved him. Wellington took care that he received his brevet within five months.

The bitterness produced by this incident was especially unfortunate as it was only at that stage of the war that it began to be possible to use the British artillery in the way in which the artillery theorists had visualised. In all the early battles the nature of the ground and the numerical inferiority of the British guns * made it difficult to use more than one battery together. In the later stages of Vitoria, Dickson was able to pound the last French position with 75 guns and, as he wrote, 'the French were generally obliged to retire e'er the infantry could get at them'.[52] At Orthez again, 'twice we had eighteen guns in line'.[53]

Waterloo was, in Wellington's words, 'a pounding match' and the artillery had a great part to play. Wellington's real feeling about their performance did not come to light until more than 50 years later. In 1872 there was published a letter he wrote to the Master-General in which, while paying a rather offhand compliment to their gallantry, he wrote: 'To tell you the truth, I was not very pleased with the Artillery in the battle of Waterloo. The army was formed in square immediately on the slope of the rising ground, on the summit of which the Artillery was placed, but to fire only when bodies of troops came under fire. It was very difficult to get them to obey this order. The French cavalry charged, and were formed on the same ground with our Artillery in general within a few yards of our guns. In some instances they were in actual possession of our guns. We could not expect the Artillerymen to remain in such a case: but I had a right to expect that the officers and men of the Artillery would do as I did, that is, to take shelter in the squares of infantry till the French cavalry should be driven off. But they did no such thing; they ran off the field entirely, taking with them limbers, ammunition and everything: and when, in a few minutes, we had driven off the French cavalry, and had regained our ground and our guns, and could make good use of our artillery, we had no artillerymen to fire them; and, in point of fact, I should have had no artillery during the action if I had not kept a reserve in the commencement'.[54]

This was not one of the angry diatribes Wellington sometimes wrote in the heat of the moment, but was dated six months after the battle. The first criticism, that it was hard to stop the guns firing at un-authorised targets, is certainly just. Captain Mercer admits that he was guilty of this and there must have been others. The accusation of running away is much harder to deal with. No doubt there were gunners, and more probably, drivers, who joined the throng from all arms who fled towards Brussels. All the evidence is that the guns were served most gallantly and Mercer's troop insisted in serving their guns, however close the French cavalry came, for fear of demoralising the square of Brunswick infantry on either side of them by running for cover. Yet it is incredible that Wellington could have invented this

* Fuentes de Oñoro was the only battle at which there were more allied guns than French due to Massena's shortage of gun teams. At Salamanca there were 24 more French guns than British; at Busaco there was a great preponderance of French guns but they could not be brought to bear.

accusation. He had a great admiration for the Royal Artillery, apart from their senior officers, and his worst enemy could not have accused him of anything but the most undeviating truthfulness. It seems probable that what gave him the impression of fading artillery support, apart from some undoubted desertions by foreign gunners, was the effect of exhaustion and recoil on the crews and their pieces. Colonel Frazer, R.H.A., wrote that the French cavalry were able to re-form under the lee of the ridge 'covered, in great measure from the fire of our guns, which by recoiling, had retired so as to lose their original and just position. But in the stiff soil, the fatigue of the horse artillerymen was great, and their best exertions were unable again to move the guns again to the crest without horse; to employ horses was to ensure the loss of the animals.' [55]

Wellington took a keen interest in the development of artillery weapons. Amidst all his troubles in 1809 he found time to write to Colonel Shrapnell to tell him that he 'had every reason to believe that . . . the spherical case shot . . . had the best effect in producing the defeat of the enemy at Vimeiro.' [56] Later his belief in Shrapnell's invention was 'much shaken, [as] I have reason to believe that their effect is confined to wounds of a very trifling description. I saw General Simon,* who was wounded by the balls of Shrapnell's shell, of which he had several in his face and head; but they were picked out of his face as duck shot would be out of the face of a person who had been hit by accident while out shooting.' [57] He was still prepared to experiment with them and three weeks later reported that 'they have been very destructive to the enemy in Badajoz when fired from 24-pounder carronades; and I have directed that some of them may be loaded with musket balls, in order to remedy what I have reason to believe is the material defect of these shells, viz. that the wounds which they inflict do not disable the person who receives them, even for the action in which they are received'.[58]

Another invention which Wellington caused to be tried in Portugal was Mr. Parr's perforated shot. This was not a success, and the artillery officer who conducted the trials had to report that, 'Out of twelve that were fired, three only burst. Supposing, however, that Mr. Parr could bring his shot to a great certainty of bursting, I confess I am at a loss to discover the utility of his invention.' [59]

Rockets were tried twice in the Peninsula, largely to gratify the Prince Regent who was a friend of their designer, Major Congreve. The first trial, against Santarem in 1811, was not successful. Wellington had not been optimistic. 'I assure you', he wrote to the admiral commanding in the Tagus, 'that I am not a partisan of Congreve's rockets, of which I

* General Simon commanded a brigade in Ney's corps and was captured, wounded at Busaco.

entertain but a bad opinion. . . . It is but fair to give every thing a trial.' [60] The rockets were withdrawn, but in September 1813 he was again offered a rocket troop. He accepted with alacrity, although it would have distressed the Prince Regent to have heard his explanation that he only accepted them to get hold of the horses which drew them, since 'I do not want to set fire to any town, and I do not know any other use of the rockets'.[61]

It must be confessed that he had good reasons for scepticism. At a trial of the newly arrived troop in January 1814, which Wellington attended, an observer noted that 'The ground rockets, intended against cavalry, did not seem to answer very well. They certainly made a tremendous noise: no cavalry could stand near them if they came near, but in that seemed the difficulty, for none of them went within half a mile of the intended object, and the direction seemed extremely uncertain. I think they would have hit Bayonne, for instance, somewhere or other, and no doubt set fire to the town; but the part of the town you could not very well choose.' [62]

In fact, the rockets were used in support of the crossing of the Ardour, perhaps because they were more easily transportable for a river crossing than field guns. They behaved with slightly more accuracy than had been expected and contributed to frightening away a timid French advanced guard.

Before Waterloo Wellington ordered the Rocket Troop to be rearmed with nine-pounder field guns, but later relented sufficiently for them to take a proportion of rockets into the field with them. On the retreat from Quatre Bras, a rocket did succeed in killing the crew of a French gun, but, wrote a gunner, 'whilst our rocketeers kept shooting off rockets, none of them ever followed the course of the first; most of them, on arriving about the middle of the ascent, took a vertical direction, whilst some of them actually turned back upon themselves— and one of these, following me like a squib until its shell exploded, actually put me in more danger than all the fire of the enemy throughout the day'.[63]

CHAPTER TWELVE

THE DUKE

We would rather see his long nose in a fight than a reinforcement of ten thousand men any day.

Captain John Kincaid, Ninety-fifth Rifles

During the Peninsular War each division of the Anglo-Portuguese army depended on three distinct lines of supply. One branch of the Commissariat issued food to the British infantry and cavalry; one issued food to the artillery 'and ammunition to infantry, cavalry and artillery; one supplied the Portuguese. The two British branches met only at the Treasury in London. The Portuguese branch, which was funded by the British Treasury, was responsible to Lisbon. It was clearly an absurd and inefficient system. Robert Craufurd decided that in his, the Light Division, it should be rationalised and issued orders accordingly. When a copy of these orders reached Wellington he wrote to Craufurd: 'I have no doubt that the whole of the Commissariat arrangements of both the British and the Portuguese army might be very much improved; and one of the improvements would doubtless be to place the whole under one regulation, and an unity of superintendence. Unfortunately, however, the orders of our own government, and various other considerations—some political, others military, and others financial—do not allow of this amalgamation. All that can be done is, that we should assist each other as much, and clash as little, as possible; and arrangements have been made by me, and directions have been given by the Commissary General to his deputies and assistants to carry these arrangements into execution. . . . You may depend upon it that there are few of the general arrangements of the army which have not been maturely considered by me; and that, although some inconveniences may attend some of them, they are the smallest that, after full consideration, it was found would attend any arrangement of the subjects to which those arrangements relate.' [1]

In these words is the key to much of Wellington's success. The organisation of the army was chaotic, the men were recruited from 'the scum of the earth', the officers of infantry and cavalry were untrained and the generals inadequate. These factors were immutable. Any field commander who devoted his energies to trying to bring the whole anachronistic agglomeration into some supposedly logical framework would have been defeated by the politicians, the civil servants, public opinion and, for the most part, his professional colleagues long before he could have brought his troops within range of the enemy. Wellington's genius lay in making the best of any situation and of the materials available. Occasionally in a private letter to one of his brothers his frustration with the petty incompetences of the government in London breaks out in an angry phrase: 'If there was any thing like a government in England, or any public sentiment remaining there, Bonaparte would yet repent his invasion of Portugal,' [2] he wrote in 1810, but for the most part he accepted them with resignation and a determination to surmount the difficulties. Six weeks before Waterloo he confessed that 'I am not very well pleased with the manner in which the Horse Guards have conducted themselves towards me' in the provision of an adequate army or staff, but having made his point he concluded: 'However, I'll do the best I can with the instruments which have been sent to assist me.' [3]

He was not an innovator. In tactics, for example, he devised nothing new. He took what was best from the various schools of tactical thought current in his day and welded it into a combination which proved unbeatable. Tactics at the beginning of the nineteenth century were dictated by the capabilities of the common musket, which was accurate only up to 80 yards, had a rate of fire of about four rounds a minute, and a misfire rate of two in 13 in dry weather and of 100 per cent in heavy rain. With such a weapon to provide its fire power, infantry had no option but to fire volleys so that, from the sheer number of rounds fired, a high proportion must strike an enemy force somewhere. Thus infantry could only go into action shoulder to shoulder, and this necessity for close order was strongly reinforced by the threat of cavalry, against which the only sure defence was an unbroken hedge of bayonets.

Professional armies of the eighteenth century were trained to fight in three-deep line, a formation calling for a very high standard of foot drill and one in which it was extremely difficult to manoeuvre. It was vulnerable to the fire of artillery and sharpshooters and almost unusable in broken country. This last defect had become very apparent to the British in the American War of Independence and some steps had been taken to train a proportion of the infantry in open-order fighting. Nevertheless, since fighting on the continent of Europe remained the principal potential use of the army, the old close-order drill remained the staple of infantry training and was codified in David Dundas' *Rules and Regulations for the movement of His Majesty's Infantry* which became the official drill book in 1792.

The French army also retained, in their drill book, regulations for fighting in three-deep line. Increasingly, however, they found that by attacking with heavy columns, using momentum to replace fire power, they were able to break through an enemy line, provided it had previously been softened up with intensive artillery fire and harassing from skirmishers, especially when the enemy morale and training were poor. Such shock action was expensive in casualties but, with the conscription and the reservoirs of manpower acquired in the Netherlands, Germany, Poland and Italy, France could afford to be lavish with men's lives provided victory was ensured.

Wellington rejected the French practice outright. Before he sailed for the Peninsula he remarked, 'if what I hear of their system of manoeuvres be true, I think it is a false one as against steady troops'.[4] Experience showed him that he had been right. Writing in 1811 after the action at Sabugal, where four British battalions had repulsed 6,000 French infantry supported by cavalry, he wrote: 'Really these attacks in columns against our line are very contemptible',[5] and a few days later: 'I do not desire better sport than to meet one of their columns *en masse* with our own line.'[6]

In the British army there were two main schools of thought on infantry tactics: the close-order school, which was associated with the name of Sir David Dundas, and the skirmishing order school, which has come to be associated with Sir John Moore. In fact, neither of these generals adopted the extreme views which their partisans and later historians have attributed to them. Dundas, the codifier of the multifarious drill systems, was by no means opposed to light infantry in their proper situation which he conceived to be 'to form advanced and rear guards, to gain intelligence, to occupy the outposts, to keep up communications, and by their vigilance and activity to cover a front'.[7] Moore, although he was responsible for a revolution in the relationship between officers and men, was not an innovator in tactics. He relied on the published works of de Rottenburg and Jarry, both approved by the Horse Guards before the camp at Shorncliffe was ever formed, and insisted that 'Light Infantry in the British service is a species of troops different from the light troops of every other nation. These seldom act in line. . . . Our Light Infantry on the contrary, not only are employed as Yägers, but act in line, and are selected to head attacks when enterprise, activity and courage are particularly required. They are in fact a mixture of the Yäger and the Grenadier. . . . Their first drill and instruction should, I conceive, be the same as that of other infantry—they should be confirmed in the exercise and movements of regular battalions before they are taught any other.'[8]

Wellington took the best from both these schools. No general appreciated more the merits of the solidarity and fire power of the line and no one used it to more effect. Equally, no one used a higher proportion of skirmishers to protect his line. In his normal Peninsular divisions one man in five was trained as a skirmisher (see p. 141 footnote) and was used as such. In addition he created the Light Division on the basis of the battalions Moore had trained at Shorncliffe and, in the second half of 1811, he seems to have tried to create a second such division from the Seventh Division.

In almost everything he did in the way of tactical handling of troops Wellington kept strictly to the approved drill books. The only exception was in his use of a line two deep instead of the three deep enjoined by Dundas. This was by no means an original idea. The two-deep line had been employed in the American war, where, in the opinion of Sir John Fortescue, it had been responsible for at least one British defeat. Sir Ralph Abercromby had used it successfully at Alexandria and Moore's troops had fought two deep at Coruña. It was, in fact, a deviation widely used and officially tolerated. The advantages of two deep were obvious—it permitted every musket to be brought to bear on the enemy, whereas in three deep the rear rank could not fire without serious danger to those in front of them. It also increased the front held by units and formations and gave the opportunity for the extreme wings to be thrown forward, enveloping the enemy. Against this 50 per cent gain in fire-power had to be set a loss in stability. There was no reserve from which to fill up gaps caused by casualties in the firing ranks and to oppose infantry two deep to cavalry was to cut the safety margin to the lowest possible point. To use it the commander had to have the highest confidence in the steadiness of his troops and it is remarkable that no continental commander was prepared to use it as a regular practice. Even Wellington, whose confidence in his infantry was un-bounded, thickened up his ranks on occasions of great danger. At Waterloo when the Imperial Guard was moving to the attack he ordered the two battalions of the British First Guards to be formed four deep lest the French should be supported by cavalry.

In the organisation of his army Wellington adhered scrupulously to existing practice, but added to it a touch of inspiration and a persevering determination to see that it worked. In his use of his staff his only departure from the practice of other British commanders was in laying more stress on the duties of the Quartermaster-General than upon the Adjutant-General. This was probably due to the higher standard of training of the officers of the Quartermaster-General's department and especially to the notable superiority of George Murray, the Quartermaster-General, over Charles Stewart, the Adjutant-General. For the rest Wellington was content to use the archaic system which denied him an operations staff,* only taking the greatest care that every staff officer performed his functions efficiently.

Again, in the supply of the army Wellington adhered to established

---

* After Waterloo, when the army had become an occupation force, the Quartermaster-General was translated into a chief of staff. This was largely done to conform with the practice of the allied armies since Wellington's headquarters acted as headquarters for all the occupying forces.

forms. The Commissariat in 1809 was scandalously inefficient. In June of that year he wrote to the Treasury: 'The gentlemen of the Commissariat are very new to their business, and I am not without grounds of complaint of their want of intelligence; but I believe they do their best, and I shall not complain of them.' [9] Before the end of 1811 he had to send home at least three commissaries whose conduct had rendered them liable to proceedings under civil law, but by the end of the war, thanks to Wellington's careful supervision and the exertions and abilities of Commissary-General Robert Kennedy, the supply system worked exceedingly well and wholly within the tiresome and unsuitable regulations laid down by the Treasury. It is, indeed, doubtful whether he would have been permitted to operate his supply system by any other rule since it was the duty of the Commissary-General to report to his masters in Whitehall over the head of the Commander of the Forces and, loyal as Kennedy was, he could scarcely have failed to act as an informer had the regulations been breached.

It was the same in every department. The existing forms of procedure were absurd and all but unworkable but Wellington made them work and made them work well. As a modern writer has said: 'Everything that he touched—and he touched everything—bore the mark of his own personality.' [10]

Intimately bound up with the regular supply of rations was the question of discipline. Being composed only of those unable to obtain employment elsewhere, the British army was a difficult force to control. 'British soldiers fight well,' said William Napier in 1807, 'but they are the greatest scoundrels possible.' [11] If the army was not regularly paid and fed, discipline went to pieces whoever commanded it and the first contribution to discipline was regular rations. Punishment in the army was savage, but not more so than under the civil penal code in England and notably less so than that used in the Royal Navy. Wellington accepted the standards of his day, provided that a heavy punishment was used as a deterrent. 'It cannot be expected that crimes will be prevented by punishments, or discipline maintained in the army, unless the example of the consequences attending the commission of these enormous offences should be of a nature to operate on the minds of the soldiers in general.' [12] Nor was he inflexible in putting the law into practice. Many a man was pardoned because of his previous good conduct or because of the good reputation of his regiment. The Judge Advocate-General tells of a soldier who 'deserted with a Spanish girl from the neighbourhood of Madrid whom he had brought away with him. On being ordered to send her off by his Captain, he appeared to have had no intention of going over to the French. . . . Lord Wellington pardoned him, from the good character of his regiment, and that which the Colonel gave him.' [13]

'It has frequently been stated', wrote a sergeant of Fusiliers, 'that the Duke of Wellington was severe. In answer to this I would say, he could not be otherwise. His army was composed of the lowest orders. Many, if not most of them were ignorant, idle and drunken. . . . Could a general, so wise, just and brave as Wellington was, suffer the people that he was sent to deliver from the tyrant Napoleon to be robbed with impunity?' [14] This view is confirmed by George Napier. 'Lord Wellington was placed in a very critical situation, and very often found it necessary to be stern and inflexible in his administration of the army; and I am sure, though he is not a man who outwardly shows any softness of feeling, that he has always felt the greatest repugnance to ordering military executions or harsh treatment of either officers, soldiers or inhabitants. . . . I think the Duke of Wellington does not get the credit which is due upon the score of feeling. He has a short manner and a stern look, which people mistake for want of heart; but I have witnessed his kindness to others, and felt it myself in so many instances and so strongly, that I cannot bear to hear him accused of wanting what I know he possesses.' [15]

Wellington, in moments of anger, could speak harshly of his troops. 'No soldier', he wrote, not without justification, in 1810, 'can withstand the temptation of wine. This is constantly before their eyes in this country, and they are constantly intoxicated when absent from their regiments, and there is no crime which they do not commit to obtain money to purchase it; or if they cannot get money to obtain it by force.' [16] But he was in no doubt where the fault lay. 'I know of no [point] more important than closely to attend to the comfort of the soldier: let him be well clothed, sheltered and fed. How should he fight poor fellow if he has, beside risking his life, to struggle with unnecessary hardships. . . . One ought to look sharp after young officers and be very indulgent to the soldiers.' [17]

It was always the officers whom Wellington blamed for the indiscipline of their men. Except for a few regiments, the officers of the army were not only untrained but showed no wish to learn anything of their profession. Their bravery could be taken for granted but their obedience to orders, except orders which would place them in direct contact with the enemy, could never be assumed. As Wellington remarked: 'Nobody in the British army ever reads a regulation or an order as if it were to be a guide to his conduct, or in any other manner than as an amusing novel.' [18] On another occasion he complained to his brother that 'British officers require an authority of no mean description, exercised with considerable strictness, to keep them in order and within due bounds'.[19]

His confidential circular after the retreat from Burgos put the blame firmly where it belonged. 'The officers lost all command over their men. Irregularities and outrages of all descriptions were committed with impunity, and losses have been sustained which ought never to have occurred. . . . I have no hesitation in attributing these evils to the habitual inattention of the officers of the regiments to their duties.'[20]

Wellington possibly put too much venom into this circular, and he was prepared to admit that occasionally he did this. 'There are some of us who cannot avoid to feel warmly for the success of the operation to which we have the charge; and to express ourselves with vehemence, and in language not perfectly correct, on the mistakes and neglects which are likely to impede it'.[21] But many, if not the majority, of the army were prepared to admit the justice of his strictures and knew in which divisions and regiments the blame lay. 'I must confess', wrote Sergeant Wheeler, 'that altho' there are several severe remarks imbodied in the order, yet I cannot say they are uncalled for. It is impossible for any army to have given themselves up to more dissipation and everything that is bad, as did our army. The conduct of some men would have disgraced savages, drunkenness prevailed to such a frightful extent that I have often wondered how it was that a great part of our army were not cut off.'[22] Major Hew Ross wrote to his sister: 'Be assured that it is thought much worse of [in England] than it deserved; and although Lord Weellington's circular is a general censure upon all, it does not with justice affect more than two or three divisions. The Light [Division] is perfectly clear of meriting it in any way, and his Lordship's remark at his own table is a proof of this. The letter became a subject of conversation when Colonel Barnard, who commands one of the brigades, said "We do not take it to ourselves", and was immediately replied to, "I know that; I never intended that you should." . . . You must not therefore suppose that the letter, which appears so harsh in the papers, had the effect of annoying any but those who ought to feel it.'[23]

The outcry about the circular was in fact the last outburst of the anti-Wellington lobby in England. No one stopped to enquire which of the generals to whom it was addressed had not scrupled to release a confidential letter to the press, and no one drew attention to the very similar wording used by Moore, the Whig paragon, in his general orders to the army on the retreat to Coruña.*

Looting after a successful siege was, by Wellington's standards, permissible. By eighteenth-century conventions a garrison which had stood an assault after being summoned in the proper form sacrificed all its rights. It was not until the day following the storm of Badajoz that he issued an order that 'it is now full time that the plunder of Badajoz should cease',[24] but even then he had limited views on the subject of

* The Commander of the forces is tired of giving orders which are never attended to . . . He was forced to order one soldier to be shot at Villafranca, and he will order all others to be executed who are guilty of similar enormities: but he considers that there would be no occasion to proceed to such extremities if the officers did their duty; as it is chiefly to their negligence, and from the want of proper regulations in the regiments, that crimes and irregularities are committed' (G.O. 6 Jan 09).

plunder. 'His definition of booty was "What you could lay your bloody hands upon and keep." ' [25] This continuation of the conventions of eighteenth-century war ran through his conduct and, in other matters, did much to alleviate the horrors of the long Peninsular campaign. During the blockade of Pamplona in 1813 the number of French wounded surviving from Vitoria was far greater than the British medical services could cope with. Wellington sent in a flag of truce to the town requesting the loan of French doctors who were immediately forthcoming. Civilities were the order of the day between the outposts of the British and French armies. 'The advanced posts always gave notice to each other when they were in danger', the Duke used to recount after the war. 'On one occasion, when the French army was advancing suddenly and in force, the French posts suddenly cried out to ours, "*Courez vite, courez vite, on va vous attaquer.*" I always encouraged this; the killing of a poor fellow of a vidette or carrying off a post could not influence the battle, and I always when I was going to attack sent to tell them to get out of the way.' [26] So friendly did relations between the outposts become that towards the end of the war a British commanding officer 'in returning from the front on a very dark stormy night, missed his way, and his horse falling over a bank, both horse and rider came clattering down heels over head into a lane, and close to a French sentry who instantly challenged. [The officer] hearing the qui vive, and the click of the musket, thought he was going to fire, and called out, "*C'est l'officier du poste Anglais—ne tirez pas!*" "*Non, non, mon Colonel*" replied he, "*J'espère que vous n'êtes pas blessé.*" ' [27] At all levels there was an easy and constant interchange between the two sides. From headquarters aides-de-camp frequently rode into the French lines with a white flag to arrange for the exchange of prisoners, with money for those officer prisoners who could not be exchanged and to negotiate for the return of non-combatants such as doctors, commissaries and, on one occasion, the Judge Advocate-General. In 1813 the Royal Navy was asked to send in from the sea to beleaguered Santoña 'to have an inquiry made of the Governor what ransom he will take for all the clothing, &c, taken in the *Margaret* [which was blown into the port in a gale], which can be of no use to him, and puts those to whom it belongs to the inconvenience of waiting for the arrival of more from England'.[28] At the other end of the scale a French sentry, on the night after Fuentes de Oñoro, did not hesitate to walk across the plank over the stream which separated the two armies for a light for his pipe.[29]

It was in his dealings with his allies that Wellington found the greatest test of his willingness to make the best use of a situation as he found it. Gneisenau was wholly wrong when he asserted that the Duke 'had so accustomed himself to duplicity that he had at last become such a master of the art as even to outwit the Nabobs themselves' (see

p. 181). In fact the exact opposite was true. The Indian potentates were devious men who had a conception of honour which did not coincide with that of an eighteenth-century gentleman. Many of the servants of the East India Company had fallen into dealing with them in ways at least as devious as their own, ways which, to say the least, belied the word 'Honourable' in the Company's .title. Wellington would have nothing of this. 'I would sacrifice Gwalior, or every frontier of India, ten times over, in order to preserve our credit for scrupulous good faith.'[30] He treated the princes with the most upright and unswerving honesty and was trusted by them accordingly.

With the Portuguese and Spaniards the process was more trying and less successful. The governments of neither country reacted favourably to honesty or to persistent endeavour. The Portuguese could to some extent be controlled. Their economy survived entirely on the large British subsidy and there was always the possibility of appealing over the heads of the Regency in Lisbon to Prince Regent John in Brazil. Despite these curbs the Regency systematically neglected the needs of their army, especially after the immediate threat to Lisbon had receded. For the most part the fault lay less in evil intentions than in indolence. 'There exists in the people of Portugal an unconquerable love of their ease, which is superior even to their fear and detestation of the enemy.'[31] 'The Portuguese really have not sufficient exertion in them; they will not work. The only answer I ever got from them, and which they imagine unanswerable, is "I wrote" or "I gave the orders"; never thinking it necessary to see or enforce their execution.'[32] It was a situation infuriating to a man with Wellington's passion for efficiency and discipline. Nevertheless he managed to keep his temper over the years and to maintain relations on a civil and usually friendly footing, although by 1811 he remarked that 'I have brought matters almost to that state that it is nearly indifferent what the Portuguese government do; and I never give myself the trouble of writing to them, or of consulting their opinion on any subject whatever'.[33] Fortunately, whatever the neglects of their government, the Portuguese troops improved out of all recognition and by July 1813 he could report, with perfect truth, that 'the Portuguese are now the fighting cocks of the army'.[34]

The Portuguese at least had a devotion to the British alliance which scarcely wavered. The Spanish government was quite another matter. They never wanted an alliance with Britain and accepted it only because they had no option. General Castaños said to his French prisoners after Baylen: 'Let not Napoleon persevere in aiming at a conquest which is unattainable. Let him not force us into the arms of the English. They are hateful to us, and up to the present moment we have rejected their proffered succours.'[35] To make matters worse there was between the Spaniards and the Portuguese 'an ancient enmity . . . which is more like that of cat and dog than any thing else, of which no sense of common danger, or common interest, or any thing else, can get the better even in individuals'.[36]

Successive Spanish governments behaved disgracefully throughout the war. 'The truth is, that it is impossible for any rational man to talk to any of them. They are visionaries and enthusiasts, who will not look at things as they really are; and although they cannot be ignorant of the truth of all we say of the miserably inefficient state of their army, they talk and act as if it was an army, till some dreadful disaster happens, and are highly offended if in any discussion the truth . . . is even hinted.' [37] 'Examine any transaction in which they have been concerned and it will be found characterised by delay, weakness, folly or treachery.' [38]

But if the governments of Spain were bad and their generals even worse the Spanish peasantry was Wellington's most effective ally. In the words of a British colonel, 'The soldiers are naturally as brave a set of fellows as exist but they have fallen so often a sacrifice to the ignorance and rascality of their generals that it has ruined their morale.' [39] Properly led and supplied, Spanish troops could meet the French on equal terms, as they showed at San Marcial, but the Spanish officers 'march the troops night and day, without provisions or rest. . . . They reach the enemy in such a state as to be unable to make any exertion or execute any plan, even if any plan had been formed; and then, when the moment of action arrives, they are totally incapable of movement, and they stand by to see their allies destroyed, and afterwards abuse them, because they do not continue, unsupported, exertions to which human nature is not equal.' [40]

There could be no question of British officers taking in hand the training and organisation of the Spanish armies as they did with the Portuguese. All that the Spaniards would agree in 1812 was that a certain number of Spaniards should be allowed to be recruited into the British army up to a hundred being permitted to join any one regiment.[41] The plan failed. It found little support amongst the Spaniards, it was disapproved of by the Horse Guards and, as a result, 'we have not got enough in the whole army to form one company; and I am sorry to add that some have deserted'.[42]

It was not, however, true that Wellington received no military help from the Spaniards. The guerrillas, which formed spontaneously and until a late stage in the war paid only formal allegiance to the government, were of the most essential service. They tied down thousands of French troops, made permanently insecure the French lines of communication and regularly supplied Wellington with information about French movements and intentions which went far to compensate for Wellington's lack of numbers. From their very form they had their limitations. 'The guerrillas, although active and willing, and although their operations in general occasion the utmost annoyance to the enemy, are so little disciplined that they can do nothing against the French troops, unless the latter are very inferior in numbers; and if the French take post in house or church, of which they only have to barricade the entrance . . . guerrillas are so ill equipped, as military bodies, that the French can remain in security till relieved by a larger body.' [43]

Wellington gladly acknowledged the debt he owed to the guerrillas, but he remained of the opinion that 'the Spanish government are really too bad'.[44] Nevertheless he maintained good relations with them no matter how often they broke their promises to him.

The same attitude of dealing only with what was possible lay behind his work for the army after the war. Once peace was re-established after Waterloo, the only thought of the politicians was to cut down on the expense of having an army. By 1821 the establishment was reduced to 101,031 of whom 31,572 were in various colonies, 19,267 in India and only 50,192 were either in the United Kingdom or on passage home. The total strength of the Royal Engineers was reduced to 140 and the only equipped artillery in the British Isles were two troops of Horse Artillery with two guns each. In such a climate it was impossible to attempt to reform the army. Neither political party would lend its support to anything but reductions. The Duke did what he could. He managed to abolish the degrading economy, which had been practised since the army became a regular force, of providing only a wooden crib for four soldiers to sleep in, and arranged that every man should have his own iron bedstead. Having first tested them in his own fowling pieces, he authorised the adoption of the percussion cap to replace the inefficient flintlock, a reform which every Master-General of the Ordnance since 1807 had refused to sanction. Towards the end of his life he approved the adoption of the rifle by the infantry of the line, stipulating only that it should continue to be known as a musket as 'we must not allow them to fancy they are all riflemen, or they will become conceited, and be asking next to be dressed in green, or some other jack-a-dandy uniform'.[45] While he was Prime Minister the first step was taken to provide a pension for old soldiers. After 21 years' service with good conduct, the veteran was to receive one shilling a day with a further halfpenny for each additional year's service. The reforming ministry of Lord Grey cut the basic rate to sixpence in 1833, and the following year the radical William Cobbett moved in Parliament for a reduction in the pay for the private soldier. In his term at the Ordnance Office Wellington carried out a thorough reform of the organisation, saving £100,000 a year and dismissing 68 redundant officers, thereby, no doubt, increasing the dislike that the Ordnance Corps felt for him.

These were all small things, but at a time when Peel, as Chief Secretary for Ireland, felt it necessary to defend the number of troops stationed in that country as being necessary 'to prevent the distillation of illicit spirits', there was little more that could have been done.

The two major achievements of the Duke's first premiership both had good results for the army. The emancipation of the Roman Catholics, a measure Wellington had advocated before the French Revolution (see p. 33) and forced through Parliament in the teeth of the opposition of his own party, resulted in some pressure being taken off the troops stationed in Ireland to keep the peace, for a time at least, and made it possible to keep them more concentrated, thus avoiding the extreme dispersion which was always such a menace to the morale and training of regiments kept there. Similarly, the creation of the Metropolitan Police in 1829 disposed, except in the direst emergency, of the army's most distasteful and unpopular rôle, that of keeping down civil disturbance. The credit for this last reform has gone largely to Peel, as Home Secretary, but there is no doubt that he had Wellington's firmest backing and keen interest and that it was Wellington who saw to it that the first Chief Commissioner was Sir Charles Rowan, formerly Assistant Adjutant-General of the Light Division, a pupil of Moore and a man brought up in the humane tradition of the more advanced regiments of the army.

The question of whether Wellington was popular with his troops has often been debated and is irrelevant. Popularity is not a safe guide by which to judge a commander—few British generals have been so loved by their troops and few have led them with such consistent wrong-headedness as Sir Redvers Buller. Wellington, with his rare but vivid bursts of temper and his icy contempt for inattention to orders, hurt many feelings but they were almost always feelings which richly deserved to be hurt. Birth and good connections were no protection against Wellington's righteous wrath. When Charles Stewart, son of a marquess and brother to the Foreign Secretary, stood presumptuously on the supposed rights of his office as Adjutant-General, Wellington reduced him to tears in a few devastating sentences but never forfeited his respect and friendship.

What was important was that, throughout the army, everyone trusted him to lead them to victory and a victory purchased as cheaply in terms of casualties as was possible. They knew too of his pride in them and of the care he took of them. When, in January 1814, a battalion discharged a man on his way to England in a penniless condition, it could not be long before the whole army knew that the commanding officer had received a very sharp letter of rebuke stating that 'no circumstances of service could justify the destitute condition in which Private ———— was sent from the Headquarters of his battalion, with a view to his final discharge. The attention of the Commanding officer, and the credit of the corps, should always be considered connected with the soldier's welfare to the last hour of his service, and omission on any points relating to that end cannot fail to prove prejudicial to the interests of the corps.' [46]

Two witnesses are enough to make this point. Sergeant Wheeler, who served under him from Fuentes de Oñoro to Waterloo, wrote in 1816: 'If England should require her army again, and I should be with it, let me have "Old Nosey" to command. Our interests would be sure to be looked into, we should never have occasion to fear an enemy. There are two things we should be certain of. First, we should always be as well supplied with rations as the nature of the service would admit. The second is we should be sure to give the enemy a d——d good thrashing. What can a soldier desire more?' [47]

The other comes from one of the many men wounded at Albuera. When visiting the hospitals after his arrival Wellington found a group of the Worcesters lying together in a ward and said: ' "Old 29th, I am sorry to see so many of you here!" They instantly replied, "Oh, my lord, if you had only been with us, there would not have been so many of us here." ' [48]

ORDERS OF BATTLE

A Anglo-Portuguese Army, 6th May 1809

Commander of the Forces, Lieut-Gen Sir Arthur Wellesley
Second in Command, Maj-Gen the Hon Edward Paget
Commander-in-Chief Portuguese Army, Maj-Gen W. C. Beresford
Quartermaster-General, Col G. Murray
Adjutant-General, Brig-Gen the Hon Charles Stewart
Military Secretary, Lieut Col J. Bathurst
Commander, Royal Artillery, Col E. Howorth
Commander, Royal Engineers, Maj R. Fletcher
Commissary-General, Comm-Gen J. Murray

MAIN ARMY (*Wellesley*)

Cavalry

Cotton's Brigade, 14th Lt Dgns (less 1 sqn), 16th Lt Dgns, 20th Lt Dgns
(2 sqns), 3rd Lt Dgns K.G.L. (1 sqn)

Infantry

H. F. Campbell's Brigade, 1/Coldstream Gds, 1/3rd Gds, Coy 5/60th
A. Campbell's Brigade, 2/7th, 2/53rd, Coy 5/60th, 1/10th Portuguese
Line
Sontag's Brigade, 2nd Bn Detachments, 97th, Coy 5/60th, 2/16th
Portuguese Line
Hill's Brigade, 1/3rd, 2/48th, 2/66th, Coy 5/60th
Cameron's Brigade, 2/9th, 2/83rd, Coy 5/60th, 2/10th Portuguese
Line
R. Stewart's Brigade, 1st Bn Detachments, 29th, 1/16th Portuguese
Line
J. Murray's Brigade, 1st, 2nd, 5th, 7th Line Bns K.G.L. Dets Lt Bns
K.G.L.

Artillery

Sillery's Battery R.A.
Lawson's Battery R.A.
Tieling's Battery K.G.A.
Heise's Battery K.G.A.

FLANKING COLUMN (*Beresford*)

Cavalry

14th Lt Dgns (1 sqn)
1st Portuguese Dgns (3 sqns)

Infantry

Tilson's Brigade, 2/87th, 1/88th, 5/60th (5 coys)
Portuguese Brigade, 2/1st Portuguese Line, 7th and 19th Portuguese
  Line (each 2 Bns)

Artillery

2 Portuguese Batteries

FORCE WATCHING SPANISH FRONTIER (*Mackenzie*)

Cavalry

Fane's Brigade, 3rd Dgn Gds, 4th Dgns
Portuguese Brigade, 4th and 7th Portuguese Dgns (5 sqns together)

Infantry

Mackenzie's Brigade, 2/24th, 3/27th, 2/31st, 1/45th
Portuguese Brigade, 1/1st Portuguese Line, 3rd, 4th, 13th and 15th
  Portuguese Line (2 bns each), 1st, 4th and 5th Cacadores

Artillery

May's Battery R.A.
3 Portuguese Batteries

Garrison of Lisbon, 2/30th

B Anglo-Portuguese Army, 1st May 1811

Commander of the Forces, Lieut-Gen the Viscount Wellington
Commander-in-Chief, Portuguese Army, Maj-Gen Sir William Beresford
Quartermaster-General, Col G. Murray
Adjutant-General, Col the Hon Edward Pakenham (acting)
Military Secretary, Capt Lord Fitzroy Somerset
Commander, Royal Artillery, Brig-Gen E. Howorth
Commander, Royal Engineers, Lieut-Col R. Fletcher
Commissary-General, Comm-Gen R. H. Kennedy

NORTHERN ARMY *(Wellington)*

Cavalry

(Maj-Gen Sir Stapleton Cotton, Bart)

Slade's Brigade, 1st (Royal) Dgns, 14th Lt Dgns
Arentschildt's Brigade, 16th Lt Dgns, 1st Hus K.G.L.
Barbacena's Brigade, 4th and 10th Portuguese Dgns
Artillery attached to the Cavalry, Bull's Troop R.H.A.

Infantry

1st Division (Lieut-Gen Sir Brent Spencer)
Stopford's Brigade, 1/Coldstream Gds, 1/3rd Gds, Coy 5/60th
Nightingall's Brigade, 2/24th, 2/42nd, 1/79th, Coy 5/60th
Howard's Brigade, 1/50th, 1/71st, 1/92nd, Coy 3/95th Rifles
Von Löw's Brigade, 1st, 2nd, 5th and 7th Line Bns K.G.L., Dets Light
Bns K.G.L.
Artillery attached to 1st Division, Thompson's Battery R.A.

3rd Division (Maj-Gen T. Picton)
Mackinnon's Brigade, 1/45th, 74th, 1/88th, 3 coys 5/60th
Colville's Brigade, 2/5th, 2/83rd, 2/88th, 94th
Power's Brigade, 9th and 21st Portuguese Line (2 Bns each)
Artillery attached to 3rd Division, 2 Portuguese Batteries (V.v.
Arentschildt)

5th Division (Maj-Gen Sir William Erskine, Bart)
Hay's Brigade, 3/1st, 1/9th, 2/38th, Coy Brunswick Oels
Dunlop's Brigade, 1/4th, 2/30th, 2/44th, Coy Brunswick Oels
Spry's Brigade, 3rd and 15th Portuguese Line (2 bns each), 8th
Cacadores
Artillery attached to 5th Division, Lawson's Battery R.A., Da Cunha's
Portuguese Battery

6th Division (Maj-Gen Alex Campbell)
Hulse's Brigade, 1/11th, 2/53rd, 1/61st, Coy 5/60th
Burne's Brigade, 2nd, 1/36th
Madden's Brigade, 8th and 12th Portuguese Line
Artillery attached to 6th Division, Rozierres' Portuguese Battery

7th Division (Maj-Gen W. Houston)
Sontag's Brigade, 51st, 85th, Chasseurs Britanniques, Brunswick Oels
(8 coys)
Doyle's Brigade, 7th and 19th Portuguese Line (2 bns each), 2nd
Cacadores

Light Division (Maj-Gen R. Craufurd)
Beckwith's Brigade, 1/43rd, 1/95th Rifles (4 coys), 2/95th Rifles (1
coy), 3rd Cacadores

Drummond's Brigade, 1/52nd, 2/52nd, 1/95th Rifles (4 coys), 1st Cacadores
Artillery attached to the Light Division, Ross' Troop R.H.A.

Independent Brigades
Pack's Brigade, 1st and 16th Portuguese Line (2 bns each), 4th Cacadores
Artillery attached to Pack's Brigade, Pinto's Portuguese Battery
Pamplona's Brigade, 6th and 18th Portuguese Line, 6th Cacadores

SOUTHERN CORPS (*Beresford*)

Cavalry
(Maj-Gen R. B. Long)
De Grey's Brigade, 3rd Dgn Gds, 4th Dgns
Otway's Brigade, 1st and 7th Portuguese Dgns
Madden's Brigade, 5th and 8th Portuguese Dgns
        unattached, 13th Lt Dgns
Artillery attached to the Cavalry, Lefebure's Troop R.H.A.

Infantry

2nd Division (Maj-Gen the Hon William Stewart)
Colborne's Brigade, 1/3rd, 2/31st, 2/48th, 2/66th
Hoghton's Brigade, 29th, 1/48th, 1/57th
Lumley's Brigade, 2/28th, 2/34th, 2/39th
Artillery attached to 2nd Division, Hawker's Battery R.A.

4th Division (Maj-Gen the Hon Lowry Cole)
Kemmis' Brigade, 2/27th, 1/40th, 97th
Myers' Brigade, 1/7th, 2/7th, 1/23rd
Harvey's Brigade, 11th and 23rd Portuguese Line (2 bns each), 1/Loyal Lusitanian Legion
Artillery attached to 4th Division, Cleeves' Battery K.G.A., Sympher's Battery K.G.A.

Portuguese Division (Maj-Gen J. Hamilton)
Arch. Campbell's Brigade, 2nd and 14th Portuguese Line (2 bns each)
Fonseca's Brigade, 4th and 10th Portuguese Line (2 bns each)
Artillery attached to Portuguese Division, 2 Portuguese Batteries (Dickson)

Independent Brigades
C.v.Alten's Brigade, 1st and 2nd Light Bns K.G.L.
Collins' Brigade, 5th Portuguese Line (2 bns), 5th Cacadores

Garrison of Lisbon, 77th

(Lieut-Gen T. Graham)

Cavalry

2nd Hus K.G.L. (2 sqns)

Infantry

3/1st Gds, Composite Gds Bn (2/Coldstream and 2/3rd Gds), 2/47th, 2/67th, 2/87th, 2/95th Rifles (2 coys), 3/95th Rifles (4 coys), Provisional Bn of 'German Deserters', 20th Portuguese Line (2 bns)

Artillery

Owen's Battery R.A., Hughes' Battery R.A., Roberts' Battery R.A., Dickson's Battery R.A., Shenley's Battery R.A.

C Anglo-Portuguese Army, 25th May 1813

Commander of the Forces, General the Marquess of Wellington
Second in Command, Lieut-Gen Sir Thomas Graham
Commander-in-Chief, Portuguese Army, Lieut-Gen Sir William Beresford
Quartermaster-General, Maj-Gen G. Murray
Adjutant-General, Brig-Gen Lord Aylmer (acting)
Military Secretary, Lieut-Col Lord Fitzroy Somerset
Commander, Royal Artillery, Lieut-Col A. Dickson
Commander, Royal Engineers, Lieut-Col Sir Richard Fletcher, Bart
Commissary-General, Comm-Gen Sir Robert Kennedy

Cavalry

(Maj-Gen George, Baron von Bock, acting)

R. Hill's Brigade, 1st and 2nd L. Gds, R.H.G.
Ponsonby's Brigade, 5th Dgn Gds, 3rd and 4th Dgns
G. Anson's Brigade, 12th and 16th Lt Dgns
Long's Brigade, 13th Lt Dgns
Bülow's Brigade, 1st and 2nd Dgns K.G.L.
V.v.Alten's Brigade, 14th Lt Dgns, 1st Hus K.G.L.
Fane's Brigade, 3rd Dgn Gds, 1st (Royal) Dgns
Grant's Brigade, 10th, 15th and 18th Hus
D'Urban's Brigade, 1st, 11th and 12th Portuguese Dgns
    unattached, 6th Portuguese Dgns
Artillery attached to the Cavalry, Bull's Troop R.H.A., Beane's Troop R.H.A.

1st Division (Maj-Gen K. A. Howard)
Stopford's Brigade, 1/Coldstream Gds, 1/3rd Gds, Coy 5/60th
Halkett's Brigade, 1st, 2nd and 5th Line Bns K.G.L., 1st and 2nd Light Bns K.G.L.
Artillery attached to 1st Division, Dubourdieu's Battery R.A.

2nd Division (Lieut-Gen Sir Rowland Hill)
Cadogan's Brigade, 1/50th, 1/71st, 1/92nd, Coy 5/60th
Byng's Brigade, 1/3rd, 1/57th, 1st Provincial Bn (2/31st and 2/66th), Coy 5/60th
O'Callaghan's Brigade, 1/28th, 2/34th, 1/39th, Coy 5/60th
Ashworth's Brigade, 6th and 18th Portuguese Line (2 bns each), 6th Cacadores
Artillery attached to 2nd Division, Maxwell's Battery R.A.

3rd Division (Lieut-Gen Sir Thomas Picton)
Brisbane's Brigade, 1/45th, 74th, 1/88th, 3 coys 5/60th
Colville's Brigade, 1/5th, 2/83rd, 2/87th, 94th
Power's Brigade, 9th and 21st Portuguese Line (2 bns each), 11th Cacadores
Artillery attached to 3rd Division, Douglas' Battery R.A.

4th Division (Lieut-Gen Sir Lowry Cole)
W. Anson's Brigade, 3/27th, 1/40th, 1/48th, 2nd Provincial Bn (2nd and 2/53rd), Coy 5/60th
Skerret's Brigade, 1/7th, 20th, 1/23rd, Coy Brunswick Oels
Stubb's Brigade, 11th and 23rd Portuguese Line, 7th Cacadores
Artillery attached to 4th Division, Sympher's Battery K.G.A.

5th Division (Maj-Gen J. Oswald (acting))
Hay's Brigade, 3/1st, 1/9th, 1/38th, Coy Brunswick Oels
Robinson's Brigade, 1/4th, 2/47th, 2/59th, Coy Brunswick Oels
Spry's Brigade, 3rd and 5th Portuguese Line (2 bns each), 8th Cacadores
Artillery attached to 5th Division, Bandreth's Battery R.A.

6th Division (Maj-Gen the Hon Edward Pakenham (acting))
Stirling's Brigade, 1/42nd, 1/79th, 1/91st, Coy 5/60th
Hinde's Brigade, 1/11th, 1/32nd, 1/36th, 1/91st
Madden's Brigade, 8th and 12th Portuguese Line (2 bns each), 9th Cacadores
Artillery attached to 6th Division, Lawson's Battery R.A.

7th Division (Lieut-Gen Lord Dalhousie)
Barnes' Brigade, 1/6th, 3rd Provincial Bn (2/24th and 2/58th), Brunswick Oels (9 coys)

Grant's Brigade, 51st, 68th, 1/82nd, Chasseurs Britanniques
Lecor's Brigade, 7th and 19th Portuguese Line (2 bns each), 2nd
  Cacadores
Artillery attached to 7th Division, Gardiner's Troop R.H.A.

Light Division (Maj-Gen Charles Count von Alten)
Kempt's Brigade, 1/43rd, 1/95th Rifles (8 coys), 3/95th Rifles (5 coys),
  3rd Cacadores
Vandeleur's Brigade, 1/52nd, 2/95th Rifles (6 coys), 17th Portuguese
  Line (2 bns), 1st Cacadores
Artillery attached to the Light Division, Ross' Troop R.H.A.

Portuguese Division (Maj-Gen Conde de Amaranthe)
Da Costa's Brigade, 2nd and 14th Portuguese Line (2 bns each)
Arch. Campbell's Brigade, 4th and 10th Portuguese Line (2 bns each),
  10th Cacadores
Artillery attached to the Portuguese Division, 2 Portuguese Batteries
  (Tulloh)

Independent Brigades
Lambert's Brigade, 1st and 3rd Bns 1st Gds, Coy 5/60th
Pack's Brigade, 1st and 16th Portuguese Line (2 bns each), 4th
  Cacadores
Bradford's Brigade, 13th and 24th Portuguese Line (2 bns each), 5th
  Cacadores

Reserve Artillery
Webber Smith's Troop R.H.A., Cairnes' Battery R.A., Parker's Battery
  R.A., 2 Portuguese Batteries (V.v. Arentschildt)

Garrison of Lisbon, 77th

Cadiz Contingent
(Maj-Gen G. Cooke)

2/59th, De Watteville's (7 coys), Chasseurs Britanniques (2 coys),
  Bn Foreign Deserters, R.A. Batteries of Hughes, Roberts and Shenley

D Anglo-Netherlands Army, 15th June 1815

Commander of the Forces, Field Marshal the Duke of Wellington
Generals commanding Corps, Gen H.R.H. the Hereditary Prince of
  Orange, Lieut-Gen Lord Hill
Quartermaster-General, Col Sir William Delancey (acting)
Adjutant-General, Maj-Gen Sir Edward Barnes
Military Secretary, Lieut-Col Lord Fitzroy Somerset
Commander, Royal Artillery, Col Sir George Wood

Commander, Royal Engineers, Lieut-Col C. Smyth
Commisary-General, Comm-Gen D. Ord

Cavalry

(Lieut-Gen the Earl of Uxbridge)

Somerset's Brigade, 1st and 2nd L Gds, R.H.G., 1st (King's) Dgn Gds
Ponsonby's Brigade, 1st (Royal) Dgns, 2nd (R.N.B.) Dgns, 6th Dgns
Dörnberg's Brigade, 23rd Lt Dgns, 1st and 2nd Lt Dgns K.G.L.
Vendeleur's Brigade, 11th, 12th and 16th Lt Dgns
Grant's Brigade, 7th and 15th Hus, 2nd Hus K.G.L.
Vivian's Brigade, 10th and 18th Hus, 1st Hus K.G.L.
Arentschildt's Brigade, 13th Lt Dgns, 3rd Hus K.G.L.
Von Estorff's Brigade, Prince Regent's, Bremen and Verden, and Cumberland Hus
Tripp's Brigade, 1st and 3rd Dutch, 2nd Belgian Carbineers
De Ghigny's Brigade, 4th Dutch Lt Dgns, 8th Belgian Hus
Van Merlen's Brigade, 5th Belgian Lt Dgns, 6th Dutch Hus
Brunswick Brigade, Hus Regt., Sqn Uhlans
Artillery attached to the Cavalry, Bull's, Webber-Smith's, Gardiner's, Whinyate's, Mercer's, Ramsay's Troops R.H.A., 2 half batteries Dutch H.A.

Infantry

1st Division (Maj-Gen G. Cooke)
Maitland's Brigade, 2nd and 3rd Bns 1st Gds
Byng's Brigade, 2/Coldstream Gds, 2/3rd Gds
Artillery attached to 1st Division, Sandham's Battery R.A., Kuhlmann's Battery K.G.A.

2nd Division (Lieut-Gen Sir Henry Clinton)
Adam's Brigade, 1/52nd, 1/71st, 2/95th Rifles (6 coys), 3/95th Rifles (2 coys)
Du Platt's Brigade, 1st, 2nd, 3rd and 4th Line Bns K.G.L.
H. Halkett's Brigade, Landwehr Bns of Bremervöde, Osnabrück, Quackenbrück and Salzgitter
Artillery attached to 2nd Division, Bolton's Battery R.A., Sympher's Battery K.G.A.

3rd Division (Lieut-Gen Charles, Count von Alten)
C. Halkett's Brigade, 2/30th, 33rd, 2/69th, 2/73rd
Von Ompteda's Brigade, 5th and 8th Line Bns K.G.L., 1st and 2nd Light Bns K.G.L.
Kielmansegge's Brigade, Field Bns of Bremen, Verden, York, Lüneberg and Grübenhagen, Jäger Bn
Artillery attached to 3rd Division, Lloyd's Battery R.A., Cleeve's Battery K.G.A.

4th Division (Lieut-Gen Sir Charles Colville)
Mitchell's Brigade, 3/14th, 1/23rd, 51st
Johnstone's Brigade, 2/35th, 1/54th, 2/59th, 1/91st
Lyon's Brigade, Field Bns of Lauenberg and Calenberg, Landwehr Bns of Nienburg, Hoya and Bentheim
Artillery attached to 4th Division, Broome's Battery R.A., Rettberg's Hanoverian Battery

5th Division (Lieut-Gen Sir Thomas Picton)
Kempt's Brigade, 1/28th, 1/32nd, 1/79th, 1/95th Rifles (6 coys)
Pack's Brigade, 3/1st, 1/42nd, 2/44th, 1/92nd
Von Vinke's Brigade, Landwehr Bns of Hameln, Gifhorn, Hildesheim and Peine
Artillery attached to 5th Division, Roger's Battery R.A., Braun's Hanoverian Battery

6th Division (no G.O.C.)
Lambert's Brigade, 1/4th, 1/27th, 1/40th, 2/81st
Best's Brigade, Landwehr Bns of Verden, Lüneberg, Osterode and Munden
Artillery attached to 6th Division, Unett's Battery R.A., Sinclair's Battery R.A.

1st Netherlands Division (Lieut-Gen Stedman)
D'Hauw's Brigade, 4th and 16th Line, 16th Chasseurs, 9th, 14th and 15th Militia Bns
De Eerens Brigade, 1st Line Bn, 18th Chasseurs, 1st, 2nd and 18th Militia Bns
Artillery attached to 1st Netherlands Division, Wijnand's Battery

2nd Netherlands Division (Lieut-Gen Baron de Perponcher-Sedlnitzky)
Bijlandt's Brigade, 7th Line Bn, 27th Chasseurs, 5th, 7th and 8th Militia Bns
Prince Bernard's Brigade, 2nd Regt of Nassau (2 bns), Regt of Orange Nassau (2 bns), Coy Jägers
Artillery attached to 2nd Netherlands Division, Stievenart's Battery, Bijleveld's Battery

3rd Netherlands Division (Lieut-Gen Baron Chassé)
Detmer's Brigade, 2nd Line Bn, 35th Chasseurs, 4th, 6th, 17th and 19th Militia Bns
D'Aubremé's Brigade, 3rd, 12th and 13th Line Bn, 36th Chasseurs, 3rd and 10th Militia Bns
Artillery attached to 3rd Netherlands Division, De Bichin's Battery, Lux's Battery

Brunswick Contingent (H.S.H. Frederick, Prince of Brunswick-Wolfen-buttel-Oels)
Advanced Guard, Det Uhlans, Jägers (2 coys), Lt Inf (2 coys)
Von Buttlar's Brigade, 1st, 2nd and 3rd Light Bns
Von Specht's Brigade, 1st, 2nd and 3rd Line Bns
Brunswick Artillery, Von Heinemann's Horse Battery, Moll's Field Battery

Nassau Brigade (Von Kruse)
1st Nassau Regt (3 bns)

Netherlands Indian Brigade (Anthing)
5th E. India Regt (3 bns), 10th and 11th W. India Chasseurs, Bn of Flank coys
Artillery attached to Netherlands Indian Brigade, Riesz's Battery

Reserve Artillery
Ross' Troop R.H.A., Beane's Troop R.H.A.

British & Hanoverian Troops in Garrison
2/25th, 2/37th, 2/78th, Field Bn of Hoya, Landwehr Bns of Mölln, Bremerlehe, Nordheim, Ahlefeldt, Springe, Otterndorf, Zelle, Ratzeburg, Hannover, Ülzen, Neustadt, Diepholz

OFFICERS WHO COMMANDED DIVISIONS AND HIGHER FORMATIONS UNDER WELLINGTON IN THE RANK OF MAJOR-GENERAL OR ABOVE
(in order of seniority)

John Hope, b. 1765; 2nd s. 2nd Earl of Hopetoun; MP Linlithgow 1790; Cornet 19th Lt Dgns May 1784; Lieut-Col 1793; Maj-Gen April 1802; Lieut-Gen April 1808; Commanded left wing of the Army Oct 1813–April 1814; Wounded and captured Bayonne April 1814

Henry Paget, 2nd Earl of Uxbridge, b. 1768; e.s. 1st Earl of Uxbridge; Educ. Westminster and Christ Church, Oxford; MP Carnarvon Boroughs 1790–96, Milborne Port 1796–1810; Lieut-Col on raising 80th Foot Sep 1793; Maj-Gen April 1802; Lieut-Gen April 1808; Commanded Cavalry in Waterloo Campaign; Wounded

Thomas Graham, b. 1748; 3rd s. Thomas Graham of Balgowan; Educ. Christ Church, Oxford; MP Perthshire 1794–1807; Lieut-Col 1794 on raising 90th Foot; Maj-Gen March 1809 (backdated to Sep 1803); Lieut-Gen July 1810; Commanded Cadiz Garrison, March 1810–July 1811; Commanded 1st Division, July 1811–July 1812 and May 1813–Oct 1813; Commanded left column of the army in campaign of 1813

John Coape Sherbrooke, b. 1764; s. William Coape, J.P.; Ensign 4th Foot 1780; Lieut-Col March 1794; Maj-Gen Jan 1805; Commanded 1st Division, June 1809–April 1810

William Payne, b. 1759; s. Ralph Payne, Chief Judge of St. Christopher, W.I; Cornet 1st (Royal) Dgns July 1777; Lieut-Col March 1794; Maj-Gen Jan 1805; Commanded Cavalry, June 1809–June 1810

Edward Paget, b. 1775; 4th s. Earl of Uxbridge; Educ. Westminster; Cornet, 1st Life Gds March 1792; Lieut-Col April 1794; Maj-Gen Jan 1805; Lieut-Gen June 1811; Second-in-command of the Army, 8th–12th May 1809; Commanded 1st Division, 11th Oct–17th Nov 1813; Wounded (lost arm) Oporto, 1809; Captured on retreat from Burgos 1812

Brent Spencer, b. 1760; s. Conway Spencer Esq.; Ensign 4th Foot Jan 1778; Lieut-Col May 1794; Maj-Gen Jan 1805; Lieut-Gen June 1811; Commanded 1st Division, April 1810–July 1811

Stapleton Cotton, b. 1773; e.s. Sir Robert Cotton, 5th Bart; Educ. Westminster and private Military Academy in Bayswater; MP Newark 1806–14; Ensign 23rd Foot Feb 1790; Lieut-Col May 1794; Maj-Gen Oct 1805; Lieut-Gen Jan 1812; Commanded Cavalry, June 1810–Jan 1811, April 1811–July 1812, Oct 1812–Dec 1812, June 1813–April 1814; Wounded accidentally at Salamanca, July 1812

Rowland Hill, b. 1772; (cr. Viscount Hill, 1814) 2nd s. Sir John Hill, 2nd Bart; Educ. privately and Military School, Strasbourg; Ensign 38th Foot 1790; Lieut-Col May 1794; Maj-Gen Oct 1805; Lieut-Gen Jan 1812; Commanded 2nd Division, June 1809–Jan 1811, and May 1811–March 1813; Commanded right wing of the Army, March 1813–April 1814; Commanded 2nd Corps in Waterloo campaign

William Carr Beresford, b. 1768; natural s. 1st Marquess of Waterford; Educ. Catterick Bridge School and private Military Academy, Strasbourg; Ensign 6th Foot 1785; Lieut-Col Aug 1794; Maj-Gen April 1808; Lieut-Gen Jan 1812 (acting rank from Feb 1809); Marshal in Portuguese Service, March 1809; Commander-in-Chief, Portuguese Army, 1809–22; Commanded Corps in Estremadura, Jan–May 1811; Commanded Centre Corps of Army, Oct 1813–April 1814; Wounded Salamanca, July 1812

George Ramsay, 9th Earl of Dalhousie, b. 1770; e.s. 8th Earl of Dalhousie; Cornet 3rd Dgn Gds July 1788; Lieut-Col Aug 1794; Maj-Gen April 1808; Lieut-Gen June 1813; Commanded 7th Division, Oct 1812–Oct 1813 and Feb–April 1814

James Leith, b. 1763; s. James Leith, Esq.; Educ. Aberdeen University and private Military Academy, Lille; Ensign 21st Foot 1780; Lieut-Col Oct 1794; Maj-Gen April 1808; Lieut-Gen June 1813; Commanded 5th Division, Oct 1810–Feb 1811, Dec 1811–July 1812, and 30 Aug–1st Sep 1813; Wounded Salamanca July 1812; Wounded San Sebastian, Sep 1813

James Randoll Mackenzie, b. 1762; MP Caithness Burghs 1806–09; 2nd Lieut R. Marines July 1778; Lieut-Col Nov 1794; Maj-Gen April 1808; Commanded 3rd Division, June–July 1809; Killed Talavera, July 1809

Thomas Picton, b. 1758; s. Thomas Picton, Esq., of Poyston, Pembs.; Educ. privately and private Military Academy in France; Ensign 12th Foot Jan 1772; Lieut-Col Nov 1794; Maj-Gen April 1808; Lieut-Gen June 1813; Commanded 3rd Division, Feb 1810–June 1812, May–Sep 1813 and Dec 1813–April 1814; Commanded 5th Division in Waterloo campaign; Wounded at Badajoz April 1812; Killed Waterloo

Galbraith Lowry Cole, b. 1772; 2nd s. 1st Earl of Enniskillen; Educ. schools at Armagh and Portarlington, and Stuttgart University; Irish MP Fermanagh 1798–1800, MP Fermanagh 1803–23; Cornet 12th Lt

Dgns Nov 1787; Lieut-Col Nov 1794; Maj-Gen April 1808; Lieut-Gen June 1813; Commanded 4th Division, Oct 1809–May 1811, June–July 1812 and Oct 1812–April 1814; Wounded at Albuera May 1811; Wounded at Salamanca July 1812

William Erskine, 1st Bart, b. 1769; s. William Erskine Esq. of Fife; MP Fife 1796–1805; Cornet 15th Lt Dgns 1786; Lieut-Col Nov 1794; Maj-Gen April 1808; Commanded 5th Division, Feb–March 1811, Light Division and Cavalry March–April 1811, 5th Division, April–May 1811, 2nd Cavalry Division, May–July 1811 and April–Nov (?) 1812; Committed suicide, Lisbon, April 1813

William Stewart, b. 1774; 4th s. 7th Earl of Galway; MP Saltash 1795; Wigtonshire 1796–1816; Ensign 42nd Foot March 1786; Lieut-Col Jan 1795; Maj-Gen April 1808; Lieut-Gen June 1813; Commanded 2nd Division, Nov 1810–May 1811; 1st Division, Nov 1812–March 1813; 2nd Division, March 1813–April 1814 (under Hill); Wounded Albuera May 1811; Wounded Pyrenees July 1813

John Hamilton, b. 1755; s. James Hamilton Esq. of Woodbrook; Ensign Bengal Native Infantry 1771; Lieut-Col Feb 1795; Maj-Gen Oct 1809; Commanded Portuguese Division, Feb 1810–Feb 1813 and Nov–Dec 1813

William Houston, b. 1766; Ensign 31st Foot July 1781; Lieut-Col March 1795; Maj-Gen Oct 1809; Commanded 7th Division, March–Aug 1811

John Slade, b. 1762; s. John Slade Esq. of Maunsel Grange, Somerset, Commissary of the Victualling Board; Educ. Westminster; Cornet 10th Lt Dgns 1780; Lieut-Col April 1795; Maj-Gen Oct 1809; Commanded Cavalry, Jan–March 1811

Miles Nightingall, b. 1768; natural s. 1st Marquess Cornwallis; Ensign 52nd Foot 1787; Lieut-Col Sep 1795; Maj-Gen July 1810; Commanded 1st Division, 2nd–6th May 1811; Wounded Fuentes de Oñoro May 1811

Henry Clinton, b. 1771; 2nd s. General Sir Henry Clinton; Educ. Eton; MP Boroughbridge 1808–1818; Ensign 11th Foot Oct 1787; Lieut-Col Sep 1795; Maj-Gen July 1810; Lieut-Gen June 1814; Commanded 6th Division, Feb 1812–Jan 1813 and Oct 1813–April 1814; Commanded 2nd Division in Waterloo campaign

John Sontag, b. ?; Cornet 12th Dgns Sep 1780; Lieut-Col Oct 1795; Maj-Gen July 1810; Commanded 7th Division, July–Oct 1811

James Dunlop, b. ?; s. John Dunlop of Dunlop; Ensign 82nd Foot Jan 1778; Lieut-Col Nov 1795; Maj-Gen July 1810; Commanded 5th Division, March–April 1811 and May–Dec 1811

Alexander Campbell, b. ?; Ensign ?; Lieut-Col Dec 1795; Maj-Gen July 1810; Commanded 6th Division, Oct 1810–Nov 1811

Henry Frederick Campbell, b. ?; Ensign 1st Gds 1786; Capt and Lieut-Col April 1796; Maj-Gen July 1810; Commanded 1st Division, July–Oct 1812

George, Baron von Bock, b. ?; From Hanoverian Service as Colonel, Dec 1804; Maj-Gen July 1810; Commanded Cavalry, July 1812–Oct 1812 and Dec 1812–June 1813; Lost at sea, 21st Jan 1814

Charles, Count von Alten, b. 1764; From Hanoverian Service as Colonel, Dec 1804; Maj-Gen July 1810; Commanded 7th Division, Oct 1811–May 1812, Light Division, May 1812–April 1814 and 3rd Division in Waterloo campaign; Wounded at Waterloo

John Hope, b. 1765; s. John Hope Esq.; Ensign Scots Brigade (in Dutch Pay) Dec 1779; Lieut-Col Feb 1796; Maj-Gen July 1810; Commanded 7th Division, May–Sep 1812

Charles Colville, b. 1770; s. Lord Colville (Scots Peerage); Ensign 28th Foot 1781; Lieut-Col Aug 1796; Maj-Gen July 1810; Commanded 4th Division, Dec 1811–April 1812; 3rd Division, Jan–May 1813; 6th Division, Aug–Oct 1813; 3rd Division, Oct–Dec 1813, 5th Division, Dec 1813–April 1814, and 4th Division in Waterloo campaign; Wounded Badajoz, April 1812

Kenneth Alexander Howard, b. 1767; s. Capt Henry Howard of Arundel; Ensign Coldstream Gds 1786; Capt and Lieut-Col July 1799; Maj-Gen July 1810; Commanded 1st Division, March 1813–April 1814 (under Graham and Hope)

John Oswald, b. 1771; s. James T. Oswald, Esq.; Educ. Military School, Brienne; Ensign 23rd Foot 1788; Lieut-Col April 1797; Maj-Gen June 1811; Commanded 5th Division, Oct 1812–Aug 1813 and Sep–Oct 1813

Robert Craufurd, b. 1764; 3rd s. Sir Alexander Craufurd, 1st Bart.; MP East Retford, 1799–1806; Ensign 25th Foot 1779; Lieut-Col Dec 1797; Maj-Gen June 1811; Commanded Light Division, Feb 1810–Feb 1811 and April 1811–Jan 1812; Killed Ciudad Rodrigo, Jan 1812

Andrew Hay, b. 1762; s. George Hay Esq. of Mount Blainey, Banff; Ensign 1st Royal Scots, 1779; Lieut-Col Jan 1798; Maj-Gen June 1811; Commanded 5th Division, Oct 1813–Dec 1813; Killed at Bayonne, April 1813

Robert Burne, b. 1753 (?); Ensign 36th Foot Jan 1777; Lieut-Col Jan 1798; Maj-Gen June 1811; Commanded 6th Division Nov 1811–Feb 1812

George Cooke, b. 1768; s. George John Cooke of Harefield, Middlesex; Educ. Harrow and Caen; Ensign 1st Gds 1784; Capt and Lieut-Col June 1798; Maj-Gen June 1811; Commanded Cadiz Contingent, July 1811–April 1813; Commanded 1st Division in Waterloo campaign; Wounded Waterloo

George Townshend Walker, b. 1764; s. Major Nathaniel Walker, American Corps of Rangers; Ensign 95th Foot 1782; Lieut-Col Sep 1798; Maj-Gen June 1811; Commanded 7th Division, Nov 1813–Feb 1814; Wounded Orthez Feb 1814

Edward Pakenham, b. 1778; 2nd s. 2nd Baron Longford; Ensign 92nd Foot 1794; Lieut-Col Oct 1799; Maj-Gen Jan 1812; Commanded 3rd Division, June 1812–Jan 1813, 6th Division, Jan–June 1813 and July–Aug 1813; Killed New Orleans, 1815

Denis Pack, b. 1772; s. Thomas Pack D.D., Dean of Kilkenny; Cornet 14th Lt Dgns Nov 1791; Lieut-Col Dec 1800; Maj-Gen June 1813; Commanded 6th Division, July 1813; Wounded Sorauren, July 1813

Edward Howarth, b. ?; Educ. Royal Military Academy, Woolwich; 2nd Lieut R.A. July 1779; Lieut-Col Jan 1798; Maj-Gen June 1811; Commander, Royal Artillery, July–Dec 1811

William Borthwick, b. 1760; Educ. Royal Military Academy, Woolwich; 2nd Lieut R.A. Nov 1779; Lieut-Col Sep 1803; Maj-Gen Jan 1812; Commander, Royal Artillery, March–Aug 1812

COMMANDERS OF THE FRENCH ARMIES OPPOSED TO WELLINGTON IN SPAIN, 1810–13

1 Army of the South

Jan 1810–March 1813	Marshal Soult, Duke of Dalmatia
March 1813–July 1813	General Honoré Gazan

2 Army of Portugal

May 1810–May 1811	Marshal Massena, Prince of Essling
May 1811–July 1812	Marshal Marmont, Duke of Ragusa
July 1812–Sept 1812	General Baron Bertrand Clausel
Sept 1812–Nov 1812	General Joseph Souham
Nov 1812–Jan 1813	General Jean-Baptiste Drouet, Count D'Erlon
Jan 1813–July 1813	General Count Honoré Reille

3 Army of the North

Jan 1811–July 1811	Marshal Bessières, Duke of Istria
July 1811–May 1812	General Jean-Marie Dorsenne
May 1812–Jan 1813	General Louis Marc Caffarelli
Jan 1813–July 1813	General Baron Bertrand Clausel

4 Army of the Centre

Jan 1813–July 1813 General Jean-Baptiste Drouet, Count D'Erlon. (Before Jan 1813 the Army of the Centre was commanded directly by King Joseph.)

The four Armies were merged into the Army of Spain under Marshal Soult, in July 1813.

BIBLIOGRAPHY

With abbreviations used in the references

AHR, *Journal of the Society for Army Historical Research*

Anton, *Retrospect of a Military Life*, J. Anton 1841. Reprinted and edited in *Wellington's Men*, W. H. Fitchett, 1900

B. & G., *History of the Life of Arthur, Duke of Wellington*, M. Brialmont and G. R. Gleig, 1858

Barnard, *The Barnard Letters* (Ed. A. Powell), 1928

Beamish, *History of the King's German Legion*, N. Ludlow Beamish, 1832

Blakeney, *A Boy in the Peninsular War. The Services, Adventures and Experiences of Robert Blakeney* (Ed. J. Sturgis), 1899

Blakiston, *Twelve Years Military Adventure*, John Blakiston, 1840

Booth, *The Battle of Waterloo by a Near Observer*, 1817

Burgoyne, *Life and Correspondence of Field Marshal Sir John Burgoyne* (Ed. Hon. G. Wrottesley), 1873

Boutflower, *Journal of an Army Surgeon during the Peninsular War*, Charles Boutflower, n.d.

Bragge, *Peninsular Portrait. The Letters of Capt William Bragge* (Ed. S. A. Cassells), 1963

Cammisc, *Some Letters of the Duke of Wellington to his brother, William Wellesley Pole* (Ed. Sir Charles Webster), *Camden Miscellany* Vol xviii 1948

Canning, *George Canning*, H. W. V. Temperley, 1905

Cintra, *Proceedings upon the Inquiry relative to the Armistice and Convention &c. made and concluded in Portugal in August 1808*, 1809

Colborne, *Life of Sir John Colborne, Lord Seton* (Ed. C. G. Moore Smith), 1903

Connolly, *History of the Royal Sappers and Miners*, T. W. J. Connolly, 1857

Cooper, *Rough Notes of Seven Campaigns*, John Spencer Cooper (2nd edition), 1914

Costello, *The Adventures of a Soldier*, Edward Costello, 1857

Creevey, *Creevey* (Ed. John Gore), 1938

Croker, *The Croker Papers* (Ed. L. W. Jennings), 1884

Dalrymple, *Memoir written by General Sir Hew Dalrymple, Bart.*, 1830

Davies, *Wellington and his Army*, Godfrey Davies, 1954

DMSS, *Dickson Manuscripts* (Ed. J. H. Leslie), 1908–09

Donaldson, *Recollections of the Eventful Life of a Soldier*, Joseph Donaldson (new edition), 1841

Duncan, *History of the Royal Regiment of Artillery*, F. Duncan, 1878

D'Urban, *Peninsular Journal of Maj-Gen Sir Benjamin D'Urban* (Ed. I. J. Rousseau), 1930

Elers, *Memoirs of George Elers* (Ed. Lord Monson and G. Leveson Gower), 1903

Ellesmere, *Personal Reminiscences of the Duke of Wellington by Francis, 1st Earl of Ellesmere* (Ed. Alice, Countess of Strafford), 1904

Fortescue, *A History of the British Army*, vols. iv–x, Sir John Fortescue, 1915–20

Foy, *Vie Militaire de General Foy* (Ed. M. Girod de l'Ain), 1900

Fraser, *Words on Wellington*, Sir William Fraser, Bart., 1902

Frazer, *Letters of Sir Augustus Frazer* (Ed. E. Sabine), 1859

Gleig, *Life of Arthur Duke of Wellington*, G. R. Gleig (revised edition), 1882

G. Napier, *Early Military Life of General Sir George Napier* (Ed. W. C. E. Napier) (2nd edition), 1886

Gomm, *Letters and Journals of Field Marshal Sir William Gomm* (Ed. F. C. Carr-Gomm), 1881

Gordon, *A Cavalry Officer in the Corunna Campaign: The Journal of Captain Gordon* (Ed. H. C. Wyllie), 1913

Grattan, *Adventures with the Connaught Rangers*, William Grattan (Ed. Sir John Fortescue), 1902

Greville, *The Greville Memoirs* (Ed. H. Reeve) (new edition), 1896

Henry, *Events of a Military Life*, Walter Henry, 1843

Hist. R.E., *History of the Corps of Royal Engineers*, Whitworth Porter, 1889

Hobhouse, *Recollections of a Long Life*, J. C. Hobhouse (Ed. Lady Dorchester), 1909

Houssaye, *1815, Waterloo*, Henry Houssaye (42nd edition), 1903

Jones' Sieges, *Journals of Sieges carried out by the army under the Duke of Wellington*, Sir John Jones (3rd edition), 1846

Kincaid ARB, *Adventures in the Rifle Brigade*, John Kincaid, 1830

Kincaid RS, *Random Shots of a Rifleman*, John Kincaid (2nd edition), 1847

Larpent, *Private Journal of Judge Advocate Larpent* (Ed. Sir G. Larpent) (3rd edition), 1854

Leith Hay, *A Narrative of the Peninsular War*, Andrew Leith Hay (2nd edition), 1832

L'Estrange, *Recollections of Sir George B. L'Estrange*, 1874

Londonderry, *Narrative of the Peninsular War*, 3rd Marquess of Londonderry (2nd edition), 1828

Long, *Peninsular Cavalry General. The Correspondence of Lieut-Gen Robert Ballard Long* (Ed. T. H. McGuffie), 1951

LWN, *Life of General Sir William Napier* (Ed. H. A. Bruce), 1864

Malmesbury, *Letters of the 1st Earl of Malmesbury, his Family and Friends* (Ed. 3rd Earl), 1870

Maxwell, *Life of Wellington*, Sir Herbert Maxwell, 1907

McGrigor, *Autobiography and Services of Sir James McGrigor*, 1861

Mercer, *Journal of the Waterloo Campaign*, Cavalié Mercer (Ed. Sir John Fortescue), 1927

Müffling, *Passages from my Life*, Baron von Müffling (Ed. P. Yorke) (2nd edition), 1853

Napier, *History of the War in the Peninsula and the South of France*, William Napier (new edition), 1852

Oman, *History of the Peninsular War*, Sir Charles Oman, 1902–30

Pakenham, *The Pakenham Letters 1800–15* (Ed. Lord Longford), 1914

Pen. Sketches, *Peninsular Sketches by Actors on the Scene* (Ed. W. H. Maxwell), 1845

Ross, *Memoir of Sir Hew Dalrymple Ross*, 1871

Ross Lewin, *Life of a soldier*, H. Ross Lewin, 1834

Simmons, *A British Rifle Man. The Journals and Correspondence of Major George Simmons* (Ed. Willoughby Verner), 1899

SD, *Supplementary Dispatches and Memoranda of Field Marshal the Duke of Wellington* (Ed. 2nd Duke), 1858–72

Smith, *Autobiography of Sir Harry Smith* (Ed. G. C. Moore Smith), 1901

Smythies, *Historical Records of the 40th (2nd Somersetshire) Regiment*, R. H. Raymond Smythies, 1894

Southey, *History of the Peninsular War*, Robert Southey, 1823–32

Stanhope, *Notes of Conversations with the Duke of Wellington*, The Earl of Stanhope, 1889

Swabey, *Diary of Campaigns in the Peninsula*, William Swabey (Ed. F. A. Whinyates), 1895

Tomkinson, *Diary of a Cavalry Officer*, William Tomkinson (Ed. J. Tomkinson), 1894

Verner, *History and Campaigns of the Rifle Brigade*, Willoughby Verner, 1912–19

Ward, *Wellington's Headquarters*, S. G. P. Ward, 1957

Warre, *Letters from the Peninsula 1808–12*, Sir William Warre (Ed. E. Warre), 1909

Waterloo Letters, *Waterloo Letters* (Ed. H. T. Siborne), 1891

WD, *The Dispatches of F.M. the Duke of Wellington 1799–1818* (Ed. J. Gurwood), 1834–39

Wellington's Army, *Wellington's Army 1809–14*, Sir Charles Oman, 1913

Wheeler, *The Letters of Private Wheeler* (Ed. B. H. Liddell Hart), 1951

Wyldmem, Memoir annexed to Wyld's Atlas showing the principal Movements, Battles and Sieges in which the British Troops bore a Conspicuous Part, 1841

Manuscript Letters of Maj-Gen Miles Nightingall, Asst-Surgeon W. M. Brookes, The Rev Samuel Briscall, in the author's possession

REFERENCES

Chapter one

1 Duncan ii 10
2 WD vii 55 to Gordon, 19 Dec 10
3 WD vi 43 to Gordon, 17 April 10
4 AG to D of Y, 27 March 93 (q. in Fortescue iv 81)
5 J. Steven Watson, *The Reign of George III* (1960), 374
6 Fortescue iv 384
7 Fortescue iv 496
8 Stanhope 18
9 Cooper 15
10 Stevenson, q. in Davies 68
11 Donaldson 86
12 *Rules and Regulations for Cavalry*, 1795
13 Blakeney, 240

Chapter two

1 q. in Maxwell i 12
2 SD xiii 2, to Sir Chichester Fortescue, 20 Dec 94
3 Stanhope 182
4 *ib.*
5 Letter of 25 June 95, q. in B & G i 22
6 SD ii 501 to HW, 8 July 01
7 Elers 120
8 SD i 152 to HW 2 Jan 99
9 *ib.*
10 SD i 187 to Mornington 29 Jan 99
11 SD i 203. 'Draft of description of our March'
12 SD i 209 to Mornington, 6 April 99
13 WD ii 345–6
14 Elers 122
15 Stanhope 103
16 WD ii 16 to Close, 19 June 03
17 WD ii 210 to Stevenson, 17 Aug 03
18 WD ii 403 to Stevenson, 19 Oct 03
19 WD i 339–40 to Munro, 1 Nov 03
20 Croker i 354
21 Blakiston i 160–2
22 WD ii 330–1 & 340. Memorandum and letter to Munro, 1 Nov 03
23 WD ii 325 to Mornington, 24 Sept 03
24 Blakiston i 167
25 Blakiston 161–2
26 SD iv 186. Letter of Colin Campbell
27 WD ii 341 to Munro, 1 Nov 03
28 SD vi 563 to WWP, 31 July 10
29 WD ii 561 to Shawe, 2 Dec 03
30 WD ii 557–8 to Mornington, 30 Nov 03
31 WD ii 561 to Shawe, 2 Dec 03
32 SD vii 112 Dundas to W., 23 April 11
33 WD iii 677
34 WD iii G.O. of 9 March 05
35 SD iv 507 to Wellesley, 3 July 05

Chapter three

1 Cammisc. to WWP, 13 Sep 10
2 Croker ii 342
3 SD v 82 to Lady Anne Smith, 10 June 07
4 SD v 61 to Sir E. B. Littlehayes, 24 May 07
5 SD v 125 to Richmond, 24 July 07
6 Q in Canning 73
7 Q in Canning 75
8 LWN 44
9 Croker i 343
10 LWN i 42
11 LWN i 43
12 Gomm 85
13 Cammisc. 1–4, to WWP
14 ib.
15 SD v 192 to Lord Hawkesberry, 20 Nov 07
16 SD v 176 to Lord Hawkesberry, 9 Nov 07
17 Southey i 347
18 Southey i 349
19 SD xiii 291 to Richmond, 21 July 08
20 WD v 607 to Craufurd, 30 March 10
21 WD iv 40 to Castlereagh, 21 July 08
22 SD xiii 291 to Richmond, 21 June 08
23 WD iv 42 to Castlereagh, 25 July 08
24 SD vi 95 to Richmond, 1 Aug 08
25 ib.
26 WD iv 55 to Castlereagh, 1 Aug 08
27 SD vi 95 to Richmond, 1 Aug 08
28 Dalrymple 52
29 Robe, 28 Sep 08, printed in History of the Campaigns of the British Forces in Spain and Portugal (1812) ii 227
30 WD iv 72 to Castlereagh, 8 Aug 08
31 WD iv 66 to Burrard, 8 Aug 08
32 WD iv 54 to Castlereagh, 1 Aug 08
33 SD vi 115 to Richmond, 16 Aug 08
34 Croker ii 122
35 Cammisc. 5 to WWP, 22 Aug 08
36 Croker ii 122
37 Cammisc. 6 to WWP, 22 Aug 08
38 Croker i 122
39 Cintra, p. 197, evidence of Torrens
40 Sherer 43
41 SD vi 122 to Richmond, 22 Aug 08
42 Cintra, 101
43 ib., 105
44 Cammisc. 7 to WWP, 22 Aug 08
45 ib.
46 Croker ii 121
47 Croker ii 123

Chapter four

1 Moore to Castlereagh, Salamanca, 25 Nov 08
2 WD iv 262 Memorandum to Castlereagh, 7 March 09
3 WD iv to Castlereagh, 1 Aug 08
4 WD iv 261 to Castlereagh, 7 March 09
5 SD vi 216 De Garay to Canning, 12 March 09
6 George III to Castlereagh, 3 Oct 09
7 SD vi 210 Castlereagh to W., 2 April 09
8 SD vi 212, Castlereagh to W., 3 April 09
9 SD vi 227 to Richmond, 14 April 09
10 SD vi 227 to Richmond, 14 April 09
11 SD vi 222 Memorandum to Castlereagh, 11 April 09
12 WD iv 269 to Castlereagh, 24 April 09
13 WD iv 274 to Castlereagh, 27 April 09
14 Return of 6th May 1809
15 WD iv 281 to Castlereagh, 29 April 09
16 WD iv 303 to WCB, 6 May 09
17 WD iv 302 to Huskisson, 5 May 09
18 WD iv 267 to Frere, 24 April 09
19 WD iv 349 to Frere, 20 May 09
20 WD iv 380 to Castlereagh, 31 May 09
21 SD xiii 370 to Buckingham, 16 Nov 09
22 WD iv 412 to Villiers, 11 June 09
23 WD iv 373 to Huskisson, 30 May 09
24 WD iv 380 to Castlereagh, 31 May 09
25 SD xiii 330 Stewart to Thompson, 27 June 09
26 Cuesta to de Garay, 3 May 09
27 WD iv 430 to Castlereagh, 17 June 09
28 WD iv 526 to Frere, 24 July 09
29 Cammisc. 16 to WWP, 25 July 09
30 Cammisc. 17 to WWP, 1 Aug 09
31 Cammisc. 18 to WWP, 8 Aug 09
32 WD iv 499 to Roche, 8 July 09
33 SD vi 364, Asst-Comm.-Gen. Gauntlett to Sherbrooke, 15 Sep 09
34 SD vi 343 to Burghersh, 1 Sep 09

35 SD vi 373 Lord Wellesley to W., 19 Sep 09
36 SD vi 412 Liverpool to W., 20 Oct 09
37 SD vi 423 to Liverpool, 19 Nov 09 (dated 14 Nov in WD v 280)
38 SD vi 484 Liverpool to W., Feb 10
39 SD vi 493 Liverpool to W., 13 March 10
40 SD vi 515 Col. Taylor (sec. to George III) to Liverpool, 21 April 09
41 WD v 150 to Roche, 14 Sep 09
42 WD v 335 to Frere, 6 Dec 09
43 WD v 89 to Castlereagh, 25 Aug 09
44 ib.
45 WD v 411 to Liverpool, 4 Jan 10
46 WD v 517 to Liverpool, 22 Feb 10
47 SD xiii 386 Berthier to King Joseph, 31 Jan 10
48 Foy, *Mémoires*, 100
49 Hulot, *Mémoires*, 303, q. in Oman iii 208
50 Ellesmere, 97
51 Nap Corr xx, 16519
52 WD vi 189 to Craufurd, 12 June 10
53 WD vi 493 to Stuart, 6 April 10
54 WD vi 555 to Liverpool, 27 Oct 10
55 ib.
56 WD vii 416 to Berkeley, 30 March 11
57 Nightingall MSS
58 ib.
59 WD vii 336 to WCB, 4 March 11
60 Pakenham. EP's letter of 20 March 11
61 WD vii 448 to Liverpool, 9 April 11
62 WD vii 461 to WCB, 13 April 11
63 WD vii 454 to HW, 10 April 11
64 WD vii 448 to Liverpool, 9 April 11
65 WD vii 417 to Stuart, 30 March 11
66 Pakenham. HP's letter of 20 June 11
67 WD vii 565 to Liverpool, 15 May 11
68 Gomm 205, letter of 24 March 11

Chapter five

1   WD viii 94 to Liverpool, 11 June 11
2   WD vii 622 to HW, 29 May 11
3   WD vii 647 to Liverpool, 6 June 11
4   SD vii 163 to Torrens, 20 June 11
5   SD vii 176 to WWP, 2 July 11
6   WD viii 118 to Liverpool, 18 June 11
7   SD vii 176 to WWP, 2 July 11
8   SD xiii 659 Bessières to Berthier, 6 June 11
9   WD viii 118 to Liverpool, 18 July 11
10 WD viii 184 to Liverpool, 8 Aug 11
11 SD vii 41 to WWP, 11 Jan 11
12 SD vii 102 Liverpool to W., 11 April 11
13 WD viii 232 to Liverpool, 27 Aug 11
14 WD viii 290 to Liverpool, 18 Sep 11
15 SD vii 228 to Liverpool, 9 Oct 11
16 WD viii 233 to Liverpool, 27 Aug 11
17 Berthier to Marmont, 21 Nov 11
18 Return of 1 Jan 12
19 WD viii 520 to Graham, 25 Dec 11
20 Berthier to Marmont, 11 Feb 12
21 Berthier to Marmont, 26 Feb 12
22 WD ix 29 to HW, 4 April 12
23 WD ix 54 to HW, 11 April 12
24 WD ix 170 to Liverpool, 26 May 12
25 ib.
26 WD ix 288 to Stuart, 15 July 12
27 WD viii 7 to Gordon, 12 June 11
28 WD ix 236 to Graham, 14 June 12
29 WD ix 241 to Liverpool, 18 June 12
30 SD vii 401 Liverpool to W., 19 Aug 12
31 SD vii 408 Liverpool to W., 22 Aug 12
32 WD ix 352 to Bathurst, 13 Aug 12
33 WD ix 367 to Bathurst, 18 Aug 12
34 WD ix 429 to Paget, 20 Sep 12
35 WD ix 429 to Paget, 20 Sep 12
36 ib.
37 SD vii 477 to E. Cooke, 25 Nov 12
38 ib.
39 WD ix 573 to Liverpool, 23 Nov 12
40 WD ix 526 to Bathurst, 21 Oct 12
41 SD vii 477 to E. Cooke, 25 Nov 12
42 WD ix 370 to Bathurst, 18 Aug 12
43 Stanhope 9
44 WD ix 370 to Bathurst, 18 Aug 12
45 WD ix 598 to Bathurst, 2 Dec 12
46 WD ix 617 to WCB, 10 Dec 12
47 WD x 71 to Gordon, 31 Jan 13
48 WD x 105 to Bathurst, 10 Feb 13
49 WD x 510 to Graham, 2 July 13
50 WD x 248 to Bathurst, 31 July 13
51 WD x 412 to Graham, 3 June 13
52 WD x 436 to Bathurst, 13 June 13
53 WD ix 495 to Popham, 17 Oct 12
54 WD x 473 to Bathurst, 29 June 13
55 WD x 495 to Bathurst, 2 July 13
56 WD xi 67 to Bathurst, 2 Sep 13
57 WD xi 35 to Bathurst, 23 Aug 13
58 Hobhouse ii 190

Chapter six

1 WD iv 270 to Castlereagh, 24 April 09
2 *ib.*
3 *ib.*
4 WD iv 309 to WCB, 7 May 09
5 Tomkinson 4
6 MS letter dated 2 June 09 from Asst.-Surgeon Brookes, 87th Foot
7 WD iv 343 to Castlereagh, 18 May 09
8 SD vi 462 Memorandum for Lord Wellesley, Dec 09
9 Stanhope MS q. in Fortescue vii 547
10 WD ix 175 to Liverpool, 26 May 12
11 WD ix 252 to Liverpool, 25 June 12
12 Tomkinson 165
13 Warre 266, letter of 25 June 12
14 WD ix 267 to Graham, 3 July 12
15 Stanhope MS q. in Fortescue viii 471
16 WD ix 283 to Bathurst, 14 July 12
17 Boutflower 148
18 WD ix 296-8 to Bathurst, 21 July 12
19 *ib.*
20 Tomkinson 188
21 Marmont, *Mémoires*, iv 136
22 Croker ii 120
23 Grattan 246
24 Leith Hay ii 53-4
25 Leith Hay ii 55
26 Leith Hay ii 57
27 Napier iv 268
28 *Rules and Regulations for the Sword Exercise*, 1796
29 WD ix 308 to Bathurst, 24 July 12
30 Ross 30
31 WD ix 308 to Bathurst, 24 July 12
32 Tomkinson 190
33 WD 308 to Bathurst, 24 July 12
34 WD ix 433 to Maitland, 20 Sep 12
35 Colborne 202
36 *ib.*
37 SD viii 744 Memorandum by G. Murray, QMG
38 SD viii 756 Memorandum by W.
39 SD vii 745 Memorandum by G. Murray, QMG
40 *ib.*
41 D'Urban 322
42 Blakiston ii 360
43 Anton 278-9
44 *ib.*
45 Blakiston ii 361
46 Colborne 205
47 Anton 280-1

Chapter seven

1 WD vii 427 to WCB, 4 April 11
2 WD vii 448 to Liverpool, 9 April 11
3 WD vii 467 to WCB, 14 April 11
4 WD vii 469 to Cotton, 15 April 11
5 Pakenham, 15 April 11
6 WD vii 515 to Liverpool, 1 May 11
7 WD vii 465 to Spencer, 14 April 11
8 SD xiii 624 Preparatory order by QMG, 30 April 11
9 Simmons 167
10 *ib.*
11 Donaldson 124
12 WD vii 529 to Liverpool, 8 May 11
13 *ib.*
14 *ib.*
15 Napier iii 149
16 Croker ii 123
17 Larpent 65
18 Wheeler 54
19 Simmons 169
20 *ib.*
21 Simmons 181
22 Ross 16. The same assertion is made by Cotton and in Pen. Sketches
23 Londonderry 512
24 Grattan 66
25 *ib.*
26 Grattan 67
27 SD vii 176 to WWP, 2 July 11
28 WD vii 587 to Perceval, 22 May 11
29 Larpent 196
30 WD x 539 to Torrens, 18 July 13
31 WD x 519 to Bathurst, 9 July 13
32 WD x 522 to Bathurst, 10 July 13
33 WD x 527 to Hill, 14 July 13
34 WD x 563 to Graham, ½ before 12 a.m., 24 July 13
35 SD viii 118 QMG to Dalhousie, 25 July 13
36 WD x 566 to Graham, 10 p.m., 25 July 13
37 SD vii 494 to Torrens, 6 Dec 12
38 WD x 596 to Bathurst, 4 Aug 13

39 SD viii 112 QMG to Cole, 23 July 13
40 Larpent 242
41 *ib.*
42 Wyldmem 113 QMG to Pack and Dalhousie, 26 July 13
43 Wyldmem 113 QMG to Picton, 26 July 13
44 L'Estrange 114
45 SD viii 121 Picton to W., 26 July 13, ½ past 8 o'clock
46 SD viii 125 Cole to QMG, 26 July 13 (misdated in SD as 27 July)
47 Wyldmem 115 QMG to Hill, 27 July 13
48 Larpent 242
49 Fortescue ix 272
50 Letter from Major Mills q. in Smythies 145
51 *ib.*
52 Kincaid ARB 72
53 WD x 602 to Wm Bentinck, 5 Aug 13
54 *ib.*
55 WD x 572 to Graham, 28 July 13, ½ past 3 p.m.
56 WD x 582 to Bathurst, 1 Aug 13

Chapter eight

1   Wellington's Army 279
2   Jones' Sieges i 344
3   Blakeney 166
4   WD ix 141 to Malcolm, 13 May 12
5   Pasley's *Elementary Fortification,* q. in Connolly i 184
6   Jones' Sieges i 10
7   DMSS, 27 April 11
8   Jones' Sieges i 71
9   Burgoyne i 135
10 DMSS. Letter of Capt. Dyneley RHA, 22 Jan 12
11 Letter after fall of Badajoz among Lord Liverpool's papers, q. in Oman v 255
12 Jones' Sieges i 12
13 *ib.* i 157
14 Burgoyne i 177
15 Jones' Sieges i 153
16 Gomm 261
17 Pen. Sketches i 305
18 Simmons 228
19 *ib.* 231
20 Gomm 262
21 Leith Hay i 296–7
22 Jones' Sieges i 212
23 Fortescue viii 583
24 WD ix 436 to Paget, 20 Sep 12
25 DMSS. 742 Robe to Dickson, 18 Sep 12
26 Ellesmere 146
27 Jones' Sieges i 275
28 WD ix 436 to Paget, 20 Sep 12
29 WD ix 446 to WCB, 22 Sep 12
30 WD ix 443 to Bathurst, 21 Sep 12
31 WD ix 470 to WCB, 5 Oct 12
32 WD ix 485 to Hill, 12 Oct 12
33 SD vii 458 T. Sydenham to HW, 16 Oct 12
34 Gomm 291 letter of 22 Nov 12
35 Malmesbury ii 319. Bowles' letter of 31 Oct 12
36 Burgoyne i 235
37 WD ix 457 to Bathurst, 27 Sep 12
38 Ross Lewin ii 44
39 WD ix 573 to Liverpool, 23 Nov 12
40 Ellesmere 146

Chapter nine

1   SD xiv 539 to Burghersh, 13 March 15
2   Creevey 135
3   *ib.*
4   WD xii 288 to Gneisenau, 5 April 15
5   SD x 20 Torrens to W., 4 April 15
6   SD x 716 Return of 23 March 15
7   SD x 167 to Bathurst, 28 April 15
8   SD x 168 to Bathurst, 28 April 15
9   WD xii 299 to Craddock, 11 April 15
10 WD xii 358 to C. Stewart, 8 May 15
11 Müffling 212
12 WD xii 288 to Gneisenau, 5 April 15
13 WD xii 375–6 to Prince of Orange, 11 May 15
14 WD xii 416 to Bathurst, 22 May 15
15 SD x 268 Bathurst to W., 9 May 15
16 WD xii 291 to Bathurst, 8 April 15
17 Creevey 136
18 SD x 424 Dörnberg to Somerset, 6 June 15
19 Fraser 260–6
20 WD x 307 to Bathurst, 20 April 13

21 q. in Houssaye 193
22 Malmesbury ii 447
23 Hist RE i 382
24 WD xii 529 to WCB, 2 July 15

25 Creevey 142
26 Booth ii 75. Letter of Rifleman Lewis
27 Fraser 35

Chapter ten

1   WD vii 567 to Liverpool, 15 May 11
2   Torrens to W., 11 Sep 10, q. in Fortescue vii 419
3   SD vi 582 to Torrens, 29 Aug 10
4   Torrens to W., 11 Sep 10, q. in Fortescue vii 419
5   WD v 384–5 to Liverpool, 21 Dec 09
6   WD v 404 to Liverpool, 2 Jan 10
7   WD vi 270 to Liverpool, 14 July 10
8   WD x 224 to Houston, 23 March 13
9   SD vii 485 to Torrens, 2 Dec 12
10 q. in Fortescue ix 88
11 SD vii 485 to Torrens, 2 Dec 12
12 WD x 269 to Cotton, 7 April 13
13 Smith 124
14 WD viii 431 to Torrens, 2 Dec 11
15 Nightingall MSS, 1 and 23 Feb 11
16 McGrigor 304–5
17 WD iv 369 to WCB, 29 May 09
18 WD ix 427 to Torrens, 13 Sep 12
19 WD viii 146 to Torrens, 25 July 11
20 Smith 118
21 Blakeney, 257
22 Swabey 165
23 AHR vol 140, 168
24 WD vii 560 to Alex Campbell, 15 March 11
25 WD viii 442 to Torrens, 7 Dec 11
26 WD xi 499 to Colville, 5 Feb 14
27 SD vii 485 to Torrens, 2 Dec 12
28 SD vii 527 Torrens to W., 14 Jan 13
29 Bragge 89–90

30 Ross 17–8
31 Leach Journal, q. in Verner ii 69
32 Napier ii 405
33 Smith 216
34 Stanhope 69
35 WD ix 398 to Torrens, 7 Sep 12
36 Larpent 238
37 Colborne 37
38 ib.
39 WD ix 109 to HW, 3 May 12
40 WD vii 91 to C. Stuart, 31 Dec 10
41 Greville iv 142
42 WD x 34 to Torrens, 22 Jan 13
43 Stanhope 190
44 Croker ii 123
45 Swabey 174
46 Wyldmem 100 QMG's Arrangements, 20 June 13
47 Wyldmem 101
48 ib.
49 Malmesbury ii 385
50 WD xi 371–2 to Torrens, 15 Dec 13
51 WD ix 278 to Bathurst, 9 July 12
52 Colborne 140
53 WD vii 124 to Hill, 17 May 10
54 Donaldson 212
55 Pakenham, 15 April 11
56 Briscall, MSS, 28 May 11
57 SD vii 176 to WWP, 2 July 11
58 SD vii 125–6 WCB to W., 15 May 11
59 Printed in Napier vi 349
60 SD vii 547 WCB to W., 12 Feb 13
61 SD vii 484 to Bathurst, 2 Dec 12

Chapter eleven

1   Ross 8 Letter of 12 Aug 09
2   WD vii 598 to Liverpool, 23 May 11
3   WD v 402 to Payne, 2 Jan 10
4   WD vii 34 to Liverpool, 7 Dec 10
5   WD viii 231 to Liverpool, 27 Aug 11
6   WD v 84 to Castlereagh, 25 Aug 09
7   WD viii 231 to Liverpool, 27 Aug 11
8   ib.
9   SD vii 504 Gordon to W., 25 Dec 12
10 Tomkinson 135
11 Kincaid RS 162
12 WD viii 58 to Liverpool, 27 June 11

13 Tomkinson 135
14 WD ix 238 to Hill, 18 June 12
15 Frazer 550
16 Wellington's Army 104
17 Long 275
18 Bragge 102
19 Vidal de la Blanche q. in Fortescue ix 513
20 Gordon 20
21 Gordon 99
22 Pakenham. H. Pakenham's letter of 16 Aug 11
23 SD xiii 720. AG to Slade, 13 Oct 11
24 WD ix 277 to Bathurst, 9 July 12

25 WD vii 503 to WCB, 24 April 11
26 Beamish ii 82
27 WD x 19 to C. Stewart, 2 Jan 13
28 SD vii 165 to D. of York, 25 June 11
29 WD ix 308 to Bathurst, 24 July 12
30 SD vii 465 T. Sydenham to HW, 28 Oct 12
31 q. in Fortescue x 332
32 Mercer 148–9
33 Waterloo Letters 131–2. Letter of Lt. S. O'Grady, 7 Hus.
34 AHR Special publication 8, p. 48
35 Waterloo letters 131–2. Letter of Lt. S. O'Grady, 7 Hus.
36 Waterloo Letters 10. Letter of Lord Anglesey
37 SD vii 166 D of York to W., 31 May 11
38 SD vii 586 to E. Cooke, 16 May 13
39 Larpent 243
40 DMSS 905
41 Gomm 299–300
42 Duncan ii 277
43 Swabey 162

44 Ross 19
45 DMSS 840, Letter of Capt Cairnes
46 Cammisc. 24 to WWP, 13 Sep 09
47 Ross 27
48 WD x 45 to Mulgrave, 27 Jan 13
49 DMSS 905. Letter of Capt. Cairnes, 11 June 13
50 DMSS 833 Letter of Capt. Cairnes, 28 Jan 13
51 Duncan ii 360
52 DMSS 916. Letter of 23 June 13
53 Frazer 430
54 SD xiv 618 to Mulgrave, 21 Dec 15
55 Frazer 559
56 SD vi 286 to Shrapnell, 16 June 09
57 SD vii 304 to Liverpool, 12 March 12
58 WD ix 28 to Liverpool, 3 April 12
59 SD vi 430 Fisher to W., 1 Dec 09
60 WD vi 591 to Berkeley, 6 Nov 10
61 WD xi 314 to Bathurst, 22 Nov 13
62 Larpent 354–5
63 Mercer 153

Chapter twelve

1 WD vi 91 to Craufurd, 5 May 10
2 Cammisc. to WWP, 6 April 10
3 SD x 219 to Bathurst, 4 May 15
4 Croker i 13
5 WD vii 427 to WCB, 4 April 11
6 WD vii 434 to Capt Chapman RE, 8 April 11
7 Principles of Military Movement 13
8 Instructions given to the battalions of Irish Militia 1798–9, q. in Carola Oman's Moore, p. 197
9 WD iv 473 to Huskisson, 28 June 09
10 Ward 163
11 LWN i 42
12 WD x 184 to O'Callaghan, 12 March 13
13 Larpent 43 and 52
14 Cooper 15
15 G. Napier 145
16 WD vi 576 to Torrens, 2 Nov 10
17 q. in Prof. Michael Howard's 'Wellington and the British Army' in Wellington Studies, 1959
18 WD ix 610 to Torrens, 6 Dec 12
19 WD ix 109 to HW, 3 May 12
20 WD ix 582–3. Circular to Officers cmd'g divisions and brigades, 28 Nov 12
21 WD viii 296 to Alex Campbell, 21 Sep 11

22 Wheeler 105
23 Ross 36
24 SD vii 311. G.O., 7 April 12
25 Hobhouse ii 202
26 Croker i 433
27 Pen. Sketches ii 336
28 WD ix 182 to Capt Collier RN, 10 Oct 13
29 Costello 125
30 WD iii 168 to Malcolm, 17 March 04
31 WD vii 102 to Stuart, 3 Jan 11
32 SD vi 361 WCB to W., 11 Sep 09
33 WD viii 143 to HW, 24 July 11
34 WD x 569 to Liverpool, 25 July 13
35 B. & G. i 186
36 WD viii 7 to Gordon, 12 June 11
37 WD viii 127 to HW, 20 July 11
38 WD viii 166 to HW, 2 Aug 11
39 Barnard 230
40 WD vii 398 to Graham, 25 March 11
41 WD ix 153. Circular to Officers cmd'g divisions, 18 May 12
42 WD ix 272 to Torrens, 7 July 12
43 WD ix 240 to Liverpool, 18 July 12
44 WD v 188 to Wellesley, 27 Sep 09
45 Gleig 398
46 SD xiv 372 AG to AAG, Right Column, 30 Jan 14
47 Wheeler 196
48 Pen. Sketches ii 331

INDEX

Wheeler, Sgt William, 232, 238
Whitelocke, Lieut-Gen John, 49
Whittingham, Brig-Gen Samuel, 198n.
Wicklow, 53
Wilson, Brig-Gen Robert, 70
Williams, Lieut-Col, 146
Wimbledon Common, 78, 213
Wood, Col Sir George, 222
Woodbridge, 212
Woolwich, 17, 26, 30, 162, 220, 221

Xeres, 58

Yonge, Sir George, 15, 16
York, H.R.H. Field-Marshal, the Duke of, 16, 25, 28, 29, 30, 31, 59, 69, 165n., 195, 215, 218

Zadorra, 205
Zamora, 77, 103, 109–11
Zarza la Mayor, 74
Zealand, 52
Zieten, Lieut-Gen Hans Ernst Carl, Graf von, 186
Zubieta, 158
Zubiri, 157–8